Against History, Against State

CULTURES OF HISTORY

CULTURES OF HISTORY

NICHOLAS DIRKS, SERIES EDITOR

The death of history, reported at the end of the twentieth century, was clearly premature. It has become a hotly contested battleground in struggles over identity, citizenship, and claims of recognition and rights. Each new national history proclaims itself as ancient and universal, while the contingent character of its focus raises questions about the universality and objectivity of any historical tradition. Globalization and the American hegemony have created cultural, social, local, and national backlashes. Cultures of History is a new series of books that investigates the forms, understandings, genres, and histories of history, taking history as the primary text of modern life and the foundational basis for state, society, and nation.

Against History, Against State

Counterperspectives from the Margins

Shail Mayaram

COLUMBIA UNIVERSITY PRESS NEW YORK

COLUMBIA UNIVERSITY PRESS
Publishers Since 1893
New York Chichester, West Sussex

Library of Congress Cataloging-in-Publication Data
Mayaram, Shail.
Against history, against state : counterperspectives from the margin / Shail Mayaram.
p. cm. — (Cultures of history)
Includes bibliographical references and index.
ISBN 0-231-12730-8 (cloth : alk. paper) — ISBN 0-231-12731-6 (pbk. : alk. paper)
1. Meo (Indic people)—History. 2. Folk literature, Hindi—India—History and criticism. I. Title. II. Series.
DS432.M35M38 2003
305.6′9710544—dc21

2003051633

∞

Columbia University Press books are printed on permanent and durable acid-free paper.
Printed in the United States of America
c 10 9 8 7 6 5 4 3 2 1
p 10 9 8 7 6 5 4 3 2 1

Contents

Illustrations

Figures

Maps

Preface

The Meo oral tradition first came to my attention in the mid-1980s. I had moved with my family to live in the Alwar District of the state of Rajasthan in northwest India, and I was struck by the overwhelming concern of the Meos with their past, voiced in their ballads and folk epics. The Meos also had a marked nondeferential stance to bureaucratic and political authority. Here was none of the reverent idiom, frequently called "feudal," characteristic of other areas in Rajasthan. On the contrary, one of their leaders had defiantly told the previous district collector when he exhorted them to adopt birth control measures, "*tujhe kyā, tere ghar kā to nahīn khāte hain*" (What bothers you? We don't eat of your household). In public meetings I heard Meos speak of how they had fought successive sultans, Mughal Badshahs, and the *angreji* (British) raj. A fragment from a Meo woman's song was evocative, "*aiṛī nīche thāṇo mero ṭhokar main sipāhī re*" (the police post is under my heel, the policeman at my toe). A Meo repeated a frequently expressed sentiment, "*mev to mullā kī nāy māne*" (the Meos do not listen to the Muslim clerics). Narratives from their oral tradition derided colonial and kingly authority and the "Turk" and the "Pathan" (Afghan), despite the fact that censuses referred to them as Muslim. I recorded story after story from Meo bards, the Mirasis. People in Alwar still cannot fathom why a mere study of "folklore" could evoke so much interest and thought it quite undignified for me to sit with low-caste musicians (regarded as "untouchable" even by their Meo Muslim patrons). But a world of meaning had begun to unfold for me in the universe of the Meo oral tradition and cultural performance.

Conflict, battle, and war constituted major themes in Meo myths. In most cases Meo heroes were the protagonists; their antagonists were the rulers and the elite of the Mughal and British Empires, the Rajput and Jat kingdoms of Alwar and Bharatpur. I began to grapple with a whole array of questions. What did such a countercultural narrative tradition mean? Was it just an imaginative world derivative from the warrior Rajput oral tradition? Or did it mean something deeper in terms of the region's history? Were these myths that expressed a group sensibility of its past? Further, was there a link between myth and action? How was collective memory being constituted? Were warrior ideologies a form of cultural capital that got reproduced as the group attempted to cope with questions of survival and marginality? In other words, what was the relation between culture, memory, and politics? Was the performing art tradition also an attempt to control the future, to constitute a community, forge the individual into a member of the collective? What was the role of metaphor and image in the making of the mythic tradition? What was the nature of medieval Meo identity? What was their relationship to the dominant "religions" of Hinduism and Islam?

A pattern of meaning seemed to emerge from the Meo narrative tradition. But slowly, only very slowly. Often it would take months to find a singer of a particular narrative of which I had a fragment and a broad outline from a Meo or another Mirasi. The cultural performance text then had to be contextualized, and the written record excavated at archives at Delhi, Bikaner, Alwar, Bharatpur, and London.

What was astounding was the way in which mythic representation was mirrored in other sources. For example, a narrative of three decades of peasant unrest in the early nineteenth century was affirmed by a description in Colonel Lockett's report to the governor general and echoed in the land records of the Alwar State. Fieldwork in the villages affected by successive revolts helped fill in the gaps, as oral family histories and the genealogy of the local Rajput family provided further fragments of evidence. Finally, I saw the architectural ruins of the Meo settlement of Kaulani destroyed by the Alwar king to break the backbone of Meo autonomy.

The mirror of the oral tradition also turned things around. The substantial corpus of Indo-Persian histories and records beginning with the thirteenth century stigmatized the Meos (referred to as Mewatis). The statist account *The Shah Jahannama* described the repression of the Mewatis in the mid-seventeenth century. But it was really the oral tradition that fleshed out the skeletal description of the historical text detailing the onslaught of the

Mughal-Rajput alliance that devastated the local community and prevented the performance of Meo women's ritual, even as it enforced revenue collection and the spread of imperial authority.

The intellectual boundaries my educational socialization had endowed me with came to be slowly but surely shaken in the process of research. The first casualty were the categories "Hindu" and "Muslim" and the attendant Hindu-Muslim binary. There was a complex expression of ethnic identities in the oral tradition. Mewati was obviously in conversation with several languages, and its cosmology drew upon multiple theologies. This suggested how cultures might participate in more than one religion, which at another level are seen as diametrically opposed. The Meos have often been seen as a group with a "syncretic" culture. Syncreticism is viewed as synonymous with (a somewhat artificial and forced picture of) peaceful intercommunal coexistence (often referred to as "communal harmony" and "national integration" in the Indian subcontinent). But the evidence of conflict in Mewat is ubiquitous. The account of feuds available in regional accounts and the Meo narrative tradition suggests also much intra-Muslim conflict, with Muslim groups frequently positioned against other Muslim groups. The oppositional politics of the Meos against the Turk, Afghan, Mughal, and Rajput ruling elites; feuds; and everyday life produced crosscutting and shifting relationships, alliances, and fissures with "Hindu" castes. Indeed the categories "Hindu" and "Muslim" rarely figure in their narrative tradition before the twentieth century. The ground-level situation made me rethink the census-oriented categories that have dominated our thinking, classification, and pedagogies in the previous century.

The textual and oral present a similar received dichotomy. Hermeneutics has traditionally been concerned with textual exegesis of written texts. But isn't a hermeneutics of oral texts possible? This dichotomization coincides with that between the classical and the folk. But the world of the "folk" is permeated by the "classical" and the written. "Folk" itself is the product of the dialogical encounter between the local and the pan-Indian, the "classical" and the "popular."

Academic boundaries have also been demolished in the process of this work. Myth, comparative religion, history, anthropology, political economy, cultural geography, and literary criticism all had to be drawn upon to start my education afresh, to cope with a universe where life is an integrated whole and disciplinary divisions are artificial. University education had hardly equipped me to handle these questions. Educated in India in the

1970s, in the positivist tradition of political science, I been taught to disregard people's narratives. They were said to represent a fantasy world woven by illiterate people, steeped in backwardness, unliberated by modernity. "Truth," instead, was to be discovered through scientific practice and by reliable modes of enquiry provided by historiographical and other appropriately "scientific" methods. This privileged the social-anthropologist, the historian, and the political scientist, just as it disparaged popular knowledge as "opinion" and preferred "writing" over orality.

And so I went first for "knowledge" of the Meos to the written texts, ethnographic and historiographical, and to administrative documents. If there was a continuity in the use of antistate symbols, metaphors, and images in the Meo oral tradition, it was as marked as the negative representation of the Meo-Mewati in written texts authored as early as the thirteenth century. Where did the truth lie about the Meos? In their stigmatized characterization as criminals, insurgents, or both in written histories or in their self-representation encoded in their myths? The only way out seemed to me to be a juxtaposition of written and oral texts. The following chapters are a record of this effort. The juxtaposition of perspectives is not a question of replacing one history with another. Indeed, a methodology involving a clash of histories is worked out in this book. This is somewhat different from reading ruling sources "against the grain," an approach identified with the Subaltern Studies group, or what Ranajit Guha refers to as the act of listening to the "small voices of history." The clash of histories is of intrinsic importance in itself, as it may provide a moment of illumination by raising questions about what has thus far been recorded in the name of universal history; it can also help give us an insight into plural universes and alternative political visions.

This book is an exploration of constructions and contestations of state and sovereignty "from below" and from a subaltern perspective. I have often reflected on a question I have been asked, What relevance does this work have for political science? I have learnt since that there are multiple ways of doing political theory that go beyond the conventional classroom focus on written "classics," and that popular, people's texts and social action can embody incisive critiques and provide alternative visions of moral and social order.

Against History, Against State has been in the making for more than a decade and reflects the various stages of my own growth. Another book, called *Resisting Regimes*: *Myth, Memory, and the Shaping of a Muslim Iden-*

tity on a chronologically later period, was published first, being a much-revised version of my doctoral dissertation. The narrative source material used in both these books will be published separately, both transcribed and translated into English.

I have drawn sustenance from a variety of intellectual enterprises going on in the contemporary world. I am grateful to Daya Krishna who patiently went through a draft; to Susanne and Lloyd Rudolph for introducing me to the "new history" when I had first recorded tentative ideas. To Ashis Nandy I owe the strengthened focus on myth as a possible source of resistance. Without Veena Das's help in sharpening the critique of ethnography and historiography, this work might have been far more diffuse. From Komal Kothari I have learned the approach of beginning with the practice and knowledge of ordinary people, usually considered "illiterate," rather than with inherited academic categories. Gananath Obeysekere's careful and close scrutiny of the manuscript contributed to a significant honing of the arguments. This work was conceived long before I became aware of the work of the group of scholars, who are now celebrated the world over as Subaltern Studies for the debates and departures they have initiated with respect to the historian's craft. I have since joined the editorial collective. A reader will sense my differences with positions taken by other members of the collective as she proceeds through the pages of this text. Nonetheless, my work has been strengthened by the paths already charted by other scholars of the collective. Even as I find the concept of "subaltern" needs to incorporate a great deal of layering (for instance, Meos are subaltern in relation to the Rajput or British power, but are hegemonic, as a dominant caste with respect to the dalit Chamars), I have drawn greatly on the subaltern and moral economy studies.

For the transcription of the narratives I am indebted to Vinay Dixit. For their translation which I have done in free verse and editorial improvement I owe much to the assistance and advice of Francine Krishna and Mukund Lath. Chapters 4 and 5 are indebted to comments from Muzaffar Alam, V. S. Bhatnagar, and Dilbagh Singh. Manvendra Singh, Sumbul Halim Khan, and Maulana Habibur Rahman contributed their familiarity with Mughal and Rajasthan historical sources. For the reworking of chapter 6, in particular, I acknowledge the contribution of Gyan Pandey, Ramchandra Guha, and Sanjay Nigam. Rajendra Joshi, Rima Hooja, and other friends have helped improve successive drafts. My Rockefeller colleagues at Chicago, Sudhir Chandra and Radhika Singha, have contributed to this work in ways they may not recognize. I am grateful to the *Contributions to Indian Sociology* and *Indian Economic and Social History Review* for permission to use articles published in volumes 25 (1) and 34 (2), respectively, and to Cambridge University Press, which is to publish a revised version of chapter 9 under the title "Kings versus Bandits: Anticolonialism in a Bandit Narrative" in the *Journal of the Royal Asiatic Society*. The hospitality of the Chaturvedis and Madhoks in Delhi, Kleins in Alwar, Jains in Bikaner, and Varmas in London underlies a good deal of my research.

To colleagues and friends at the Delhi School of Economics, Centre for the Study of Developing Societies, the Nehru Memorial Museum and Library, Delhi, the Institute on Culture and Consciousness in South Asia of the University of Chicago, and the Institute of Development Studies, Jaipur, I owe an intellectual ambience that defies description. The hospitality extended to me as a visiting scholar by the Advanced Center for History, Aligarh Muslim University, made possible consultation with Irfan Habib, Iqtidar H. Siddiqui, Satya Prakash Gupta, Shireen Moosvi, Iqbal Hussain, and Habibullah's assistance with my nascent Persian. Similarly, Marc Gaborieau's hosting of a visit to Paris made possible discussions with several colleagues at the Ecole Des Hautes Etudes en Sciences Sociales. I am grateful to audiences organized by the University of Cornell, the Indira Gandhi National Centre for the Arts, and the International Conference on Rajasthan at Jaipur to whom I presented sections of the manuscript and to colleagues who participated in a Subaltern Studies editorial group meeting. This research has been made possible only because the frontiers of history and anthropology have already been expanded by scholars working in India and elsewhere.

My husband, Arvind, is really a part of this work, having witnessed each moment of its painful yet excitement-filled growth. From Arvind and my children, Aniruddh and Abhinav, I have received strong and silent support. To Daya I owe a training of relentless questioning, and to Amma, Daddy, and Mum enormous emotional support. Jijji and Papa have been like an additional set of parents to me. To my family, both inherited and acquired, I acknowledge the sense of confidence that has made this work possible. What underlies much of my work is an unstated debt to the warmth and hospitality of my numerous Meo, Mirasi, and other friends, Abdul, Fateh Singh, Sulaiman, Islami, and Dalpat, to name just a few.

I am grateful to Rupayan Sansthan for a grant that enabled initial recordings of the oral tradition in 1988. The Indian Council for Social Science

Research supported the project from 1989 to 1991 through a general fellowship enabling further fieldwork and analysis, during which period I was affiliated with the Centre for the Study of Developing Societies. A.M. Shah supervised an early master's of philosophy thesis at the Delhi School of Economics. My debt to the staff of the National Archives of India; the Rajasthan State Archives at Bikaner and Alwar; the India Office Library, London; to Jim and Bill of the Regenstein Library, Chicago cannot go unacknowledged. The Villa Serbelloni at Bellagio provided a paradisial ambience to rework the draft manuscript. For assistance with texts and documents in Persian, Urdu, and Mewati I am grateful to Kali Charan Bahl, Maulvi M.A. Subhan, Maulanas Ilyas and Rahim Baksh, Rakesh Chaturvedi, Pankaj Chaturvedi, and Suraj Chaturvedi, Harish Chandra Dixit, Syed Tahir Ali, Sannu Khan Mewati, and to Satyendra Chaturvedi, Jugmandir Singh Tayal, Chandra Shekhar, and C. M. Naim. To Rajan, Manish, Rachel, Neeru, Somoti, and Nair, thanks for help with indispensable software, hardware, and secretarial assistance. During the last birth pangs of the book I joined the Centre for the Study of Developing Societies. Vijay Chaturvedi, Ashwini Parashar, Himanshu, Diwan Singh, Mohan, Neti Ram, Umesh, Ramu, and so many others have assisted this life process of regrafting. Returning to the Centre has been a homecoming. As I walk the forested Delhi Ridge across from my office I realize that this was the landscape the Meos inhabited in the twelfth and thirteenth centuries before its colonization by the successive cities of Delhi.

Abbreviations

AGGR	Agent to the Governor General in Rajputana.
ASAR	*Alwar State Administrative Report.*
ASRA	Alwar State Records, Bikaner.
ASSR	M. F. O'Dwyer, *Final Report on the Alwar State Settlement, 1900–1901* (Lahore: Mufid-I-'am Press, 1901).
BSAR	M. F. O'Dwyer, *Bharatpur State: Assessment Report of Tahsils of Gopalgarh, Pahari, Kaman, and Dig, 1898–99* (Simla: Government Central Printing Office, 1898).
BSARCT	M. F. O'Dwyer, *Bharatpur State: Assessment Report of the Four Central Tahsils of Bharatpur, Kumher, Akheygarh, Bhartpur, Nagar, 1898–99* (Simla: Government Central Printing Office, 1898).
LRSGD	F. C. Channing, *Land Revenue Settlement of the Gurgaon District* (Lahore: Central Jail Press, 1882).
CIS	*Contributions to Indian Sociology.*
DG	*District Gazetteer.*
ED	Henry M. Elliot and John Dowson eds., *The History of India as Told by Its Own Historians: The Muhammadan Period* [Allahabad: Kitab Mahal, 1963–64] (1867–77).
EPW	*Economic and Political Weekly.*
ERSA	Eastern Rajputana States Agency.
FC	Foreign Consultations of the Foreign Department of the Government of India, National Archives of India.
FD	Foreign Department.

FPF	Foreign and Political Files of the Government of India.
GOI	Government of India.
IESHR	*Indian Economic and Social History Review*.
Legis. Dept. Progs.	Legislative Department Proceedings of the Government of India, National Archives of India, New Delhi.
MT	'Abd-ul-Qadir Bada'uni, *Muntākhab ut-Tawārīkh* (Persian), (reprint ed., Patna: Academica Asiatica, 1986).
OAGGR	Officiating Agent to the Governor General in Rajputana.
Offg.	Officiating.
OPA	Officiating Political Agent.
PA	Political Agent.
Proc.	Proceedings of the Foreign Department, Government of India.
r.	ruled.
RA	Files of the Rajputana Agency, National Archives of India.
RSAB	Rajasthan State Archives, Bikaner.
Secy.	Secretary.
SGOI	Secretary, Government of India.
TA	Khwajah Nizam al-Din Ahmad, *Ṭabaqāt-i Akbarī* (Persian), 3 vols, ed. Brajendranath De (Calcutta: Asiatic Society of Bengal, 1911–36).
TF	Mohammad Qasim Firishta, *Tārīkh-i Firishta* (Persian), 3 vols, ed. Mir Kheirat Ali Khan Mushtaq (Kanpur: Nawal Kishore, 1864–84).
TFS	Ziya'-ud-Din Barani, *Tārīkh-i Fīrūz Shāhī*, (Persian), ed. Shaikh Abdul Rashid (Aligarh: Aligarh Muslim University, 1958 [1862]).
TMS	Yahya bin Ahmad, *Tārīkh-i Mubārak Shāhī* (Persian), ed. Mohammad Hidayat Husain (Calcutta: Asiatic Society of Bengal, 1931).
TN	Minhaj-us Siraj Juzjani, *Ṭabaqāt-i Nāṣirī*, (Persian), ed. Abdul Haye Habibi (Kabul: Anjuman, 1924).
TNR	Abu-'l-'Umar-i-'Usman Minhaj-ud-din, Maulana *Ṭabakāt-i Nāṣirī: A General History of the Muhammadan Dynasties of Asia, including Hindustan from* A.H. *194* (*810* A.D.) *to* A.H. *658* (*1260* A.D.), trans. Maj. H. R. Raverty (Delhi: Munshiram Manoharlal, 1970 [1872–81]).

A Note on Transcription and Transliteration

The romanization of words and titles of books in Persian and Urdu follows the *ALA-LC Romanization, Tables, Transliteration Schemes for Non-Roman Scripts,* ed. Barry Randall (Washington: Library of Congress, 1991). The consonant *v* is romanized as *w* since it is the dominant usage. The ʻ and ʼ are used for ayn and hamzah, respectively, but no diacritical marks are used for *ghain* or *khā,* the ninth and twenty-second letters of the Persian-Arabic script.

As there is no established system for transliterating Rajasthani languages, the Library of Congress system is also used to transliterate the Mewati narratives transcribed in Devanagari (they can be and indeed have been transcribed in Pakistan in the Persian-Arabic script). A dot under d and r represents the harder sounds of the Indian languages, and ḷ is the Rajasthani retroflex. The anusvāra and anunāsika are transliterated as n and ñ respectively without exceptions.

Diacritics are used for most non-English words and authors' titles with the exception of proper nouns, names of castes, and administrative units and positions. Words that are not part of common English usage are italicized and their meanings explained only the first time they appear in the text in the glossary; otherwise they appear in normal typeface without diacritical marks. On the whole, I have depended far more on the popular than on the classicist approach to language. Local usage has been retained as far as possible. Thus the al-Din of Shahab al-Din Ghuri in Persian is replaced by ud-Din in the case of Sufis such as in Shaikh Nizam-ud-Din. Meo and

Mewat rather than Mev and Mevat, and Khanazada rather than Khanazad are used, as the English rendering has become fairly lasting. Hence also Ahlad Singh, Jawahir Singh, Rai Bhan, and Suraj Mal rather than Ahladsingh, Jawahirsingh, Raibhan, and Surajmal. So also I have used the colloquial *gadar* rather than the Urdu *ghadar* for the revolt of 1857.

Against History, Against State

1 Introduction

Seldom in world history have successive states been resisted for seven hundred years or more. This book is about a group in India called the Meos who did not themselves form a state, but who were marginalized by consecutive states. From the sultanate, through the Mughal and British Empires to the regional Rajput and Jat kingdoms there is a continuous, if interrupted and sporadic, history of Meo resistance. Of this resistance there are no Meo records. Had there been no Meo oral tradition this history would have been lost. Had there been no Meo cultural memory the fragmentary accounts in the Indo-Persian histories might have been far less meaningful. Meo self-articulation suggests a remarkable continuity in their response to different states. Conversely, there is a conspicuous connection in the stigmatized representation of the Meos in the written records of the sultanate, and the Mughal and British States, and in those of the Jaipur and Alwar kingdoms. There is also a persistence of strategy comprising modes of direct repression across states. State and history are against the Meos. But their own agency comes into play as they position themselves against states and against history, both in terms of the unfolding of events and processes and the written narratives that come to be called "history."

Two dramatic instances from the Meo oral tradition illustrate this. In the mid-seventeenth century when the Mughal-Rajput ruling alliance insists on the subservience of the local Meo clan, the women assert their right to perform their rites and beat the drum. In similar fashion Antigone disobeys the command of Creon, King of Thebes, and performs the rite of burial for her rebel brother, Polynices, and then hangs herself. Death and destruction for the Meo clan likewise follow from the performance of the rite. In another story from the early nineteenth century, when the Meos are coerced into paying revenue, a Meo leader refuses to pay and, following his example, the others take back their contributions. He is the symbol of Meo defiance of the kingdom's fiscal demands and reminds his clansmen of their recurrent resistance in the past. Other cultures have countered state systems. But in most cases, cultures have not preserved accounts that suggest their past is imbued with violence and what Wachtel calls the vision of the vanquished.[1] A few have, however, such as the letter of the American Indian chief and the orally communicated memory of the Meos.[2]

Social science has traditionally privileged the written over the oral. Although oral art forms are centuries older there has been a relentless dominance of textuality in the history of civilizations. This comes from the association of reason, writing, and truth.[3] Derrida, however, maintains that Western metaphysics locates truth in speech as it purportedly gives an unmediated access to the autonomous self. Speech and voice express the spontaneity and authenticity of the self that is the bearer of consciousness and the source of originary meaning. He critiques the logocentrism of Western thought that privileges speech and treats the written word as a mere record of the spoken.[4] Derrida ignores a parallel stream of Western thought that has viewed speech as effervescent, subjective, open to recanting, to altered positions and perspectives.[5] Lord's seminal work sees orality in terms of fluidity, so that there is no "original" text from an oral point of view, as each performance is original. Homeric traditions are called song rather than poetry. Lord's ideas have exercised a wide influence on the study of oral traditions.[6] This parallel, if not dominant, tradition in Western thought is characterized by the valorization of writing and of the record as the bearer of objective rationality. The hierarchization is implicit in binary classificatory categories such as folk/classical, oral/written, myth/history, little tradition/great tradition.

Oral accounts have been considered "mythic," inauthentic representations, and distorted versions of "reality." The written word is seen as providing the possibility of scientific discourse, whereas the "oral" is relegated to "folk" and "lore." Thus not only are certain groups subordinated but also their modes of knowledge and articulation, their political forms and languages, their experience and perspectives are marginalized. History primarily recognizes the powerful, the victorious. Much history comprises narratives written from the perspective of the state.

As recent research has brought out, however, oral traditions have been very important to cultures with or without writing. These are an invaluable resource in understanding people's categories and textures of consciousness. No culture is really ahistorical. All peoples locate themselves in time. In a sense, all groups use memory to organize the past. Human memory interprets, classifies, evaluates, and organizes. Even the ability to forget is an integral part of memory. This work investigates the mythic mode of organizing and transmitting memory, in particular, the subject group's perspective on state formations.

The Meos were constituted subjects by different states, imperial (used in this work to refer to the sultanate and Mughal Empire), colonial, and princely. Official memory is available to us as the histories associated with these state formations. The question is how to bring the margin into representation that exists only as the stigmatized other in these texts? This work attempts to do this through an analysis of narratives of oppositional practice. These narratives construct and reconstruct identity and social being, and also order the past through broken histories.

The Meo oral tradition suggests at ways in which knowledge systems might be politically marginalized, yet retain their vibrance within a cultural context enabling resistance across centuries. The narrative exploration of the past indicates alternative forms of the historical imagination, modes of structuring power, and the changing nature of identity, bonding, and conflict over time.

The Meos, who are estimated to number more than 10 million persons, have been one of the largest Muslim communities of the Indian subcontinent. They have inhabited for at least the previous seven centuries the region called Mewat. Even after the diaspora that accompanied the partition of the subcontinent, the largest concentration of Meos continues to be in this region. Mewat, which means the "land of the Meos," lies southwest of Delhi and because of its contiguity to the imperial capital has constantly been affected by the politics of the center. In the early part of the twentieth century Mewat was territorially part of the kingdoms of Alwar and Bharatpur in Rajputana, indirectly under the British, and the British-ruled district of Gurgaon in the Punjab. A large number of Meos also inhabited the United and Central Provinces and Baluchistan. The Meos of Mewat are organized into what I call a Pal Polity comprising thirteen close-knit, territorially based, patrilineal clans as well as nonterritorial lineages, all connected through the exchange of women, social relations, and their sense of a shared past. The clan itself includes all those related by ties of descent to a common male ancestor. The Meo polity like the Rajput polity is governed by patrilineages rather than clans. The Meos were one of the many pastoral-peasant communities and had close relations with other groups such as the Jats, Gujars, and Ahirs.

Details of the Meo past are discussed in the following chapter. Following an almost continuous resistance to the rule of the Turkish-Afghan sultanate between the thirteenth and fifteenth centuries, the Meos were brought briefly under central control by the Afghan Lodi dynasty after 1451 and in a more sustained way by the Mughal Empire after 1527. Over this period of nearly four centuries the warrior group was transformed into a settled peasant community. Even as the state enhanced its control through the period of Mughal, Rajput, and British rule, the animosity between state and community was a prominent aspect of the historical process.

This account is not directly concerned with the literary-musicological character of the Meo oral tradition or with the rhythms of group life as in a conventional anthropological monograph. It is also not a "history," breaking as it does continuously the linearity of the historical narrative. The Meos provide a point of entry into a theoretical terrain of knowledge systems and power relations. Their struggle against history and state enables questioning of a set of assumptions that have been held as axiomatic in current thinking, such as the distinction between orality and writing, myth and history.

Orality and Writing

Since the "Enlightenment," cultures have been seen as either preliterate or with writing and therefore with literatures. From this flowed the possibility and likelihood that cultures with writing also had more evolved political forms such as the state. Writing and statehood created the ground for the development of religion and history. Thus these cultures constituted civilizations. Their "other" are the dark and less-evolved cultures of continents that are without writing and characterized by mere orality. These cultures are constructed by contrast, that is, without either history or religion, as being stateless and deficient in reason that might have enabled the development of sciences. They are conceived in terms of an absence. The shadowy area that blurred this careful construction was civilizations such as of India.

Writing and domination have been closely associated over much of human history.[7] Levi-Strauss points out the violence of civilization associated with writing. Derrida criticizes his valorization of phonetic writing and of an innocent Rousseaun state of nature, but likewise stresses the violence of *écriture*, or writing in its broadest sense. The world of writing overdetermines speech, erasing its "presence" and substituting it with an absence and a new presence. At a later historical stage in the history of civilizations, writing is embodied in forms of print such as treaties, new laws and rules, court pronouncements, in revenue and forest settlements, in census documents and gazetteers, all backed by growing structures of coercion. The "Turk" and "Mughal" and "Meo" of the oral tradition are reconfigured by the "Musalman" of colonial ethnography and history. Writing profoundly affects people's imagination and articulation. The Meo oral tradition in its struggle against the state simultaneously contests the universe of writing and history.

Nonetheless, the tendency to constitute orality as the other of the written must be cautioned against. This approach has been represented by several scholars. Goody, for example, refers to the interface of written and oral traditions and to their dialectical relationship, but treats the latter as non-ideological. He maintains that writing makes possible "the rise of 'an organized body of intellectuals,'" and with it "its complement, the differentiation of ideas into ideologies, the fragmentation of the world view, the conflict of ideas."[8] The presence of ideologies is the criterion, which Goody, following Gellner, uses to differentiate preliterate, tribal religions.[9] He argues that logical thought involving syllogistic reasoning is only possible with writing.

Writing has been identified with inscription, whereas orality is regarded as belonging to the domain of speech. But "speech" itself covers a range of articulation, and a distinction needs to be maintained between spontaneous speech as in a conversation and the transmission of knowledge and memory, which has a greater fixity. The transmission of Vedic traditions, Buddha's *vaçana* (utterance), Mahavir's *vāṇī* (speech), and Muhammad's *ḥadīth* (authentic traditions of the sayings of the Prophet) all assume that there has been greater fixity than assumed by mere speech and presuppose an enormous attention to mnemonic conventions. Similarly, the use of poetic rhymed verse by oral literary traditions suggests a striving for a measure of "fixity" to ensure its transmission across generations. Moreover, the fixity of written texts themselves has also been brought into question in debates on authorship or, say, in the search for an Ur text.

The problem then that arises in conceptualizing orality is the constant resort to dichotomous categories. According to Goody, writing is visual whereas orality is based on hearing. But the visual is also very important in oral traditions since nonverbal modes such as gesture are central to the communication of meaning. Indeed this is why transcription is such a reductionist exercise since orality is what infuses texts of the Meo oral tradition with life for both the singers and the audience.[10]

The writing/orality binary has been challenged by recent research that shows how orality is not displaced by literacy. It exists in contexts of state power and is simultaneous with writing as in the telling of scripture.[11] The study of popular culture shows how written and oral texts intersect and interpenetrate. Writing transcribes the oral, and the oral simultaneously borrows from, refers to, and opposes written texts. In bardic verse of northwestern India composed in the literary language of Pingal, as in many African oral traditions, the field of literature spans the oral and the written.[12] The genre called *bāt* that is the musico-poetic form used to express Meo collective memory explicitly mediates the worlds of orality and writing.

The "oral," in this case, is no autonomous aesthetic but is permeated by forms, metaphors, and images from both Sanskrit and "vernacular" literary conventions. Poets and performers are also influenced by the Indo-Persian tradition of history writing called *tārīkh*, or chronicles, and Meo collective consciousness is imbued by colonial histories. Memory arises in the context of intense intercultural encounter. Meo ideas of power internalize the symbolic world of Rajput ideologies of honor and dishonor as well as a courtly vocabulary that derives from the medieval Indian Empires, even as the Meos fight against sultans and Rajput kings. A complex intertextuality is at play within the oral. It is with these qualifications that the following pages explore how the Meo oral tradition offers what Terdiman calls a "counter-discourse" to hegemony or is a source of Foucauldian countermemory.[13]

Consider the question of why the term "text" has been identified with inscription (read, writing). Ricoeur defines a text as having a referential dimension, that is, as revealing a world. But if a folk text (narrative, performance) can also be seen as having a referential dimension it fulfills the criterion of a text, in which case his restricted definition of text, as that which is inscribed, collapses.[14] Nonliterate cultures thus have their texts and modes of transmitting them. Although, as Ganesh Devy points out, these are mostly regarded as "paraliteratures," which do not qualify for the literary canon.[15]

Myth and History

Another dichotomy endowed by the Enlightenment is that of myth and history. Myth has been seen as radically distinct from the rational sciences being viewed as the other of the empirical with respect to its truth claims. Whereas myth has been assumed to characterize primitive and traditional societies, ideology has been identified with the developed industrial West. The latter is even described as having gone beyond ideology.[16] A university course/text on ideology typically looks at "isms," a contribution of post–Renaissance Europe. The discussion of myth, on the other hand, has generally referred to totemic and primitive societies and traditional societies such as India, China, Japan, and others. Modern societies are often assumed to be bereft of the processes of myth making and traditional societies of all ideological components. In the Third World, ideologies such as Liberalism, Marxism, or African Negritude are considered to be a consequence of European intervention, which presumably transformed what Campbell calls the "archaic" Oriental mind. In the "rational" Occident he considers the mythological problematic to have long since (in A.D. 613) been transformed into the ideological one.[17]

One of the major contributions of Levi-Strauss was the rejection of the duality of thought and action and the study of myth as an ideological system. Regrettably Levi-Strauss tended to identify myth with "cold" or primitive societies that were without history and without writing. This reinforced the dichotomous view of myth and history even as he also reified the conflict between orality and literacy. These became parallel to the contrasts between myth and science and nature and culture.[18]

Although much of this book is about the mythic contestation of history, it must be emphasized that history and myth are not completely exclusive modes of representation. Historiography creates its own fictions despite its claims to embody "objectivity." Myth stands for another, deeper mode of understanding and representing experience. Myth can also appropriate historical time by framing a narrative and ordering the episodic structure in linear time. The order of representation, however, tends to be metaphorical. The mythohistorical narrative thereby combines both linearity and symbol, and also a heterogeneity of temporal experience.[19] This can make myth a particularly powerful source of collective representations that celebrates collective memory.

This does not mean that myth and history are epistemically identical. Indeed, one of the problems with the path-breaking, early work on oracy done in Africa by scholars like Ruth Finnegan and Jan Vansina was the historicization of myth. For Vansina the oral tradition must be at least a generation old to be used as a source of history. He seeks to distinguish the chaff of eyewitness reminiscences from the historical kernel.[20] But to glean the "oral history" from myth seems to me an unaesthetic activity of disaggregating networks of meaning.

The traditional anthropological conception of myth as a charter for social institutions and ritual à la Malinowski denies ways in which myth can be a source of cultural and institutional critique. Michael Taussig, for instance, shows that a magical figure such as the devil arises from "folk politics" and embodies a folk critique of capitalism. Jonathan Hill argues that the "subject" position of myth be seen as a source whereby the perceptual and experiential dimension of consciousness can be investigated.[21] The structuralist approach to myth, which sees it as atemporal objectified thought, is also problematic in that it isolates it from the historical conjunctures that produce myth and give it meaning. Much recent work, however, views myth as providing an alternative ontological perspective that displays the multiple centers wherein peoples articulate, produce, and shape their worlds.[22] These accounts are a significant resource in the attempt to reconstruct social and cultural textures of the past, although not necessarily precise representations of "fact" or "event" in a conventional sense. An exciting body of work has emerged in this area from Africa, Asia, and the Americas.[23]

Myth suggests a culture's coding of truth-values through narrative. It refers to a set of sequentially arranged images each of which is, in turn, a dense network of meaning and reference. The mythic imagination weaves together cosmologies, categories, moral values, and visions of the past. Barthes views mythologies as a "nauseating mixture of common opinions," but for Nietzsche "every culture that has lost myth has lost its natural healthy creativity. Only a horizon ringed about with myths can unify a culture."[24]

Clearly, myth can provide a space to access resistance. This is particularly so when it expresses communal memory and becomes a contestatory site with respect to the official memory of the state. The latter purports to be universal or national memory or History but subsumes and silences a plurality of individual/group memories/histories. What Halbwachs calls the collective memory is umbilically linked to community identity.[25] Jewish existence, Valensi argues, is molded not by theology or a shared history, which they lacked being a dispersed people, but by memory, an untiring recall of the events of the past.[26] Jewish memory worked as a powerful force that countered other processes of history.

For Levi-Strauss, concerned with the structural similarity of myths collected in different regions, their content was of negligible importance. The science of myth was made possible by its breakdown into constituent units. Interested in the formal properties of myth that are universal, he argued that myth as an underlying structure is composed of relations of binary oppositions. He saw myth as "timeless," as it explains the present, the past, and future, and in opposition to politics, which has replaced myth in modern societies.[27] The universality that is imputed by structuralism, however, denies the relation between myth and memory. To look at myth as memory, however, suggests the politics of remembrance. Indeed, it is only the mythic location in time and space that can help us understand how myth can be a source of resistance, a form of oppositional practice.

State Formation

Political desire, to paraphrase Lacan, is the desire for the other.[28] A desire attained through conquest and control. The process is universal and familiar and intensified by the technologies of governance and violence available to the modern state. A contemporary example is the Baltic states of Latvia, Lithuania, and Estonia, whose populations were decimated by Stalin, yet whose resistance persisted. Latvia was recolonized by Russia, a tenth of its population deported to Siberia and reduced to 54 percent of the general population. Death, rape, or deportation affected at least one person in every family. Taussig puts it far more dramatically when he describes how the U.S. Plains Indian bears the brunt of primitivism that testifies and draws out the otherwise inarticulable magic and sacred design of the modern state. The image of the Indian is a key to the state's sacred interior that he refers to as the magicality of the state.

State formation has yielded a range of forms such as the kingly, imperial, colonial, the modern nation-state, and others, and one of the attempts made in this book is to historicize the state. A large body of state-centered literature exists focusing on institutions, exchange relations, dynasties, centralized or decentralized units, big and little kingdoms, coercive and ritual aspects of sovereignty. This considerable research highlights the difference between the premodern and the modern states.

Are Asiatic states best characterized as segmentary state formations on the

African model, as Stein suggests? Or the theater state that Geertz identified in Bali? Tambiah advances an "indigenous" conception of the galactic polity. He sees Southeast Asian kingdoms in terms of a multicentered political galaxy comprising principalities and dependencies from the late thirteenth through the eighteenth century.[29]

In the South Asian context the Dumontian framework gained considerable ascendancy. Although Dumont identified a division between the brahman and the king, he saw Indian kingship as encompassed by the brahman. The social order is grounded on the principle of purity and pollution. The king is subordinate to the brahman who is the highest embodiment of purity. The thesis of the all-encompassing sacred was challenged by what has come to be called the Chicago School, which foregrounded the autonomy of the political. Represented by Dirks it contested Dumont's dominance of the brahman by highlighting the centrality of the king and of the political order. In this alternative model the king was the font of social hierarchy organized through the royal activity of prestation including of land, honors, and service tenures.

The range of literature on the subject is fascinating. The issues contended with include the literature on state and kinship but also on caste. Both the Dumontian and Dirksean models depend on a topdown construction of authority. Further, the thesis of ritual sovereignty provides a theory of order and obedience but does not allow or explain dissent and protest.[30] Tambiah's otherwise outstanding work is a representative example. He sees legitimacy as derived from two sources. One from the claim of the ruler to being a cakkavatti or universal monarch or a dharmaraja or righteous ruler on the basis of personal achievement and commitment to Buddhist norms of kingship. The second relates to "the possession of *palladia* and *regalia*, which are enduring sedimentations and objectifications of power and virtue."[31] In Tambiah's view legitimacy flows from the imperial center. It derives from the claims of the ruler to descent from a lineage but more important, as Tambiah rightly emphasizes, from his claims of personal achievement and of rule in terms of righteousness and justice. In this analysis, there is no reference to the fact that the claims of the ruler must be counterposed with the evaluation of the state of the many subject groups of the realm. Claims of righteousness and justice are then scrutinized. The subject's response may range from acceptance and identification to rejection and rebellion. In Tambiah's view the flow of sovereignty is outward and downward. But the subjective construction of power and legitimacy is complex, multilayered, and individuated or communitarian. A differentiated construction of state and sovereignty might come not only from priestly orders and merchant communities but also from subaltern groups. Certain groups such as the Meos through the period characterized as medieval perceived the terror of the state. Clearly the magicality that Taussig identifies with the modern state has its antecedents in premodern times.

The category state "formation" that has dominated historical sociology and comparative politics then is deceptive: suggesting a creative act of an entity coming into being, of becoming. It does not indicate how other institutions, forms of political practice, and modes of political being are negated by states. State formation renders the subject invisible, but if population is one of the four "elements" of the state according to traditional Western political theory surely the subjective view of the state cannot go unconsidered. We return to the old philosophical question as to whether the state is an object in itself independent of perception. This is not merely an epistemological question but also an ethical one. The state is constructed, reproduced, and challenged in people's narratives, in cultural performance. There is a need not only to work with multiple models of the state but also to see the differentiated character of even a single state for the different groups that inhabit that society. For instance, a Mughal or British administrator perceives the state differently from a peasant group or a group characterized as criminal or itinerant (such as gypsies).

In this book the state imaginary of the Meos is juxtaposed with the Meo imaginary of the state. The concern is how state and sovereignty are constructed and redescribed. The state is not a mere set of institutions and procedures. Indeed, political practices are culturally constituted. Recent work suggests how the state is manifest in technologies of governance and activities such as talk. Later sections of this work engage with debates on kingship, the Mughal imperium, and colonialism.

The relation between knowledge and power has been foregrounded by contemporary theory. Narratives of the state and its others, which have been called history or ethnography, are also aspects of the production of stateness. The professional discipline of history has been overwhelmingly oriented to monarchy, thereby ignoring the institutions of people who did not achieve statehood. History isolates the study of the past from the present, masking the concerns of the state or of the historian. The ethnographer has often tended to sever the present from history, exoticising or demonizing subjects. Fabian suggests the rhetorical devices whereby ethnography deprives subjects of their contemporaneity. Tribalism spatializes time just as evolutionism naturalizes it.[32]

Is this a Foucauldian reading that identifies power and knowledge, a reader may well ask? Yes and no. Certeau's corrective to Foucault is profound and restorative of the life within, what he refers to as the "cadavers" of the city seen from the panoptic perspective. Certeau presents a powerful critique of the Foucauldian panoptic perspectives, which he states is similar to the elevation offered by the (erstwhile) World Trade Center or to the cartographic impulse where "a solar Eye, [is] looking down like a god." Certeau goes on to ask the question of the forgotten and ignored itineraries of the pedestrians of the city that are obliterated by the panoptic perspective from "out there" and "high above." He emphasizes the importance of everyday stories that people use to (re)construct the space around them and that are omitted in the modern geographical form of the map and in the other human sciences like history and ethnography. Like maps these disciplines are founded on spatializing assumptions that in naming and classifying an area also colonize it rhetorically. Following Merleau-Ponty, Certeau attempts "to locate the practices that are foreign to the 'geometrical' or 'geographical' space of visual, panoptic or theoretical constructions" that constitute an "'anthropological,' poetic and mythic experience of space." Certeau details the "murky intertwining daily behaviors" that continually disrupt the order of the city as individuals continually transgress the "stable" and "isolatable" divisions through which the state attempts to co-opt their subjectivity.[33] In a sense then, myths and stories might not only reimagine institutions such as the state by providing a poignant sense of its powerful interiority but also provide an alternative perspective on both space and time. Say, the multiple possibilities implicit in the territoriality of the nonstate polity or their perspective on conquest that is rendered a past of struggle.

The question that Certeau does not pursue, however, is the possibility of rewriting the archaeology of disciplinary terrain, particularly its compartmentalization. This is the project of how to retrieve the presence of the footprint and the stories of travel in the map from which the map arose. Or how the reinsertion of mythopoetic might reconfigure "the opacities of history everywhere." How might the objectified subject of ethnography be replaced by the historicized subject with her complex and often contradictory baggage of conceptual and emotional experience? And how can the subjectification of the abstract universal subject by the state be reconfigured in the domain of politics? The project Certeau does not work through involves the erasure of the erasure, a recall of the forgotten, a bringing into view of what is outside and beyond what the state has reduced and conquered and history othered.

In medieval historiographical representation the Meos become the elements of disorder while kingship epitomizes order. The Meos are held responsible for a continuous war that ruptures the peace that has to be constantly reestablished by the state. They are described as threatening Delhi so that its gates had to be closed against them. This is only one example of the construction of the mythology of the sultanate as a weak state. It is echoed in the construction of Mughal and British sovereignty. The assertion ignores the nature of Meo existence and their marginalization in terms of land and power.

Needless to say, postcolonial academic scholarship to this day draws considerably upon the statist perception of Meo resistance. Amir Ali writes, "Time and again, several rulers of Alwar, the names of Bakhtawar Singh and Jai Singh being more prominent among them, had to fight against the Meos and bring peace to the region."[34] There is little awareness of the role of the state in the constitution of marginality as also the resistance of the margins.

Marginality and Resistance

A rich reflection on marginality is available that shows the cultural construction of domination, difference, and otherness.[35] Regrettably there has been in postcolonial writing a tendency to reduce the making of marginality to colonialism. The sources of marginality are more pervasive than the constructivist position allows. Marginality arises from a comprehensive association between writing, state, history, and religion.[36] Combined they constitute the center in contrast to the periphery that supposedly comprises (nonstate) community characterized by orality, illiteracy, myth, nonreligion, or corrupted and deviant forms of belief and practice (mostly beliefs in spirits and ancestors). Marginality has to do with distinctive and unequal subject positions within fields of power and knowledge. The combination of state power, history, and ethnography constructs the other as a ferocious and backward people far removed from "religion" and civilization.

Marginality is a source of both powerlessness and power, and results in subordination and resistance. As the Meo oral tradition makes apparent it is not accepted passively. The Meos challenge and resist their exclusion. Their agency emerges in the context of resistance.

The margin is a space that is simultaneously imbued with both violence and creativity. Rosaldo refers to border crossings as "sites of creative cultural production."[37] The margins are inhabited by populations perceived as dangerous.[38] In the Meo case the impurity of culture (the "syncreticism" of a confused bricolage of Hinduism and Islam) adds to the danger of the insurgent and the itinerant criminal. The Meo narrative tradition reveals how this space is a site of discursive contestation. The margin bears within it resistance to the idea of "religion," of history and writing as the embodiment of truth, of the state as the authoritative exponent of legitimacy, and intimates the counterimagination of a decentralized polity. It constantly demonstrates how the community is embedded in an open-ended dialogue even as it internalizes hegemonic perspectives.

What is the source of a critique to a dominant and comprehensive knowledge system such as historiography or ethnography? Languages that are called "vernacular" or *apabhraṇṣa* (the deprecating terms of English and Sanskrit, respectively) provide access to lived history. Devy persuasively argues that one of the problems that has beset Indian intellectuals is their preoccupation with the ruling languages of either Sanskrit or English.[39] Mewati is the spoken language of the region of Mewat. Termed a "dialect," it has no script of its own and can be written in both the Persian-Arabic and Devanagiri scripts. Its status is neither that of classical or śastric languages such as Persian and Sanskrit nor of the Indian regional *bhaṣa* languages such as Marathi, Rajasthani, and Bengali. The Mewati oral tradition counters the construction of sovereignty and its other in Persian and English texts.

In the subcontinental context there is a close relationship between oral literatures, memory, and performance. Mukund Lath points out that in the Indian context most of the arts such as music, poetry, and drama have been closely related.[40] Oral traditions are usually performed. Mythic representation is particularly powerful because of the intensive communicative modes and dramatic quality of the cultural performance and the rhythmic-poetic form set to music. Tune, melody, *tāl* (rhythm), and *rāga* are an integral part of the creation of *rasa*, or emotion. The performance of Mewati narratives highlights the centrality of the cultural tradition in constructing and reproducing community and in sustaining resistance over centuries.

Resistance emerges at the interface of memory and imagination. The relative autonomy of memory enables marginalized groups to engage in struggle. The role of imagination suggests how memory is not a representation of the past but a *re-presentation*. Within the world of their own culture they re-present their own history. This follows a pattern that departs from the conventional historical work that is written and that organizes time chronologically (as ages, eras, reigns, etc.). Memory mythologizes the Meo past as it is told as multiple stories in the present. The focus is episodic (such as on battles) and heroic, and oriented to a construction of masculinity. The time of the story is distinct from the external, chronological, and linear time of clocks and calendars. But it frequently intersects with the historical time of the community. A narrator, thus, often sets a historical frame: "In the time of Shah Jahan, . . ." "At the *darbar* of Akbar, . . . " "Under the rule of (the Jat raja) Jawahir Singh. . . . " In the representation of the past, history is not consciously "secularized" as was done in Europe following the Enlightenment. Memory is constantly sacralized, hence the repeated references to Hazrat Ali, the Prophet's cousin and son-in-law, and the gods, Mahadev (Shiva) and Kṛishna.

Meo oral texts counter the Persian and English texts by inverting their categories. Persian has an extraordinarily rich vocabulary for the state and its others. The idea that the Meos are "*mufsid*" (rebellious) and "*zorṭalab*" (insurgent) becomes the commanding image of the medieval Meo. This is countered in the Mewati oral text called the *Pāñch Pahāṛ kī laṛāī* by showing how the Mughal-Rajput army moves into the area to appropriate the agrarian surplus in the seventeenth century. Revenue collection is backed by the coercive power of the imperial regime. The Rajput noble comes in as the revenue collector at the head of an army. Meo women are troubled, elders insulted, men slaughtered, and local conditions of scarcity and famine overlooked to maximize the coffers of the state. To underscore Meo women's subordinate status, they are not allowed to perform a rite of childbirth. The Mughal-Rajput army has already besieged the area and the narrative ends with the tragic slaughter of virtually the entire Meo clan in a battle. In English ethnographies the Meos are epitomized as the looters. Who are the looters, the narrative seems to ask? Is not the treasure of the Mughal regime the booty of conquest or surplus appropriated from the peasantry? Then who is really guilty of the unrighteousness that the Mughals attribute to the Meos? Conversely the Meo narrative imputes *julam* (derived from the Persian *ẓulm*) meaning tyranny or oppression to the imperial state system.

The written record of the sultanate and the Mughal Empire in its interstices substantiates the Meo view. It indicates the territorial displacement of the Mewatis, as they are then called, by Rajputs and Turks from the twelfth century if not earlier. It evocatively portrays the constant struggle of the Meos against central rule and in defense of local autonomy and control over land

and resources. The battle described in the *Pāñch Pahāṛ* is one that is repeated time and again from sultanate to Mughal Empire between the twelfth to the seventeenth centuries. Archival sources from the mid-seventeenth through the early twentieth centuries likewise demonstrate sustained Meo resistance.

In the narrative of *Ghurchaṛī Mev Khāñ* contextualized in the late nineteenth century, the regional princely state of Alwar is seen in collusion with the colonial state. This bandit story articulates Meo dissent against the ruling Rajput monarchy legitimated by birth and divine right. The colonial ethnographic tradition, however, translated peasant concerns as criminality. The entire Meo group was stigmatized as a "criminal tribe." The Meos demonstrate what Erikson calls a negative identity: what is stigmatized becomes a matter of glorification. Looting and banditry become a consciously heroic act. It is not indexical of criminality but of critique. The Meo oral tradition contests categories through counterimages and lexical reformulation: in contrast to the extractive Rajput regime the narrative demonstrates the "goodness" of the Meo bandit brothers who assist the poor and oppressed. This is a common device used all over the world in stories of this genre.

The center and the margin are not exclusive spaces but always constantly shifting and changing. There are also centers within the margin as it asserts hierarchy and masculinity with respect to caste and gender within its own regional social organization.

The oral tradition constructs the site of narration as a male, public arena from which women are excluded. The feminine voice is a powerful one in Meo narratives although it is always mediated through a male narrator. Rajput women frequently defy their husbands and emerge in strong defense of the Meos. The queens of the Rajput maharajas, Mangal Singh and Jai Singh of Alwar, in the narratives *Ghurchaṛī* and *Yāsīn Khāñ* plead for the Meos and are soundly admonished by their husbands. The English official's wife even falls in love with the Meo bandit-hero Ghurchari, drawn to his sexualized power. In Meo narratives the Rajputs and the imperial-colonial regimes are often in alliance. Their women, however, are able to reach across boundaries of caste, class, gender, and power. The marginalized of both patriarchal and political systems are narrativized as part of a subaltern alliance.

This work looks at three languages, English, Persian, and Mewati. The languages are not homogenous, noncontradictory idioms but have a plurality of voices, of genres. Mewati can be seen as a site of struggle over the past and an arena where ruling ideologies pervade, and its representations are both internalized and battled by the community. It is important to qualify the reading of the oral tradition as resistance with the recognition that like other languages Mewati is polysemic, the site of conflict and contradiction and considerable ambivalence. Resistance, moreover, is rarely the response of the unified community and might not even move the majority.

Unlike the written texts of the medieval–early modern period where ethnic identities are often frozen, the oral tradition both unravels these identities and exposes the fractured "community." Although the brothers Ghurchari and Mev Khan challenge princely rule, their own uncle is described as a close friend of the Maharaja Mangal Singh, the ruler of Alwar. In the *Pāñch Pahāṛ*, likewise, even as the Pahat clan defies the Badshah Shah Jahan, Gadai, a Meo from Sikri, is present at the imperial court, advising the Mughal ruler and communicating "intelligence" against the Meos to the empire. We know that a large number of Meos were continuously co-opted into collaborative roles within the imperial and regional state systems. The tendency to romanticize resistance may be forestalled with the remark that it is simultaneous with evidence of both collaboration and passivity.

The next chapter details the sources of marginality. Chapter 3 outlines the vision of the Meo polity and the organization of self-governance, which provide an alternative to kingship and the state. Chapter 4 traces the intellectual genealogy of Mewati otherness that reverberates through many Indo-Persian historiographical texts written between the thirteenth and the eighteenth centuries and in the administrative documents of the Mughal Empire. This is counterposed with the Mewati perspective on the Mughal Empire (chap. 5). Chapter 6 demonstrates the colonial construction of the Meos. This builds on and supposedly gives a scientific basis to the construction of the Meo in Indo-Persian histories. Their own folklore is appropriated by colonial ethnography as evidence of their criminality. The colonial idea that the Meos were a "criminal tribe" has left a permanent impress on popular, administrative, and academic imaging of the group. Watson writes, "[They] converted to Islam yet [they] did not give up their thieving and plundering propensities and to this day are the most determined of cattle lifters." They are referred to as "Ishmaelites" — suggesting the Christian category for outcasts. Writing increasingly permeates Meo life worlds and speech and affects their self-description in terms of wildness and criminality. Chapters 7 and 8 focus on the self-representation of Meo action in terms of differentiated categories of feud, banditry, and resistance that writing collapses as disorder and crime.

This work is about the Meos and their ways of thinking, acting, living, resisting, forgetting, and remembering. It is part of a larger enterprise, however, attempting a critique of state forms and their associated textual discourses of ethnography and history. The universe of the Meo mythic tradition enables access to their internal world of ordering events, categories, and hierarchies. The oral text is thereby linked to actual practices involved in the relation of ruling as well as to social being that is on the cusp of religious traditions that we now call Hinduism and Islam. This is not to say that we have encapsulated their world but merely gained a passage to it that enables new questions to be asked, new methods to be sought.

2 The Making of Meo Marginality

The Meo past has been one of migration and sedentarization, displacement, and marginality. Historical detail for the period before the establishment of the sultanate in the thirteenth century is somewhat hazy. Are the Meos the "Mid"? The Mid and Jat were the two major migratory groups of northwestern India between the seventh and the eleventh centuries.[1] Arab writers refer to clusters of these groups inhabiting the swamps, mountains, and deserts of Sind at the time of the Arab conquest. These two groups, who were the oldest inhabitants of Sind, had divided the region among themselves and frequently fought each other.

Arab sources suggest that the frequent Mid and Jat raids on seaports and the maritime trade of the Persian Gulf and the western Indian Ocean caused the Arab conquest of Sind. Gardizi describes the al-Mayd and the al-Zutt as sea pirates of the coastal region from Daybul (originally Debal) to Kathiawar. Daybul was then part of the kingdom of Dahir, son of the brahman ruler Chach.[2] Muhammad al Qasim, son-in-law of the governor of Iraq, invaded Sind in A.D. 711 when the Khalifa declared war against Sind and Hind. Arab sources explain the conquest on grounds of protecting the commerce of the Persian Gulf against alleged piracy, an argument that scholars like Wink seem to accept.[3] But one needs to remember that all the preceding Khalifas had sent expeditions to prospect the conditions in Sind. Further, that this was a period of vibrant Arab expansion in Syria, Persia, Central Asia, and Spain. Mid piracy is a weak argument.

The Arabs introduced processes of control oriented to sedentarize the pastoral-nomadic groups in Sind. Discriminatory practices were enforced on the Jats that prohibited their chiefs and elders from riding with saddles, and wearing shoes and clothes of silk and velvet. They were made to go about bare headed, their bodies tattooed, and accompanied by a dog for the sake of identification. Revenue obligations and the *jiziyā*, or tax, on non-Muslims were imposed on them. Already on the fringes of brahmanical society, they were explicitly hierarchized as non-Muslim subjects under Arab rule. Rebellions and armed conflicts were constant.[4]

Up to the mid-ninth century the governors of Sind continued to raid the unsubdued areas of Sind, took large numbers of prisoners and slaves, and made inroads into transhumance. While certain groups of Jats compromised and were converted, the Mids concentrated in southeastern Sind persisted in their hostility. Jats were extended *amān*, or immunity, after their submission; they subsequently joined Arab armies and were deployed against the Mids. The Arabs killed three thousand Mids in an expedition and attacked their sources of water by constructing an embankment *(sakru-l med)*. With the help of Jat chiefs they brought seawater through a canal to their tank, making their water saline, and also sent out marauding expeditions against them. Al-Baladhuri also mentions that an Arab group proceeded with sixty or so ships against the Mid and killed a number of them. The Mids continue to be described as robbers by Arab geographers through the ninth and tenth centuries. During the tenth and eleventh centuries there are references to frequent clashes of the Mids with the Muslim kingdom of Mansura (Sind). The Arabs, however, seem to have been unable to permanently repress the Mids. Expeditions against the Jats and Mid continued till A.D.844.

Wink argues that Islamic thought and historiography have projected a false contrast between *jihād*, or the holy war, that is against infidels and therefore legitimate and *fitna*, or internal strife, that is illegitimate civil war against Muslim or non-Muslim groups. This rhetoric has led to the bias of Western historiography that Islam is in essence a warrior religion. Wink points out that early Islam was much more a "political" than a "moral" or "religious" affair. So-called jihad often culminated in compromise with locally established powers.[5] I agree with Wink's argument that fitna was a normal mechanism of state formation so that the extension of sovereignty was made possible by intervening in and making use of existing local conflict. Further, that the distinction between outside "enemy" and internal "rebel" cannot be maintained. But the suppression of fitna did not always result in conciliatory politics. True, in some cases immunity was given to defeated populations who submitted or converted, as in the case of the Jats.

But this was not always the case. Indeed, fitna also authorized strong state action against local populations, as epitomized by Arab action toward the Mids. Further, one needs to distinguish between the range of Muslim polities across space and time. Compromise and conciliation were far more characteristic of the early phase of Arab rule in India and the Mughal polity than in the rule of the Turko-Afghan sultanate.

Arab geographic-history written from the point of view of the sedentary state constructs pastoral groups as the other of the political order. What is understated in the narrative are vital details, for instance, that the Jats and Mids are involved in the active commercial life of the Persian Gulf. The *Chachnāma*, which castigates the Jats and other tribes as "detestable people" *(makrūh khalqan)*, "highway robbers," "thieves," "pirates," with the "wild nature of brutes" *(waḥshī mizāj)*, also mentions that they are employed in the armed forces of the Sindian kings and as guides of caravans. The Mid are described as sailors of the coastal regions of Makran, Sind, and Kathiawar. Was it that these groups were "predatory" as Wink maintains or that the Arabs were attempting to dominate the trade of the Gulf? As he himself points out, trade and piracy were closely related.

The question of migration remains open and conjectural. It has been suggested that the Jats migrated from the Indus Valley in lower Sind to the northeast into the Punjab and Multan, where they seem firmly established and sedentarized by the early eleventh century.[6] Between the ninth and eleventh centuries the Mid wandered along the banks of the Indus, Sind, Kutch, and Kathiawar, reaching the frontier of Makran. Both Jats and Mid were among the most important mobile and migratory populations of this period. Arab geographers refer to their movement from Multan to the sea and across the desert. They formed a large population "unconverted to the faith," who occupied pastures on the fringes of the desert and along the Indus, cultivating camels and goats.[7] Another group might have moved eastward from Sind across the Thar desert to the Doab, the alluvial plain between the Ganga and the Yamuna Rivers. The clan form of organization was associated with a mode of production that involved transhumance in search of grazing lands and water.

The areas of Rajasthan known as Mewar and Merwara are said to have had an association with the Meos. Mewar, Tod tells us, was traditionally known as "Meḍāpaṭa," meaning the country of the Medas. Interestingly, both Meo historians and contemporary genealogists of the Mers of Ajmer claim that the Meos of Mewat are a section that migrated from the settlements of the Mers in the central Aravallis.[8] Elliot maintains that the Mers of the Aravalli Mountains and Kathiawar along the Gujarat coast are descendants of the Mids. He deduced from the thesis of identity one of criminality.[9] The derivation of identity from place-names, however, is somewhat weak evidence.

Successive invasions and the rise of a series of monarchical states in the early medieval period resulted in the displacement and marginalization of several tribal, pastoral, and peasant groups like the Meos.[10] According to Meo histories there was a considerable concentration of Meos in the fertile delta between the Ganga and Yamuna Rivers called the Doab.[11] Meo settlement in this area by the tenth century is recorded by the gazetteers of the United Provinces as also their displacement by Rajput clans such as the Dors, Tomars, Bargujars, and Chauhans. These Rajput clans were characterized by a tremendous mobility and search for territory.

The Chauhan (Cahamanas) Rajputs had emerged in the later tenth century and established themselves as a paramount power, overthrowing the Tomar Rajputs. In 1151 the Tomar Rajput rulers (and original builders) of Delhi were overthrown by Visala Dev, the Chauhan ruler of Ajmer. After the Chauhan ruler Prithviraja III's victory over the Turks in 1191, a part of the Punjab and a considerable part of the area inhabited by the Meos was brought under the Chauhan Empire. During Prithviraj's rule Meo lands in Aligarh, Bulandshahr, and Meerut are said to have been taken by the Rajputs. The Bargujar Rajputs were also victorious over the Meos, Chandellas, and Bhihars.[12] Another dislocation of the Meos is attributed to the Turkish conqueror Mahmud Ghaznavi, who made seventeen raids on northwest India between A.D. 1000 and 1025.[13] In the first half of the eleventh century Salar Masud, his nephew and general, conquered Delhi and Meerut. Meo memory refers to their displacement from the Doab, the crossing of the Yamuna River, the movement westward, and then farther to the south and southwest of Delhi.[14] As in the case of Meo migration from the Sind, the evidence of displacement from the Doab is conjectural rather than definitive.

There is more conclusive evidence of the Meos being pushed out of Delhi by Turk and Afghan conquerors. Mu'izz al-Din Ghuri, the founder of the Ghurid dynasty and leader of the Turkic Muslims, having destroyed Ghaznavi and conquered Multan had moved on to take over Delhi and virtually all of north India. Mu'izz al-Din's "slave"-general, Qutub al-Din Aibak, conquered Meerut and Ajmer. After defeating the Chauhan Rajputs, the Turks occupied Delhi in 1192.[15] Aibak's declaration of independence from the Ghurids after the death of his master in 1206 established the sultanate that was ruled by the "slave" or Mamluk sultans up to 1290. The Mewatis also seem to have been adversely affected by the early Mongol invasions in the thirteenth century.[16]

The establishment of the sultanate and its capital at Mehrauli (south Delhi), which was one of the most important cities of its time, affected the Meos, being seen by them as the appropriation of Meo land. Not surprisingly, their earliest raids were incursions into the new capital, attacking traders, pilgrims, and the water carriers at the city's major sources of water. The concentration of Meo settlements when they forge their presence onto the pages of history in the mid-thirteenth century is in the region south of the capital called Mewat. Mewat derives its name from the ferocious Mewati. In the mid-thirteenth century they inhabited settlements around the periphery of Delhi, in the Siwalik hills (in the contemporary state of Haryana), Bayana, and in the Kohpaya.[17] The Kohpaya includes Bharatpur, Dholpur, and a part of Jaipur and Alwar that stretches up to Ranthambhor. This became the heartland of Meo resistance.

What was the ecology of resistance? Rajasthan is an area isolated from the subcontinental heartland. The region is internally differentiated, including both arid and semiarid tracts with a considerable variation of economy and culture that helped sustain the fragmented political sovereignties. The parallel ridges of the Aravalli mountain range cut across the semiarid region north to south. The low rocky mountain chain that begins from Paharganj in Delhi and extends through Tijara and Alwar in Mewat are part of the Raialo series. The gray color of the soft, slatey stone lent it the name Kala Pahar. But more than that, as dalit novelist Bhagvan Das points out, the name Kala Pahar (literally Black Mountain) became a virtual metaphor for the region's wildness. The landscape includes some fertile valleys due to a relatively high (for Rajasthan) average rainfall and seasonal streams that run down the hills and fall into alluvial catchment valleys called *ḍahar*. It has had a fairly thick forest cover consisting mainly of dry deciduous species such as the *ḍhok (Anogeissus pendula)* and a variety of wildlife, including the tiger and panther.

In the recesses of the Aravalli mountains the Meos carved out their settlements and small areas of control. The inaccessibility of the terrain rendered conquest and imperial control difficult. It fostered autonomy and the sustained resistance of Meo ruler-warriors to conquest, control, and centralization. It gave them constant refuge from the armies of the central and regional powers.

The area from the Sutlej River to Hariana was referred to as *jangaldesha*, or land of the forest, in the tenth and eleventh centuries. Vast tracts of land around Delhi and in the Doab were forested until they were reclaimed by the sultanate in the thirteenth century. Warfare was an important activity for warrior lineages and raiding was frequent. Settled agriculture grew slowly in the dry, inhospitable countryside peopled by cattle herders. Mewat had a large cattle population. There are references to a cattle market in Kaman in A.D. 905.[18] At what stage the transformation from a pastoral to an agricultural economy occurred cannot definitively be postulated. It was possibly parallel to the sedentarization of the Jats that took place between the eleventh and sixteenth centuries and continued even after that. But pastoralism and agriculture are not mutually exclusive modes of production and cohere instead in a symbiotic relationship. Agriculture and animal husbandry were simultaneous and alternating activities depending on climatic variables. The clan form of organization was associated initially with a mode of production that had involved transhumance in search of grazing lands and water. Meo social organization continued to retain a "tribal" character involving multiple, intermarrying clans even as they acquired a semisedentary status and metamorphosed into a caste.

The crucial overland trade routes connecting Delhi to Punjab that went beyond to West and Central Asia traversed through Mewat, and sultans periodically attempted to assert their control over the area. Although they battled Mewati lineages for a century sultanate control over the area was discontinuous. It was interspersed with what was from the state's perspective "rebelliousness." From the Mewati point of view, however, the challenge was to overthrow an "illegitimate regime," to which, at best, they paid regular tribute. The repression initiated by the slave kings continued through the brief rule of the Turkish clan of Khiljis (1290–1320). The greatest and most powerful sultan of Delhi, Ala al-Din Khilji (r. 1296–1316), who saw himself as a "second Alexander" continued Sultan Balban's policy. Following a prolonged conflict with local chiefs, a part of the area called Rajasthan was brought under the sultanate (see map 1). All turbulent chiefs and rais were suppressed in the region of Delhi and forced to pay tribute; rebellions were dealt with severely.[19] In the "disturbed areas" groups of soldier-farmers were settled who were both informers and checks on local administration.

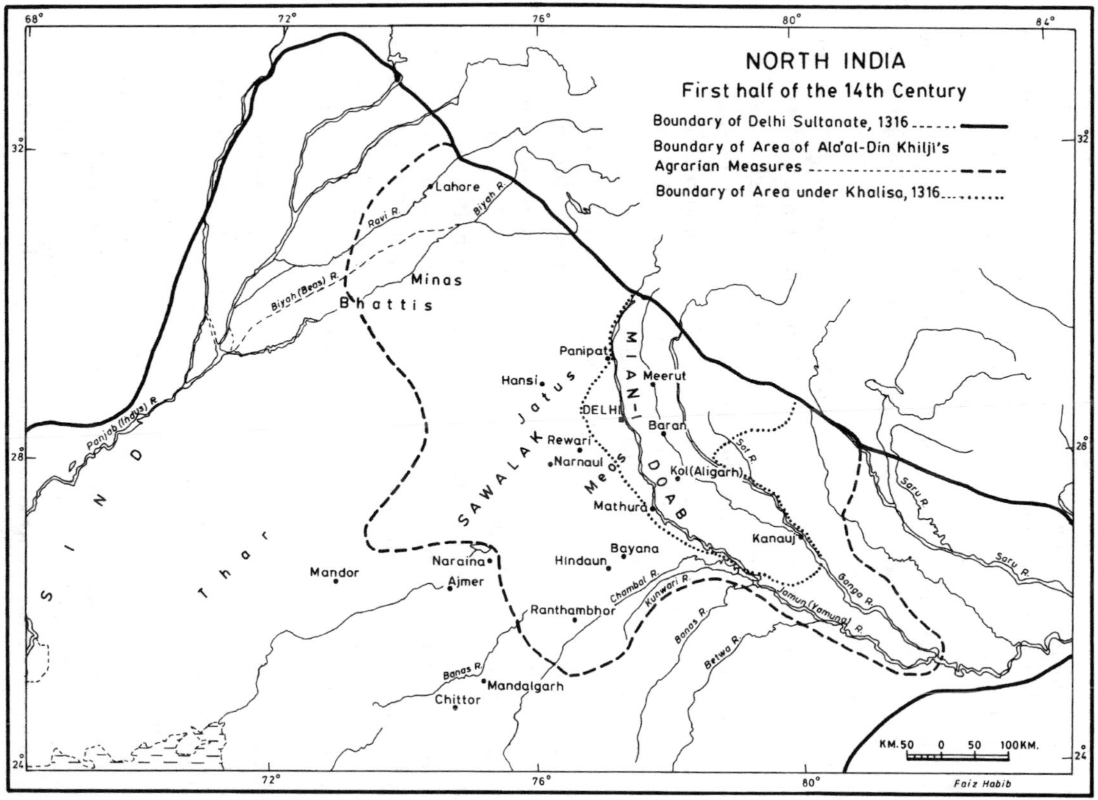

MAP 1 North India in the First Half of the Fourteenth Century.

Ala al-Din Khilji introduced administrative reforms, including a uniform rate of assessment for all classes. As a result, the trade route from Gujarat to Delhi was rendered relatively secure.

Firoz Shah Tughlaq (r. 1351–88), the great ruler of the Tughlaq dynasty that ruled through the fourteenth century, is described as facing a great deal of turbulence as the maliks and local chiefs had once again asserted their independence.[20] Simultaneously there was a shift in sultanate policy following his accession to a use of more complex ruling strategies involving both coercion and co-optation.

A Mewati lineage under a chief called Nahar Singh had risen to prominence in the mid-fourteenth century. His father, Lakhanpal, had ruled a small tract around the area of Firozpur Jhirka. Nahar Singh arrived at a compromise with the Tughlaq sultan, converted to Islam, and assumed the name of Nahar Khan. After the presentation of tribute and *peshkash* (offering), his lands were restored to him. The lineage continued the use of the name Khan and came to be called Khanazad(s) (and later still Khanazadas). Under Bahadur Nahar "the brave lion" as he is popularly called, the Khanazadas emerged as a ruling power in the area in Tijara (in the present-day Alwar region). Bahadur Nahar is described as one of the most powerful chiefs in the neighborhood of Delhi.[21] He ruled from Sarheta, four miles east of Tijara. A regional history attributes his adoption of Islam to either a change of heart or to a tactical move dictated by sheer survival, that is, to forestall a likely beheading and save his lands from being annexed.[22] The latter seems more plausible, and Bahadur Nahar considerably expanded his territorial jurisdiction and sphere of influence and became an active player in court politics.

Khanazadas today claim independent and distinct genealogies, but the evidence suggests they were part of the larger group called the Mewatis that included ancestors of Meo clans. Yahya bin Ahmad, the historian, makes it quite clear that the followers of the "Khanazada" Bahadur Nahar are Mewatis or Miwan. Bahadur Nahar's own grandson is referred to as Jalal Khan Meo. Later British writers distinguished between the Meos and the Khanazadas, but they became differentiated only at this stage of Mewat's history, when for a brief period the Khanazadas were co-opted by the sultanate. Both groups claim descent from the Jadon Rajputs of Bayana, a branch of which had relocated themselves in northern Alwar after their defeat by Ghuri.[23] The Khanazada chiefs were active in court politics, and Bahadur Nahar played a prominent role in a succession dispute, switching sides to enhance his own maneuverability.

Sultanate authority disintegrated in the mid-fourteenth century under the later Tughlaqs and Sayyids whose influence extended but a short distance beyond Delhi. A couple of Mewati lineages flirted with competing court factions, promoting one side or other. But central control had greatly weakened after the death of Firoz Tughluq, and the ineluctable struggle of the period between the imperial and regional powers resurfaced. Between 1390 and 1428 there were intermittent rebellions against the Tughlaqs and the Sayyids. Mewat continued to be divided internally into areas of control of different lineages. From the mid-fourteenth up to the mid-fifteenth century several tracts continued to resist the imposition of centralized rule and harbored insurgents. Successive sultans ravaged the country even as the *mawās*, or wilderness, resisted and refused to pay tribute. During Timur's invasion Mewat was devastated in 1398–99 and again in 1411–12. Bahlol Lodi (r. 1451–88) once more asserted control over northern India on behalf of the Afghan Lodi dynasty. But the Lodi claim of conquest over Mewat was fragile and only repeated the Sayyid history of several expeditions and campaigns against the defiant Mewatis. The scattered Pathan tombs in the area suggest the Lodi attempts at control. Dynastic changes meant not only shifts in the ruling coalition but also in the nature of the state and in the practices involved in governance.

Military posts and towns in the region multiplied, associated with the sultanate's constant attempts to assert its authority over Mewat. Small towns were usually fortified administrative centers. Rewari, Jhirka, Taoru, and Tijara became well-established urban centers by the mid-fourteenth century. Merchant castes, Hindu, and Jain settled in these towns. Other centers such as Indor, Sarheta, and Kharol became identified with the struggle of Mewati warrior lineages. The area was populated also by other castes such as the Rajputs, Jats, and Ahirs.

The Mughal invader Babur (r. 1526–30) defeated a coalition of Rajput-Mewati factions in the battle of Khanva. As the Mughal Empire was consolidated, Meo status as landholders rather than chiefs and warriors became firmly entrenched. Mewat was brought under imperial rule by the Mughals and divided into the administrative units of parganas subsumed under five *sarkars* that were governed by the Agra and Delhi Subas. The largest concentration of Meo population was in the Agra Suba, particularly in the Alwar Sarkar that incorporated southern Mewat, while north central Mewat was administered by the Tijara Sarkar. By the mid-sixteenth century the Meos seem to have been firmly sedentarized and reduced from a warrior, self-governing group to a revenue-paying, landowning caste. The agricultural expansion that took place under the Mughals, the growth of a money economy, and cash crops in the seventeenth century seem to have benefitted certain communities but bypassed others like the Meos.[24]

The Mughal Empire consolidated its authority in the sixteenth century by alliance with preexisting kingships based on the clan structures of Rajput warriors who were themselves involved in both raiding and ruling. The Mughal-Rajput alliance, which was one of the pillars of the grand imperial design, underwrote Meo marginality (see map 2). The kingdom of Kacchavaha Rajputs at Amber (later Jaipur) established its power largely on the grounds of its ability to "manage" the troublesome Marathas, the rebellious Jats, and the Meos. When Bharamall, its Kacchavaha Rajput ruler had submitted to the Mughal emperor Akbar in 1562, the state possessed only a single pargana.[25] Akbar (r. 1556–1605) accepted the Rajput's offer of a marriage alliance with his daughter and gave the title Amir-ul-Umara to Bharamall's son, Man Singh. Man Singh of Amber emerged as a great Mughal general and played a major role in helping Akbar defend the northwest frontier in the troubled times when there were simultaneous uprisings in Bihar and Bengal. His reward was being elevated to the privileged rank of mansabdar of five thousand *(pāñch hazārī)*, which was later increased to the rank of seven thousand. The Kacchavaha Rajputs were involved in all military expeditions during Shah Jahan's reign (including against the Meos) and were a major prop to the empire. The Rajputs conceived their role in terms of their own ambitions for land and power.

The reign of Jai Singh (r. 1622–67) saw the beginning of the rise of the Kacchavaha principality of Amber to the position of the dominant kingdom in Rajasthan in the early half of the eighteenth century. The Kacchavaha Rajputs took leases *(ijāras)* from Mughal employees or jagirdars to whom revenue from the area had been assigned in lieu of salary and also gave ijaras on sublease. They used the ijara system to undertake a vast extension of territory and to colonize lands that were difficult to administer. The Jaipur rulers were able to legitimate the extension of territory by claiming to bring recalcitrant Mewati zamindars under control. By the mid-eighteenth century Amber (now called Jaipur) was one of India's largest and most populous states, with an area of twenty thousand square miles that incorporated tracts of Machari (Alwar), Tonk, Shekhawati, and Jodhpur. In 1802–3 it had an estimated income of 10 million rupees.[26]

Jagirs were granted by the Amber ruler to his Kacchavaha Rajput kin such as to the sublineage of the Naruka Rajputs. A remarkable transfer of land

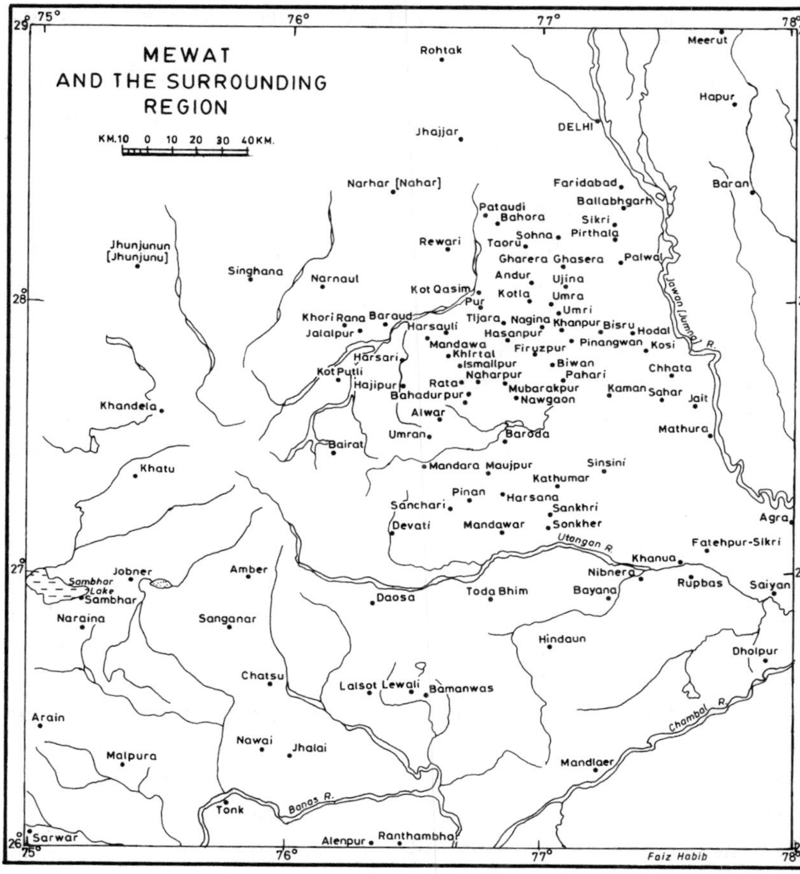

Map 2 Mewat and Surrounding Areas in the Sixteenth Century.

Based on Irfan Habib, *An Atlas of Mughal India* (Delhi: Oxford University Press), map 6A.

occurred in which much land passed from Khanazada and Meo owners (both being Muslim groups) to the new Rajput gentry that was expected to provide a more loyal base to state formation. The rising power of the Naruka Rajputs and Jats during the seventeenth and eighteenth centuries adversely affected Meo landholders. Often with Mughal support, the Naruka Rajputs acquired extensive land rights in villages through coercion or by usurping the rights of Meo and Khanazada clans.[27] Mughal and Rajput aggrandizement was fiercely resisted by the Meos.

The weakened rule of the later Mughals enabled the rise of groups such as the Jats and the Sikhs. While no Meo clan was able to establish overriding power, a lineage of the Sinsini Jats achieved preeminence in the Mathura-Agra region. In the last quarter of the seventeenth century, the Jats made sustained raids on the Mughal Empire (plundering even Akbar's tomb). By the eighteenth century they had carved out a powerful Jat State with land from the area of Mewat. Badan Singh, the great Jat raider-conqueror, Churaman's successor, became raja of Dig in 1722. Suraj Mal took over Bharatpur by capturing its fort in 1733 and ruled up to 1763. The Jat rulers are said to have practiced considerable cruelty on the Meos in the process of extending their rule to the south and southeast.[28] A brief period of Maratha rule over Mewat was followed by another spurt of Jat conquest. The Meos fought against both the Marathas and the Jats. They raided Maratha battalions. According to a local history, the Jats attacked the Meo clans of the Ghasera and Baghora, troubling the Meos each day.[29] The oppositional stance of the Meos to the Jat State was qualified by the collaboration of the Meos *within* the Bharatpur kingdom. In a Meo narrative, the ruler of Bharatpur, Jawahir Singh (r. 1764–68), is referred to in kin terms by the chief of a Meo clan, leading to his alliance in battle with the Jats against the Rajputs of Amber. The Rajput ruler had prevented Jawahir Singh from ritual bathing at the ancient pilgrimage site of Pushkar near Ajmer. Eventually the Naruka Rajputs carved out the independent kingdom of Alwar from the Amber State in 1775.

The transitions from the thirteenth to the eighteenth century reduced the Mewatis from a self-governing, relatively autonomous group to one with a mere peasant-pastoral status. Due to their numerical strength and land control, the Meos grew to be what sociologists call a dominant peasant caste in Mewat and the pivot of the *jajmānī* system that defined hereditary patron-client relations with castes such as the brahmans, Mirasis, and Nais, or barbers.[30] The term "dominance" is generally configured in terms of land ownership and the patronage of dependent castes but erases what might be a long-term political marginalization.

Marginality had both a political and spatial manifestation. It led to a remarkable contraction of the territory called Mewat. What is called Mewat today is far smaller compared to its spread in the early medieval period. The medieval historian Minhaj Siraj Juzjani refers to Mewatis inhabiting the area up to Ranthambhor in the thirteenth century. Under the rule of the Afghan Lodi dynasty, Mewat included the countryside around the urban centers of Kotila, Rewari, Narnaul, Tijara, and much of Alwar and Bharatpur. Ahmad writes that Mewat began eighty miles east of Amber and extended up to the Yamuna River or the region of Braj in the west. During the period of Mughal rule, whereas most of Mewat became part of the Agra Suba, the important centers of Narnaul and Tijara were deliberately transferred to the Delhi Suba. This was in 1656, just before the end of Shah Jahan's reign.[31] Even during this period the Mewatis are described as inhabiting the rural terrain between Delhi and Agra. Over time Narnaul and Rewari were detached from Mewat. By the nineteenth century the region was reduced to a seventy-five-hundred-square-mile area.[32] The postcolonial state continues with Mughal and Rajput practice strategically dividing it into administrative units and electoral constituencies. The fear of a united Mewati power survives even after their forced diaspora following a genocide against them in the aftermath of the partition of India.

In the nineteenth century the British became a major player in the region (see map 3). Treaties with sovereign "native states" brought them under British protection. The transfer of government from The East India Company to the Crown after the suppression of the 1857 revolt led to the establishment of the British as the paramount power. In 1858 the East India Company was dissolved and the last Mughal Emperor deposed as Parliament assumed direct control of British India. The new treaties were no longer among equals. Colonialism definitively emasculated the region by maximizing extraction and overwriting local institutions. This was done both through direct administration and by transforming the authority of the "Indian princes," as the kings came to be called, of more than 650 kingdoms. British policy undermined the territorial basis of communities and converted erstwhile local chieftains into dependent landlords, revenue collectors, or both, even as it introduced major legal changes to individuate group entitlements.[33] By the nineteenth century the largest concentration of Meos lived in the Gurgaon District of the Punjab that was directly administered by the

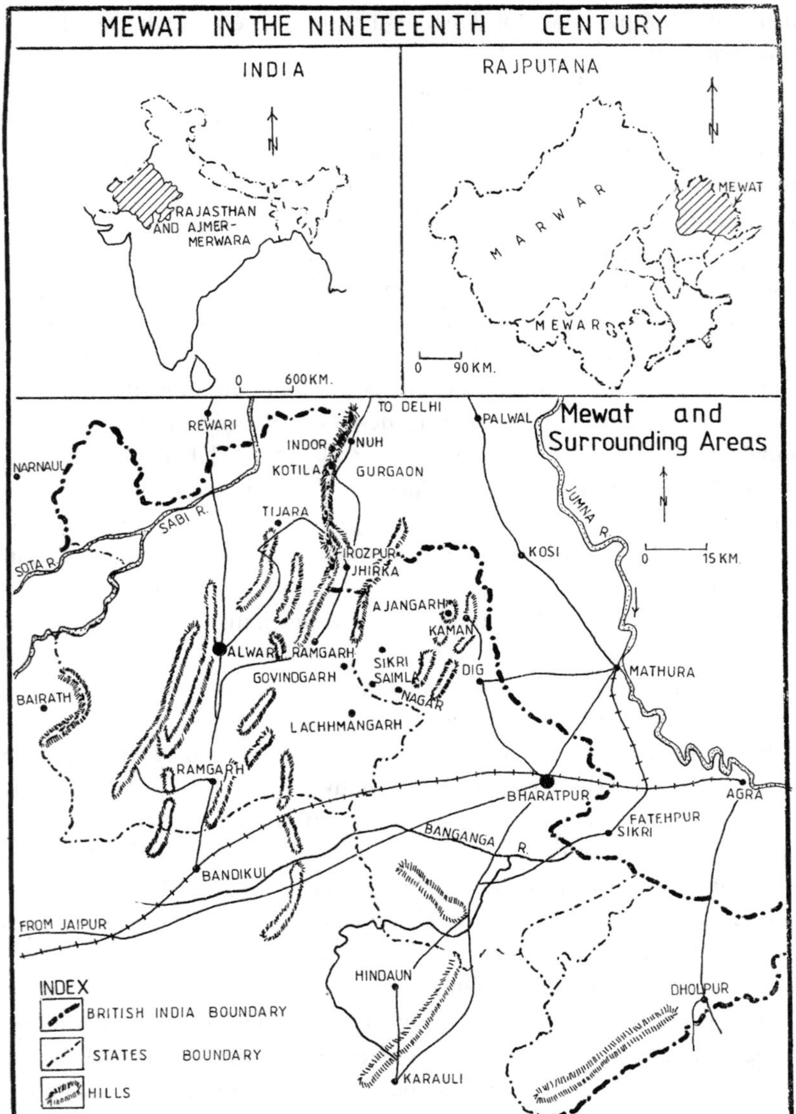
MEWAT IN THE NINETEENTH CENTURY
INDIA
RAJASTHAN AND AJMER-MERWARA
0 600 KM.
RAJPUTANA
MEWAT
MARWAR
MEWAR
0 90 KM.
Mewat and Surrounding Areas
0 15 KM.
TO DELHI
REWARI
NARNAUL
INDOR
NUH
KOTILA
GURGAON
PALWAL
JUMNA R.
TIJARA
SABI R.
SOTA R.
FIROZPUR JHIRKA
KOSI
AJANGARH
KAMAN
ALWAR
RAMGARH
SIKRI
SAIMLA
NAGAR
DIG
MATHURA
GOVINDGARH
BAIRATH
LACHHMANGARH
RAMGARH
BHARATPUR
AGRA
FATEHPUR SIKRI
BANGANGA R.
BANDIKUI
FROM JAIPUR
HINDAUN
DHOLPUR
KARAULI
INDEX
BRITISH INDIA BOUNDARY
STATES BOUNDARY
HILLS
ROAD
RAILWAY

MAP 3 Mewat in the Nineteenth Century.

British and in the Alwar and Bharatpur kingdoms (now called "princely" states) of Rajputana ruled by Rajput and Jat lineages, respectively.

The Gurgaon District near Delhi had once consisted of considerable wooded tracts and wildlife but was gradually rendered into "wasteland." After brief periods of Jat and Maratha conquest, part of the Gurgaon area of Mewat was taken over by the English in 1803. Another part was given to the nawab of Firozpur and Loharu, and brought under direct British administration in 1836 on grounds of the alleged assassination of Colonel Fraser, an English resident, by Nawab Shams-ud-Din. Rewari, Nuh, Bahora, and Sohna had already been brought under direct rule in 1808–10 after Lord Lake's conquest.

Why did Meo and Jat histories assume such a different trajectory? After all, in the period between the eighth and nineteenth centuries they shared a similar social status. For one thing the Jats were a widely dispersed and much larger group. Indeed "Jat" had been a generic term for a peasant in the Punjab. Because Meo resistance was sharper and more localized it was subject to greater repression by the sultanate and Mughal Empire. Jat lineages were eventually in a much better position to carve out for themselves states in Punjab and in Rajasthan.

The nineteenth-century story for the Meos became one of growing impoverishment and indebtedness since land that became alienable under colonial rule could be used as security for loans. This was in contrast to the Jats to whom benefits accrued from the canal-irrigated areas and who were consequently constructed as loyal peasants. Water was similarly seen as having a civilizing effect on the Gujars of the Upper Doab. In the mid-nineteenth century high rates of fertility made the Meos the largest group in the district population. They were followed by the Chamars, Ahirs, Jats, brahmans, baniyas, Gujars, and Rajputs (see tables 1–3). In 1849 the Meos numbered 110,000 persons constituting about one-sixth of the population. The Meos held land in the southern part of the district of Gurgaon in the Mewat tehsils of Nuh and Firozpur Jhirka.

The Jat-ruled kingdom in eastern Rajputana called Bharatpur consisted of a well-cultivated alluvial plain and hills with substantial forest cover. It had a good rainfall, and two-fifths of the area is described as irrigated at the turn of the nineteenth century by either wells or rainwater and small dams that enabled double cropping. The Meos inhabited the northern part of the state, which consisted of well-forested hills broken up by a fertile alluvial plain.[34]

TABLE 1 Decennial Census of Meo Population

Year	Rajputana	Punjab and Delhi	United Provinces	Total
1868	—	130,385	—	—
1881	45,946[a]	116,227	13,246	—
1891	145,258	120,578	67,000	656,986[b]
1901	168,596	146,666	58,000[c]	671,767[b]

[a]The census figure for the Rajputana Meos in 1881 seems to include only the population of the Bharatpur Meos and is highly dubious.
[b]These totals do not include scattered Meo populations in areas such as the Central Provinces and Baluchistan.
[c]Major population concentrations in the United Provinces consisted of 22,576 Mewatis in Meerut, 7,316 in Agra, and 16,129 in Rohilkhand.

Source: A Report on the Census of the Punjab, 1868 (Lahore: Indian Public Opinion Press, 1970); *Census of the Native States of Rajputana 1881* (Bombay: Examiner Press, 1882); *Census of India 1891*, vol. 26, *Rajputana* (Calcutta: Office of Superintendent of Government Press, 1892), 27–28; H. A. Rose, *Census of India 1901*, vol. 17A, *Punjab and North West Provinces* (Simla: Government Central Printing Office, 1902); A. D. Bannerman, *Census of India 1901*, vol. 25, *Rajputana* (Lucknow: Newal Kishore Press, 1902), 168; E. A. H. Blunt, *Census of India, 1911*, vol. 15, *United Provinces of Agra and Oudh* (Allahabad: Government Press, 1911), 222, 377.

A lineage of Rajputs called Narukas ruled from Alwar State that began thirty-five miles southwest of Delhi. Mewat comprised over a third of its territory.[35] The author of a settlement describes Mewat as one of its natural divisions, with villages concentrated in the north and east. The extent of Meo sedentarization is reflected in the ethnographer Crooke's statement describing them as a "large agricultural tribe settled in villages and leading a fairly peaceful life."[36] In the Alwar State they formed the largest caste group, comprising one-eighth of the population and owning approximately 448 villages.

The character of the margins was simultaneously effaced and underwritten by the classificatory practices of colonialism practiced both in the British Empire and the princely states. In this schema one had to be registered as either Hindu, Muslim, or Other. Take the case of Bharatpur where in 1901

TABLE 2 Regional Population by Caste, 1901

Caste	Region			
	Gurgaon	Alwar	Bharatpur	Rajputana
Ahirs	78,329	65,740	4,675	159,434
Baniyas	33,507	—	—	—
Bhangis	21,000	14,230	8,919	77,218
Brahmans	54,582	79,045	65,243	1,140,311
Chamars	87,095	92,320	100,752	716,949
Gujars	24,948	46,046	44,875	492,731
Jats	75,753	35,650	93,242	845,909
Mahajans	37,197	45,081	31,197	754,317
Malis	10,888	27,879	20,788	313,349
Meos	128,861	113,142	51,546	168,596
Minas	826	49,245	12,098	477,129
Mirasis	4,240	2,456	—	14,442
Rajputs	27,565	33,833	11,931	638,573
Sheikhs	10,422	19,614	16,037	242,046
Total Population[a]	746,208	828,487	746,208	9,853,366

[a]Numbers in this row include miscellaneous castes not listed in the table.

Source: H. A. Rose, *Census of India 1901*, vol. 17A, *Punjab and North West Provinces* (Simla: Government Central Printing Office, 1902); A. D. Bannerman, *Census of India 1901*, vol. 25, *Rajputana* (Lucknow: Newal Kishore Press, 1902), 168.

the population is said to have been 81 percent Hindu and nearly 18 percent Muslims, of which the Meos comprised 8 percent.[37] The Alwar Census of 1872 recorded 598,334 Hindus and 180,225 Muslims, of which 96,861 (12.4 percent) were said to be Meos.[38] The group is described as an "agricultural class" and as almost all Muslim. In 1891 the total Meo population in Mewat comprised more than 266,184 persons. In 1901 Meos numbered a total of 671,767, with 385,584 Meos in Baluchistan, Andamans, Punjab, the United and Central Provinces, and Rajputana. Thus more than half the total number of Meos were resident outside Mewat, with a major concentration in the United Provinces.

TABLE 3 Regional Decennial Census of Population by Religion

Year	Religion	Region			
		Alwar	Bharatpur	Gurgaon	Rajputana
1872	Hindus	598,334	—	480,307	—
	Jains	—	—	216,147	—
	Muslims	180,225	—	114,693	—
	Tribals	778,596	—	696,646	—
1881	Hindus	526,115	535,367	439,264	8,839,243
	Jains	—	—	—	—
	Muslims	151,727	105,666	198,610	861,747
	Tribals	682,926	645,540	641,848	10,100,399
1891	Hindus	582,690	528,629	455,045	10,192,458
	Jains	—	—	—	—
	Muslims	180,426	107,260	209,931	991,351
	Tribals	767,786	640,303	668,929	12,220,343
1901	Hindus	618,378	510,508	499,373	8,089,513
	Jains	4,919	3,321	3,909	342,595
	Muslims	204,947	112,621	242,548	924,656
	Tribals	828,487	626,665	746,208	360,543

Source: A *Report on the Census of the Punjab, 1868* (Lahore: Indian Public Opinion Press, 1970); *Census of the Native States of Rajputana 1881* (Bombay: Examiner Press, 1882); *Census of India 1891*, vol. 26, *Rajputana* (Calcutta: Office of Superintendent of Government Press, 1892), 27–28; H. A. Rose, *Census of India 1901*, vol. 17A, *Punjab and North West Provinces* (Simla: Government Central Printing Office, 1902); A. D. Bannerman, *Census of India 1901*, vol. 25, *Rajputana* (Lucknow: Newal Kishore Press, 1902), 168; E. A. H. Blunt, *Census of India, 1911*, vol. 15, *United Provinces of Agra and Oudh* (Allahabad: Government Press, 1911), 222, 377.

Religion and Identity

Even as governmentality forced groups into boxes, Hindu and Muslim, the cultural articulation of Meo identity is deeply and disturbingly contestatory. There are many questions relating to Meo practice, some of which can elicit only speculative answers. What was the religious culture of the margins? How did their conversion come about? What was the extent of the influence of Ismailism, a branch of Shi'ite Islam, on them? Or did the Mids like the Jats follow Buddhism then dominant in the Sind (and Afghanistan and Baluchistan) and became one of the first Indian groups to convert to Islam?[39] What did conversion mean? How was Meo religious practice and belief viewed by the theologians?

Early Turkish raids not only brought Islam to a major part of India but also created an upheaval of populations. Diverse explanations are available regarding Meo conversion. Certain accounts see conversion as one-time, complete, and associated with conquest.[40] There is also some memory of forced conquest. Varied Meo accounts attribute it to Sultan Balban, the Mongol conqueror Timur, Sultan Firoz Tughlaq, and the Mughal emperor Aurangzeb.[41] Mirasi Abdul told me that the Meos were among the first communities to adopt Islam in India. Memories of possible forced conquest are also transformed through narrative. Salar Masud, the general of the Turkish conqueror Ghaznavi, for instance, who is remembered for his attack on Taragarh (Ajmer) is revered by the Meos as the saint Ghazi miyan, the virgin martyr. An oath taken in Ghazi miyan's name ensures that a Meo will speak the truth.

The adoption of Islam was partly an outcome of political compromise. Meo lineages that later came to be known as Khanazadas began flirting with sultanate court politics in the mid-fourteenth century. The first recorded conversion, described earlier in this chapter, is that of Nahar Singh who assumed the title of Nahar Khan during the rule of Sultan Firoz Tughlaq around 1359.

Conversion is often only partial as communities continue their preconversion practices and is also differentiated within the same community. Indeed, there is a need to rethink the very notion of "conversion." It presupposes a binary logic, as well as a transformation of religious belief and practice "from" one given state "to" another. In the case of the Meos we have hardly any idea of their preceding ("Hindu"?) practice, which certainly cannot be derived from later practices. Conversion did not bring about a major shift in their attitude toward the central authority.

Persian records and the Meo oral tradition yield a highly complex and textured field of religious belief and practice. Persian inscriptions suggest the settlement of saints and Sufis in various parts of Rajasthan from the thirteenth century.[42] The Chishtiyya Silsila established an early presence followed by the Naqshbandi. The founder of the Chishtiyya Silsila, the celebrated Sufi Khwaja Mu'in-ud-Din Chishti (d. 1235) along with his successors significantly aided the establishment of Sufi ideologies in the thirteenth century. Mu'in-ud-Din is locally referred to as the "pir of pirs." Rizvi argues against Nizami's contention that the Sufis worked at converting non-Muslims, pointing out the absence of evidence, epigraphic or textual. Regional sources, however, do attribute *dāwa* and *tablīgh* (preaching) to Sufis.[43] Shaikh Farid-ud-Din Masud Ganj i-Shakar (d. 1265) worked in Hansi and later Delhi. He was succeeded by Shaikh Nizam-ud-Din Auliya (1238–1324) and then by Shaikh Nasir-ud-Din Chiragh of Delhi (1276–1356). The Meo saint Shah Musa, whose dargah is near Nuh, was one of the latter's *khalīfās,* or preachers. Shah Chokha who came from Khurasan spent considerable time in Mewat. Akbar is said to have sought his benefaction along with that of Shaikh Salim Chishti for an heir to the throne. A *khānaqāh* (Sufi religious center) was made in his honor by Akbar but left incomplete with the emperor's death. Stories of Shah Chokha's *karāmāt,* or miracles, as well as the food and shelter provided by the khanaqah may have given some Meos a greater familiarity with Islam. His throwing of grains in three directions is held to be responsible for the prosperity of the Meo clan known as the Chiraklot Pal. Some Meos possibly frequented the ideologically more orthodox Naqshbandi Khanaqah in Kot Kasim of Firozpur Jhirka, which emphasized Islamic law and rejected the *'samā,* or mystical music so important for the Chishtiyyas.

The Qadiriyya Silsila became popular in Narnaul and Mewat particularly with Mulla Ibrahim Ruhi in the seventeenth century. He was a disciple of Miyan Mir, a follower of the mystical doctrine of *waḥdatu'l-wujūd,* or the doctrine of the unity of being derived from the great Sufi Ibn al-'Arabi. Ruhi was both a scholar-theologian *('alim)* and a keen traveler who was extremely popular. The Qadiriyya became the most powerful silsila in the nineteenth century, with a large number of followers among the Meos. A Dhaingal Meo, Miya Raj Shah, became particularly well known in Gurgaon.

Clearly the Meos had diverse ideological affiliations. The Punjab Census of 1901 mentions the existence of thirty-two Sufi orders. In Gurgaon the Chishtiyyas far outnumbered the Qadiriyyas.[44] The towns were the centers for the dissemination of Sufi and other Islamic ideologies but the extent of their influence on the countryside is difficult to estimate. The khanaqahs probably had a greater impact on the Muslim nobility. The peasantry, more likely, approached them primarily for *tā'wīz* (protective amulets). Meo writers suggest an elaborate world of silsilas that define Meo belief, but they are rarely mentioned by their oral tradition. There were scattered mosques in the area. Meos more often than not believed in pirs, faqirs, and darveshes to whom were attributed magical and healing powers. Pir Shah Alakh, whom we encounter again in an anti-Mughal narrative, is said to have enabled the ruling dynasty of the Jadon Rajputs to reestablish themselves at another center after their defeat at Bayana by Shahab al-Din Ghuri. Alakh Pir is referred to as Alakhniranjan by the Nath Yogis and his well is believed to have healing properties.

Some Meos became followers of what the clerics referred to as "heterodox" sects. 'Abdu'r-Rasul Shah, a darvesh of the eighteenth century, became *peshwā*, or leader, of a wandering sect recognized by a handkerchief worn on the head. Headquartered in the hills near Alwar, its ascetic adherents followed ecstacy-inducing practices and were prohibited from sleeping at night. Renowned for miracles, Saiyid Rasul Shah is said to have had a large number of adherents, including the first Alwar raja, Pratap Singh (1740–91).[45] The disciples of the Rasuli branch were similar to Qalandars, darveshes who wandered in a state of *sukr*, or mystic intoxication, and were indifferent to bodily needs and social norms. The Rasulshahis described themselves as Chistiyyas but came into conflict with both Chishtiyya and Suhrawardiyya saints.[46] They often shaved bodily hair, and some went about clad only in a loincloth. They redefined *kufr* (being an infidel) as the pursuit of *nafs*, or the lower or appetitive soul, and considered the settled life of the khanaqah sinful.[47] Like the Nath Yogi ascetics some Rasulshahis had great influence over kings and governors, but they also faced persecution as their practice was alleged to be un-Islamic. The Rasul Shahi khanaqah and tomb were destroyed by Maharaja Bakhtawar Singh and Maharaja Jai Singh, Alwar rulers of the early nineteenth and twentieth century, respectively.

Meos were exposed to a variety of Islamic ideologies. These ranged from the Qadiris who combined theological and mystical knowledge (sharī'at and tarīqat) to the Madariyya Tariqa. Theologians referred to the latter disparagingly as "bi-shar," or without law, pointing out that the Madariyya Tariqa did not believe in the Islamic religious law.[48] Like Hindu mendicants its members wore no clothes and covered themselves with ashes and consumed hemp leaves (hence the derivation from *mad*). The warrior-saint Salar Masud was worshiped in every village on Shab-i-rat, but his popularity was rivaled by that of Shah Madar and Ajmer's Khwaja sahab. The Husainis had a presence in Gurgaon, with more female than male followers. Another group of faqirs were followers of Banda Nawaz. They were said to leap up in the air repeating lā-īlah-illallāh, work themselves into a frenzy, and fall down exhausted. The Sarwardiyya were followers of Hasan Basri of Basra near Baghdad. The adherents were said to chant Allāha with a suppression of breath and effort that culminated in a faint.

Religious sects were considerably open-ended and their membership fluid, as there seems to have been constant lateral movements of Meos drawn to Vaishavism, the Nath Panth, *nirguṇ bhakti* (the worship of a formless God), or to Islamic sects. The Meo *auliyā*, or saints, included such highly popular figures as Lal Das (1540–1648) and Chudh Sidh, who reinterpreted bhakti and Islamic traditions in the region. The followers of both included Hindus and Muslims. Chudh Sidh was the offspring of a Meo man and a woman from the Nai or barber caste who lived in the reign of Aurangzeb. The hagiographies of both saints have several references to the "oppressions" of local Mughal officials including of the governor and the tax collector. The Nath tradition also played a significant role in Mewati religious life. Mughal documents indicate the existence of Nath Yogis in each pargana. Narnaul was a particularly important center. There is evidence also of some persecution of the Nath Panth, as Uda Das and Udhav Bairagi were beheaded by Aurangzeb and two Rajput disciples by the Qazi of Shahjahanabad.[49]

Clearly the region fostered an immense diversity of belief and practice. The discourse of "religion," however, constitutes the margin in terms of deviance, ignorance, spuriousness, and so on. Its inhabitants are said to be confused because they mix and creolize. On occasion the Meos are even described as animists or people without religion. An early nineteenth-century colonial text identifies them as being Hindu, Muslim, and having one section with no religion who became renouncers of various kinds referred to as darveshes, jogis, jangam, sevra, sanyasis, and paramhans.[50] This is not dissimilar to the ways in which the center constituted tribal peoples the world over. The anthropologist's gaze likewise sifts Hindu from Muslim practice, and when it fails lumps heterogeneity into the singular category of "the syncretic." As though "world religions" were somehow pure and non-syncretic.

Censuses portray conversion as having been achieved by recording the Meos as Sunni Muslim. In 1891 there are said to be 145,184 Muslim Meos in Rajputana. There is also the significant category of Hindu Meos, although they number only 74 by then. Contrary to the perspective of the theologian and the census taker, which views conversion as accomplished in the early half of the second millennium, late nineteenth-century ethnographers describe the Meos as nominal (and inferior!) Muslims. Ethnographers' indices are defined by the "great traditions" of Islam and Hinduism. Powlett writes that "as regards their own religion the Meos are very ignorant. Few know the *kalima* [the profession of faith in Allah's unity and the prophethood of Muhammad] and fewer still the regular prayers." Until recently the *nikāh* marriage ritual, burial, and circumcision were the only Muslim customs. Powlett refers to them as "half-Muslim." He mentions the few mosques in their area and the shrines common with their Hindu neighbors. These included those dedicated to the Panch Pir or five Pirs, the Bhomia responsible for protecting the village, and the Chavand or Khera Deo where sacrifice is offered to the goddess.[51] Watson and Kaye mention that though converted to Islam the Meos professed "a spurious character of that faith." As in the case of the Rangar and Bhati (Muslim) Rajputs of the North West Provinces a brahman fixed the days of marriage and betrothal. Although marriage was performed by a qazi, Hindu castes played ritual roles. Watson and Kaye mention also the practice of levirate (the custom of an older brother's marrying the widow of his younger brother that was prevalent in the Punjab) and describe their clothing as being Hindu not Muslim.[52]

Mewati narratives suggest the shared culture of pastoral-peasant groups. Meo rituals of marriage, childbirth, and succession were similar to those of most other Hindu castes. Like Hindu castes, the Meos observed rules of purity and pollution with regard to low castes. They avoided eating beef in some areas, and vegetarianism was widespread among them.[53] The Meos were known to celebrate festivals such as Holi and Sankrant following the spring and winter harvests; Govardhan, a festival of cattle worship; and Tij, Amavas, Janmashtami, and Diwali associated with the worship of Hindu gods and goddesses such as Parvati, Krishna, and Rama. They also worshiped gods and goddesses of the village, water, and disease.

The author of a revenue settlement refers to the Meos as "lax Mohamedans" who "rarely observe the fasts or attend prayers in the mosque, drink spirits and are quite willing to reverence the same deities as their Hindu neighbours." He mentions the spread of Wahabi tenets among them from the center of the sect at Bhaunri in Bharatpur's Pahari tehsil.[54] Powlett, the colonial ethnographer for the Alwar State, however, mentions that a Wahabi teacher came once but his doctrine was distasteful and caused offense.[55] The Islamic ideology of Wahabism (originating in Saudi Arabia) condemned pilgrimage and the cult of the saints as akin to idol worship. Clearly communities were not static in terms of sectarian influence. Across time there emerged a strong attachment to land as a component of Meo identity. The community derived its multiple identities from various sources, including a remembered past of autonomy, from a ruler-warrior status, from pastoral and other migration, from interaction with other state forms, from gender relations, and from a religious culture that was simultaneously Hindu, Muslim, and regional.

The Meo Oral Tradition

Orality has often been the linguistic associate of marginality. Around A.D. 1000 the Rajasthani language branched in three directions, western, southern, and eastern. Mewati became the spoken language of eastern Rajasthan.[56] The politics of language constituted it a "vernacular" and "dialect." Mewati included four variants: standard Mewati, Rathi Mewati, Nehera Mewati, and Kather Mewati.[57] The oral is, however, saturated by the written. Mewati is a highly porous universe demonstrating the influence of Brajbhasha, Haryanvi, and even Persian and English texts, genres, and metaphors.[58]

In a complex web of intertextuality, oral and written texts constantly influence each other. Mewati narratives are called *bāt* following the Rajasthani genre of *vāt* meaning "tale" or "epic" or prose narrative that derives from the Sanskrit *vārtā*, or account. Grounded in the oral tradition, vat are authored, preserved, and transmitted by specialist castes like the Charan, Bhat, Mirasi, and Rao. The English referred to these groups disparagingly as bards, but they performed a complex role, as they were panegyrists and historian-poet-musicians as well as satirists. Their compositions often mirrored their patrons' perspectives, but they also used their literary power to bargain with patrons and on occasion could be quite critical of them. There is then a need to interrogate the very category "bard" that derived from the European downgrading of orality, performed traditions, and narrated pasts. In form, rhyme, and meter *vāt sāhitya* (literature) is not very different from written poetical composition and exposes the artificial dichotomy between the oral and the written, the folk and the classical.[59] Images are shared, as when a woman's delicately molded fingers are likened to a bean pod *(moṭha phaḷī sī āñgaḷī)*, the shape of her arm to a rolling pin *(belan belī bañh)*, or her head to a coconut *(sīs baṇo nārel sū)*.

In fact, it is difficult to see bat in terms of an exclusive genre since what characterizes it is generic heterogeneity and an intense relation between orality and writing.[60] There are no generic boundaries, as Malinowski would have us expect, between legend, saga, folk epic. Instead most bat were at the junction of *kāvya, itihāsa,* and *sangīt,* or a generic compound of mythopoetic history, epic narrative, genealogy, and music.

The *lok gāthā* (literally, folk narrative) was a highly developed tradition in the Indian subcontinent, especially after the twelfth century, and was simultaneous with the growth of apabhransa, the literary languages of India that derived from Sanskrit and the Prakrits. This developed into the *deśa bhāṣā,* or popular languages, such as Old Western Rajasthani (OWR) or Marubhasa, Bengali, Gujarati, and so on. The traditional language of Rajasthani bards is Dingal (from *ḍing,* or arrogance), a literary and archaic form of old Marwari. It was replaced by the more popular Rajasthani (which Grierson calls old Gujarati) that detached itself from western apabhransa about the thirteenth century. This language was the first of all the bhasas of northern India to possess a literature. The Dingal of the Rajasthani bards is the literary form of that language and the ancestor of the contemporary Marvari and Gujarati.[61] Most vat literature used a combination of OWR and Pingal. This was the language of the Bhats, while the Charans or Rajput bards used mostly Dingal. The themes of vat literature were both heroic and romantic.[62]

Several poetic narratives were composed in regional languages. In western India, and Rajasthan, in particular, a large body of literature in both prose and verse ranges across genres such as lok gathas, *khyāts* (chronicles), *vaṇśāvalīs,* and *pīṛhīāvalīs,* comprising genealogies, clan, lineage, and biographical histories.[63] Many of these have been referred to as indigenous forms of recording history and are written rather than oral. The Mewati oral tradition draws upon these written genres. It also shares with apabhransa traditions the centrality of the heroic. The hero may be superior in kind or in degree to others as is the case with other Rajasthani narratives such as *Pābūjī, Bagṛāvat, Gogājī, Tejājī, Ḍūngjī-Javārjī, Ḍholā Mārū,* and others. The limits of the genre of the heroic narrative lie in its eulogization of the past. Marginality is thus overwritten, defeat transformed into victory. The literary, even as it encodes the past, also veils it in a masculinist overwriting.

Certain Mewati narratives also memorialize the past. In this respect they are close to the genre of the historical narrative, a widely prevalent form in several parts of the world as the Norwegian, Irish, and Icelandic sagas indicate. "*Ye mevon kī tārīkh kahte hain*" (they tell the history of the Meos), a

Meo told me, suggesting how collective memory is framed by the Persian genre of history writing as well as by the Indian genre of *itihāsa-purāṇa*. Mythic metaphors also draw upon Persian story-telling genres of the *dāstān* and the *qissā* and from the Rajasthan *vāt*.

The liminality of patrons and performers, the Meos and the Mirasis, mirrors each other. The population of Mirasi performers estimated at 241,660 persons was spread over Rajasthan, Jammu, and Kashmir, Punjab, North West Provinces, United Provinces, and Rajputana. At the turn of the nineteenth century the Mirasis were mostly Muslim, with some Hindus and a few Buddhists and Sikhs. The Mirasis of the Meos are poet-historian-musicians and a ritual service caste that have an exclusive and hereditary patron-client relationship with the Meos. The Mirasis are a highly creative (although mostly illiterate) literati and also the agents of cultural transmission. As professional specialists they are responsible for composing and transmitting the vigorous Meo oral tradition, which consists of a vast gamut of material including a large corpus of narratives. These are recited and sung at ritual occasions involving social gatherings. Memory is ritualized by performance during the Mevon *ke sāye* (calendrical period over the summer season auspicious for marriages). Performances begin in the evening and once spanned the few days and nights that the bridal party stayed in a village. Performative groups can range from a single lead singer accompanied by instrumentalists to a group of Mirasi singers.

Mewati bat are performed in the style of *dohā dhānī,* that is, two-lined rhymed verses set to music. They might also include other metrical forms such as the *chappā* (consisting of six lines that end in a doha) and the *sorṭho*. The doha is a rhyming couplet in which each line consists of half lines made up of feet of 6 + 4 + 3 and 6 + 4 + 1. The sorṭho, or *sorṭhā*, is the name of a poetic meter consisting of a rhyming couplet in which the first and second half lines contain 11 and 13 matras, or metrical instants. The narratives consist of an alternation of prose and verse. The dohas are usually in a mix of poetic Rajasthani combined with Brajbhasha (Pingal *kāvya*), and the prose that explicates them is in colloquial Mewati. Narratives are usually not anonymous unlike several other oral traditions and might even be dated. There are undoubted variations in the performative context, and no two performances are ever the same.[64] The sequence of verses is often rearranged. Nonetheless, there is a striking continuity between versions.

Sometimes the narrative becomes immobilized in tape or print, creating a displacement of speech by writing. But the performed text is grounded in

FIGURE 1
A group of Mirasis: authors, composers, performers of the Meo oral tradition.

orality and governed by the rules of oral communication. The *batkāvan*, or commentary, plays a vital role in bringing memory alive in the present. Poetry itself has mnemonic possibilities, but the prose makes it possible to establish sequentiality and make the past contemporaneous. Sometimes, however, levels of meaning in the text are not known even to the performer, indicating a loss of cultural memory.

The oral tradition sustained by *jajmānī* patronage often assumes a panegyric character. The author imagines dialogue, fantasizes encounters, and can provide desired endings. The poet-genealogist has a magnifying role, structured, as Burghart puts it, "both in relations of reference and address."[65] In the *Pāñch Pahāṛ* the fearsomeness of the Meo clan is deliberately exaggerated, and the Rajputs are described as worried by the fierce Meo challenge. The patron rewards the Mirasi appropriately for his praise, and he usually obtains a share of the harvest. Although the Mirasis are conservers of the cultural tradition and collective memory, they have a markedly low social status in an agrarian economy that has come to privilege land.

The narrative tradition constructs a male public arena. This excludes women as performers and as audience. They might listen but in seclusion on the periphery. Heroic narratives are engendered by being called *mardānī*, or masculine. Most narratives are performed with single or multiepisodic extracts, which are often centered on a *laṛāi* (battle) that builds up the *vīr rasa* (heroic mood or emotion). The Mirasis often begin with an invocation to the Lord (Khuda) or *vandanā* (hymn) to Bhavani, the goddess responsible for poetic creativity. As in epics, the characters are bounded and preformed rather than layered. Unlike the novel, the oral tradition's primary concern is not with exploring individual subjectivity and consciousness.[66] Although most of the Mewati bat are differently authored they frequently refer to each other, suggesting the cumulative process of collective memory. In a narrative on the early twentieth century called *Harsānā*, seventeenth-century events of the *Pāñch Pahāṛ kī laṛāī*. are referred to where the Meos claim to have "looted the Badhshah's treasure with seven hundred thousand swords" *(sāt lākh talvar hī mārā bādsāhan kā māl)*. The transfer of images and phrases across texts and the coherence between the versions of different performers probably comes from the frequent interaction of performers at cultural performances. Though a Mirasi might not know the entire narrative, he might quote fragments and dohas. Some of the better-known verses might be recited in chorus by Mirasis and even by the Meos present at a performance. The interjections, comments, and chorus of the audience *(hunkārā)* are a conventional part of the cultural performance as also the frequent "Ah" and "Ha" of the performer. Cultural memory is a complex interplay of singers and audience.

The narratives are mnemonically preserved, and the tradition is passed on from generation to generation unless the son opts for a different livelihood. Cultural performances constitute the link between the oral tradition and individual memory. The bat undoubtedly project an idealized image of the past, almost as though to prevent forgetting. For example, the Meo relation with the Mughals is constructed around a battle. The antistate thematic that runs through several narratives suggests that they portray a selective interpretation of the past and also structure a system of collective representations into which individual Meos are then socialized through their reiteration at Meo rites of passage. Writing, it is said, creates fixity, but one may well ask does not orality also offer a fixity of image as it totalizes the category of Rajput or Mughal?

Marcel Proust mentions how time erases the past but memory is able to restore it. He points out that the past cannot be recalled with voluntary memory but comes back with involuntary memory. His description of the episode of dipping a madeleine into a cup of tea is now famous; it recalled for him a complete picture of the past — his aunt, the garden, the town, and its paths.[67] It is as though the past were preserved against the erosion of time, of oblivion, and results in a release from the finite world. Nonetheless, one also needs to remember that memory is also about selection and forgetting. As a contemporary poet expresses it:

one memory
Certainly hides another, that being what memory is all about.[68]

Like all narrative traditions the Meo suffers from inconsistencies and contradictions; it articulates a definite point of view and explicates a plurality of time. Linear time is telescoped and coalesced with sacred time. Multiple histories intersect, and authorial voice plays a major and undisguised part in the narrative.

This work is not concerned with the facticity of the oral tradition or its correspondence to actual events. That would be to historicize myth. On the contrary, its starting point is the interweave of the imaginary and the real that the oral tradition represents. It is thereby able to capture a perspective on the contested past, indicate shifts in the group perspective over time, and reveal a besieged sensibility that the written record fails to reveal.

The performative approach of folklore, which involves recording and comparing variants of the same narrative or analyzing a single performance, has deliberately been avoided.[69] A purely textual or structural approach would have been unsuitable since the analysis moves back and forth between the text and the historical context. The aesthetic-musicological aspects of the text have been underemphasized in favor of cultural analysis to bring out the larger meaning of the folk text for Meo history and society. Fieldwork in the region has been discontinuous and mobile because of the requirement of recording divergent performance contexts.

I have drawn upon several narratives from the Meo oral tradition recorded from Mirasis during cultural performances in Mewat. Nonetheless, only a section of the Meo cultural universe and oral tradition has been used to throw light on the time frame of this work. The narratives under review are essentially oral, both in terms of composition and transmission. Some of the tapes and transcripts used here are now part of the archives of the Rupayan Sansthan, Jodhpur.

This book is about strategies of representation both in oral and written genres and the processes of marginalization and resistance that derive from them. Marginality exists at many levels. The community on the margin is also implicated in the constitution of marginality. It reproduces the ritual hierarchy of caste based on principles of purity-pollution, excluding the "untouchable" castes. There is also the cultural construction of male and female worlds in the oral tradition that reinforces a public-private division. But it becomes increasingly apparent as the millennium unfolds that the Meos inhabit a world that is not organized by them; a constant violation of their territoriality takes place; they face repeated and deliberate attempts to break up their political unity as a community; and the juridic-institutional order that takes shape by the nineteenth century is regarded as alien by them. Their voices are suppressed in a world of textually mediated discourses that often are of foreign origin; their protests are ignored by systems of military, bureaucratic, and intellectual rationality. I move in chapter 3 to a discussion of the Meo political alternative to the state, and detail in chapters 4 to 9 the constitution of marginality.

3 Antistate: The *Pāl* Polity

The historiographical discourse treats the achievement of kingship as indexical of political performance in premodern times.[1] It tends to negate the pasts of groups who developed alternative political forms. The large pastoral-peasant groups of northern India such as the Jat, Gujar, Ahir, and Meo in several cases did not confer ideological legitimation to monarchy and were incompletely integrated into states. Only for a brief interlude and in a limited geographical area between the eighteenth and twentieth centuries did the Ahirs and Jats form kingdoms at Rewari, Bharatpur, Dholpur, and in the Punjab. On the whole, however, one can see the institutional arrangements of these and other groups such as the Pakhtun in Afghanistan in terms of dispersed rather than concentrated power. Rather than looking upon these groups in terms of their politico-historical *failure* to attain state and sovereignty, one needs to see the alternative political possibilities that they represented. My concern is how to grasp and write about different forms of political being and practice, particularly in view of the fact that they were considered insignificant by states and by social science given the virtual absence of an archive.

Critics have pointed out the imposition of a European model of state formation with respect to African and Asian societies. The territorial state, it is argued, is a Eurocentric notion.[2] In other areas of the world and during various periods of history, different modes of political organization were developed based on kinship or caste. Sovereignty and bureaucracy did not necessarily characterize these. Burton Stein forcefully contests the Eurocentric political formulation that sees the modern state as *the* state with all other political forms merely progressing toward this universal type. This is an approach that views the absolutist centralized monarchies of France, England, and Spain as paving the way for the emergence of Europe from a "parcelized" sovereignty. Asia has known states as general political formations as early as Europe, if not earlier. Communitarian institutions and their politics and nonmonarchical modes of governance have had a long history here, predating and surviving the formation of states.[3]

The distinctive Meo contribution to the diversity of Asian polities might be characterized as a pal polity.[4] The absence of "sovereignty" in this polity did not mean an absence of territoriality, legitimate rulership, or political organization, which Evans-Pritchard declared characterized the so-called stateless African tribal polities.[5] One of the problems with early political anthropology is the conception of stateless societies in terms of a "lack." But these societies, as Clastres points out, may have resisted the emergence of monopoly forms of power that generate the state and social stratification.[6] This is not to say that the kin-based community is without its own hierarchies of status and rank or that the striving for kingship is completely absent. But the working of the Meo polity can be conceived of as a different political form rather than as demonstrative of anarchy or political underdevelopment. Political forms antithetical to kingship often provided the context of resistance to state formation and one can characterize them negatively as "antistate." The political history of the subcontinent might be better understood as the dialectic between state and antistate rather than as a progressive movement "from lineage to state." The last phrase is derived from Thapar's characterization of the period from 800 to 400 B.C. and the subsequent period of state formation that saw a proliferation of lineage-based janapadas, or clan-based states.[7]

The "pal" is the basic unit of the Meo polity that potentially decenters monopoly sovereignty. Mewat is, more or less, divided into thirteen pals (see map 4). The pal polity can be seen as an alternative political structure that resisted assimilation by successive state formations and indeed frequently challenged them. One might speculate on the relation of bards to types of state. Bards and oral traditions have related to both monarchical and nonmonarchical modes of organizing power. In the case of the latter they advanced mythic claims to political equality with ruling groups, such as the Rajputs.

Lineage and the genealogical organization of politics were important for

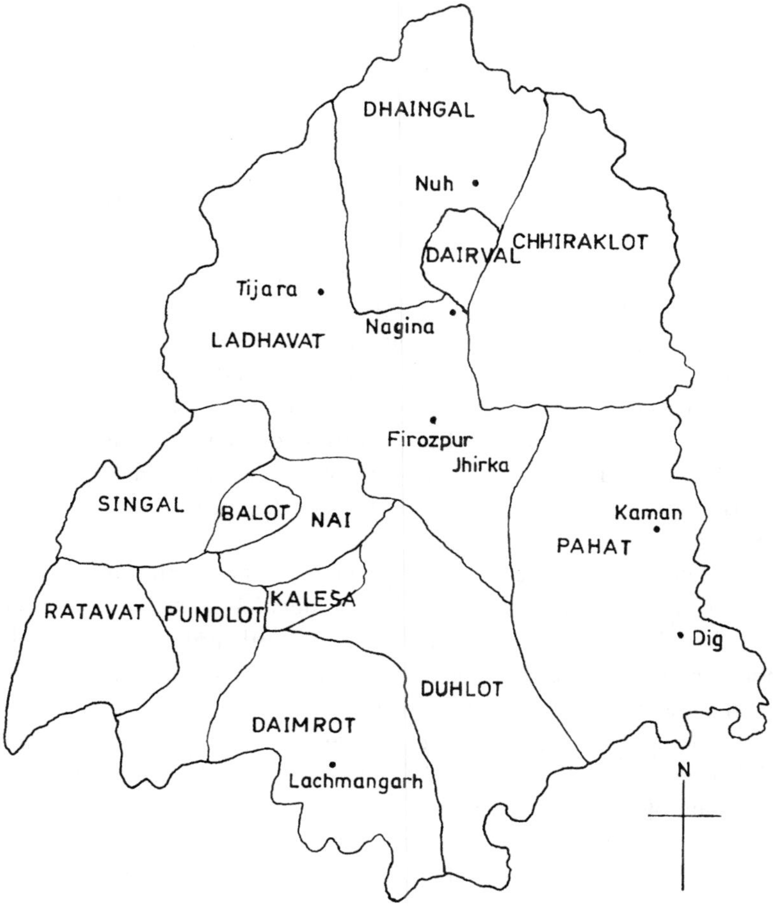

MAP 4 Map of Meo Pals.

Pratap Aggarwal, *Caste, Religion, and Power: An Indian Case Study* (New Delhi: Sri Ram Centre for Industrial Relations, 1971), 20.

several political configurations in north India and not merely for ruling groups like the Rajputs. In this chapter I examine a narrative account of the group's "origins." Levi-Strauss demonstrates a similar link between the song of the Borroro Indians of South America and their clan structure.[8] I use the text to make an incision into aspects of Meo political society and their ideology of governance.

The *Pālon kī Bansābalī*, or the "Genealogy" of the Pals

The *Bansabali* is a short account of the Meo pal system that describes the ideal units of both its kinship system and segmented polity.[9] The title literally means the genealogy of the pals. The use of genealogies by Hindu, Muslim, and Jain castes is widespread throughout India.[10] This belongs to the larger tradition known as itihāsa-purāṇa that was extensively used by several communities in India (itihasa, referring to a somewhat didactic history, and purana, meaning ancient tale) following the fifth century B.C. This genre is a complex of remembered pasts, genealogies, real and imagined, and panegyric.

The Meo *Bansabali* then is not a pedigree or "the account of one's descent from an ancestor or ancestors by enumeration of intermediate persons."[11] A useful distinction is made between the pirhiavali and a vamsavali. Although both comprise genealogical forms, the former is an account of the series of generations, while the vamsavali is a detailed account of the line of descent tracing it through blood ties or fictive kinship to an ancestor and possibly even to the clan founder. Moreover, the record of the actual links in the chain of descent recorded in the *bahīs*, or ledgers, is maintained for the Meos by the caste of Jagas or genealogists (as the Bhats do for the Rajputs). The vamsavali, on the other hand, is the work of the poet-historian-musician.

The *Bansabali* is more in the nature of an "origin myth" than an account of the line of descent. It only mentions the respective "founders" of the Meo pals and important persona. The final "signature" verse of the author, Kanvar Khan, alludes to the purpose, which is to have described the family of Meo clans. This is called the '*bāvan-bārā pāl* and the *pallākṛā* (fifty-two *gots* or *gotras* and twelve pals and a thirteenth pallakra). The Meo pal-got social structure is outlined as consisting of five pals of the Jadu Meos; five of the Tanvar (Tungar) Meos; two of the Kacchavaha Meos; one pal is said to come from the Rathors; and the thirteenth or the pallakra of the Pahats is said to derive from the clan of Nirban Chauhans. All thirteen pals (including the pallakra) are clustered into five groups each of which has a Rajput bans *(vansh)* name.[12]

The very first verse establishes the territorial center of the *Bansabali*, which is presumably Mewat, for the region of Braj is described as southward:

alal kuṇḍ dakhan disā mathurā maṇḍal gāñv
birajpat thepī rājā kisan nai likhī rājā rām sinh kai nāñv

Beyond the tank of Alal
to the south, in a village of the Mathura region.
Raja Kisan established power over Braj,
and wrote it in the name of Raja Ram Singh.

Raja Kisan, or the popular cowherd god Krishna, later treated as one of the incarnations of Vishnu by Hindus, is believed to have established rule over Braj, the area that adjoins Mewat. Memory is spatialized, as it is anchored in topography and material objects, thereby rendering it meaningful. The oral tradition returns again and again to this marking of sacred space around the area of Braj.

According to the Sanskrit Mahabharata, Krishna's clansmen are said to have been liquidated following an orgy of mutual killing in fulfilment of the curse of Gandhari. But the Meo narrative describes the Jat raja, Ram Singh, as having descended from Krishna's clansmen, the Jadu ksatriyas. Even as the narrative maps a distinct Jadu bans exclusively for Meo clans, it legitimizes the ruling Jat lineage of the eighteenth-century kingdom of Bharatpur and suggests a distant kinship of the Meos and Jats. Kinship links with the Khanazadas are also indicated, and significantly one of the Meo saints mentioned in the genealogy has a mother who belongs to the "service" caste of barbers. Even as the Meos elaborate their ksatriya identity, their kinship linkages to the non-twice-born castes such as the Jats and the Nais are not denied.

The poet next refers to the rule of the Jadu (Jadon) Rajputs:

sarhad nāpī samand jūñ jahāñ lag sūrsen kā nāñv
chappan kūṭ jādū huā jinko mathurā maṇḍal gāñv

He [Krishna] ruled the region extending up to the sea
so far as the name of Surasena was heard.
The Jadus whose village was in the Mathura region
had fifty-six forts.

Surasena refers to an ancient region named after a Jadu raja who is believed to have lived before Krishna. Bayana (near Mathura) from where the Jadus ruled in the tenth century was included in Surasena. The Surasena dynasty whose capital was at Mathura also claim to belong to the Jadu/Yadu vansh. The narrative suggests the layers of "archaeology" that comprise cultural memory.

Kanha (Krishna) "whose praises the *gopīs* [milkmaids] sing" is the founder of the five Meo pals of the Jadu bans. The Meo pirs or saints, Chudh Sidh and Lal Das, belong to this bans. The five pals of the Jadu Meo bans are the Duhlot, Chiraklot, Daimrot, Pundlot, and Nai-Nasr.

Krishna is also the founder of the four Meo Tanvar clans. In this lineage are the Kairu-Pandu, that is, the Kauravas and the Pandavas, the cousins of the Mahabharata epic and the parties to the great fratricidal war, to whom most Meos ascribe their "origin."[13] Arjulla (Arjuna) of the Pandava brothers is the ancestor-hero of the four Meo Tanvar Pals that include the Dairhval, Rattavat, Balot, and the Ladhavat *chatrīs (kṣatriyas)* of Baghora.[14]

The other epic tradition of the Ramayana is also woven into this Meo kinship myth. The Meo Kacchavaha bans is said to have descended from Rama.

kachavāhā rājpūt ramchandar kā potā
jānai rāvaṇ kūñ bas kiyā diyā durjan ke gotā

The Kacchavaha Rajputs
are the grandsons of Rama
who vanquished Ravana,
and destroyed the bad men.

The Kacchavaha Meos include the Dhaingal and Singal Pals who are said to descend from Rama:

raghubaṇsī insūñ kahaiṇ saccā karūñ bayān
haiṇ ye dhaiṇgal yāi bans maiṇ bañkāñ barġūjar balvān

Raghuvanshis they are called,
my testimony is all true.
The Dhaingal are in this line,
the brave Bargujars too.

The relation of hero-gods and Meo pals is explicitly established, the chain of descent being from Rama through Kacchavaha ksatriyas to the Dhaingal and Singal (Bargujar) Pals.

The description of the twelfth pal (Rathor) and the thirteenth or the pallakra of the Pahat is brief. Only a single line of a single doha is sketchily devoted to each, "The brave Kalesa Pal, they are the brave Rathors." "The thirteenth pal is the pallakra; with the Pahats my story is complete."[15]

The *Bansabali* is a significant statement on identity and establishes Meo bonding with the area of Braj. We have in this "genealogical" account of the Meos the sociopolitical ordering of people belonging to a single group; the organization of territorial space; the construction of time, events, and heroes in a single myth; and a clue to the structural frame of kinship. In the process of fixing identities, however, genealogies also transform them. The "founding myth" is noticeably an exercise in historical amnesia negating an older past of migration to the area, of settlement and dispersal. It privileges an imagined geography of a region that merges into the sacred terrain of Braj. The narrative tends to silence the extensive horizontal linkages that arose from Meo intermarriage with Rajputs, Jats, Minas, and even the "untouchable" Chamars. Forgetting is implicit in the very act of remembering.

The historian and anthropologist's readings of genealogies in India see them as fabrications indicative of what anthropologists have called sanskritization/ksatriyaization. Genealogies were very common in eighteenth- and nineteenth-century India and even earlier. Romila Thapar points out that sudra and brahman families demonstrated ksatriya status through "fabricated genealogies, linking them to Suryavaṃśi and Candravaṃśi lineages, which lineages seem also to have been an invention of a particular historical time." Surajit Sinha asserts that genealogies demonstrate the assimilation of tribal groups of Central India by Rajput state formation.[16] A similar reading can be made of the Mewati narrative. By the late nineteenth century virtually all castes in Rajasthan claimed either ksatriya or brahmanical status. While the literature on genealogies views this as an attempt to sanskritize or imitate upper castes and therefore "fabricate," the hermeneutics of genealogies have to see them as far more complex statements. One can, for instance, glimpse in the Meo claims to ksatriya status a sense of loss, of the erosion of power and an erstwhile autonomy.

Genealogies also represent claims to status and power. The larger question is whether, in their claim as descendants of Krishna and Rama the Meos are merely appropriating Rajput lineages. I stress another reading: that the very rendering of bans in terms of non-Rajput groups demystifies monarchical cosmologies and the Rajput's exclusive right to rank and authority. The issue is not one of mere fabricated identities that historians and anthropologists have seen lower castes and tribals as claiming. Meo countervailing claims and affirmation of ksatriya status are also an assertion of the right to rule. The self-address of "raja" as well as references to the political insignia of *darbār* (court) and *fauj* (military force) and horsemen suggest an accent on local autonomy and the corrosion of the exclusive Rajput right to rule. The Meo chief, Masand, claims, "Kingship is in my lineage." The use of the term "king" to indicate men of superior rank suggests, as Price puts it, that kingliness constitutes the honorable status toward which men strive. It therefore "is fluid and subject to constant challenge."[17] Genealogies then also represent assertions of power of nonruling groups and hence a contest over the very category ksatriya. The folk epic *Bagaṛāvat* is a similar account with respect to the pastoral-peasant Gujars.[18] *Ḍholā,* the epic of the Jats, like the Meo genealogy, suggests how non-twice-born or the sudra castes made persistent claims to ksatriya status.[19] Skaria's account of the Bhil "forest polity" brings out how the Bhils in the Dangs region of Gujarat imagined themselves as rajas and ksatriyas.[20] Not surprisingly, the category "ksatriya" historically proved to be the most open-ended of the four varnas, or caste clusters.

The *Bansabali* indicates the presence of different, even conflicting, principles of political association within a given area. These principles may be derived from the categories of Meo political structure that are well defined in the narrative. A pal is defined as a territorial got that is believed to have descended from a mythico-real ancestor. The entire area of Mewat is spatially demarcated into thirteen tracts or pal territories. The bans have exclusive and common ancestors (Jadu: Krishna; Tanvar: Krishna and Arjuna; Kacchavaha: Rama; Rathor and Pahat: unmentioned). But in the case of the Meos it is the pal rather than the bans that is the more important unit of their social structure. The bans is not significant as a unit in Meo kinship nor does it have a political organization such as the panchayat, unlike the territorial pal.

We have within the *Bansabali* an explicit four-order division suggesting the different layers comprising a political system (see table 4). The first order is that of the Meo community with a patrilineally organized polity. All Meos who belong to one of the pals are called *pāliyās*; the rest are *nepāliyās* who only belong to a got. The second, third, and fourth orders are those of bans, pal, and got, respectively. The latter two being maximal lineages are exogamous units. In kinship terms the pal is an expanded got, that is, a numerically significant clan.[21] Territoriality, however, is the major distinguishing feature of the Meo pal since each pal has a defined or imagined territory. The lines of division are both sustained and mediated by the rules of exogamy. Meo males continue in the gots ascribed to them by birth, and women are subject to exchange transactions between men that occur across gots.

The other levels that are not mentioned in the *Bansabali* are those of the household, *paṭṭī*, village, and the *thāmā*. All the pals are divided into thamas each of which traces descent to an actual ancestor known as *dādā (ek hī dādā kī aulād)*. The thamas are named after the ancestor or after the original village of the ancestor.[22] The thama, which includes several villages, usually has a *chaudhari*, or headman, whose position is hereditary. All these levels, of the pal, got, thama, and the household constitute lineal branches. As in the case of the Punjab, Meo villages are divided into pattis each of which is a localized got. The number of households in a patti vary considerably. Frequently each patti has its own leader who generally comes from the most important household in the patti. The *kunbā* is the minimal lineage consisting of several households who own fields adjacent to each other. It often consists of a group of agnates who hold rights to ancestrally inherited property in a subdivision of the village. The corporate descent group comprises a localized patrilineage that also has effective land control in the area. Members of a got may also be dispersed, but usually a cluster of contiguous villages are inhabited by *sehgotiās* (people of the same got).[23] The Meo kinship structure is closer to the Jat system prevalent in Punjab and Rajasthan where the subcaste comprises segmented exogamous intermarrying gots rather than to the Muslim system in which women are retained within the descent group.[24]

Most Meo villages have been complex, multicaste entities. The membership of a village has historically been quite fluid. Meo males moved to other regions as warrior lineages and in search of sustainable livelihoods that might be immune to the disruption of drought and famine. Under Mughal rule, pahis and paltis were migrant peasants who came from other villages

TABLE 4 Meo Sociopolitical Structure

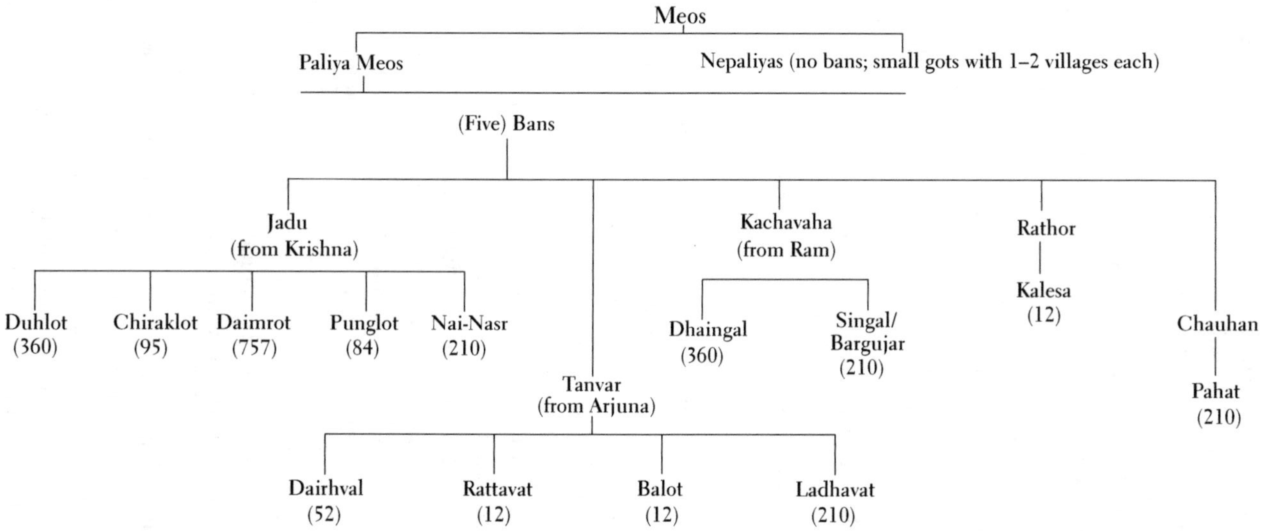

Note: Figures in parentheses denote number of villages.

Source: Pratap Aggarwal, *Caste, Religion, and Power: An Indian Case Study* (New Delhi: Sri Ram Centre for Industrial Relations, 1971), 26–27.

to cultivate land. The constant splitting of households and lineages enabled the establishment of new villages and the colonization of land.

Decentering Power: The *Pāl* Polity

Why this long-winded account of a mere genealogical text? Even a cursory reading would suggest how the ground is elaborately laid out for political plurality. The sacralization of Meo political structure within the narrative makes it a charter of authenticity for dispersed power. It also makes difficult the unification of the group unless by conquest or an overriding theory of divine kingship.

The debate between centralized forms and decentralized ones is an old one in Indian political theory. The *gaṇa rājya,* or the "republics," of ancient India were often in conflict with monarchy. In the Mahabharata, Jarasandah, the powerful king of Magadha, is in favor of monarchy, whereas Krishna defends the republican form and even leaves Mathura for this reason.[25] The political ideal of the cakravartin or imperium was also a contested one. But the tension between state and antistate or forms antithetical to it has been a far more pervasive one that has persisted across state formations, medieval and modern. Meo warrior lineages did endeavor periodically to establish semblances of kingship. But these were only intermittent attempts to consolidate power. The self-governing Jats similarly demonstrated an apathy to monarchy, and scholars have commented on their more participatory political processes.[26]

The principle of division rather than of hierarchy is involved in the pal polity since the pals unlike castes are not hierarchically integrated. All pals are equal in status, at least theoretically.[27] In practice, distinctions of size, population, power, and proximity to regimes worked as significant variables in the rise and fall of pals.

Meo narratives offer considerable clues into the operation of the pal polity, bringing alive the changing perspectives, coalitions, and crosscurrents. Power was not only dispersed among the segments of the polity but also extended within the clan to other heads of lineages who shared the authority of the chief. Inasmuch as the pal was a territorial entity, the jurisdiction of its chief (referred to as rao, mal, or sardar) extended over a given number of villages. His authority to declare war and summon the pal panchayat was exercised consensually, in consultation with elders of other households and lineages and other chiefs who were members of the *bhāī baṇdh,* or brotherhood. A narrative refers to a battle being declared after the entire clan had been summoned for a feast. Rai Bhan, the chief of the Pahat clan, is described as a "tiger" but other powerful persons are named, including Masand, Mavasi, and Ruda Sultan who are heads of their thamas or patrilineages. Kinship linked them to the chief to whom they also owed military service even as the chief's personal power was circumscribed by these other chiefs of countervailing power.

The parallels with Bhil raj or the forest polity of the Bhils that Skaria discusses are striking. Skaria remarks that the Bhil style of kingship diverged from dominant understandings; "Such kingship, with its privileging of wildness and very distinctive forms of political power, often constituted a powerful alternative to Brahman or Kshatriya-centred claims to social power." What brahman or ksatriya-centered models are is not quite clear, unless what is implied is an alternative to monarchy. According to Skaria, "widespread participation in Bhil kingship was associated with a politics of lack — a lack, this is to say, of self-sufficient loci for kingship. Because of this lack of self-sufficient loci, kingship resided in no one place, and there were multiple hierarchies of kingly authority." Skaria does not see the absence of a center, of a clear hierarchical apex to political power as an alternative model to kingship itself, hence his imputation of a "lack." But his material certainly seems to suggest a different organization of power, and the association of the entire (male) community with political power as power was widely shared.[28]

The multiple markers of a Meo chief's authority included the *pagṛī,* or turban, representing the chief as head of household, lineage, and possibly clan; the use of *nagāṛās* (kettledrums); and a *nishān* (flag/insignia). His residence was called *nākā* and more occasionally *gaṛhī* in the case of the presence of a "fortress." Authority derived from the chief's skills in battle, his leadership of peasant warriors, and later from the extent of land owned and the power and influence he wielded. The *Palon kā jas* (praise verses of the pals) refers to the preferred characteristics of the chief, which are not only his superiority in his lineage but also his personal character that ought to be *bahādur aur dātār* (valorous and generous).

In the Meo oral tradition *dāna* (ritual prestation) is extolled as an attribute of the chief and derives from Hindu conceptions of kingship. "*Laṇk luṭāve*" is a metaphor for generous gifting akin to the giving away of all that existed in Lanka, the legendary city of gold. This image derives from but is not part of the original Ramayana. *Kaulānī* refers to the Meo chief Baksa as a great *sākī* or *dānī,* that is, the giver of gifts. One of the modes of participation in authority in both monarchical and nonmonarchical polities is through receiving royal gifts. Over a period of time power became rooted in entitlements to land and resources. But power is visualized as essentially redistributive.

Dumont defines dominance territorially. A caste is dominant "because it enjoys main rights in the soil" and reproduces the royal function at the village level.[29] The strong brahman-ksatriya relation or the purity-pollution principle that Dumont identified in the subcontinent and as the basis of the hierarchy of castes is considerably qualified. Among the Meos, the brahman did not play the major priestly role of the person who conducts and protects the sacrifice and instead had a minor ritual role as occasional astrologer and genealogist. As in some Rajput States, in the Meo polity the ideological role of the brahman might even be substituted by that of the Charan bard or the Nath Yogi, both groups identified with the non-twice-born castes.

Raheja has argued that Dumont, Trautman, and Heesterman fail to perceive the central importance of evil and inauspiciousness in Hindu social life. This is removed, she maintains, through a particular ritual procedure or through a set of dana prestations made by the dominant landholding caste in the village. This caste wields temporal power, and the notion of dana provides for the well-being and auspiciousness of the donor and the village through the ritual transference of evil and inauspiciousness from donor to recipient. The dominant caste has a center-periphery relation with other castes rather than a hierarchical ordering. Raheja is challenging Dumont's contention that the brahman-ksatriya relation derives from the distinction between purity and temporal power.[30]

While Raheja's emphasis on auspiciousness-inauspiciousness is valid, her argument raises the question as to why one would want to transfer inauspiciousness. Moreover, why would this be acceptable to the recipient of the gift? Surely then logically *kanyādāna* (literally, the gift of the bride) by the bride-givers would invert the normativity of the hierarchical ordering of the bride-takers over the bride-givers. Along with the gift of the bride-girl they would be able to transfer inauspiciousness to the bride-receivers. Moreover, the idea of dana has far more positive connotations of the acquisition of personal merit, reciprocity, and incorporation, which Raheja seems to overlook.

Pal literally means "to nourish" and "to look after" and the style of face-to-face relations of the pal polity needs to be foreground. Not only was land and its surplus shared, so were the products of raiding such as Mughal treasure or camels. Warfare and raiding were important occupations for men, particularly in the period of transition to sedentarization. Meo narratives give us a strong sense of the dispersal of coercive power in rural society, as there are frequent references to "guards" or an armed and mounted peasantry that might fight enemies such as the Rajputs or the Mughals. This force was recruited largely on the basis of kinship but often the mobilization was of more than one clan or even of the male, adult members of the entire community and could also include persons belonging to other castes. The version of *Dariyā Khāñ* that Kalu sings describes the Meo and Mina chiefs Todar Mal and Bada Rao as *dauṛā*, or raiders *("do dauṛā mevāt maiṇ ṭodar mal bādā rāv")*. Todar Mal is said to have had five hundred warriors and Bada Rao another nine hundred.

The sources of raiding have been conventionally seen in terms of the mobility of pastoral and tribal communities. Was raiding a mode of creating a fiscal base for a polity in the imperfect transition from pastoralism to subsistence agriculture characterized by single crop cultivation and frequent failure of rains? Related to this is the question, What was the resource base of the Meo polity? The political economy explanation might see Meo raiding in terms of the failure of wheat- and millet-producing subsistence agriculture. Raiding has generally been seen as disruptive of statist order. More recently there has been considerable review of the politics of raiding. Historical research has demonstrated for one the close relationship between state formation and raiding. Plunder was an important mode of tax collection, and states themselves were involved in raiding either directly or through the employment of gangs of marauders. This has been shown with respect to the Mughal Empire, Rajput and Maratha kingdoms, and other polities. Skaria challenges the association of raids with failed monsoon or poor cultivation and points out the importance of raids for forest polities. "Dangi [Bhil] raids on surrounding settled agricultural areas were not only attempts to get resources for state-making. Rather there was a distinctive culture around them, and they were often celebrated for enacting a particular kind of masculine wildness." Celebrations of raiding were central to Bhil imagining of themselves and their enactment of masculine wildness since "the very act of leading raids was crucial to imagining a raja, his bravery and daring. To rule, in other words, was to raid."[31] To a lesser extent a *dhaṛ*, or raid, was also about particular claims to power by Bhil chiefs: it could be about demonstrating a raja's authority, challenging other chiefs, or a demand for haks, especially for giras haks that were shares paid by villages to Bhil chiefs and distributed by rajas.

In the case of the Meos, raids were also an aspect of oppositional subaltern discourse, for instance, when in 1257, the Meo chief Malka robbed the sultanate's army of a number of camels. The spoils enabled the chiefly gifting, as the animals were redistributed among resistant groups through the Kohpaya and up to Ranthambor. Raiding is narrativized as an act of play, of daring, of sheer *jouissance* as when the chiefs are told, "Masand, Mavasi, Rai Bhan / Rura listen to this. / The [Mughal] camels go to Akbarabad, / take them if you can." Jahangir's revenue was raided at Kosi (between Agra and Delhi) when it was being taken to the capital under military protection.[32] So was Shah Jahan's, the Mughal treasure being shared even with the Mirasi bards. Raids, however, gradually became infrequent and were extinguished, as in the Bhil case, with the consolidation of colonialism in the nineteenth century.[33]

The persistence of feuds and the institution of dispersed power ensured political plurality. But the impetus to hierarchy and patrilineal authority was always present. Genealogies help establish, but do not circumscribe, the field of political alliances. They can produce lineage solidarity but can also cleave the group as when brothers lead two opposing factions. The elements of blood, birth, and ancestry described in the *Bansabali* create a sense of cultural bonding as well as denote the internal divisions of the community as a large number of conflicts were fought between clans.

Warfare, ruling, alliance making, agriculture, and cattle rearing were primary occupations for men. The care of the farm and animals in addition to multiple tasks involved in household work devolved on women. The exchange of women was essentially a male transaction between clans. Controversies relating to incest and sexuality generated frequent feuds. On one occasion the "abduction" and marriage of a girl of the Kalesa Pal with a man from the Nai Pal led to a major dispute. The story goes that when their children were returning to the Nai village they were attacked by the Nais thinking they were coming to claim territory. The Kalesa Pal was virtually wiped out in the ensuing battle. Subsequently the Nai Pal moved from Bharatpur and conquered some area of the Kalesa Pal. Another long-standing feud in the nineteenth century was between the Jadu Bans and the Tanvar Bans over a Tanvar woman who had married a Jadu Meo but then eloped with a Meo of the Nauhan got, who refused to bring her back, leading to much enmity between the clans.[34] Patriarchies intensified with the agrarian mode of production grounded in control over women's labor and their sexuality, and many battles were fought over competing claims to women. A degree of sexual choice was available to a woman, and she could leave her husband, but it was incumbent on her new partner to compensate her husband for the loss of bride wealth and her labor.

The sexual division of labor made the "public," the arena of the sardar (chief), the darbar, and of the administration of justice, a male sphere. Although ritualized convention excluded Meo women from the "public" space with its communitarian institutions, women's voices and choices were not insignificant. For instance, in the *Pāñch Pahāṛ* the women of the clan prevail over the chief in the matter of performing a rite of childbirth, and the men are forced to battle the Mughals. Nonetheless, there is in the oral tradition on occasion a construction of femininity as *patinatā* (from *pativratā*, meaning devoted wife) and a woman might be referred to as *ḍheṛhī rāṛ* (foolish woman, *dheṛhī* being used for an "untouchable" of the leather-working Raigar caste). Sometimes women are referred to as not being intelligent enough to give proper advice, although they are constantly imaged as doing so. Often it is a woman who makes a moral statement or shows the way to resolve a dilemma.

The village community can hardly be nostalgically rendered an egalitarian society and instead incorporates hierarchies of status, gender, and power. The term *ḍhāḍhī* refers to the low-caste minstrel or bard in Rajasthan. The *jajmānī* system created a complex asymmetry and bonding between castes, in a relationship that was both economic and related to ritual activity. The blacksmith (lohar) for instance, traditionally brings an iron bangle to tie around the newborn's leg; circumcision is done by the barber (nai); and the Balai, occupationally a shoemaker of a polluting caste (like the barber and Mirasi), performs a major ritual role. The will to power is certainly not absent among Meo pals and is evidenced by the history of constant feuding. In chapter 6 I explore the Meo sense of power vis-à-vis other communities such as the Minas.

Genealogy, Memory, and Community

The oral tradition simultaneously reproduces and problematizes community. Even as the idea of a common descent reinforces and renews identity and solidarity, the narrativization of identity exposes the fragility of community and suggests complex lines of alliance between communities. The history of Meo feud is one of considerable conflict between and within clans and castes over land, power, and women. The Ravat Jats of Palwal had an intermittent feud with the Chiraklot Meos concentrated in the west because of the former's claim to land rights around the area of Kot. On one occasion the Chiraklot Meos allied with the Surot Jats and Rajputs of nearby Hathin to attack the Ravats on both flanks. The fight continued for months. The Meo headman of Kot eventually strayed into the Ravat area, where he was beheaded, as a result of which the Meos of Bahin kept their drum inverted, symbolizing the cessation of celebration. A colonial official describes the intervention of the British force on behalf of the Ravat Jats who were plundering Meo villages. The British were forced to retreat when a strong force of "hostile mutineers" appeared, killing many Ravats. The official was mystified that the Jats and Meos could sit together after dusk and the suspension of hostilities for the day and smoke the *hukkā*, or waterpipe, together.

Soon thereafter there was a shift in alliances. Around 1857, the Meos were cleaved by a feud between the two closely related Chiraklot Meo Chaudharis of Firozpur, Chand Khan of Bazidpur and Kabir of Bukharaka, over an assassinated headman. Each burned and plundered the villages of the other side in an eight-day battle.[35] The territoriality of the pal meant that even Jat and Mina villages within a given pal were mobilized in feuds with another pal. Fighting was simultaneous, with strong observance of the rules of the feud: hostilities were halted to eat the food brought by the women; captive prisoners were treated well and released; and when ammunition ran short, combat was interrupted until further supplies could be procured.

Despite the feuding among the Meos the united front of the pals was always a desired goal and frequently achieved in the face of an external challenge. The young Pahat Meo tells the Rajput representing the Mughal Empire, "listen to me, Ahlad, I will fight you with the fourfold strength of the sixty-four" that is, the combined strength of the twelve pals and fifty-two gotras *(suno nā ahlād tosū chauṇsaṭh chauguno jaṇg jorūṅgo)*. The reference is to a combined Meo front against the Rajput-Mughals.

Although caste endogamy and clan exogamy defined by the incest taboo underlie the *Bansabali,* in practice it was violated along with caste endogamy; the evidence for this comes from the narrative traditions of the Gujars, Meos, and Jats. The *sagāī* (proposed marriage) was used as an instrument of alliance to create kinship relations that aided the pursuit of politics. In one Mewati narrative Rao Bada Mina and the Meo chief Todar Mal arrange the marriage of their unborn offspring. Todar Mal tells the Rao:

bāvan gaṛh ke rāj hī sunre bāñkā rāv
taine maiṇ ādhā sū sāro karo merā tū dhan re bādā rāv

Ruler of fifty-two forts
listen bravest of Raos.
From the strength of halves we will have one whole
you are blessed Bada Rao.

The alliance is finalized. Even as the boy and girl in question fall in love, the two fathers develop a bitter enmity and deny marital consummation, until the couple elopes and the decision is out of their hands. Clearly the political system is not reducible to the kinship system, but it uses the kinship system.[36] Thus new clans were formed not only by the subdivision of older clans but also by marriage with other groups. The Bansabali also does not indicate that kinship is far more than a matter of blood, descent, and marriage. The idea of the *pagṛī palaṭ bhāī,* or brothers, constituted through the ritual exchange of turbans that seal a friendship bond, made possible the creation of "kinship" relations across clan, caste, and community.

In Mewat the layers of the political-jural system were reflected in the panchayat system. Commentators have remarked on the resilience of the framework. Each village continues to have its panchayat consisting of elders of important families headed by a chaudhari. At higher levels of jurisdiction are the thama, the got, and the pal panchayats. The pal panchayats, headed by their respective chaudharis, are higher courts of appeal invoked after the lineage elders have failed. Meo panchayats still have jurisdiction over all castes in the area, in contrast to the monocaste panchayats of other castes. Anthropological monographs describe how its decisions are potent and effective in case of both inter- and intracaste disputes.[37] The thama panchayats are still headed by the thama chaudhari and include the *ḍhīngs* (headmen) of that area. Because of the smaller area of jurisdiction, the thama panchayats were more frequently convoked than the pal panchayats. But the pal panchayats continue to be powerful even today.

Pals gained and lost in power over time. The Balot were once very powerful, but during the nineteenth century the Chiraklot and the Pahat Pals located largely in the Gurgaon and Bharatpur areas of Mewat, respectively, emerged as the two most powerful pals, which they continue to be today.[38] The Dhaingal and Baghora Pal areas around Kishangarh are considered inferior in terms of their agricultural productivity, unlike those of the Duhlot, Daimrot, and Nai Pals settled around Ramgarh, which were more prosperous.

What is the relation of the *Bansabali* to actual villages is a question one might well ask. A certain number of villages are associated with each pal: 210 with the Pahats; 52 with the Dairhval; 84 with the Pundlot, and so on. Thus a pal such as Pundlot is often referred to as "*chaurāsī gāñv*" (84 villages) or the Pahats as "*do sau das pāl*" (pal of the 210), representing idealized numbers. The Daimrot are said to have had the most villages and the Rattavat the least; hence, they are still referred to as the largest and smallest pals, respectively. Although there is considerable fluctuation of both pal boundaries and power, there is an explicit identification of terrain and pal.[39] Individual Meos' ideas of local geography are considerably imbued with the topography of pals.

In contrast to the dispersed Gujar and Jat castes, the Meos were far more concentrated. The Jats stretched along the loamy west bank of the Yamuna called the bangar from Mathura northward to Ambala merging with the Punjabi Jats. This was the region of small proprietors and Metcalf's world of Indian "village republics." In the case of the Jats, the clan or got was too dispersed in pockets and interspersed with settlements of other clans to function as a meaningful political entity. Eventually the *ṭappā* that was primarily a territorial rather than a kinship grouping worked as a political unit with jurisdiction over the castes living in adjacent villages. It was also the unit of the feuding that was constant among the Jats. Stokes points out that in 1857 the Jat kinship organization was insufficient to supply supravillage organization and was displaced or rather modified by the tappa.[40] The tribal Bhils have a markedly similar social structure to the Meo characterized by *tembā* or *phaḷā* (the equivalent of Meo thamas and pals) covering a cluster of villages belonging to a single lineage.

In the pre-Mughal period Meo clans had a considerable degree of autonomy. Meo narratives express a sensibility of constant intrusions into autonomy during Mughal-Rajput rule. Meos attribute the creation of the pals, described in the *Bansabali,* to Akbar's (r. 1556–1605) attempt to divide the Meos. A gathering of Meo leaders is said to have been convened and Akbar's supporter, the Meo Balot chief Kakurana, divided them into pals. The pallakra of the Pahats was constituted so because of the late arrival of its chief, hence the term has connotations of smallness and inferior status. This despite the fact that his clan was large and important and the Pahat self-image is of being an exceptionally brave pal.[41] Is this a myth of internal differentiation one wonders.

Although there were tensions with both Mughal and Rajput states, there is also evidence of co-optation and collaboration. Certain Meo chiefs such as Todar Mal are even said to have attended Akbar's court. Chiefs were transformed into headmen and made responsible for the collection of revenue so that Mughal revenue collecting apparatus was superimposed onto an existing patrilineal kinship structure.

The Rajput polity, unlike that of the Marathas, did not develop the idea of shared sovereignty with surrounding powers. The path-breaking work of Wink, Gordon, and Skaria has demonstrated how the Marathas operated with a conception of shared sovereignty operationalized through raids and coshared villages. The assistance the Bhils rendered the Marathas during state formation enabled, in turn, the extensive participation of the Bhil "brotherhood" in kingship. Thus both the western Indian Gaekwad-ruled state of Baroda and Bhil rajas, or chiefs, could simultaneously exercise rights over the same villages. Bhils collected a share of dues and were also gifted turbans by the Gaekwad rulers. The dues and revenues received by Bhil Dangi chiefs were redistributed so that even ordinary Bhils received turbans and shares of giras dues, however nominal. Skaria writes about the Bhil raja: "To extend or maintain his dominance, he had to enter into alliances with other bhauband, and this involved sharing his resources and authority — it was the very process of sharing authority that constituted his kingship."[42]

It was British rule in India that destroyed autonomy at the local level. It decisively altered the nineteenth-century character of the village consisting of coparcenary agricultural communities. The British were quite unused to villages headed by a raja, ravat, rao, or chaudhari, and indigenous political structures such as tappas and pals were marginalized. The local clan under its *mālik,* or traditional head, was initially drained of all political and administrative authority.[43] But without the intervening layer of a gentry, the British or princely administration had to deal directly with them. The imposition of taxation meant an assertion of sovereign power. As revenue settlements were worked out in British India, the advantage of using traditional leaders, accepted by the community, became apparent to the British. Their position was recognized, and muqaddams or lambardars were subcontracted local power and made responsible for collecting revenue. In Gurgaon District the *zaildārī* system was introduced at the Second Regular Settlement of 1882. The entire district was divided into *zails*, and people who were recognized as natural leaders of village communities were appointed *zaildārs*. The Mewati chaudharis of Bichhor, Nagina, Akbarpur, Bisru, Nuh, Ujina, Hathin, Bahin, and other villages were inducted into the colonial system. For their efforts they received an allowance of 1 percent of the land revenue of their respective zails.[44] In the princely states, certain chaudharis sometimes even worked as informers for the government and had minor punitive powers. Colonialism had intensified stratification.

In the nineteenth century Mewat was deeply affected by the colonial revenue bureaucracy, greater monetization, market linkages, commercialization, altered crop regime, land tenure arrangements, and a range of new legislation and institutional structures such as courts and jails. Colonial rule intensified processes of state formation in the princely states manifest in the replication of the institutional apparatus in these states.

Meo narratives present suggestive fragments of resistance to state formation. The Mewati story *Akhay Singh* describes rebellion in the Alwar kingdom. The phrase "*tilak terai tīn sau sāṭh*" refers to the recognition signified by the mark of the *tilak* on the forehead given to Chaudhari Akhay Singh of Chandoli by the Alwar ruler. The vermilion mark symbolized ritual incorporation by the sovereign of the subject and his reciprocal obligation to pay taxes. But he defied the collection of revenue *(lāg churāī)*, raided the goats belonging to the state *(rāj kī bakrī kar dī baṇd)*, and reclaimed local authority over Chandoli. For the regime his behavior was defiant *(amāī)*, but his heroism is acclaimed by the narrative tradition that states, "Ah, a Chaudhari must be like Akhay Singh" and views him as another *vīr* (brave) Vikramajit, a reference to the semilegendary king of Ujjayani (sometimes called the King Arthur of the East). His wisdom and his sense of justice are celebrated in the Sanskrit tales that became famous by the title *Baitāl Pacisī*. In pursuit of his promise to a Jogi renouncer, Vikram brings to him the *baital* (vampire) hanging in a tree. The Samvat era, which began in 56 A.D., is named after him. The Ahir ruler of Rewari, Rao Tula Ram, took over the government of the parganas of Rewari and Bahora in 1857, but the powerful

Meos of Bahora refused to accept his authority. The Jats and brahmans sided with the Ahirs in a two-day battle against the Meos.[45]

The situation was not unlike that of the precolonial Tamil country where boundaries of the state constantly expanded and contracted as local communities acceded to or resisted kingly authority. Shulman demonstrates how the authority of precolonial Tamil kings was constantly being challenged "by an endless series of potential rivals and replacements, each with his own claim to legitimacy and equal power."[46]

Despite the Meo-Rajput struggle, Mewati narratives suggest a shared discourse of honor with the Rajputs. Warrior raiding and war making were a common idiom of political expression between the Meos, as a dominant landholding group, and the Jats and the Rajputs, who were trying to reduce them to the position of subordinate cultivators. The reference to brave (Meo) men who "kill and bring wealth and distribute it" *(lāvai dhan ko mār kai bānṭai dhan khair hamesh)* represents a competitive aspiration toward valorous raiding and chiefly generosity.

Price has argued that the cultural diffusion of ideas of honor and competition for honor fostered segmentation. She maintains that the utilization of ideologies of honor was an important element of those practices that allowed for the reproduction of social and political segmentation. It was only the consolidation of colonial rule that destroyed networks of ritual exchange at regional and subregional levels as centralization and bureaucratization offered an alternative model of political authority and precolonial monarchical cosmologies became fragmented.[47] Price's framework sees an ideological continuity between the center and smaller segments reminiscent of Geertz's view of the Balinese kingdom.[48] While her model allows for competition, it cannot accommodate more than a very limited resistance to the center. Resistance, however, can itself reinforce the thrust toward segmentation and lead to very loose ties with a given center. The failure to account for more sustained resistance is possibly because Price's approach is grounded in an elite perspective.

Is subaltern resistance possible given the incorporation into a larger cultural pattern such as a shared ideology of honor? This is the question Price raises. But even if this is so, it is certainly conceivable that the substantive content of what constitutes honor is disputed. Thus the same ideology of honor could then serve as critique, the raja being castigated for his failure to act in accordance with what constitutes honorable conduct appropriate for a king.

In the case of the Meos the shared ideologies of honor with the Rajputs did not prevent their resistance to the Rajput kingdom or curb the constant striving for autonomy. Gyan Prakash shows how the myths of low castes internalize ideas of caste hierarchy and other notions from the great tradition. He demonstrates how the oral traditions of these "unclean" castes simultaneously incorporate and question the primordialism of caste hierarchy. By going back to a past in which they were warriors and *acquired* an unclean status, caste is interpreted as historical not natural.[49] Shared ideologies can have facets of both reproduction and resistance to dominant ideologies.

Nineteenth-century English writing sponsored an image of segmented village communities, the so-called unchanging republics upheld by Marx and Maine. The Meo oral tradition suggests the vacuity of this fiction. The village/pal was no isolate. Even in preceding centuries, communication between the pals was constant, undertaken by a system of messengers responsible for *chiṭhī phernā* (transport of message) or by modes such as the *ḍhol*, or drum. Attitudes toward writing were not of awe since courts of various levels had been using literate retainers. The village was in constant interaction with the outside world: its isolation broken up by trade, sectarian networks, pilgrimages, and fairs. It was visited by brahmans, genealogists, ascetics and faqirs, performers of bat and *khyāl* (musical plays), entertainers, and acrobats. The web of marriage alliances and kinship created both networks and fissures, as did the politics of battles, feud, alliances, uprisings and revolts, and contested land and tenancy rights. Battle did not mean a rupture in dialogue. Verbal exchange persisted even during fighting, which is in large measure face-to-face. Meo narratives bring out the use of the *ṭāmakh*, or large drum, as an instrument to enable intervillage communication and also the mass mobilization of the pal.

It would be wrong to conclude on the basis of the *Bansabali* that the Meos had a "Hindu culture," as Sharma claims. It is true that the *Bansabali* establishes, to begin with, Hindu referents of identity. Krishna, Rama, and Arjuna, gods and heroes of the Hindu mythological tradition, are described as founders of the thirteen Meo clans. But simultaneously a distinctive spatial context (Mewat) and identifiable group (Meo) organized into thirteen clans is described. That this founding narrative was highly significant in constituting a cohesive community is also evident from the frequently strongly stated view of the Meos that they are different from both Hindus and Muslims.

Meo narratives demonstrate a conscious attempt to create a mythology distinctive from Hindu and Islamic mythological systems, although it draws upon both. This mythology relies to a great extent on constructions of the Meo past. Myth and memory are closely entwined to create an ideology that differentiated the Meos from other Muslims like the Mughals and also from neighboring Hindu groups with whom cultural beliefs and practices were shared. Collective memory is an inextricable aspect of constituting and reproducing corporate identity. The common thread running through most Mirasi-authored narratives is a conscious and deliberate attempt to create a sense of community. This also orients the personal sense of belonging. In this analysis I try to demonstrate how a group is internally structured at the ideological level; how its sociopolitical organization and origin myth establish its distinctiveness from other social groups. A text such as the *Bansabali* also suggests the possible sources of conflict as it marks competing levels of identification. Thus identities are both common and different.

Contemporary critical anthropology has raised the question of boundaries that the anthropologist's enterprise tends to privilege. The *Bansabali*'s concerns are clearly with cognizing and marking sacred space, and relating hero-deities like Krishna and Rama with political-kinship structure. But there is a mythic affinity here between the Meos, the Ahirs, and the Jats — all claiming to be Jadubanshis, ksatriya, or both. This mythic affinity makes for the possibility of dialogue between groups of the region.[50]

When I first conceived this work, my initial formulation saw only the state as the site of violence. I now recognize how deeply communities are also implicated in violence. This becomes clear from the pervasiveness of the feud as well as from the sexual politics of the community. Thus feminine desire must be overridden by an assertion of patrilineal masculinity. The community is defined by men whether it is by male leaders or in performed narratives by male performers. The female persona Sasbadni, whose marriage is not consummated because of the Meo-Mina feud, is the first-person narrator of a Mewati story, although her "voice" is mediated by the male composer-performer. The glimpse of her narrativized biography shows how human passions, in this case male-female desire, disrupt the fragile community and require intervention at the level of narrativizing identities, the telling and retelling of memory. The community, by definition, is always an imperfect one, its boundaries, if any, always fluid, porous, and subject to encroachment.

The *Bansabali* leaves us at the point where it indicates the segmentation of Meo society into the territorial pals. In this case, ethnography both confirms, elaborates, and counters our text, as we have accounts of the pal organization from nineteenth-century and contemporary ethnographers. The Mirasis then are not mere genealogists who catalog the lineage of descent groups nor are they mere mythographers who legitimate social status and upward mobility. They are far more: a literati who help create and transmit ideology and collective memory for the Meos. An ideology that underlies the pluralized polity; a mythic memory that girds their sensibility of the past.

Oral and mythic traditions are, however, neglected in both the Western and Indian reflection on the state. The former traditionally emphasized aspects such as territory, population, and the coercive apparatus. The Indian theorist Kautilya pointed out seven elements of the polity. But even he does not recognize the poetics of power.[51] In premodern polities bards, genealogists, and chroniclers not only contributed to the making of the state but also *were* the state.[52] The Mewati case suggests that they were just as important to the polities that constituted the antistate.

4 Toward a Critique of Indo-Persian Historiography

Balban, Firishta writes, put a hundred thousand Meos to the sword. Barani is also one of the foremost historians of the sultanate. The description that precedes his account represents them as lawless plunderers, raiders, robbers, and assaulters who had virtually besieged Delhi.[1] This becomes the legitimation for the slaughter of numerous Mewati men, women, and children in the thirteenth century; for the deforestation of a large tract of forest; for the razing of the area of Mewat by "sword and fire." Yet Sultan Balban (r. 1266–86) is credited by historians for the "achievement" of "consolidating" the sultanate. With respect to the Mewatis the pattern is repeated in the description of events under successive ruling dynasties of the sultanate and Mughal Empire such as the Khiljis, Tughlaqs, Sayyids, Lodis, and Mughals. In the history written from the point of view of the ruling group, the vanquished have hardly any voice. The brutalization of conquest and coercion is euphemistically called "state formation," which valorizes processes such as centralization, militarization, and surplus extraction. The tremendous human costs of overcoming dissenting groups are rarely acknowledged; the processes of dispossession and marginalization hardly ever documented.

The historiography available to us in the written Persian texts frames Mewati history as a narrative of disorder and rebellion. Sultanate and empire, on the other hand, are rendered the protagonists. Their acts are overwritten by the doctrine of the "innocent state" whereby the state is represented as besieged and under constant attack by the turbulent and aggressive forces of society. In the state-as-order versus society-as-anarchy construction à la Hobbes, the lived history of the subject group is erased, and the actual processes of Turko-Afghan and Mughal-Rajput state formation are obliterated.

The overwhelming focus on the historiography of the colonial state has tended to obliterate the experience of precolonial empires. Variants of postmodernism, deconstructionism, and postcolonial writing privilege the colonial moment and that of decolonization. Marginality, displacement, and diaspora are associated with colonial and postcolonial cultures. Gates points out that Spivak can see "nothing outside (the discourse) of colonialism" and that Spivak's argument entails the corollary that all discourse is colonial discourse."[2]

The critique of orientalism provided a significant framework to understand the colonial experience. The powerful deconstruction of orientalist writings shows how Western systems of knowledge produced the orient as an object of power and knowledge. The Eastern world was categorized by Marx, Weber, Wittfogel, and others, as despotic, collectivist, otherworldly, and irrational.[3] According to Said, the most influential exponent of the critique of orientalism, it arose in the twentieth century because of the political necessity to understand the Islamic world, then a colonized population.[4] There is, in addition, a tendency to presume the passivity of the colonized as well as to assert a denial of the very possibility of the representation of the subaltern condition. Hence Spivak's rhetorical question, Can the subaltern speak?[5]

The limitations of the critique of orientalism, however, are both temporal and spatial. The critique does not address the precolonial and non-Western imperial experience. The Indo-Persian historiographical tradition closely associated with the Turko-Afghan sultanate, for example, also produced alien, conquered peoples in similar ways. The Persian tradition of knowledge was founded on a basic division between the rulers and the ruled. Thus it is important to recognize that there are several concentric circles of orientalism: the West produces the "Orient" but parts of the "Orient" also produce other parts.

Both this and the subsequent chapter relate to the Meos between the thirteenth and the eighteenth centuries. The discussion is divided into three sections. The first section involves an exegetical reading focusing on the semantic field of selected historiographical texts in Persian that refer to the Meo/Mewatis. Historical representation is examined both for the use of language and categories. Koselleck shows how historical writing since ancient times has been structured into asymmetric counterconcepts such as Hellene and Barbarian, Christian and Heathen. These binary categories seek to classify humanity and define the other negatively as spatially and culturally alien. The political function of historical-political semantics, according to Koselleck, is to define and promote a condition of domination. Language works as a technique of negation that penetrates conflicts. I have found Koselleck's framework particularly helpful in analyzing Indo-Persian texts.[6]

Chapter 5 analyzes administrative documents in Persian of the seventeenth and eighteenth centuries relating to imperial and regional state policies vis-à-vis the Mewatis. Third, the Mewati oral tradition is accessed for a redescription of events in Mewat during the period of Mughal rule. These accounts hint at the character of imperial and regional state formation and the sensibility of the medieval "Mewati," and give us an insight into the cultural psychology of resistance. Although the focus is regional, the questions are universal, for this is a story that has been repeated the world over. time and again. I draw upon fragments in English, Persian, and Urdu texts to recapitulate the available history of the Meos.

The making of territorial and political marginality is mirrored in the writing of history. Author after author constructs Mewati "otherness" and invests it with lawlessness. As early as the twelfth century the Mewatis are rendered "the *most turbulent* of all the Hindu groups of the Doab and the Ganges."[7] In 1195 Sultan Mu'izz-al-Din set the pattern by making a punitive raid on Mewat. The processes of state expansion and consolidation and a consequent displacement are implicit in the historical representation of the Mewati.

Mewati Otherness in Indo-Persian Historiographical Texts

History writing, it has been claimed ever since Thucydides, is capable of rendering "truth" and provides an "objective reporting" of an external reality that is totally independent of the human subject. The positivist tradition of history writing dominant in Europe in the nineteenth century conceived the discipline in terms of linearity, causality, and objectivity in what was purported to be a neutral act of describing the past. German historiography, in particular, stressed the ability to represent the past as it really was (fact), causal relations, and its scientific aspects.[8]

Recent critiques of historiography arising from an antifoundationalist perspective deny or minimize the difference between literature and history. The Ranke school's position that history is a narrative of "things as they actually happened" has been severely criticized. History, like ethnography, is regarded as akin to fiction. Like a work of literature, a historical account can be examined in terms of narrative structure, the use of language and rhetorical tropes, authorial voice, and the positioning of the subject. Roland Barthes maintains that "by its structures alone, without recourse to its content, historical discourse is essentially a product of ideology, or rather of imagination." Barthes points toward the paradox that narrative structure, which was originally developed within the cauldron of fiction (in myths and the early epics), was appropriated by history.[9] Postmodernists have attacked the claims of objectivity and scientificity of historiography and indicated the ideological function of the narrative mode of representation. Hayden White argues that historical discourse can be seen in terms of literary genres and tropes. Through emplotment the historian structures the plot as a tragedy or comedy in the explanation.[10] Certeau's powerful statement identifies history as representing an exotic otherness, an aspect of the practice of writing that is itself an alienated form of representation. He maintains that the constitution of myth by history as its other has become the myth of our times. In fact, there has been a convergence between history and literature since the Enlightenment so that fiction and history have become quasi identical.[11]

Ricoeur denies the absolute identity of fiction and history but simultaneously challenges the conventional view that sees fiction and history as mutually exclusive literary genres. He treats both as the two great modes of narrative. The past is always a reenactment in the present and is therefore never truly the "past." This reenactment forces the imagination to step in, and this combination of history and imagination generates narrative fiction — stories, in essence. He argues that history uses fiction to "refigure" or "restructure" time by introducing narrative contours into the nonnarrative time of nature. It is the act of imagining *(se figurer que)* that effects the "reinscription of lived time (time with a present) into purely successive time (time without present)."[12] The historian reinscribes lived time into natural time by the act of narration. History is also oriented to "reverential commemoration" for the deeds of those whom Hegel called history's great men, horror and loathing being the negative pairs of admiration and veneration. This is an ideological function that legitimizes domination. "Fiction then carries history back to their common origin in the epic."[13]

The tenor of poststructuralist/postmodernist critiques that have dominated the critique of history have contextualized the historical text in terms of its literariness. It might be more useful to see history as a form of itihasa-purana, an Indian concept that constructs history in terms of a generic combination of genealogy, myth, and history. This, in effect, locates the individual in the social world. And, indeed, this is what the Greek, Persian, Arab, and European modes of history writing do. This is not to say that itihasa-purana is *the* only genre of Indian history writing. It is important to recognize that the histories written in the subcontinent include the Indo-Persian, the many competing itihasa-purana traditions, and narrative traditions of the groups that have been variously called adivasi, dalit, sudra, itinerant, criminal, and so on.

History writing has come a long way from the Rankean view that history describes the past "as it really was" or Collingwood's notion that history is a reenactment of past thought. Certainly the various ways in which the Indian past has been appropriated and reconstructed dispels the fiction of ideological neutrality. The missionary and orientalist, as Cohn shows, viewed the past as a "fall" from a golden age.[14] Others have viewed Indian civilization as apolitical, mystical, and otherworldly.[15] Mercantilist historiography investigated the relation between government and landed property in the precolonial period. This was to enable the East India Company to maximize revenue from conquered territories, which would finance seaborne trade.[16] The colonial historian emphasized the "feudal decline" of the medieval period, in particular, the decadence of the eighteenth century up to the British advent.[17] The nationalist historian continues to foreground a glorious antiquity.

The Indo-Persian chronicles are characterized by their own ideological moorings. Power structures and interests have defined both the categories and the concerns of history writing. Elliot, lauding the work of Barani, tells us, however, that the Persian tradition of historiography is "close to the European." Dodwell states that "Muslim chronicles are far superior" to (English) medieval chronicles. They filled a lacuna, as India according to J. S. Mill, Elliot and Dowson, and others was an ahistorical civilization.[18] Several studies of Indo-Persian historiography have recognized the theological orientation of the Persian texts.[19] They underplay, however, the relations of power between ruled and subject that they embody.

When the Turks came to India they brought with them the well-developed genre of historical writing of the Islamic world. Indian historical works written between A.D.1206 and 1440 derived from preexisting categories of Islamic writing. The history of Islam in India was regarded as a direct continuation of universal Islamic history.[20] The initial and terminal moments of the narrative frame were those of the creation of Adam and Muhammad's prophecy. A sovereign God delegates power to a partnership between prophets and kings, and the world is seen as an arena in which good and evil coexist in mortal combat.[21]

Unlike the Arab historiographical tradition that was centered on religion and civilization, the Persian emphasis was far more on the state, because of the long history of the state in that region. So while Persian historiography, in general, was grounded in Islamic traditions, it also drew significantly upon the Persian pre-Islamic past, particularly the Sasanid tradition of monarchical domination and imperial rule dating to the third century, which contrasted with the more egalitarian Arab tribal *majlis*. The state was the primary and active agent in history as well as the site of all history. The primacy of the state was unchallenged, and any form of "rebellion" or "defiance," including refusal to surrender to the state (the state with which the particular historian identified himself), could only call for denunciation. It was this tradition that migrated to India, hence the statism of medieval Indian historiography.

Since the ruler was central to the polity, human volition comprised for the historian causal explanation in history. Mukhia points out that the advocacy of a strong state in this historiography created a tension between Islam and kingship.[22] Indeed, the Persian chronicles often become kingly hagiographies. Hardy argues that they reflect the hostility of the nobility, who together with the sultan constituted the ruling class, to the local population and their chiefs and headmen including rais, rajas, khuts, and muqaddams. "Rebels" and "disrupters" of the order of the state, including Mewatis, Rajputs, Bundelas, Marathas, and others, were all denounced and even abused in the strongest terms.

The proximity of the chroniclers to the regime and the events they narrated has been repeatedly demonstrated by commentators. Barani and Minhaj, for instance, belonged to the ulama. Hence, the valorization of conquest, violence, and conversion in works written from the perspective of the court. Reigns and revolts are, of course, a major concern. Bada'uni was exceptional in not being attached to the court.

Religion and kingship, Ziya' al-Din Barani, one of the foremost Indo-Muslim historians, wrote in the *Fatāwā-i Jahāndarī*, are twins. Kings must use their power to protect and maintain Islam. The crown is thus central to the Persian historiographical texts, as Aron has also shown with respect to Thucydides. History was clearly in the service of sovereignty embodied in the Shahenshah. Certain historians have challenged Hardy's contention that for Barani history is a branch of theology. Hasan asserts that Barani saw history rather as a "science of the social order" that was based not on religion or tradition but on observation and experience. Within the Islamic tradition, however, religion and science are not distinct, and it is difficult to conceive of a secular history. Siddiqui foregrounds instead Barani's elitist view of history, which violated principles of Islamic egalitarianism.[23] Elitism was particularly manifest among the Turks, who it has been pointed out adopted Islam around the tenth century primarily to satisfy their ambition for power. It was this orientation that influenced Indo-Persian historians from Minhaj Siraj Juzjani to Khafi Khan. The Turks had migrated to India with the Ghurids or had been turned out by the Mongol invasions. The maliks and servants of the sultans were generally Turks and Tajiks. In their anxiety to retain their racial identity, they also nurtured prejudices against Indian Muslims, especially those regarded as having lowly origins.[24]

In Arab historiography and hadith literature the *isnād* method had been developed. This traced the original source of each piece of information through all the successive stages of its passage, appraising its authenticity or fabricated character in accordance with the law of witness. In contrast, writers of the Indian Persian chronicles tended to rely on prior authority and did not develop rigorous criteria of evaluating evidence. In Minhaj's work, for instance, no attempt was made to assess the reliability of sources, and former works were unquestioningly incorporated. Similarly, Yahya bin Ahmad's *Tārīkh-i Mubārak Shāhī* derives largely from Barani and Amir Khusrau's writing.

The discussion that follows undertakes a discursive analysis of texts that represent the Mewatis, including Minhaj Siraj Juzjani's *Ṭabaqāt-i Nāṣirī*, Ziya' al-Din Barani's *Tarīkh-i Fīrūz Shāhī*, Firishta's *Tārīkh-i Firishta*, Nizam al-Din Ahmad's *Ṭabaqāt-i Akbarī*, Yahya bin Ahmad's *Tārīkh-i Mubārak Shāhī*, 'Abd-ul-Qadir Bada'uni's *Muntākhab ut-Tawārīkh*, and Babur's *Tuzak-i Bābarī*. These writers, even in the early period of the establishment of the Turkish sultanate, project a strong image of the rebellious Mewati.

Minhaj Siraj Juzjani (b. 1193) gives a contemporary account of Balban that is particularly enlightening with respect to state policy toward the Mewatis. The *Ṭabaqāt-i Nāsirī* has been highly celebrated by both Persian and

English historians.[25] It is a history from the earliest times to 658 H./1259 and compiled a year later. Minhaj and his father had both been Qazis.[26] Sultan Nasir al-Din Mahmud even presented Minhaj with a turban and horse. He was engaged as a preacher to the army and clearly concealed facts unfavorable to Balban. Minhaj asserts that Balban is like Sohrab and Rustam in battle and his body like that of an elephant. Balban is credited with vanquishing forts, making roads, and capturing infidels, rais, and ranas. Not unjustifiedly, Irfan Habib describes Minhaj as a panegyrist to Balban.

As minister or wazir (1246–66) of Sultan Nasir al-Din Mahmud, Balban exercised tremendous power. Known by his title "Ulugh Khan" during the reign of Nasir al-Din, he was the sultan's na'ib, that is, the officiating sultan when the sultan was away at battle. Ulugh Khan had charge of the *iqṭā'*, or the fief, of Hansi and Rewari and undertook a series of campaigns against the Mewatis.

The Mewatis are identified as a source of danger given their proximity to the capital. According to Minhaj, the Mewatis defy authority and are the chief disturbers and mischief makers *(jamā'at-i-fasādā)*. They inhabit the hilly terrain known as the Kohpaya in the Aravalli Mountains. They are said to be highway robbers *(qaṭ-i-tarīq)* and dacoits engaged in looting and plundering the belongings of Muslims. The Mewatis attack villages in Haryana, the Siwalik hills, and Bayana, where they disturb cultivators by their looting *(tārāj-i dihā)*, especially of animals. Minhaj describes the Mewati leader Malka as a mischief monger and the chief of the rebels *(mufsid)*. He is arrogant, disobedient, refractory, and rebellious *(nāfarman, sarkash)*, and an infidel *(gabrī)*. He refuses to accept authority and is dangerous like the devil *(dev satī hindāh)*.[27] In 1257 Malka robbed Balban's followers of a drove of camels and a number of people on the outskirts of Hansi. Malka and his people redistributed the camels among the Hindus from the Kohpaya up to Ranthambhor. This caused great difficulty for Ulugh Khan, his maliks, amirs, and army who needed to transport goods for battle. But they could not retaliate because of the onslaught of the Mongols (elsewhere described as "kafirs from China") against the cities of Sind and Punjab.

Balban had attacked the Mewati rebels of Kohpaya and Ranthambhor in 1248 and again in 1258–59. After the Mongol attacks were dealt with Minhaj writes:

> on the 4th Safar 658 H [20 January 1260] Ulugh Khan attacked the Kohpaya. In the first march they advanced fifty kos and took the rebels

> by surprise. The Muslims killed the inhabitants of that mountainous area with its rugged terrain of valleys, rivers and streams. For twenty days Ulugh Khan attacked the Kohpaya from all directions. The villages and habitations of the mountaineers were on the summits of the highest hills and rocks almost as though they were near the sky and stars. These were like the wall of Alexander but were taken by Ulugh Khan. Their inhabitants who were Hindus, thieves and dacoits were all slain.
>
> Ulugh Khan ordered that any Musalman soldier who would bring back a single head would be rewarded with one tanka and anyone who brought back a single living man would be given two. In pursuit of the truth and in accordance with the command of Ulugh Khan the army traversed the valleys and gorges and began bringing in headless captives. In particular, the Afghans exhibited great bravery and brought hundreds of Hindus from the mountains and forests. Each Afghan was like an elephant and buffalo. . . . The Afghan soldiers consisted of three thousand horsemen and footmen. The entire army including maliks and amirs, Turks and Tajiks, demonstrated great bravery. Stories of their bravery will be remembered for many years. Ever since the arrival of the Musalman army in Hindustan, no one had ever penetrated and defeated this area. The rebel Hindu who had taken the camels was captured along with his family and two hundred fifty rebel chiefs. One hundred forty-two horses were taken from them for the royal stables and six bags of tankas amounting to thirty thousand tankas were taken from the ranas of the hills and sent to the royal treasury.

In twenty days Ulugh Khan accomplishes this feat with great bravery and then returns to court. A grand court is organized for him by the sultan near Hauz Rani. The maliks, amirs, men of wealth, and wrestlers have been gifted with the *khil'lat,* or valuable robes of honor, on the previous day. Ulugh Khan along with the maliks and amirs who wear them prostrate and kiss the earth.[28] All those who had achieved victory and success in battle are rewarded by the sultan.

Evidently the victory is a shallow one, for two days later another "religious war" has to be undertaken against the Mewatis: "The army departed from Hauz Rani with the order that elephants who can cause instant death be used against the infidels. The blood-shedding Turks got their swords ready to kill the rebels. Several rebels were killed under the feet of the elephants.

Several hundred rebel Hindus were skinned with knives. Their skins stuffed with straw they were hung over the city gates. Such stringent punishment had never been given at Hauz Rani or in front of the gates of Delhi, nor had anyone ever heard tales of it having occurred previously." All this enhances the prestige of Ulugh Khan who for Minhaj is the "Badshah of the world."

The Mewatis, however, continue to be defiant. Minhaj writes that in the new year (13th Safar 658 H./January–February 1260) Ulugh Khan-i Azam is sent into the hills of Delhi to suppress the Mewatis, "who terrorize even ghosts." About ten thousand brave horsemen in armor were with him. The next day great wealth was taken and many cattle captured.

Despite the war and harsh punishment inflicted by Ulugh Khan, the relatives of many of the "rebels" flee, escaping the sword. They seek refuge in different areas of the Kohpaya. Once again they begin to rebel, plunder Muslims, and terrorize people. Spies are sent forth to identify their location. On 24 Rajab 658 H./5 July 1260 Ulugh Khan leaves with the royal army and the maliks. In one stretch he covers fifty kos or more. His attack takes them by surprise, and twelve thousand people, including women, children, and men, are taken captive. In this way, Minhaj comments, the entire mountainous region is made secure by the sword of Islam, and great wealth and property are obtained.

Aspects of sultanate state formation are explicit here. The sultan and the hierarchy below him consisted of khans, maliks and amirs, and sipahsalars (chief commanders of armies). The khans, maliks, and amirs were each qualified by their wealth and the respective number of horsemen under them. The sultan owned twenty thousand slaves.[29] The coercive apparatus included a large army *(lashkar)* of cavalry and infantry, people responsible for manning the city walls, forts, and police posts, as well as spies. Besides this was the fiscal regime and religious establishment. The ruler's authority was also ritually created, and state ritual was particularly important during Balban's rule. The gift was used extensively to signify incorporation into sovereignty. This could be of the khil'lat robe or the reward of titles, honors, land, or animals. Minhaj was rewarded with a horse and villages by Ulugh Khan and received forty slaves and one hundred ponies from the sultan. The state was also defined by symbols and practices of exclusion: elephants, for instance, could only be possessed by those permitted by the Badshah. The defeated were skinned and beheaded. Those who were not killed were captured and most likely sold in the large and thriving slave market.

Historiography was an aspect of the construction of stateness, with metaphors derived from Arabic and Persian. Minhaj's stigmatization of the Mewatis and particularly their leader, Malka, is stark. The *shaks-i Malka* and the Mewatis merge into evil, the Persian *dev*, or devil.[30] The Arabic metaphor of poisonous snakes *(ifrīt-i marẓadah)* is used for them. They are terrible people who can inject poison into other bodies. In the series of transformations that are made by the Persian texts, war is read as disorder, and power is masked by the claims to establish the social contract.

Minhaj constructs the Mewatis as given to raids and plunder. He acknowledges their continued defiance of authority expressed in their raiding of cattle and camels and in their creation of commotion among other Hindus to whom all land up to Ranthambhor has been distributed. This indicates a possible alliance of the Mewatis with the Bhatti and Chauhan Rajputs. The category of *fasād,* or disorder, is, however, inappropriate as the context for the Mewatis, and Siwalik rajas was one of a war for which any means were legitimate. Ordinary notions of crime that apply within the context of a single state system with clearly defined boundaries were not applicable. Guerilla warfare is the politics of the last resort. It involves a desperate and hence violent critique of the conquering state.

Ziya' al-Din Barani's *Tarīkh-i Fīrūz Shāhī* is in many ways a continuation of Minhaj's *Ṭabaqāt-i Nāṣirī,* completed a century later, around 1358.[31] This work is a history of the sultans of Delhi from Balban's accession (662 H./1266) to the sixth year of Firoz Shah Tughlaq's reign (758 H./1357). The *Tārīkh* was a highly influential text, since it was also the chief source for both Firishta and Nizam al-Din Ahmad.[32] The text falls, according to Hardy, in the category of "the *manāqib* or *fazā'il* type of prose eulogy, usually, but not necessarily of the ruler."[33] Even Elliot acknowledges Barani's eulogistic tone, which is not surprising as he was related to important officials of the sultan.[34] Mukhia points out that while for Minhaj history assumed the form of a narrative and the source of causation was human will (often divinely inspired), history unfolded a pattern for Barani, the study of which could teach one lessons. He attributed causation to the nature of the sultan that manifests itself in the entire reign.[35]

Barani begins his work by highlighting the relation between Balban's personality and the policies undertaken during his twenty-two-year reign. He describes Balban's rise from the band of Forty Slaves and the militarization of the new state as Balban reorganized his army and cavalry. Once the coercive machinery was in a state of readiness, Balban could undertake the tasks of expansion and consolidation.

Destroying the Meos, who were a major source of disorder, was his most important priority according to Barani.[36] More than Minhaj, Barani builds up the legitimation of Balban's incisive military action. The Meos are described as having grown in numbers. They have become emboldened and a particularly threatening force because of the dissolute habits and incapacity of the elder sons of Shams al-Din Iltutmish and the immaturity of his youngest, Nasir al-Din (Balban's immediate predecessor), who had become sultan at the age of twenty. The populace, in general, has become disorderly. Barani writes, "after the death of Shams al-Din none could control the rebellion of the Meos. For this purpose Balban left the city and camped outside it."

The use of the term *mufsidān* for the Meos, derived from Minhaj, continues; the image becomes an indelible one, "At night they would attack the city, plunder homes, giving all kinds of trouble to subjects so that people could not even sleep. They had destroyed houses in the neighborhood of Delhi." The routes to the city from all four sides are closed. The caravans of grain dealers and the merchants dare not come because of the disorder.

The Meos are described as having been one of the major sources of disturbance for the capital. For fear of their plunder the western gates to the city have to be closed after the afternoon prayer. The Punjab route is closed. None dares to emerge after the evening prayer to go to the tank of Hauz Sultani or visit the graves of ancestors for pilgrimage as they are prone to being disturbed by wayfarers *(rāhzan)*.[37] Several Meos gather in the evenings at the time of prayer around the Hauz, where they trouble the sakkas, or water carriers, and take away women's clothes. The fear of Meos has caused great commotion in Delhi.[38]

This stigmatization was not uncommon and extended to other groups such as the Jats, the Kaitharis, and the Marathas.[39] The state is represented as weak and passive; the Meos are the aggressors, wrecking the fragility of the newfound state. They are the fasadis who upset the "order" of Delhi personified by the sultanate, which is the agency to counter disorder. They rob highways and disrupt trade and travel; virtually besiege Delhi; upset sacred prayer and pilgrimage; assault people at work; and worse, molest women.

The logic is explicit: Meo behavior necessitates fierce reprisal by the state so that order can be restored. It takes Balban a year to implement his military solution: the sultan's sword delivers many followers of God from the assaults and killing of the enemy *(ulfe tegh)*. An inversion is involved in Barani's description where the Mewatis have been constructed as the source of violence. The contrast is to the sultan, the harbinger of peace who delivers the city from their attacks *(farāgh)*, bestows lawfulness, and protects the populace from the "den of robbers," which becomes a guard house. In fact, there was a large-scale massacre of Meos.

The Meo menace is the justification for further militarization. A fort is built at Gopal-gir, and several (police) posts are established near the city in the charge of Afghans who are also given assignments of land (for their maintenance). Barani completely ignores the disruptive effects of empire. Nonetheless, we can gauge that this must have been so from the information that cultivated land is appropriated to support forts and garrisons. Barani tells us also that Balban hands over the towns and villages of the Gangetic Doab to distinguished persons and orders them to destroy all the villages of the rebels, kill them, take captive their women and children, cut down the forests, and suppress the rebellion. Some of the important amirs (nobles) set about this task with large armies and put an end to rebellion. The forests are cut and the public thereafter becomes law abiding and obedient. Barani reinforces the impression left by Minhaj: those who claim to maintain order are themselves responsible for looting the villages and killing the inhabitants *(nahab-o-tārāj/qaṭl-o-ghārat)*. Thereby the roads become secure. Forts such as that of Jalali in the Doab are established, which help in the suppression of a Mewati rebellion in 1242.

One can only estimate the far-reaching impact early medieval state formation had on the countryside and on peasant, pastoral, and forest communities by examining the interstices of the written record, focusing on the phenomenological space of the historiographical construction.

In the name of Mewati repression Balban was also responsible for one of the systematic acts of deforestation that we know of in medieval India. Barani writes that in the very first year of his reign Balban begins cutting the forests near Delhi in order to destroy the Meos, a task that lasts an entire year. The rebels of the Doab and other areas of Hindustan had been taking refuge there and indulging in looting and dacoity. Firishta informs us later that "the jungle in the neighbourhood" is an eight-mile tract of forest. The ecological and human brutality associated with the reign of Balban is masked by the language and narration of Barani's *Tarīkh*. State action is necessitated in "retaliation" against the Meo "menace." Militarization, deforestation, appropriation and transfer of the revenue of land to the nobility as iqtas' (which was essentially the king's right), and the destruction of villages are thereby rendered legitimate. This was done to the subjects or *ri'āyā* whom the state was expected to look after according to the Islamic theory of kingship.

A series of contrasts are nurtured by Barani's historical writing. The sultan who is protector of the populace and sustainer of order is the opposite of the "lawless" robber. City and forest are similarly contrasted. The city is the arena of the orderly, the law abiding, and disciplined, threatened by the wildness of the forest. The destruction of the forest by the city is inevitable in the name of upholding the legal institutional order. Resistance is crushed; the regime triumphs; law and peace prevail *(zabt-o-nazm, jahāndārī)*. At least, Barani claims, till the death of Balban, when all security of life and property is lost and no one has any confidence in the stability of the kingdom.

Elliot considered the *Tārīkh-i Firishta* superior to all other general histories of India. Firishta (b. 1570) was a Shi'ite who spent his early life in Ahmadnagar. He left for the court of Bijapur where the king asked him to write the first general history of Muhammadans in India that included a description of the south. He was later at the court of Ibrahim Adil Shah. Firishta follows Barani in spatializing the sultanate and Mewat, using the counterconcepts of city *(shahar)* and forest *(jangal)*.[40] Firishta reiterates the tired theme that the Mewatis are a people characterized by anarchic disorder: they indulge in plunder *(ghārat-o-tārāj)* and property *(daulat)* is threatened as they loot the goods *(māl)* of the city's inhabitants. They imperil also the sources of water of the city by attacking women and water carriers at Hauz Shamsi, Mehrauli, the main source for the old fort (Lal Kot). They prevent pilgrimage to the saints' shrines on the outskirts of the city. The Mewatis create such terror *(khauf)* in the city that the gates have to be closed against them.

Firishta takes us back to one of Balban's first attacks on Mewat on 25 November 1247 (6th of Shaban 646 H.). He returns with a large number of prisoners. The establishment of the sultanate implicitly assumes the liquidation of alternate centers of power characterized as defiant. Categorization and state policy mirror each other. The category of *mutamurridān* used by Barani symbolizes the rebellious Mewati. The term *mutamurrid* is used for a person who is stubborn, disobedient, rebellious, beardless, who does not have faith, who resists and negates everything.[41] The group's resistance is also signified by the category of mufsid implying a group that is mischievous, pernicious, destructive, indulges in fasad (conflict, disturbance) and is the author of evil. The otherness has a religious dimension as well since the *kuffār* (plural for *kafir*) are in contrast to the Islami army. The Mewatis signify opposition to the regime both within and without. They are in a state of insurrection *(ṭughyān, sarkashī)* from the perspective of the state although for the "rebels" the context is one of war.

From the sultanate's point of view the order of the city must be diffused to the countryside. The rebels must be wiped out *(gaushmālī)*, the insurgency crushed.[42] Twelve years later (in 658/1260) Balban undertakes a campaign toward Ranthambhor and the mountains of Mewat. An announcement *(munādī)* is made in the military camp: one tanka is promised for every dead *(murdā)* Mewati and two for every live *(zindah)* one. With this incentive, 300 to 400 of the enemy *(ghanīm)* are taken prisoner *(asīr)* each day. After subduing the rebels, Balban returns to Delhi. The next year he once again takes his army toward the Siwalik and Ranthambhor, where the rajas and Rajputs of Mewat and the Siwalik have begun rebelling. His large army consisting of horsemen and foot soldiers plunders and destroys the countryside. The Mewatis retreat to their strongholds in the mountains, where they cannot be reached. The areas inhabited by the Mewatis are razed, ruined *(kharābī)*, and plundered *(ghārat)*, their strongholds flushed out. The region is subject to repression *(kalkumā)* for months with fire and sword. Having been rendered desperate, they collect all their forces and rush down from the mountains on the sultan's army. The confrontation is described as violent and terrible. Eventually after much difficulty and slaughter Balban succeeds in making his enemy retreat. Many brave Muslim officers are killed as were 10,000 Hindus, while 250 of their *sardars*, or chiefs, are made prisoner, in addition to a large numbers of common soldiers. The chiefs are put in yokes and paraded before the Badshah and at his order killed in Delhi's bazaars.

Firishta gives us a far more vivid picture of Balban's reprisal than Barani. In 664 H./1265 the army is ordered to exterminate the plundering Mewatis, who have occupied an extensive tract of forest about eighty miles southeast of the capital, toward the hills, from where they make incursions up to the gates of Delhi. In the first year of his accession one hundred thousand Mewatis are annihilated by the sword *(dafā, talwār kī ghās)*. The writ of the state means compliance with orders *(hukm, amr-i farmūd)*. The process of domination requires a repressive apparatus *(muzāḥamat)* established through a network of police and military posts *(thanās)* set up under the nobles. The army is supplied with hatchets and other implements and clears the forests for a circumference of one hundred miles. The hilly, forested region beginning from Mehrauli is brought under agricultural cultivation *(kisht, zarā'at)*. After this clearing the area provides excellent arable land and becomes well cultivated.

Conquest, violence, and the sedentarizing impetus of state formation are recurrent themes.[43] Firishta almost completely replicates Barani's account.

Like Barani, Firishta represents Balban's actions as defensive, masking the sultanate's unabashed expansionism. Firishta also eulogizes Balban for his many great qualities and the justice and wisdom of his administration. The cruel twist of his personality, including the murder of his erstwhile collaborators, the Group of Forty (that included the most powerful Turkish slaves of Iltutmish), the massacres that accompanied his reign are glossed over and the qualities of a distinguished general underlined.

The nature of reproduction of Persian historiography through well-entrenched images is apparent from Bada'uni's work. According to one commentator, Bada'uni's history, though embellished with additional facts, is an abridgment of the *Ṭabaqāt-i Akbarī* and *Tārīkh-i Mubārak Shāhī*.[44] Bada'uni (b. 1540) describes Sultan Nasir al-Din Mahmud's and Ulugh Khan's campaigns against the "rebels."[45] Following his campaigns Balban is said to have handed over the territory of Mewat in the Doab to strong governors with orders to put the rebels to death. Some were killed and others imprisoned. The patterns of rhetorical writing are well established. Ulugh Khan is said to have marched toward the hills of Delhi to quell the insurrection of the robbers of Mewat who are a terror to the devils. The metaphors are derived from Minhaj.

Yahya bin Ahmad describes in some detail events in Mewat under the Tughlaq and Sayyid dynasties. The *Tārīkh-i Mubārak Shāhī* is a crucial account of Sayyid policy in Mewat and is dedicated to Sultan Mubarak Shah (r. 1421–33). The *Tārīkh* is a history of the Delhi sultans from the time of Mu'iz al-Din to 838 H./1434. Hardy maintains that the didactic text is largely an account of reigns and revolts. Further, that Yahya relies on authority and the testimony of eyewitnesses and employs no critical technique. Events are understood according to the dogma of divine decree, and there is no explanation of why they happen.[46] Elliot, however, considered Yahya a "careful, and apparently an honest chronicler," and Rizvi remarks that he does not unduly praise the Sayyid rulers.[47] The *Tārīkh* is such a significant source that the *Ṭabaqāt-i Akbarī* and the *Tārīkh-i Firishta* consist of substantial reproductions of parts of it. The work of Bada'uni is also largely based on Yahya's account.[48]

The context of Yahya's account is the fierce factional struggles among the later Tughlaqs. In 1399 Sultan Nasir al-Din Nusrat Shah (Firoz Tughlaq's grandson) faced a strong challenge from a faction led by Iqbal Khan. Nusrat Shah received some support from a Meo group led by Shahab Khan Mewati, who supplied him with soldiers and ten elephants. The sultan occupied

Delhi, but Iqbal Khan set up a capital in Firozabad and gradually gained control of Delhi, overthrowing the sultan.[49] The Mewati chief Bahadur Nahar is said to have presented two elephants as peshkash at his accession and acknowledged his suzerainty.[50] In 1405 Iqbal Khan died in battle with Khizr Khan, and Sultan Mahmud Shah succeeded him. The sultanate was restored when Khizr Khan captured Firozabad and in 1414 established the Sayyid dynasty, which ruled till 1451. The influence of Sayyids, however, was restricted to the Gangetic Doab.

Yahya describes the Tughlaq onslaught on Mewat. Sultan Muhammad Shah attacks and ravages Mewat in 795 H./1393.[51] The reason for the attack is again legitimated: it is *because* Bahadur Nahar attacks and plunders villages in the vicinity of Delhi. Bahadur Nahar's support for the candidacy of Nasir al-Din Nusrat Khan as sultan causes a further attack on Mewat by Muhammad Shah. Yet another battle is fought at Kotila in 1397.

In 814 H./1411 Sultan Muhammad Shah arrives at the town of Narnaul under the jurisdiction of Khan Bahadur Nahar and wreaks havoc. Yahya explicitly uses the terms *nahab* and *tārāj*, or loot and plunder, for the acts of the ruler. The Mewatis close themselves in the Kotila fort, raise their flag, and prepare for *jang*, or war. But they are defeated in the first attack. As they flee into the hills, the Badshah's flag is raised. After the towns of Sarhath (Sarheta), Tijara, and Kharol, and other Mewati centers are ruined *(kharāb)* the sultan returns to Delhi. The context is explained by Yahya as the lack of order *(fatūr)* and stability *(qarār)* within the country, a situation the Badshah presumably aims to rectify. But the result of the devastation *(kharāb-o-abtar)* was large-scale exodus from the area.[52]

The image of the state as the primary agency of plunder and destruction rather than the source of order is repeated in Yahya's description of the Sayyid ruler Khizr Khan's role in Mewat. Insurgency is said to have prevailed. Yahya acknowledges, however, that the context is one of war. Similar attacks are made against the fitna caused by the fasadi people of Kol, Delhi, and Etawa. Yahya tells us that "[i]n 824 H./1421 Khizr Khan took control of Delhi and marched against the Mewatis.[53] Some Mewatis shut themselves in Bahadur Nahar's Kotila fortress while others battled. Kotila was besieged. The Meos fought but were defeated. Kotila was destroyed and the Meos fled to the mountains."

Bahadur Nahar surrenders and is arrested.[54] The battle cannot have been all that easy, however, for in the same battle the noble Malik Taj-ul-mulk is killed, and Malik Sikander has to be appointed vazir, or prime minister.

> In 828 H./1424 Saiyyad Mubarak Shah [described as Khizr's "capable" son and successor] headed for Mewat following news of a Mewati rebellion. Fighting continuously the sultan reached the outskirts of Mewat. He destroyed most of the area but was unable to vanquish the Meos. They scorched their terrain and took refuge in their impregnable stronghold in the mountain of Jahra [Jhar, Jhara according to some Persian manuscripts]. As food grain was scarce the army returned to Delhi with the wealth it had looted. . . .
>
> The next year in 829 H. the sultan again attacked Mewat. Bahadur Nahar's grandsons, Jallu and Kaddu, and some other Meos followed a "scorched earth" policy and retreated to the fort of Indor [or Andvar, the strongest of the Mewati forts located ten miles east of Tijara]. The "rebel" leaders were besieged for some days. When the victorious royal forces demonstrated their strength, Jalal and Kadar Khan were driven out of Indor to the mountains of Alwar. The next day the lord of the world destroyed the fort of Indor and followed them to Alwar. Jallu and Kaddu were besieged and attacked continuously for several days until they were compelled to surrender. The request for protection was granted. Kaddu submitted to the sultan but once again attempted to escape to the mountains. He was caught and made prisoner. The sultan sacked the region of Mewat and its villages. He remained in the Kohpaya until he had to return because of the scarcity of grain and fodder.[55]

Bahadur Nahar's son, Mubarak Khan, who had supported Iqbal Khan's claim to the throne had been put to death. Bahadur Nahar's grandson, Kadar Khan, and other Meos, who had allied themselves with Sultan Ibrahim Sharqi, ruler of the regional kingdom of Jaunpur and refused to present *peshkash* also met a similar fate.[56] Thus ended an abbreviated period of collaboration with the Delhi sultans.

Saiyyad Mubarak's repression of the Mewatis is lucidly described by Yahya, Firishta, and Nizam al-Din Ahmad.[57] In 1428 Malik Sarvar-ul-mulk is sent with an army to suppress the rebellion in Mewat. He destroys some towns and villages located in the forest. Jalal Khan Mewati, Ahmad Khan, Fakhr al-Din, and other chiefs gather in the fort of Indor with their horsemen and armies. Eventually the Mewatis have to negotiate an agreement. Jalal Khan submits to Malik Sarvar-ul-mulk giving him tribute, gifts, and slaves. But the story is not over. In 836 H./1432

> the Sultan camped right in the mountains of Mewat. Fighting continuously he proceeded to the qasba of Taoru. When Jalal Khan learnt of this he closed himself up with a large part of his army in the fort of Indor. The next day even as the Sultan prepared his attack, he set fire to the fort from within and departed to Kotila. The army managed to acquire the grain, cloth and other resources that had been collected by Jalal Khan as preparation for a prolonged siege. The Sultan now moved to the town of Tijara and devastated most of Mewat. Jalal finally acknowledged defeat and was forgiven after he paid the wealth and taxes demanded.[58]

Certain ideas deserve special attention: that state formation created its antithesis in resistance; that the so-called rebels and insurgents were expelled from their own lands, the countryside run over; that they repeatedly refused to pay tribute; and that the Mewatis' strategies were those of a desperate people. For the sultans, ruling was more a punitive exercise than one of eliciting consent. Defiance must be substituted by subjection for a "peaceable" populace is a subjugated and submissive one that regularly pays tribute. The cost of resistance was the crushing of the "rebels," the ravaging of their strongholds, and attacks on their precarious subsistence. The authority of the state was fragile and, hence, subject to constant rupture.

The making of marginality then derives from the tortured history of Mewat that emerges only from the interstices of Persian historiography: Balban's plunder of the Kohpaya, its repeated sack by successive sultans; and the destruction of all potential centers of power such as Bahadur Nahar's Kotila.[59] It is reproduced by the rhetorical strategies of a series of historians. The Mewatis are no match for the Turko-Afghan power structure. Historiography thereby becomes the narrative of state formation.

With Nizam al-Din Ahmad's *Ṭabaqāt-i Akbarī* the image of the Mewati has become iconic. Sultanate historians exercised a powerful influence on Mughal historiography. In a sense the *Ṭabaqāt-i Akbarī* is a sequel to the major chroniclers and weaves together the work of Al-'Utbi, Hasan Nizami, Minhaj, Amir Khusrau, Barani, Yahya, Firishta, and others. The *Ṭabaqāt* describes the history of India from 377 H./986–87 to 1002–1 H./1590, the thirty-seventh year of Akbar's reign. As the first comprehensive history exclusively of India, it was regarded by several writers, such as Elliot, Erskine, Lees, Ranking, Wolseley Haig, and Beni Prasad, as one of the best Persian histories and a most reliable source of information. Written around 1590, it in turn became the authority on which several later historical works were based.

Khwaja Nizam al-Din Ahmad (1551–94) was known for his orthodox leanings (hence the approval of Bada'uni). His father was an important government official, a diwan during Babur's rule and vazir during Humayun's. Nizam al-Din was Bakshi during Akbar's reign and played an important role in Mughal military campaigns in Gujarat. He was particularly successful in subjugating resistant groups such as the Kolis and Garasias in the region of Ahmadnagar and set up the military-police apparatus of thanas, forts, and military posts, as had been done in Mewat much earlier.[60] For Nizam al-Din Ahmad (as is the case with Barani, Firishta, Bada'uni and Yahya) the ruler is the epicenter of the state apparatus. He undertakes campaigns to enhance state power all over the country and to demolish power bases, other kingdoms and chiefdoms.

Mewat continued, however, to be an independent territory even during Lodi rule. It was claimed that the territory ruled by the Mewatis included Rewari and briefly Sonah in Gurgaon adding up to 1,484 towns and villages extending over Mewat.[61] But the hold of the sultans was temporary and tenuous as the fifteenth-century history of Mewat is again a repetitious narrative of expeditions.

Bahlol Lodi established an Afghan-ruled kingdom in Delhi. His first movement was toward Mewat. Ahmad Khan Mewati, who then ruled an area near Delhi stretching from Mehrauli to Ladhu Sarai, was forced to submit to Lodi authority. Seven parganas were taken from him and given to Tatar Khan who established himself at Tijara. Ahmad Khan's uncle, Mubarak Khan, was given a permanent appointment with the sultan.[62] Afghans were settled in the area to control the Meos. Following Bahlol Lodi's death, however, Meo chieftains became independent once again and defied the rule of the local governor. Till the mid-fifteenth century several tracts did not acknowledge central rule even nominally.[63] Delhi was ruled by the Lodi clan of Afghans until the defeat of Bahlol's grandson, Ibrahim Lodi, by Babur at Panipat on 20 April 1526.

Babur's autobiographical account is one of the most lucid expositions of the arduous establishment of the Mughal Empire in India. Although the *Tūzak-i Bābarī* is written in Turki, it may be regarded as a continuation of the Persian discourse: the orientations, the images, and the equation of revolt with plunder are repeated here. By a sleight of language the invading group becomes "defensive," and the subordinated peoples become "oppressors" and "plunderers," violators of the contract whereby revenue is to be paid to the rulers. Babur writes: "Every time that I have entered Hindustan, the Jats and Gujars have regularly poured down in prodigious numbers from their hills and wild, in order to carry off oxen and buffaloes. These were the wretches that really inflicted the chief hardships, and were guilty of the severest oppression in the country. These districts in former times, had been in a state of revolt, and yielded very little revenue that could be come at."[64] Babur's last line of this passage indicates the context of revolt: "On the present occasion when I had reduced the whole of the neighboring districts to subjections they began to repeat their practices." Following his victory over Ibrahim Lodi, Babur had taken Delhi and Agra. He continues: "When I came to Agra it was the hot season. All the inhabitants fled from terror, so that we could not find grain nor provender either for ourselves or our horses. The villages, out of hostility and hatred to us, had taken to rebellion thieving and robbery. The roads became impassable."[65] Rebellion and crime were clearly caused by popular hostility toward the latest group of invaders.

One of Babur's first expeditions following the victory of Panipat was against Mewat. According to Babur, Mewat was not included in the kingdom of Bahlol or Sikandar Lodi who could never really subject it. But his memoir, *Babur Nama,* mentions the revenue yielded by Mewat. According to him, Hasan Khan Mewati and his ancestors had ruled it for a hundred years or so and were only nominally under the sultans. Because of the hilly area, neither conquest nor administrative control had been accomplished.[66] When Hasan Khan did not submit, Babur sanctioned the looting of Mewat. In Babur's view Hasan Khan was an ungrateful infidel who preferred *rebellion* to a position in the lower rungs of the Mughal hierarchy. He writes that after his conquest of Hind, following the example of former sultans, he had given considerable encouragement to Hasan Khan. Yet the ungrateful infidel did not acknowledge the kindness and generosity that had been extended to him. Instead he became the promoter and leader of all the rebellions and commotion that ensued, and joined forces with other infidels.

Babur's attempt at developing a collaborative relationship was rejected by the Mewatis. Ahmad Yadgar describes the "rebellion" of Hasan Khan and Rana Sanga.[67] Babur undertook his first jihad against the "pagans" and encamped at Sikri. A battle was fought at Khanua, 37 miles west of Agra, on 17 March 1527 with the Rajput confederacy, which included 7 rajas, 9 raos, and 104 chieftains. Babur confronted the large force with a "light force." Hasan Khan and his allies were defeated. Ahmad Yadgar mentions that

Hasan Khan fled and was later killed by his own servant.[68] Following this, Babur marched through the terrain, where immense numbers of the dead bodies of the infidels had fallen in their flight, all the way to Bayana, and even as far as Alwar and Mewat.

Babur wrote, “I resolved on the reduction of Mewat.” Political control over Mewat began with his defeat of the Rajput-Khanazada coalition. Babur camped at Alwar where the capital was shifted from Tijara. The Alwar fort was conquered; its treasure and possessions were handed over to his son, Humayun. The region around Alwar and Tijara was distributed among Babur’s other followers, and a few parganas were assigned to Nahar Khan, Hasan Khan’s son who swore allegiance to Babur. The *Akbar Nama* mentions that Mewat was administered by Tardi Beg Khan.[69]

The Mughals made a more sustained attempt to co-opt the Khanazadas by marital alliances. They were given a separate area. Humayun married the elder daughter of Jamal Khan, Hasan Khan Mewati’s nephew. The powerful Turkish noble Bairam Khan married the younger one. A Meo history states that a distance began to develop between the Khanazadas and the Meos as the former began to intermarry with other Muslim groups and increasingly began to adopt Islamic ritual practices.[70] During the brief rule of the Afghan Sher Shah (1538–45), the government of the sarkars of Jodhpur, Nagaur, Ajmer, and Mewat was entrusted to Khawwas Khan, governor of Rajputana.[71] Later Humayun handed over the “mulk,” or country, of Mewat to his brother, Hindal.

Through the rule of sultanate then one can see the steady erosion of Mewati power and autonomy. Until the fifteenth century there was a marked tension between the sultanate attempt to control and the Mewatis claim to and persistent assertion of their autonomy. Mewati chiefs possessed their own signs of counterpower, such as fortresses and warriors. These texts mark the passage of a section of the Mewatis from autonomy to incorporation and co-optation by the Delhi rulers. This section of Mewatis began to play court politics, thereby sapping their own ability to resist. But there was a split within the group as the major section rejected reconciliation.

In the past few decades there has been an intense discussion of the colonial British state and of colonial historiography in India but far less of the imperial state systems (the sultanate and the Mughal Empire and their knowledge systems). The Persian language comprises the dominant discourse with respect to the Mewatis in the medieval period, as English did in the nineteenth century. Categories that classify the other in the intellectual systems of dominant groups, however, tend to become fixed icons that structure modes of cognition. These are not only passed down generationally but also are inherited by new ruling groups and influence their modes of classification. Hence the intertextuality of written texts in different languages. The idea of the Mewati qua rebel was readily assimilated by British ethnography and historiography. Filtered through the nineteenth-century evolutionist and essentialist ideas of Western "science," the "rebel" Meo group was reincarnated in the colonial doctrine of the criminal tribe.

5 Imperial State Formation and Resistance

It is not inappropriate to begin an account of Mughal state formation and Mewati resistance with an extract from *The Shah Jahannama of 'Inayat Khan*, as it bridges the following account with that of the previous chapter. The Mewati narrative I describe relates to the same locale (Kaman in northern Bharatpur, Agra Suba) and the same period. The two texts, written and oral, statist and communitarian, present divergent perspectives on the question of Mewati resistance. According to the *Shah Jahannama*:

> Murshid Quli Khan had recently gone to punish the rebels of Kaman Pahari; and after arriving on that frontier, he daily attacked one of the formidable hills or forests in which those villains were congregated, slaying a number of them. In fact, in the course of a few days, he put 300 to death and took 400 prisoner; whilst on the royalist side, Ghiyas al-Din 'Ali, grandson of Yamin al-Daula the commander in chief, and a few of the latter's followers attained the glory of martyrdom. The remnant of the rebels dispersed and sought safety in flight, and the Khan and his comrades returned to court.[1]

Imperial officials represent the coercive aspects of governance. To begin with, the Mewatis inflict a setback, hence, the "martyrdom" of a section of the army although eventually, the Mughal forces triumph.

The same text describes the deployment of the Rajputs (shortly after 6th of Rabi II 1060 corresponding with the 19th of Farwardin or 8 April 1650) to suppress the "rebels":

> In these days, as the refractory Mewatis of the sectors of Kaman-Pahari and Koh-Mujahid, which lie between the great capitals of Akbarabad and Shahjahanabad, were indulging in predatory habits, the surrounding *parganas* began to be desolated through their rapacity—to the great detriment of the *jagirdars* of those places. His Majesty, the Shadow of God, consequently invested Raja Jai Singh's second son Karan Singh with an appropriate *mansab* and bestowed the *parganas* of Kaman-Pahari and Koh Mujahid on him in *jagir*, as his fixed abode. At the same time, the Raja was ordered to overthrow those rebels, who so richly deserved destruction. Moreover, after utterly exterminating them without the least compunction, he was instructed to transfer a colony of people from his own part of the country to occupy their place.[2]

The Rajput raja of Amber was "to crush the rebels of Kaman and Pahari" for which Raja Jai Singh was rewarded with the Pargana of Hal Kaliyana (Chal Kalana, Sarkar Narnaul, Agra Suba) worth 7 million dams.

Domination is represented through divergent strategies, such as the historiographical, visual, and architectural. A painting of approximately 'Id al-Qurban 1044/27 May 1635 depicts the Emperor Shah Jahan (r. 1628–58) hunting deer in the famous imperial hunting grounds of Rupbas, also in Bharatpur. It illustrates the text cited above (see fig. 2). The miniature suggests a forested terrain with considerable wildlife symbolized by the deer. The miniature combines the presence of both forest and field. Sovereignty is personified by the image of the emperor with the nimbus. Gun in hand he points toward the hapless deer in flight, while he is watched by a deferential nobility, Muslim with the exception of one, all wearing the distinctive turban known as the *shāhjahānī pagṛī*. The pageantry of power is underscored with the peasantry at work in the distance possibly plowing the fields. The imperial terrain needs to be safeguarded for royal pursuits like the hunt, among other reasons.

The Mughal-Rajput alliance consolidates itself against the Meos. An imperial *farmān* from Shah Jahan to Raja Jai Singh of Jaipur directs him to uproot recalcitrant Meos from Kaman-Pahari and to instruct jagirdars to capture or kill them.[3] Two months later another farman decrees that action

FIGURE 2

Mughal miniature of Shah Jahan hunting deer near Rupbas in Sha'ban or Zi'l-Hijja 1053 (November 1643 or February 1644).

should immediately be taken against the troublemakers of Kaman and Pahari. A *nishān* dated 3 October 1651 rules that the troublemakers of Kaman and Pahari be replaced by Rajputs. The *faujdārī*, or imperial military-administrative authority, over the Mewat parganas is given to Jai Singh's son, Kirat Singh (Kesri Singh of Khafikhan), with a brief to crush the Meo and Jat rebels.[4] He has jurisdiction over forty-four mahals in the jagir of Jai Singh, thirty-seven of which were in the sarkars of Rewari, Alwar, Tijara, and Narnaul.

The Mewati terrain intervening between the capitals of Delhi (Shahjahanabad) and Agra (Akbarabad) was an ever-present threat on a crucial imperial route, hindering trade and the movement of the army and imperial treasure, and requiring obliteration. That a major section of the Mewatis were Muslim does not seem to have mattered. The shared religion with the Mughals hardly figured as a constraint on either side. What is indicated instead is the management of population through both extermination and colonization.

The inquiry into structures of power is incomplete without an account of the ways in which they are contested, that is, the Mewati perspective. The *Pāñch Pahāṛ kī laṛāī.* is the story of a battle between the Pahat clan of the Meos and the Shah Jahan's Mughal-Rajput army in the seventeenth century. The battle is said to have taken place near the village of Ajangarh in Kaman pargana, then part of the Sahar Sarkar in the Agra Suba. The narrative describes metaphorically the subordination of the Meos to imperial rule, the violence that accompanied state formation, and the antagonism it generated in the region.

The discussion begins with the historical context and moves from imperial to regional state formation. A further section analyzes the construction of the Mewatis in the administrative record of the eighteenth-century kingdom of Jaipur. The state perspective manifest in the historiographical and administrative discourse is then counterposed with a Mewati narrative.

State Formation: The Mughal Empire

The imperial state established by the Mughals brought an end to Turko-Afghan rule in India. The processes of military conquest followed by the administrative subordination of the Mewatis and their intensified sedentarization (like that of the Jats and Gujars in the Punjab) resulted in a considerable erosion of their autonomy.[5] From a former ruling group consisting of rais, raos, and other chiefs, the Meos were now mere landholders and referred to as "zamindars" in the sense of cultivators. They did not figure in the imperial bureaucracy as mansabdars and jagirdars or constitute the new gentry. The *A'īn-i-Akbarī* shows their substantial landholding in the following areas: 12 out of 43 parganas in Sarkar Alwar, 14 out of 18 parganas in Sarkar Tijara, and in all 4 parganas of Sarkar Sahar. In the remaining parganas they did not possess any significant zamindari rights and had virtually none in the Sarkars of Rewari and Narnaul.[6] They were at best a major peasant caste in Mewat and the largest single caste group among the peasantry that included Jats, Ahirs, Gujars, and Minas.

There has been a fierce historiographical debate on the nature of the Mughal State. Before closing this chapter I return once again to the positions that have been taken on the question. To illustrate, Tariq Ahmad argues that the state was "benevolent": jagirdars did not possess absolute power over the people; the qazi, who had judicial power, was independent of him; and the qanungo checked that no irregular exactions were made from the peasantry.[7] Ahmad has attempted to counter Irfan Habib's contention that the Mughal State was itself the principal instrument of exploitation.[8] Nonetheless, the systematic collection of revenue by the Mughal Empire was bound to create resistance, as is borne out by the story of regional records, agrarian revolts, hagiographical accounts, and folk traditions.[9]

For the Mughals, land control was particularly important, because land was the source of power and revenue as in other agrarian empires. Habib holds that the empire's appropriation of the surplus produce created the great wealth of the Mughal governing class and left the peasant at the level of bare subsistence. The imposition of permanent *dastūrs* meant that revenue rates were divorced from the quality of the actual harvest in any year. The *Dastūr-al 'amal* manual, or schedule of land revenue rates, applied after 1679 fixed a high revenue demand.[10] In addition to this, new imposts were also constantly being added. Stratification had intensified: in contrast to the condition of the lower ranks of the peasantry, the emerging elite peasantry had benefited from the extension of arable land, productivity, new markets, the inflationary spiral through the seventeenth century, and favorable schedules of revenue rates.[11]

Not surprisingly, a number of agrarian uprisings took place in northern India during imperial rule. Akbar's rule witnessed 144 uprisings.[12] In some areas fighting occurred every time the Mughals attempted to collect taxes, and even routine administration required the use of force.[13] These caused and accelerated the decline of Mughal imperial authority.[14] In north India there were several revolts of zamindars against the mansabdars; brigandage due to economic distress had increased in the southern Telugu-speaking area; and there was long tradition of peasant and tribal uprisings in the northeast.[15] Agrarian revolts among lower castes like the Jats, Mewatis, Gujars, Wattees, Dogars, and others, spread across the three Mughal subas of Agra, Delhi, and Ajmer in the seventeenth and early eighteenth centuries. These were concentrated in the areas of Braj, Mewat, Ajmer, and Ranthambhor.

In 1683, 1704, and 1709 there were major disturbances of zamindars and peasants as Minas, Gujars, Jats, Narukas, Gojhas, Panwars, Jadams, Solankis, Tunwars, and Meos rebelled.[16] Entire villages refused to pay land revenue, plundered highways, robbed and occupied villages, and looted traders. Rana comments that Mewat was one of the regions where massive revolts occurred with zamindar and peasant uprisings in Bayana, Nagar, Sahar, Khohri Rana, Kol, and so on.

State Formation: The Rajput Kingdom

Mughal expansion reinforced the rise of the Rajput-ruled kingdom of Amber. Jai Singh was appointed subedar of Akbarabad (Agra) and faujdar of Mathura in 1631.[17] After 1640 he was referred to as Mirza Raja. The Amber raja gradually acquired substantial territory: in 1643 he obtained 14 mahals (parganas) of Mewat in *tankhwāh jāgīr,* that is, land in lieu of salary.[18] Aurangzeb granted Jai Singh a *manṣab,* or rank, of 7,000 *zāt* and 7,000 *sawār* in 1661, the highest possible achievement for any noble. Jai Singh also acquired a large area on *ijāra* (lease) from other predominantly Muslim imperial mansabdars in addition to his *waṭan,* or ancestral domain. In 1650 he held jagirs worth 82 million dams.

The Mewat parganas under the ruler of Jaipur included those of Khohri, Pahari, Gaji ka Thana, Jalalpur, Maujpur, Wazirpur, Atela Bhabra, Piragpur, Pindayan, and Harsana.[19] Much of this area was given in subassignment to his Kacchavaha Rajput kin, particularly the Naruka Rajputs in jagir. To begin with, the Amber raja had only revenue-collecting power, and the administrative structure continued to be Mughal. Later, however, he obtained both faujdari and *thanedārī* rights over the Mewat parganas and appointed a faujdar over the entire *chaklā* of Mewat.[20] The latter enabled the setting up of police *chaukīs*, or posts.

Jai Singh founded the city of Jaipur in 1727. During Sawai Jai Singh's reign (1688–1743) the Jaipur kingdom became even more powerful and obtained a large area in tankhwah jagir, inam, and on ijara. Several parganas of Mewat had been taken on lease with Mughal consent in the first quarter of the eighteenth century.[21] Thus far the Jaipur State had been a complex of Mughal and non-Mughal political practice, suggesting strains of a multiethnic culture apparent in court ritual, language, and religious ideology. The tremendous territorial expansion of the Jaipur State was accompanied by rising ambitions of the ruling class, an increased use of regional language rather than Persian as evidenced by the Jaipur records, the emergence of the state as patron, and a shift in sectarian affiliation deriving from the seventeenth-century Vaishnava revivalism that took place in the wake of the growing popularity of the devotional poetry of Tulsidas.[22]

The Jaipur kingdom suppressed competing regional powers on its periphery, such as the Jats and Meos, by granting members of Rajput clans land and revenue-collection rights and military jurisdiction through faujdari powers.[23] This was in addition to modes of symbolic assertion such as the exclusive Rajput right to horses. Horses had come to symbolize social status. This was a continuation of an earlier trend deriving from Ala al-Din Khilji's rule in which zamindars who ride horses are described as presumptuous. It was not so much that the Rajput was defined as being mounted, but that they sought a monopoly over horses, which up to then had been possessed by groups like the Meos and Jats. We know, for instance, from Minhaj that the Mewatis had horses as early as the thirteenth century. When their chief, Malka, was captured, 142 horses were taken for the royal stables. A Mewati narrative (contextualized in Akbar's period) describes the Meo warrior-hero as spending most of his time riding horses.[24] In 1709 Meo rebels at Naugaon are described as creating disturbances and indulging in looting along with other sawars (horsemen). The open procurement and use of horses is what the Jaipur State sought to circumscribe: a later royal order explicitly prohibited both Ahirs and Meos from being mounted on horses.

The process of Rajput state formation involved the dispossession of several erstwhile ruling groups such as the Meos, Minas, and Bhils. Treachery had been used by Rajput chiefs to defeat the Mina and Bhil rulers of Jaipur and Bundi. This was later overwritten by the mythology of the chivalric-heroic Rajput tradition embellished by Charan bardic skills and Colonel Tod's

Rajput-oriented account of the early nineteenth century.[25] The Mina and Bhil ruling groups were displaced by the Rajputs, as the Meos had been by the sultanate and the Mughal Empire. The Minas, however, like the Ahirs, became an important peasant group. They became leaders and patels of the village communities and were given authoritative positions.[26] A similar compromise was not affected with the Mewatis.

During the seventeenth and early eighteenth centuries the rising power of the Jats and Naruka Rajputs (a sublineage of the Jaipur Kacchavahas) that led eventually to the respective establishment of the Alwar and Bharatpur kingdoms further undermined the position of the Meo zamindars.[27] New zamindars called bhomias appropriated the land of zortalab (recalcitrant) Meos on the pretext of their "seditious activities" and by undertaking to reestablish order. For instance, Meo zamindars in the villages of Neekatpura, Bhada, Todarpur, Pran Nath, Vaisachh, Jai Singh Pura, and Ram Singh Pura of pargana Khohri were deprived of their zamindaris on the ground that they had been unable to submit the land revenue of these villages to the jagirdar.[28] Bhardwaj points out, "Many of the subjugated zamindars were reduced to the rank of *khudkashta*, or self-cultivating peasant proprietors."[29] Other zamindaris came into existence through the settlement of new villages or the rehabilitation of the old ruined villages. The new zamindars embarked on a policy of heterogenizing the caste composition of the villages. Jats, Gujars, and Ahirs were encouraged to settle in Meo villages in order to disrupt caste solidarity. A large number of peasants, referred to as *pāhīs*, were brought in from outside the village to colonize land.[30]

Although there was a marked expansion of the cropped area because of the digging of wells, the beneficiaries were only an upper crust of rural society. The remaining peasantry continued to be subject to the vagaries of climate, fluctuation in crop productivity levels, and famine.[31]

The peasantry were divided along caste lines into the *ri'āyatīs* (literally, favored persons) and *rai'yatīs* (also termed *palṭīs* or *asāmīs*, who were less favored). The former included high-caste groups such as brahmans, Rajputs, Mahajans (moneylenders), and village officials such as the patel, chaudhari, qanungo, and patwari. Although revenue assessment varied from pargana to pargana and from the spring to the winter crop, the ri'ayatis enjoyed privileged land tenure rights. Under the land tenure arrangement, they had to pay only a fourth of the crop. They were generally owners of large family holdings, hired outside labor, and leased out livestock and equipment that yielded a relatively large income.[32] The raiyati included middle peasant castes such as Jats, Meos, Ahirs, Gujars, Minas, and so on. The majority of them were wholly dependent on the village mahajan, zamindar, patel, and other rich ri'ayatis for the supply of credit and bullocks, plows, seeds, and other crop inputs.[33] They generally cultivated land on the basis of *baṭāī* (share-cropping) but were often also landowners eking out a living on subsistence food crops.

The position of the rai'yatis was considerably depressed. A distinct *dastūr*, or schedule of land revenue rates, was applied to them. They paid the *hissā dīwān*, or state share, at the rate of 40 to 50 percent of their gross produce and had to bear the entire burden of the common village expenses.[34] Additional cesses related to the costs of assessment and collection of revenue, the remuneration for the watchman and revenue officials (including *salāmīs* and *bhaiṇt*, i.e., salutation tax and ritual prestation), expenses incurred on fairs, travelers, pilgrims; maintaining the diwan's office; house and marriage taxes; access to wood *(lakṛī)* and pastures *(ghās)*; and so on. These were in violation of the prescriptions of the dastur manuals.

Famine conditions frequently prevailed. The failure of successive harvests caused large scale desertion and migration in 1665, 1694–95, 1704–5, 1709, 1716–17, and 1724.[35] The peasantry's capacity to cope with the cumulative demand was greatly reduced and resulted in arrears, increased indebtedness and dependence on the mahajan, and frequent refusal to pay land revenue.[36] This caused the intermittent eviction of lower pargana officials for their inability to pay revenue. In Nivai pargana, the Rajavat (Rajput) landowner released captive patels only on condition that they collect the shortfall in the revenue collections. In Malarna pargana likewise peasants accused ijaradars of collecting unauthorized dues.[37] The *arhsaṭṭā* revenue records of some areas reveal the discrimination against the Meos in favor of castes like the Ahirs who had to pay lower rates of revenue. In Khohri pargana, Meo peasants of twelve villages complained to the Amber raja that they were being forced into paying land revenue and other cesses at a higher rate than the Ahirs of the same villages.[38]

The administrative record indicates a deliberate attempt by the Mughals and Rajputs to destroy the position of the Meos as the dominant community of Mewat. Bhardwaj comments on the systematic campaign of the Amber raja "to destroy the socio-economic base of the Meo zamindars so that they could not offer any effective resistance to the growing ambitions of the Kacchavaha Rajputs in the region." As a result of Mughal and Rajput policies the Meos were reduced to the position of middle and low level peasant proprietors. In contrast, the Narukas and Jats gradually became a force to be reckoned with in the area. The Jats emerged as powerful zamindars with control over a large number of fortresses and police posts. Both Narukas and Jats encroached upon Meo zamindaris and appropriated the land revenue while the Meos were unable to counter them. Unlike the Jats and the Narukas they were small zamindars with meager resources. They also lacked fortresses for better self-defense and were unable to mobilize other peasants against the state.

Ironically, the subassignees of the Jaipur jagirs did not prove to be malleable, as expected by the Kacchavaha ruler. But later moves to withdraw the temporary jagirs caused widespread uprisings. The plundering activities of Rajput and Jat bhomias ruined crops and desolated entire villages that were already troubled by famine.[39] They disrupted trade routes and prevented the access of grain traders to Mewat and through them the supply of food grains to the urban centers of Agra and Delhi.[40] In some cases involving withdrawal of temporary jagirs, the Rajputs insisted on bhom, or permanent land rights. They constructed fortresses and continued to collect taxes from the peasants and traders, leading to considerable conflict with the Amber ruler.

The Persian Administrative Discourse

The historiographical construction of the "Mewati" is reproduced in the administrative record of the Jaipur State. The following account is based on a reading of these documents that are mostly in Persian.[41] They reveal a recurring concern with Mewati rebellion and disorder (fasad) in the latter half of the seventeenth and early half of the eighteenth century and give a strong sense of the responses of the regime to what the state perceived was the growing problem of *zamindāran-i zorṭalab*, or rebellious zamindars.

The Meos are referred as "recalcitrant elements" that are the cause of disturbance *(bāis fasād)* and must be curbed *(rafa-i fasād)*.[42] Disturbances have been created by the Mewatis at Rewari that the administration is not able to suppress.[43] Food grain prices have risen in Agra due to the upheaval caused by the Meos in the Mewat area.[44] The akhbarat records identify the Mewatis as plunderers of traders.

Invariably the administrative discourse views the Mewati as "mufsid," or rebel. The historiographical and administrative discourse in the case of writing in Persian thus coincide. This is in contrast to the colonial English discourse, where the ethnographic construction of criminality is unsupported by police and settlement reports, administrative and travel accounts, and the documents of the Thagi and Dakaiti Department. The mufsid is the source of "fasad," or disturbances, disorder, insurrection.[45] The term might characterize the entire group *(mufsidān mewatiyān)* or refer to the entire region *(mufsidān mewāt)*. "Zortalabi" is a term also used frequently to refer to dissenting groups such as the Jats, Meos, or lower echelons of Rajputs. Although it has similar connotations of rebelliousness it refers more specifically to groups from whom revenue has to be forcibly appropriated. Mawas and fitna (Arabic for sedition) are also used to define groups negatively.[46] The otherness of these groups is seen as constituting a spatial boundary that Heesterman calls the "inner frontier."

Zortalabi has implications for state action involving both the identification and naming of a tract/group and its reconquest by the imperial and regional states. The command to local officials is to tighten the coercive apparatus *(mewāt par intazām taināt kiyā jāye)*. That this is accomplished emerges from several reports of vakils, who are virtual ambassadors of the Jaipur kingdom stationed at the Mughal court. Baroda (Mewat) is said to have been "conquered" and the rebels humbled by Hari Singh who is later rewarded.[47] Raja Ram Singh is requested to depute an army as ordered by the emperor to help him in apprehending the "rebels of Mewat."[48] A later report mentions a "scheme of suppressing the Mewati rebels" organized by the jagirdar Mohammad Akram.[49] Clearly *both* the Mughal and the regional state are involved in the repressive antimufsid campaign.

Officials are authorized to suppress the rebels of Mewat and undertake *qatl* (killing).[50] Thakur Mohan Singh and Sahu Anand Ram, who have been specially deputed to quell the rebels of Mewat, appoint Vaqar Khan, the thanedar of Bahadurpur, against whom a strong protest results.[51] Vazid Khan, faujdar of Narnaul sarkar, and Izzat Khan, the imperial commandant, are sent as faujdars to repress the Meo rebels. Gobind Chand expresses his desire for the faujdari of Mewat and the lease of the police posts of Alwar.[52] Local functionaries repeatedly ask the Jaipur ruler for military assistance to suppress the Mewatis. Mohammad Chain asks for an additional force of one thousand horsemen. Military support is requested for Rewari since force is the only way of suppressing the *"fasād mewān."*[53]

Rebellion and peasant resistance are closely related. After 1707 it becomes increasingly difficult to collect revenue.[54] There are reports that the faujdar of Narnaul "is oppressing the people very much in the collection of revenue."[55] In addition to the normal revenue demand, peshkash, or tribute, is also collected. Nusrat Yar Khan, faujdar of Nagaur, is to proceed to Mewat with fourteen to seventeen men to do *vasūlī*, not collect but extract revenue.[56] Rao Banai Singh requests the maharaja to "send a force of 4–5000 to put down the disturbance created by the Mewas and to help in the collection of peshkash and other dues."[57] Maharaja Jai Singh is petitioned to send a force to settle the matter peacefully.

Throughout Mewat, the peasantry and village leaders including patels, patwaris, and chaudharis protest the stringent collection of revenue and other dues. The patels of Khohri and Maujpur report to the emperor in Delhi that an unjustified peshkash of Rs. 17,300 has been imposed upon them.[58] Villagers from the parganas of Khohri, Khilohra, Baroda-Meo, and Rewari visit Delhi to petition the emperor against the oppression of the jagirdars, ijaradars and their agents, and other regional state officials.[59] The peasants of Khohri go to Amber to protest against the *virād* levy, under which head a variety of taxes are being collected.[60]

Although the peasantry appeals to the emperor, the imperial regime is also complicit in the violence. Frequent expeditions are made by the imperial faujdar against the Meos.[61] Strong protests are lodged against faujdar Rahimulla Khan, who was sent to "protect" them but has joined the Jat leader, Churaman, in the "*lūṭ mār*" and has divided the loot. Churaman Jat is reported to have conspired with the faujdar of Mathura to plunder Atrauli, Mathura, and Kaman.[62] There are complaints that the faujdar Abdul Rahim Khan's brother, Bazid, has forged an alliance with the Jats and established his own thanas. Alliances between Jats and Mughal officials in the context of a weakened Mughal Empire enhanced the onslaught against the peasantry.

From mid-1650 onward the Rajputs are a major target of complaint. Patels and peasants accuse them of being plunderers and oppressors of the villages.[63] The Naruka Rajputs are held responsible for the upheaval in Maujpur, Jalalpur, Bharkol, and other parganas.[64] The behavior of the mutsaddis is also regarded as arbitrary and cruel by the peasantry. At Bahadurpur, along with the faujdars, they are regarded as the most troublesome officials. In Amber peasants are forced to leave their villages.[65]

Thus a dual burden was imposed on the people involving both high revenue rates and the tyranny of the local officials. The continuous petitioning of the Amber and Mughal rulers suggests a popular perception that a redress of grievances was possible. Nonetheless, the power structure that emerges from these documents seems distant and alien from the people. Mewat was under a regional state but that system itself was perceived as part of the larger imperial one. Indeed, the practice of giving land grants in lieu of salary by both the Mughal and Rajput State intensified the burden on the peasantry. Peasants frequently protested when they perceived that a moral economy of a peasant society was violated; they resorted to nonpayment of their revenue dues and either fled or threatened to flee their village. But the conflict was a losing one for the Meos. Mohammad Daulat, the son of Wazid Khan, described his conflict with Sewa and Hira Meo, the Meo leaders. His six thousand sawars confronted the sixty sawars of the Meos. They were chased and defeated, their leaders killed, and much treasure *(bahaut sā māl)* appropriated.[66]

The metonymy of the three kinds of texts, historiographical, administrative, and oral, therefore, needs to be underlined. In all three cases the outcome is the same, tragic from the Meo point of view. Both the historiographical and the administrative record raise certain questions. Who are the looters? Who are the victims — the Meo peasantry or the state?

Pāñch Pahāṛ kī laṛāī: An Anti-Imperial Narrative

The area the Meos call the Panch Pahar (Five Hills) is located in Kaman in northern Bharatpur. Parallel chains of the Aravalli hills that run north and south enclose an alluvial and fertile valley with exceptionally good grazing lands. The light, sandy soil is inundated by hillside drainage and streams. This is the area of Pahatvad that sustained the Pahat clan of Meos said to have been spread over 210 villages. The village of Ajangarh is the *derā* (headquarters) of their clan, or *pallakṛā,* meaning half a pal. Pahatvad is part of a larger terrain of Brajbhumi associated with Krishnite mythology.

The spatial and temporal contextualization establish the *Pāñch Pahāṛ* as a historical narrative. "In the *darbār* of Shah Jahan thirty-six chairs used to be occupied. Shah Jahan Badshah was the ruler." The Mirasi performer Dina Rai's opening statement uses the past tense unlike most of the narrative. The narrative is about "those days." Dina Rai says, in the concluding *bhog kā dohā,* that the *qissā* of Pahatvad (the region of the Pahat Meo Pal) is at an end, the Alakh well *sākā* (story) complete *(sāko pāñch pahāṛ ko kath kai gāvai dāṛhī bāj).* Saka refers to an unwinnable, almost sacrificial, bloody battle of honor in which soldiers fight till they die. The genre is identified as that of a qissa (historical narrative) rather than that of the fictional *kahānī*. The well where women worship and the men are martyred is named after Shah Alakh, the darvesh who, pleased by the Jadon Rajput raja Bandhpal's *khidmat*, or service, helped him establish the settlement of Ajangarh, near Kaman. The Jadon Rajputs had fled after Shahab al-Din Ghuri vanquished them at Bayana in the twelfth century.

In this and the subsequent chapters the narrative is indented to distinguish the narrator's account from my own voice. The following excerpt from Dina Rai's performance indicates how the framing of the *Pāñch Pahāṛ* establishes its claim as an articulation of Meo collective memory.

> In the darbar of Delhi thirty-six clans *[kuṇbā]* of Rajputs used to be seated. Shaikh, Saiyyad, Mughal, and Pathan also sat. Shah Jahan was the ruler of Hindustan at the darbar of Delhi. His horses, loaded with gold, were passing by Ajangarh. The Pahat Meos learnt of this. In those days in the Pahat Meo Pal of 210 villages there were many brave warriors who used to challenge kings, all twenty-four hours. This was their duty. There was Masand of Godolia, Rai Bhan of Ajangarh, Badal Kalaliya, and Mavasi. They were all chiefs *[sardārs]* of their *kabīlās* [clans/tribes], of their pals.
>
> *masand mavāsī rāi bhān rūṛā tū sun le*
> *uñṭ to jāṇy akbarābād kūñ tam sūñ liyā jāṇy to le*
>
> *Masand, Mavasi, Rai Bhan,*
> *Rura listen to this, "The camels go to Akbarabad,*[67]
> *take them if you can."*
> *"The Badshah's camels are going.*
> *It is your duty to loot them."*
>
> The Pahats confront the army, kill all the soldiers, and loot all the camels. Only one wounded soldier remains alive. He crawls out from under the corpses and complains at the Delhi darbar, "A disaster has befallen us." "All your treasure *[māl]* that was coming has been looted. All your men have been killed."
>
> *(badsāh) mev mugal bheḷā huā rāṛ mañḍhī bhallī*
> *adlī kā darbār maiṇ ṭopī paṭkī rajab alī*

(badsāh) vāne terā chatar batar sab bas kara dakhaṇ joṛi rāṛ
mev anītī karat haiṇ māne nāy pāñch pāhāṛ

Badshah, Meos and Mughals
collected and fought fiercely.
In the court illumined by Adli[68]
Rajb Ali threw down his cap.[69]
Badshah, they have captured our force
starting a great battle in the south.[70]
The Meos are unrighteous
the Panch Pahar refuse to heed.

Images of conflict between the Mughal-Rajputs, on the one side, and the Meos, on the other, pervade the narrative. "The Pahat clan and their chiefs confront Badshahs" *(badsāhon se ṭakkar lete haiṇ)*, states Dina. The Mughal army *(fauj)* is defied by the chief's warrior-peasant force. The terms *bheḷā, sāmanā, rāṛ, raṇ,* and *jaṇg* allude to the Meo-Mughal relationship as one of confrontation, conflict, and battle. The Meo clan challenges the order of the empire, the Badshah, and his darbar.

For the Pahat Meos, the looting of the Mughal camels is not a simple criminal act but the defiance of a group that claims a symmetry of power and status. The safe and peaceful passage of treasure, army, and animals symbolizes imperial authority. The destruction of the accompanying Mughal army and the appropriation of the Mughal camels and treasure has serious implications, for "among commoner and patriarch, the tiger Rai Bhan has caused an uproar."

The authority of the empire is at stake. The emperor throws the challenge to the entire darbar: "Is there anyone who will go to Ajangarh and bring the treasure back?" The Rajput thakur accepts the challenge. For the rest of the story the emperor remains a shadowy figure in the background, and the Chauhan Rajputs represent the imperial system in the region.

The elements of the construction of the Meos in Persian accounts are replicated early in the myth: "the Meos are unrighteous and do not listen," that is, are not deferential to state authority, and indulge in lut mar (looting and killing). The categories that define the Meo in historiographical and administrative works such as fasad and mufsidan are reformulated in the Mewati text as *anītī* (unrighteousness). Resistance is foregrounded in the countering of the otherness of the other. The apparent contrast to the Meos, characterized by aniti, is the *Adlipat* Badshah. He is the giver of *'adl,* or justice, an idea central to the Persian theory of kingship, and foundational for Mughal ideology. Adlipat represents the symbolic construction of the ruler as upholder of order and justice in contrast to the forces of aniti that violate it. The binary categories established by Minhaj and Barani, of order and fasad, of city and forest, sultanate and Mewat, penetrate the Mewati "vernacular," which translates them. The asymmetric categories adlipat-aniti embody the Mughal self-image as also the otherness of the Mewati in the Persian knowledge system.

The narrative movement is from the Mughal statement of Meo aniti to a Meo statement on Mughal *julam* (from the Persian zulm meaning tyranny or oppression). What results is an image of the powerful Mughal-Rajput alliance as the hinge of the imperial system. The Rajput Sammat Singh of the Chauhan clan has four *rājāī,* or principalities, with a force of twelve thousand men each. Over a period all four Rajput jagirdars, Ahlad Singh, Dharam Singh, Hamir Singh, and Pauhap Singh move into the area with their respective armies. Ahlad Singh takes up the challenge to suppress the Meos and recover the treasure and imperial revenue. His actions in the region are oriented to conquest and control *(bas karnā, kābū maiṇ lānā, fateh karnā).* He threatens the Meo chief, "O Rai Bhan, on your head I'll make a fortress" *(tere sir par gaṛhī basāī).*

The Mughal-Rajput attempt at domination is to depoliticize the Meos and peasantize them, that is, reduce them to mere landholders. Ahlad Singh writes a succession of letters of "brotherly feeling" cajoling the Meo chief, "plow the fields, sow your crops Rai Bhan, but return the horses to us" *(haḷ joto khetī karo rāibhān ye ūñṭ haman kūñ de)*; "return to us the treasure you have looted and look after your fields" instead. Ahlad Singh offers Rai Bhan a friendly meeting with the Badshah and a position in the Mughal system. When the offers are angrily rejected, Masand is tempted by the offer of the tract of Braj in jagir. Such bargaining was a common practice in contemporary politics, suggesting how the fulfillment of desire for land and power was a mode of incorporation. The Meo leader responds to Ahlad Singh's inducements by reprimanding the Rajput for the attempt to create *phoṛ* and *phūṭ,* or dissension among the Meo brothers, which was probably an ever-present possibility and actuality given the extensive evidence of intra-Meo feuds and the inducements of darbar politics.[71]

Now that the Mughal claim has been countered, a narrative shift takes place. The remaining part of the narrative is an inversion that demonstrates Mughal-Rajput otherness from the Meo perspective. A powerful image of the Mughal regime is constructed in the episode on revenue collection to show its extraction and exploitation. In the Alwar-Bharatpur area the crops of *khāklā* and *sīngal* have failed, indicating a fodder and food famine.[72] Despite this the revenue is collected and taken to Delhi. Its collection is backed by the politico-military might of the state. Dharam Singh, Ahlad Singh's wife's brother, arrives with his force of twelve thousand. The Meo Kutba chaudhari takes the revenue to the fortress where Dharam Singh is camped. The eighty- to eighty-four-year-old man quirks his moustache up and then down in contempt of the Rajput's behavior. He is beheaded and Dharam Singh appropriates the collection. We have here a sense of the despised Mughal revenue official. The chaudhari's son, Hari Singh, vows not to touch water or grain till his father's death has been avenged by beheading Dharam Singh. For seven days he takes to his bed, not eating or drinking. His limbs become numb; his body turns yellow.

The soldiers of the imperial army trouble the Meo women. Hari Singh's wife complains to her nephew, Badal Kalaliya, "our well has been surrounded" *(merī paṇghaṭ rākhā gher)*. "My entire clan is dying of thirst," she laments. A note on the mode of Mughal revenue collection is deliberately interposed by the narrator in first person, "Tax collectors come to the villages and tease the Meo women by throwing stones at their water pitchers which shatter, drenching them completely." The narrator's comment here is, "the Mughals have been reduced to this."

The images of mutual violence are vivid. To avenge the killing of Kutba chaudhari, the Meo Badal Kalaliya kills the Rajput Dharam Singh. His severed head is sent to Ahlad Singh with a threatening letter from Rai Bhan: "if I do not erase your place of worship *(chāvanḍ)*, my name is not Rai Bhan." Ahlad Singh is equally prepared to retaliate. Rai Bhan, in turn, vows to fight with a might sixty-four times stronger *(kahai lāl pāhaṭ merī suṇo nā ahlād tosūñ chaunsaṭha chauguṇo jaṇg joṛūñgo)*.

Another force of *bārah hajjār*, or twelve thousand, is mobilized to retrieve the imperial treasure. Later Raja Ahlad Singh's rani brings as reinforcement the army of her son, Kanvar Hamir Singh. The description of the Mughal-Rajput battle with the Meos is bloody for "corpse falls on corpse, swords clash and blood streams like a river."

jvān jvān sūñ bhiṛ rahā jodhā ariyan de de mūñḍ
(bhaī) dhūmlot aise paṛāñ jaise koī gaj hastī kī sūñḍ

Young men attack young men
warriors penetrate their army.
Limbs circle and fall[73]
strewn like severed trunks of the elephant.

The Meos are slaughtered and so is the Mughal-Rajput force. Badal Kalaliya slays the force of twelve thousand. Hamir Singh is killed and his wife commits *satī* (self-immolation).

The Meo myth has thus far described the martial superiority of the Meos. But how is the actual historical subordination of the Meos to be accounted for? This is done by showing a turn of events that culminates in the defeat of the Pahat clan. The eventual defeat of the Meos is explained not by any intrinsic weakness of the Meos, such as inferior technology or absence of a unified state. It is instead attributed to a Meo woman's *haṭ* (obstinacy). Rai Bhan's older daughter-in-law taunts the younger one, Lali, to whom a son has been born, saying that there will be no celebration of the birth of the child. The motif suggests the kinship rivalry between the daughters-in-law of the household. But Lali is the "crazy woman" *(tiriyā bāvḷī)*, who insists on the worship of the well for her newborn child. Mark the contrast between the Rajput Ahlad Singh's wife who restrains him from hasty action and Lali, the Meo Jodh Singh's wife, who spurs the Meos to action that is heroic albeit self-destructive.

The climax of the conflict is the Rajput prevention of the Meo women's rite of worship. According to Meo practice, on the sixth day of childbirth the rite of *chaṭhī* (literally, sixth day) is performed. This life cycle ritual is one of the nonsanskritic, indigenous rites practiced by most castes in the region. For the Pahat Meos of the Panch Pahar, the rite was performed in Ajangarh at the sacred site of the well of Alakh Pir. Most Meo life cycle rites involve celebration, the playing of the dhol, and singing by women. Lali refuses to eat, drink, feed, or hold the baby till the rite of the sixth day is complete. And "only when the drum beats and the women sing," she asserts, "will the [rite of the] worship of the well be complete." Lali knows that Ahlad Singh has besieged them and has allowed Pahat women access to the well but explicitly forbidden the playing of the dhol. But she asks rhetorically, what is the use of worshiping at the well till the drum does not resound?

The Mirasan or woman ritual specialist and singer is called, the drum placed around her neck, and she is told to conduct the Pahat Meo women's worship at the well. The drum begins to beat, and all the women proceed to the well signifying the assertion of their right to perform their traditional modes of worship. Ahlad Singh recognizes the defiance and orders "kill or die, but do not let the well be worshipped" *(marto marai kaṭto kaṭai kuāñ nahīṇ pūjne denā chāhiye)*. The Meo men now intervene to support the women and are once again embroiled in battle with the Mughal-Rajputs.

The folk tradition mythologizes Meo heroism. Baj Khan, the younger son of Rai Bhan, descends "like a vulture" with his three-and-a-half-foot-long sword upon the force of twelve thousand. He slays many men but is killed by Ahlad Singh. Badal Kalaliya kills many Mughals and Rajputs. His *bhābhī* (older brother's wife) celebrates his valor: "your courage will always be remembered, the day the battle [with the Badshah] was fought at Ghatla" *(jā dinā raṛ maṇḍhī hai ghāṭḷai lāliyā tū hī yād karo)*. She refers to the earlier battle fought over revenue collection. The Badshah's force is severely depleted but he has another reserve of twelve hundred men armed with maces. The Pahat Meos are eventually defeated and only five men survive.

The *Pāñch Pahāṛ* can be seen as an allegorical and explicitly political narrative. The confrontation between the Meos and the Mughals underlies the episodic structure as the Meos consistently repudiate their subordination to the regime. Since the narrative is an embodiment of power relations, it is important to look at the insignia of power, that is, its signs and symbols. The territory and military system of the Mughal Empire are symbolized by the "baīs sūbā" (twenty subas or provinces) and "bārah hajjār" (the force of twelve thousand). Its institutional and symbolic apparatus are referred to in Shah Jahan's title, "Adlipat Badshah," and his darbar that seats the Muslim *ashraf*, or aristocracy, of Shaikh, Saiyyad, Mughal, Pathan, and the Rajputs. The narrative also refers to the prebendal system on which the empire was based of land grants in return for military service; a decentered army led by the jagirdars; a system of justice, reward, and punishment; a network of imperial revenue officials and messengers; imperial treasure and animal transport; and a monetary system. The ritual aspects of sovereignty are emphasized, say in the transaction of the giving of betel leaf by the ruler to darbaris. Its acceptance expressed the latter's willingness to accept his superiority and to undertake a task for the expansion of the state.

The elements of Rajput identity are defined in the narrative. They are the military nobility who provide the Mughal army that extends the Mughal frontier. As warriors they are involved in fighting and killing, and they worship Sakti, the mother goddess who guarantees their power.[74] As jagirdars they are the owners of jagir and "rajai," or principalities, and governed by a

FIGURE 3

Meo villagers at the well of the twelfth-century saint Pir Alakh. Called Alakhniranjan by the Nath Yogis it is said to contain fragments of bangles worn by Meo women who committed sati following the prolonged siege and eventual defeat of the Pahat Meo chiefs by the Mughal-Rajput army in the seventeenth century.

FIGURE 4
Ruins of the settlement at Ajangarh.

FIGURE 5
Meos of the Pahat clan.

code of honor *(rajpūtī kī lāj)*. Their weapons, drums, and horses signal their status. Women are the public demonstration of that code/status: confined to the *ḍolā* (palanquin) when they are taken out in public and called upon to perform sati after defeat in a battle.

Architectural signs of control, particularly the building of police posts, forts, and fortresses, mark local space. Dharam Singh camps at a fortress; Ahlad Singh occupies Dalmod's fortress and is in the process of building another at Ghatla. He further threatens Rai Bhan, "O Rai Bhan, on your head I'll make a fortress." The practices of Rajput power are evocatively produced in the following verse:

terā gaṛh kūñ auṇdho mār dūñ meṭūñ nām nishān
terī banī kāṭ ke phūñk dūñ jab pakṛūñgo rāi bhan

I will turn your fort upside down
destroy it, leaving no sign.
I will cut and burn your forest
when I catch you Rai Bhan.

The assertion of power extends to both land and natural resources such as forests and sources of water like the village well.

Challenging the kingly order is the Pahat Meo Pal. The Pahat self-image is constituted by terms such as "*bahādur*" (courageous), "*sūrmā*" (brave) and "*jodhā*" (warrior). It merges with the image of the Meo group as a whole, whom the Rajput thakur's wife refers to as a "*tagṛī kaum*" (strong race/people/group). The Pahat Meo are described as a kingdom *(rāj)*, and Ahlad Singh and Rai Bhan address each other as "raja."

The Meo claims to "chatri," or ksatriya status, and the performance of sati by a Meo woman contest established hierarchy and the exclusive Rajput claim to status and power. The Meo chief responds to the Rajput claims by insisting upon his own attributes of rulership such as a fort, a fighting force of armed peasants, territoriality (as the clan is spread over two hundred and ten villages), and bards who transform conflicts into commemorative events and must be generously gifted by their patrons. Political alliances are forged through kinship networks: for instance, the Pahat are related to the Pundlot Pal, and the Meo chief's daughter-in-law comes from the Saugan got. The alliance network and hypergamous marriages that have been associated with the Rajputs were characteristic of several castes. The counterinsignia claimed by the Pahat Meos include a throne and furnishings in the darbar; a *kachahirī* (the court and surroundings where complaints and conflicts are attended to and justice administered), and a *koṣa* (treasury), which is one of the attributes of statehood in traditional Indian political theory outlined in the *Arthaśastra*. Power is also symbolized by musical instruments such as the dhol, the *kunj*, and *rīṛ*, the latter two being elongated wind instruments and the chief's nishan or flag; it is proclaimed by bard-panegyrist-historians.

The chief's own personal attribute is that of *pratāp*, or light and fervor, that radiates from authority. Besides "nobles" he has guards, horses, and elephants, the animals signifying royal power.[75] The sovereignty of the Mughal Empire is acknowledged by the Meos, but only under compulsion. It exists in uneasy tension with their own regional autonomy. The persistent claim to the coeval status of Meo chiefs and other Mughal and Rajput kings underlies the narrative.

The *Pāñch Pahāṛ* is quite obviously a thoroughgoing indictment of the "dominant" system, which is that of the centralizing empire. It builds an explicit contrast between two types of political systems and their ideologies. The imperial system's marked ability for negotiation is suggested in the Mughal alliance with the Rajputs who mediate the imperial and local levels. It is an extractive system, as indicated by the treasure going to the capital that could either be the booty of conquest or the collection of the imperial revenue system. In either case it involves an appropriation of local sources of wealth or revenue and the intrusion of a state apparatus to enforce revenue collection. In the Meo view, the system is based primarily on military power and violence, symbolized by the recurrent images of the force of twelve thousand, the vicious Mughal-Rajput soldier, a dishonorable attitude toward women and peasants, and the disruption of women's ritual worlds.

The narrative suggests the emergent practices of power of the regional Rajput State. These had been reinforced by their rank and service in the Mughal Empire. The Meos were denied the right to keep horses. Those who possessed horses were required to surrender them immediately.[76] This was to prevent the dispersed use that was being made of horsemen in confrontations with state officials. A similar assertion of sovereignty was the monopoly over the drum. The right to play the dhol refers to its symbolic association with power and local authority in a large area of western India.[77] The oral narrative, commenting on the seventeenth century, demonstrates the conflict and tension of a group intent upon maintaining its relative autonomy against the imperial and regional power.

Contrasted with the imperial system is the Meo pal, which is the territorial unit of the relatively autonomous self-governing community. Its legitimacy is derived from custom and consent, and it is characterized by close ties of kinship and direct, face-to-face relations. Its ideology is that of patrilineal rule where the elder male succeeds to the authority of the father. Hierarchies of status and gender exist within the local system, and there is strong gender-based differentiation that is given a cultural legitimation. The two systems are juxtaposed as competing models.

At the core of the narrative is an inversion of the dominant categories fasad/mufsidan/aniti that emanate from the Persian knowledge system and the corresponding power relations. These can be juxtaposed by three categories that resonate through the Mewati text, of jang, julam, and jama. The Meo-Mughal relation is one of jang, or war. To loot, retaliate, and attack the Mughal army is a wholly legitimate exercise. The term "fasad" used in the Persian texts is, hence, inappropriate in a struggle for power where subordination itself is challenged. There is irony in the adlipat-aniti formulation and the conception of the Badshah as "Adlipat" or "giver of justice" since it is Shah Jahan who places the naked sword in his court symbolizing the urge to conquer, control, and dominate. For the Pahat Meos it also means death and destruction. The forced collection of jama called vasuli is the symbol of the extractive Mughal State, the illegitimate claim of a disputed sovereign. The moral economy of famine and subsistence is overlooked in the coercive collection of revenue that resorts to wilful slaughter. The Rajputs not only besiege Meo villages but also interfere with the everyday life of women, including their tasks of collecting water for the households and their modes of worship and celebration. The narrative counters the Mughal self-image of providing peace, order, and justice, and instead shows how it makes inroads into the local polity's territoriality and autonomy; appropriates local surplus; and subjects Meo women and elders to oppression. "Julam" sums up the narrator's description of the Mughal-Rajput system in contrast to the legitimacy of the local polity. The paradox that underlies the narrative is in the figure of the Badshah. His legitimacy is derived from the ideal of the king as the provider of justice, but he is ultimately responsible for injustice, violence, and dishonor.

An antagonistic posture vis-à-vis imperial domination is, therefore, necessary in terms of the local community's survival. The raiyat subject must retaliate against the Mughal-Rajput jagirdar-soldier. Within the Meo code it is the duty of the leaders to respond with aniti and lut and to defend the pal to the extent of self-annihilation. The narrative is tragic even as it is subversive.

Meo individual memory is deeply permeated by this myth. In the popular consciousness of the Meos of Ajangarh, the battle of Panch Pahar is considered to have actually taken place. Many persons told me about the fragments of broken bangles that still lie scattered at the bottom of the Alakh well. "All the Pahat women," I was told, "committed sati after the men were slain by the Mughals." I was taken to the hill overlooking the village nestling in the valley to be shown the ruins of the Pahat fortress of Rai Bhan. The lonely ruins and the well of Alakh Pir inscribe space with the memory of the annihilation of the entire clan by the Mughal Empire.

Time also inscribes a more polysemic memory for the Meos. The evidence of Meo collaboration with the Mughals and Rajputs is suggested by some accounts. *Dariyā Khāñ* mentions the participation of Meo chiefs like Todar Mal at Akbar's darbar. Both Todar Mal and the Mina chief Rao Bada are said to have contributed their respective forces and worked together to suppress the revolt of the Dholpur ruler against Akbar and eventually destroy his kingdom. According to Meo accounts, it was Akbar who began the appointment of Meo chaudharis, tied the *chaudharī kī pāg* (turban), and tried to co-opt them *(chumkārā)*. Kakurana Meo, who was a spy for the Mughals, was rewarded with the fort of Dhavan near Mehrauli for "breaking" the Meo. Up to then they had been divided into the Jadus and the Tonvars. Kakurana subdivided them into pals and gotras. The power of the Meo pals was broken *(tākat nā rahī jo pahle kī)*.[78] Irrespective of the facticity of this event, the identification of the Mughals and their agency with the breaking of their collective strength is significant.

I have long been self-conscious about not presenting an ahistorical view of the Mughal Empire. Possibly, the Meos had a different view of Akbar, who is eulogized by historians as "the great" Mughal, that might be a departure from their castigation of Shah Jahan and Aurangzeb. After all, even the brahman Gosvamis of Vrindavan conceded that Akbar was a brahman in his previous life and was reborn as a Muslim when he had accidentally drunk a cow's hair in a glass of milk! Contrary to my expectation, I found Mewati space inscribed with memory of Akbar's destruction of a village, abduction of a Meo woman, and the slaughter of an entire clan of the Malak Khanazadas. The Mewati *Dādā Bāhar kā qissā* describes Akbar's appropriation of a Meo woman and her later rescue by a Meo hero from a fort. The animosity with the Mughals inscribes geography and clan/family histories. The following comment and recitation by a Meo suggests their otherness: "Mughals were *gair mulkī* [foreigners], and the Meos did *baghāvat* [rebelled] against their collection of revenue. They took a Daimrot girl from Bisru called Rajni."[79]

charḥī bādsāh kī fauj bhondar ā tharrāī
mugal huā asvār bisrū jākar chāī
ḍaimrot kī pāl maiṇ dukhī huā nar nār
rajnī phāns gaī jhāṛ maiṇ yāpai lego uṭhār

The Badshah's force advances
halts at Bhondar.
The Mughal riders
shadow over Bisru.
The men and women of the Daimrot Pal
are full of sorrow.
Rajni is caught in the bushes
she is taken away.

Categories such as the "Mughal" and *rāñghṛā* referring to the tyrannical Rajput totalize the world of medieval Mewati subjecthood, as well as of Mughal-Rajput domination. The men and women of the Daimrot Pal collectively perceive the *dukh* wrought by the state.

How does the Mewati material comment on the historiographical debate on the Mughal Empire? The extent of centralization under the Mughals has been fiercely debated. Eisenstadt argues that the Mughal Empire falls within the category of the centralized bureaucratic empires positioned in between patrimonial societies, feudal societies and city-states, on the one hand, and modern societies, on the other.[80] The Aligarh "school" of Mughal historians has, by and large, taken the position that the empire represented a strong and centralized state that appropriated a large quantum of agrarian surplus through the land tax.[81] A group of scholars who have been termed "revisionist" maintain a different position. Blake questions Eisenstadt and Wittfogel's arguments regarding the presence of a powerful centralized bureaucracy and cautions against conceiving of the Mughal Empire in the image of the colonial state. He argues that it represents a patrimonial-bureaucratic empire on the Weberian model, rather than a case of bureaucratic despotism. Blake views the empire as dominated by the patrimonial household and as an extended patriarchal system. Rudolph and Rudolph point out that the imperial system was quite different from the absolute state that emerged in Europe in the fifteenth century, as there was a large degree of decentralization within the Mughal Empire. Heesterman argues that the roads and market towns provided the basic framework of the empire. Streusand likewise asserts that the Mughal regime in the provinces "did not reach the individual peasant, or even many villages. It consisted of a series of relationships between Mughal officials and the zamindars."[82] More recently Alam and Subrahmanyam have challenged approaches to the Mughal State that view it as unitary, centralized, and all powerful, on the one hand, and as segmentary, on the other. Alam and Subrahmanyam recommend a "patchwork quilt" model, rather than the dominant "wall-to-wall carpet" approach, which will bring out its regional and local diversity and that will not reduce a complex political system to its agrarian fiscal aspects.[83]

Alam and Subrahmanyam's point about the differentiated character of Mughal rule is well taken, particularly that its control was weak outside the "regulation" territories that included the provinces of Allahabad, Awadh, Agra, Delhi, Lahore, and Multan. Nonetheless, the Mughal Empire was based on a hegemonizing principle. Richards remarks that the Mughal empire was one of the largest centralized states known in premodern world history.[84] Ludden points out that the Mughals built South Asia's first empire of agrarian taxation.[85] As a conquest state, its central concern was the extraction of an agrarian surplus to pay for the mansabdars and troopers.[86] Streusand refers to the four elements responsible for the Mughal "transformation": the increasing centralization of power, the growing acceptance of Akbar's position as imperial sovereign and of the Mughal constitution, the change in the sovereign cult of the empire, and the development of the mansabdari system and the class of mansabdars. Like Iqtidar Alam Khan, Streusand suggests a shift from a Mongol "tribal" political theory to a Turkish absolutism. Both point out that the Ottoman, Safavid, and Mughal dynasties displaced the collective sovereignty of the Timurids.[87]

The folk text supported by a mass of documents decries the assertion that imperial rule did not affect the peasant-pastoralist or that its influence was restricted merely to towns and roads. The perception of power at the local level suggests a well-organized administrative apparatus. Not only was there a fiscal regime in place that enforced revenue collection but there was also a constant transmission of information about dissenting sources that enabled swift state action. In popular consciousness there was no absolute distinction between the imperial state and regional state, as they reinforced each other. Even as the story dwells on the coercive aspects of the Mughal State, it goes beyond a binary formulation, suggesting the complex relations between the imperial and local levels. The Mewati narrative enables us also to go beyond the dominant fiscal orientation of the Aligarh historians and identify the nonmaterial aspects of power, which were an important aspect of both imperial and regional state formation.

Part of the controversy regarding centralization has arisen because the criterion of evaluation has been either an ideal type oriental despotism or the colonial and modern state. In fact, the standard has to be provided by the preceding state, in this case, the sultanate. The Mughals built on the sultanate and Afghan polities but went far beyond the attempts of the Khiljis and Afghans at administrative systematization. Athar Ali emphasizes the importance of the creation of a composite nobility as one of the major structural changes that the Mughal rulers brought about.[88] Once the Mughal Empire was established, state formation centered on the problem of subordinating numerous segments at various levels — provincial, regional, and local. The attempt to impose a uniform administrative structure, land control, a single official language, and the concentration of power in the office of the governor were unprecedented. The relatively plural or "anarchic" character of the subcontinent was under pressure. The tension between competing sovereignties was a constant dialectic of the Mughal period even in the early sixteenth century, long before its "decline." Nonetheless, the Mughal Empire did not seek to intrude into the customary practices of most communities. The onslaught on systems of education, law, and knowledge would begin with colonial rule.

6 The Construction of Meo Criminality: Toward a Critique of Colonial Ethnography

Sovereignty unfolds its attributes in the construction of criminality. Problems of governance have led many states in history to classify particular groups as criminal. In the case of the colonial regime in India, however, ideas of "criminality," "tribe," and "caste" were overwritten by science. They were represented as empirical and objective accounts of Indian society. But the manner in which crime was viewed was closely connected with British views on Indian society as a whole. Crime was associated with groups rather than individuals. Colonial notions acquired their theoretical legitimacy from the evolutionary theory of society and the ethnological classification of the human species into racial types dominant in the nineteenth century.

This chapter explores colonial discourse and the way in which British notions of criminality were extended to encompass the Meo population. Meo indictment was sealed because of their regional contiguity with what had been deemed to be the "criminal tribe" of Minas and the reasoning that contagion would inevitably result from the Meo-Mina association. In addition, the Meo oral tradition was itself held indexical of their criminality. The narrative of *Dariyā Khāñ* was considered "proof" that they intermarried with the Minas. Since they shared the substance of blood with the Minas it was believed that a common criminal essence imbued them both.

On Criminality

Around the late nineteenth century, when the first ethnographic works on the Meos were written, criminality had become a major preoccupation of British administration. The problem of brigandage, which existed all over India in the first quarter of the century, led to setting up the Thagi Department under F. C. Smith and his assistant Captain W. H Sleeman (later major general) in 1829. This department was virtually defunct by 1863 but was actively maintained by the Government of India for the princely states. The Thagi and Dakaiti Department later developed into the Criminal Investigation Department (CID) as the nationalist movement gathered strength but the Special Branch lingered on.[1]

In 1869 the Habitual Criminals Act was passed in England. This legislation assumed an internal differentiation within the working class in that the labor aristocracy was seen as distinct from the habitual offenders of the working class. Transported to India, however, criminality was conflated with the categories of caste and tribe. Criminality became a threefold notion implying that it was dangerous, pervasive, and irreversible.[2] A major epistemological departure from Victorian England took place, since crime was seen as the hereditary predisposition and occupation of entire groups. Because it was dangerous, state activity was to be oriented to its containment and control.

In 1871 the Criminal Tribes Act was passed, which imposed the idea of the "containment" of criminal groups in enclosures. An entire administrative strategy was worked out that set up police posts, which maintained registers of members of the group. They were kept under surveillance and subject to roll call and a ticket-of-leave system. Attempts were made to "reform" the erstwhile criminals by appointing them village watchmen and members of militia, and by introducing education for their "uplift." The stress on regulatory control and resettlement of the act invoked a metaphor of quarantine. It was amended in 1897 and 1911. Simultaneously the legislative and administrative undertaking was supported by a knowledge enterprise that worked out the sources of criminality in terms of hereditary impulses.

During the 1870s bandit gangs were perceived as criminal "tribes." Administrative activity involved the listing of "criminal" groups. In the North West Provinces, the Aherias, Bahalias, Banjaras, Sansis, Jogiahs, Nuts, Bowrias, Sonoriahs, and others were described as "dangerous classes." A draft bill for their control and surveillance was proposed. In the Central Provinces, groups such as the Bauriahs, Sanorias, Harbwahs, and Maghiya Doms had been identified as criminal by the Criminal Tribes Act of 1871. In western India the Bhils, Kolis, Kanjars, and Minas were increasingly regarded as criminal. Other communities were similarly classified in Nagpur and Oudh, Bihar and Bengal, in Hyderabad and the Madras Presidency.[3]

The activity affected several million people in British India and the areas of indirect rule. The kingdoms of Rajputana followed the legislative example of the government of India with respect to the Criminal Tribes.[4] By virtue of certain members who were "criminal" or insurgent the entire caste or tribe was treated as "criminal." They were seen as "dangerous classes" comprising "born and habitual offenders" and as "morally depraved" and "vicious."[5] This concern with criminality constituted the frame for the colonial ethnographic discourse on the Meos.

Criminality thus became a particularly powerful motif in terms of which a group's identity could be seen, its essence characterized, and the group's past, present, and future understood. The disorderly groups also reinforced the evangelizing role of the British vis-à-vis Indian civil society. The thesis of criminalization legitimated the colonial state's intervention, which now increasingly used reestablishment of law and order and control of the subject population as a pretext to make inroads into domains hitherto regulated by civil society. Meo "otherness" that characterized ethnographic writing on the Meos was established with the help of stigmatized categories such as "criminality."

The remnants of intellectual practice remain in postcolonial India. The "ex-criminal tribes" still continue to figure in state action and in the media. Cases of thievery, dacoity, and murder are often attributed to "former criminal tribes" such as the Bawarias, Sansis, Kanjars, and others, rather than seen as the activity of gangs. Members of these formerly criminal tribes are among the first to be arrested by the police. In an episode of violence in September 1994 by the landed Jats in Sinsini (Bharatpur) against the Bawarias, it was easy to transform the Jat attempt at appropriating land into retaliatory action against the petty thievery of the erstwhile criminal tribe. In Jaipur even Kanjars (who are settled, possess land, and have varied livelihoods) are often mistaken by the police for "vagrants" and arrested. The former "criminal tribes" have sometimes protested their exclusion from citizenship. Nomadic groups like the Guhadia Lohars and Kanjars are still unable to exercise their political rights. Decriminalization still has a long way to go.

On Colonial Ethnography

Colonial governmentality led to a phenomenal knowledge-building exercise in the nineteenth century. This resulted in numerous surveys, censuses, ethnographies, gazetteer, settlement, and other reports, and culminated in the *Imperial Gazetteer of India*.[6] Reasons of state were apparent in these works. The division of groups into those who were pliable and those who were resistant became the epistemological basis for the classification as "criminal" of whole groups. Much of the ethnographic writing on the Meos was a part of this elaborate taxonomic classification of Indian castes and tribes.[7]

The influence of literary criticism has demonstrated how ethnography as the recording or writing of cultures constructs and, in a sense, transforms them.[8] The work of Asad, Said, and Inden on orientalism has effectively highlighted the simultaneity of commentary, classification, and description in numerous texts.[9] Power relations are masked as was the case with Evans-Pritchard's *The Nuer*, which obliterated the impact of the violence of the world war.[10] Narrative tropes such as metaphor, authorial voice, and figuration are central to ethnographic writing.[11] The activity that tends to be monological rather than dialogical privileges the voice of the ethnographer-anthropologist.

While ethnography purports to be a faithful representation of "reality," I examine how that "reality" is apprehended, selectively appropriated, and refracted by the ethnographer. The power structure creates knowledge for the ruler and also the self-knowledge of the other. That is, hierarchies of power and status are both created and reinforced through knowledge systems. And if the links between power and knowledge were characteristic of colonial ethnography, the question must be asked whether postcolonial historiography and social anthropology have transcended this. With respect to the Meos this has not been the case. Indeed contemporary social anthropology and history still bear the burden of inherited images.

In the case of ethnographic writing on the Meos, the story of the marriage of a Meo boy and a Mina girl called *Dariyā Khāñ* was appropriated to prove Meo-Mina intermarriage and thereby the criminality of the Meos. From the series of associations that were made, the ethnographic argument may be formulated as follows:

1. *Dariyā Khāñ* was an actual case of Meo-Mina intermarriage. From this instance, the general prevalence of exogamy between the two "tribes" is construed. (The "fact" of a single case is held to be socially valid.)
2. From exogamous practice a "common origin" is established. (From the imputed universal prevalence both a past and a lineage are deduced.)
3. As the Minas are an acknowledged criminal group, the Meos are likewise "dangerous" and "predatory," given the blood relationship. (A shared history and common biological "traits" imply the conditioning of social action.)

This chapter juxtaposes British ethnographic writing with the very narrative that is held as evidence of Meo criminality. If criminality is the central concern of Meo colonial ethnography, the idea of community is indicated by a symbolic reading of the narrative. I attempt an alternative reading of *Dariyā Khāñ* based on a metaphorical interpretation.[12] The Meo community is defined quite explicitly in the story as a distinct group in terms of territoriality (common habitat), a shared past, and common religious and cultural practices. Crucial to the definition of the Meo self is the signification of Mina otherness. The narrative begins with a relationship of alliance between a Meo and a Mina chief symbolized by marriage. The sequence of events that climaxes in a battle between the Meo bride-takers and the Mina bride-givers and the latter's defeat suggests a major shift in the narrative structure from symmetry to hegemony in the representation of the Meo-Mina relationship. This shift is crucial to the sense of Mina otherness and, hence, to the symbolic construction of the Meo community.

The Ethnographic Construction of Meo Criminality

In Mewat, ethnographic data on the region was first collected by Major P. W. Powlett. This work was the primary resource that later ethnographic compilers drew upon and constituted in many ways as their starting point. Powlett, like many other ethnographers, had held positions in the military, police, and administration.[13] He worked as assistant general superintendent of the operations of the Thugee and Dacoitie Department in Upper Rajputana between 1869 and 1871. He was appointed settlement officer at Alwar in 1872 and conducted the Sixteen-Year Settlement in 1876. Powlett was political agent at Alwar for a year and a half between 1874 and 1875. Clearly colonial administration facilitated vertical mobility between the military and civil administration, between appointments in political, crime, and revenue administration that was highly significant for the intertextuality of the administrative discourse. Powlett writes in the *Gazetteer of Ulwar*: "The Meos claim to be of Rajput origin [but] there are grounds for believing that many spring of the *same stock* as the Minas. The similarity between the words Meo and Mina suggests that the former may be a contraction of the latter. Several of the respective clans are identical (Singal, Nai, Pundlot, Dingal and Balot), and *a story of one Daria Meo and his lady love Sasbadni Mina seems to show that they formerly intermarried*."[14]

A definite commentary may be discerned underlying this apparently descriptive statement. First, Powlett rejects the Meo's own claims to ksatriya descent. This is difficult to reconcile with Powlett's later statement that "apostate Rajputs founded many of the clans as the legends tell." Second, his concern is obviously with a common racial stock. Powlett reflects a major problematic of nineteenth-century European anthropology and ethnology that centered on questions of race and racial classification in accordance with physical appearance. The essentialist view of human nature can be seen from his attempt to establish the identity of both tribe and clan names. "Meo" is even seen as a contraction of Mina. The evidence, however, indicates that up to the nineteenth century the Meos were referred to as "Mewatees." In Powlett's work we see a deliberate attempt to establish a Meo-Mina relationship. He describes the Minas as a former ruling group who are the "famous marauders which the Thuggee and Dacoities Suppression Department had claimed were notorious robbers and whom Major Impey, Political Agent of Alwar, had placed under surveillance."[15]

The *Rajputana Gazetteer* states, regarding the Meos, that "they may possibly have some Rajput blood in their veins; but they are probably, like many other similar tribes, a combination from ruling and various other stocks, and there is reason to believe them *very nearly allied with the Meenas who are certainly a tribe of the same structure and species*."[16] Though this very interesting statement acknowledges the possibility of "some Rajput blood," it also accepts that the Meos are like most tribes a "combination" implying that there are no "pure" tribes. At the same time the Minas and Meos are seen as sharing the "same structure and species."

What is meant by structure and species is elaborated by the *Rajputana Gazetteer* with two arguments. First, it is said that the Meos (as Powlett also argues) have twelve clans or pals, the first six of which are identical in name and claim the same descent as the first six clans of the Minas. Second, it is claimed by the text that "*intermarriage between them both was the rule until the time of Akbar* when owing to an affray at a marriage of a Meo with a Mina the custom was discontinued." This is obviously a reference to the narrative of *Dariyā Khāñ* . But we can see that there is a subtle shift here from Powlett's position that more tentatively hypothesized that "the story seems to show," "there are grounds for believing," and "the common names suggest," and so on.[17]

In the *Rajputana Gazetteer*'s version the story now acquires the status of an event. The event itself becomes demonstrative of a rule of exogamy (that can also be called endogamy), which is crystallized as a social fact. The necessity of establishing Meo-Mina sameness became a denial of other realities such as the fluidity of groups and both Meo and Mina intermarriage with other local groups. For the *Gazetteer*'s narrative it mattered little that Meo-Mina intermarriage (according to its own testimony) had been suspended during Akbar's rule. Even after a three-hundred-year interval the unity created once by the "substance" of blood made them identical in "structure and species." Having thus assimilated the present into the past, the social mores of one group into another, criminality becomes imbued with a timelessness. The "Gazetteer of Bharatpur" then draws the conclusion that the mode of life of both Meos and Minas was similar, as both tribes were notoriously predatory."[18] The essence of both groups is thereby captured: all action, past and future. is to be is framed by "predatoriness."

Certain influences were decisive. The Indo-Persian historiographical discourse was a significant source of the historiographical and ethnographic image of the Meos as "plundering banditti." K. D. Erskine's draft *Imperial Gazetteer* article on the Meos and Mewat is preceded by a series of extracts from Briggs's translation of Firishta, Caldecott's *Life of Baber*, and Elliot and Dowson's compilation of Muslim historians. A long extract from Powlett consists of his quotations from Persian sources.[19] These sources untiringly reiterate the resistance of the Mewatis to the sultanate: the repeated raids, plunder and insurrections they were prone to, and the numerous reprisals and massacres that successive rulers of Delhi had to undertake against them.

The statist orientation obliterated the relation between resistance and marginality.

Skinner's *Tashrīh-ul-Aqwām* constitutes a "bridge" text between Persian historiography and English ethnography.[20] The visual representation that goes with this text published in 1824 shows a nearly naked (read primitive) Mewati clad in a loincloth, a sheet, and a turban (see fig. 6). The sparse clothing is in contrast to the fully clothed visual of the Jats and that of the partially clothed Ahir peasant with a plow. Mark the substantial drapery of the means of violence, including a gun and dagger. In addition, the text adds that the Meo carries a *barchī* (lance that has a long wooden handle), *bhālā* (mace), and *salakh*, a sharp weapon. The peasant-pastoral character of Meo lifestyle is obliterated in the reincarnated warrior Mewati.

Skinner uses a sexual metaphor to describe Meo-Mewati origin: the fallen semen of the raja-renouncer Basu, descendant of the god, brahma and the moon, and a ksatriya woman (literally and metaphorically) impregnates a fish. The fish who is the courtesan Maneka from the divine Indra's court gives birth to a human child from whom descend the Matsyas (Sanskrit for fish), the ancestors of the Mewatis. The origin myth suggests the connection to the Matsyas who settle in the country to the west of Chanderi called Mewat. But genealogy is invoked in the text to aid a "mixed" caste explanation (that is almost racial in its connotations): the crossbreeding of human and marine species creates a genetic variety that is warlike, criminal, and treacherous. Incidentally Skinner himself had a mixed parentage derived from a marriage between an Englishman and a Rajput woman.

Powlett was decisively influenced by the emphasis on Mewati "otherness" of the "Persian histories" that he held were the most reliable sources of information.[21] He begins his work with a historical account that relies almost wholly on Barani, Abu'l Fazl, and Firishta. Because of their "troublesome" character, the repression of the Mewatis is described as necessary. Images once produced acquire their own logic: Crooke represents the Meos as residing in "wild" uninhabited tracts, and O'Dwyer repeats the weary metaphor of the Mewatis as a "thorn" for Delhi.[22]

The inherited image of Meo otherness was really not decisive until it was confirmed by the colonial state's own experience of the Meos. This was exemplified by their anti-British role in the events of 1857. Until then it is apparent from the files and correspondence of the Foreign Department that although the British were preoccupied with Mina and Bhil "predatoriness," the Meos hardly figured in the administrative concern with tribal "outrages,"

FIGURE 6
Mewati peasant.

From Col. James Skinner, *Tashrīh-ul- Aqwām* (Persian, British Museum, 1824).

"excesses," and "aggression." Thereafter the Meos move to the forefront of administrative concern.

From the British point of view, the narrative of the mutiny confirmed the (Persian) historiographical image of the Meos. Watson and Kaye sum up the administrative perspective when they remark that "in the Mutiny and rebellions in some districts especially around Agra they were more troublesome than the Goojars adding to their *original evil disposition the blood thirstiness of Muhamaddan fanatics*."[23] Race and religion are conflated in the making of evil and J. Malcolm described them in a similar vein of them as "*the most desperate rogues in India*."[24] Colonial ethnography, thus, constituted them a "criminal tribe," "notorious for their thieving propensities."[25] The "original evil disposition" was presumably a result of their original Mina blood exacerbated by their Muslimness, so that they became "the most desperate rogues." Ethnographic "truth" fed into further historical construction. Faulkner's *History of Alwar* quotes an unidentified source referring to them as "singularly savage and brutal" and "never to be reformed and subdued."[26]

Powlett's work then was vital in constituting the British perspective on the Meos. Ibbetson writes that they are so excellently described by Powlett in his *Gazetteer* that he can do no better than quote the passage in full.[27] Sherring concludes his account with a statement of "fact" that "the Meos intermarried with Meena families until lately."[28] In the *Rajputana Gazetteer*'s version "until lately" had meant Akbar's reign. Here "until lately" conveys the impression that Meo-Mina exogamy was practiced till the nineteenth century. Within a few decades Powlett's more hypothetical remarks are transformed into conclusive evidence.

Cunningham goes a step further and ascribes a common origin to the Meos and Minas. He writes that "the acknowledgment of previous intermarriage seems to offer rather a strong proof that the Meos must have been a cognate race with the Minas, holding the same social position — higher, perhaps, than the Ahirs and other agricultural classes, but decidedly far below the Rajputs, from whom they claim descent. I am inclined therefore, to agree with Major Powlett that the Meos and Minas may have had a common origin."[29]

I have suggested earlier that the Meo clans emerged from a history of migration and intermarriage with many groups. Local populations were far more fluid than they are today.[30] Like the Meos, the Minas intermarried with several other groups such as the Jats, Gujars, Rajputs, Bhils, and others.[31] The Meos have several nepaliya gots that are said to have been a consequence of Meo intermarriage with Rajputs, Bhatiaras, Nais, and persons from other groups. Particularly toward the south of Alwar where the Minas are concentrated there seems to have been a close relationship between certain Mina and Meo clans. Four Meo chiefs are said to have married Mina women.[32] But to establish the Meos and Minas as a "cognate race" with a "common origin" is a denial of difference. It would be as mistaken to identify the Meos with the Minas as it would be to see them as a cognate race of the Rajputs. Although colonial ethnographers attributed the suspension of Meo-Mina marriages to the former's conversion to Islam and, hence, conferred a sectarian reading, in fact, Meos recall occasional marriages between the two groups till as late as 1947 when they were suspended by the partition genocide against the Meos. The marriage rites could include both the *pherās* and the *nikāh*, that is, a combination of Hindu and Muslim ritual.

The stigmatized image of the Meos intersects with their hypothetical tribal status. Risley claims that "among the Meos and Minas of Rajputana a strain of Bhil blood may be discerned."[33] He derives both from their aboriginal Dravidian blood — a substance that presumably oriented them to crime. In the *Imperial Gazetteer*'s reference to them as "almost pure aborigines" one can witness a self-consciously racial theory of human nature and an evolutionist underpinning of social change. The antecedents of this thesis come from administrator-historian-cartographer Col. James Tod's writing much earlier in the century. The "Bhil blood" factor is then upheld as proof of Sir John Malcolm's contention that the Meos are a proud, thievish, and "debauched race."[34] Whereas "thievish" might be concerned with criminality, the adjective "proud" indicates that the Meo defiance of authority had other sources. But the demonstration of Meo-Mina exogamy was a significant functional contention. The circle of "lawless turbulence," which up to then had comprised the Bhils and the Minas, was now expanded to include the Meos. Ethnography thereby spatialized the tribe to the margins of Indian civilization and temporally constituted it a "primitive" other.[35]

The ethnographic discourse is not univocal. Indeed, the ethnographic perspective on the Meos of Punjab and Rajputana has markedly different resonances. This is not unrelated to the different ecologies and political economies of the directly administered and princely regions, respectively. But the divergences reveal the internal contradictions within the ethnographic thesis. In contrast to some writers who view the Meos as thriftless, extravagant, and lazy,[36] O'Dwyer describes the Meos of Alwar as a "prolific and prosperous race." His *Settlement Report* for Bharatpur comments that

Mewat is the most prosperous part of the Bharatpur State and the Meos the most industrious group. Drake-Brockman who remarks on their "thieving and plundering propensities," also states that Bharatpur's revenue, which is higher than that of many states of equal and greater area in Rajputana, is largely due to the Jat and Meo peasants.[37]

Powlett's work percolated through the "vernacular." One of the earliest Indian-authored ethnographies of Rajputana refers to the *Dariyā Khāñ* narrative as a "case" and to the Meo "*peshā*" (occupation) of "*chorī dhāṛā*" (thievery). The "proof" of this is the Persian histories, which reveal the constant Meo tendency to indulge in looting and killing. Balban's unabashedly expansionist sultanate is described as having been "forced to attack" the Mewatis. Ala al-Din Khilji is mentioned as a great ruler, but even he had to "close the gates of Delhi" against them.[38]

The colonial perspective continues to structure postcolonial anthropology and historiography. Sharma refers to the Meo "predatory tradition," and Sharma and Srivastava mention the "predatory habits and plundering acts of the Meos which caused their perpetually strained relations with the Muslims."[39] Amir Ali, a writer commissioned by the independent Indian State's prestigious organization the Planning Commission's Research Programmes Committee, inquiring into the "morals of the Meos" describes them as "prone to prowling, theft and robbery."[40] The vocabulary of British administration permeates the ethnography of both colonial and Indian writers. Mark the stigmatized vocabulary of Haig's *Cambridge History of India*, which uses terms such as "infested" and "depredations" with regard to the Meos. In 1260, he writes, they expiated with a terrible punishment a long series of crimes. Even a historian like Wink remarks that the Mid were notorious for their predatory activities down to 1821 when the British subdued them.[41] Aggarwal, a major social anthropologist of the Meos, describes their "antisocial activities" and their "*vocation*" of "stealing cattle and looting pilgrims."[42] In a later work he confesses his naive acceptance of the colonial "bias" without indicating what made him abandon his earlier views.[43]

The idea of their being a criminal tribe has also insidiously penetrated Meo conceptions of the self. Fateh Singh, an important Meo leader, told me that the Meos had been a "Scheduled Tribe" during princely rule whose occupation had been "*chorī*" and "*dakaitī*" (thieving and dacoity) "like the Minas." There was "reservation" for us in the army, he added.[44] Fateh Singh's ideas of the Meo past are widespread among Meos, as when they refer to themselves as the "Ismaelites of the Upper Doab."[45] They show the strong hold of colonial modes of classification exemplified in the census and other ethnographic works. Writing in English thereby constitutes the dominant discourse. It pervades the Hindi gazetteer and historical and social anthropological accounts. It also orients the memory and identity of the Meos.

The Evidence of Meo Criminality

The question to be asked is whether Meo criminality is confirmed by the juridical-legal record and the administrative and police reports of the period. Interestingly, Lockett's report to the governor general on the "predatory associations of Rajputana" in 1831 negates their stigmatization. He records no complaints against Mewati "plunderers" by either the Alwar minister or the people. In the paper sent to him by the raja, which lists the cases of depredations alleged to have taken place within the last five years, there is no mention of their criminal activities.

On the other hand, Lockett's indictment of localized gangs comprising Minas and Rajputs, particularly in Kotputli, Jaipur, and Shekhawati, is quite explicit.[46] He writes that "the Meenas of Butteesee have practiced robbery as a profession from time immemorial, and in skill, dexterity and address in their predatory calling are considerably inferior to no gang of any kind in upper Hindoostan." Of the bands of armed robbers in Rajputana, he states that the "most notorious are the Sulhedees, Larkhanees, Beedawuts, Bawureeas and Meenas" and that "almost all the marauding tribes in Shekhawatee employ Minas in their plundering incursions.[47] Clearly Minas were deployed as instruments to settle interzamindari disputes among Rajputs.

In the pre-1857 period the administrative concern with the Minas had been a constant. They were outlawed in Mewar following "depredations" in Sirohi and Marwar, and Captain Brooke led an expedition against them. Orders were issued to seize or execute all the Minas of Mewar or Sirohi who ascended the Ghat of Mewar without a pass.[48] In the late 1850s the intensity of their activity was described as increased, with robberies at Mewar, "outrages" at Ajmer and Tandla, and incursions into the British district of Jawed Neemuch.[49] Strategies worked out by the British to manage the Mina menace involved the twin aspects of repression and reform. But despite their increased surveillance and enlistment in local militias such as the Jodhpore Legion and an independent Mina corps, several administrative and police sources described crime as persisting.

In the decades following 1857 the concern with the Minas intensified. The Bharatpur and Punjab police reports catalog their activities at length.[50] Younghusband's Berar police report likewise mentions that "heavy robberies and dacoities which had long been rife in the Hyderabad territories and in the Dakhin, were almost invariably perpetrated by the Minas residing in Shahjehanpur in Gurgaon, and in the States of Alwar and Jaipur adjoining. Their gangs are said to leave home in the autumn for the North West and the Central Provinces, Hyderabad and the Deccan, for plunder and dacoity sometimes for a year or two." The need for their control and surveillance is constantly emphasized. Similarly, the Five-Year Report of the Thagi and Dakoitie Department's Operations in the Native States expresses its concern with the "Meena Chowkeydar land pirates," who are held responsible for the opium robberies in Central India and dacoities in Rajputana, Deccan, and Gujarat.[51]

In contrast to the criminality of certain Mina gangs, which is quite clearly inscribed in the record, the Meos are nowhere mentioned as an organized and habitual criminal group. No suggestion is made to place them in Schedule A of the Act of 1871 that lists the criminal tribes. Police reports register no list of sustained criminal activities such as cattle stealing, pickpocketing, burglary, housebreaking, highway robbery, petty theft, and so on.[52] Page after page of Hervey's report catalogs the activities of the Minas, yet we draw a blank regarding similar cases by Mewatis. Of the 277 Thug and 19 Dakoit cases, Hervey mentions only 3 cases by Mewatis, while 6 cases are attributed to Jats and 10 to brahmans. The Mewatis also go unmentioned in the report on Alwar.[53] Hervey's report describes 72 authenticated acts of dacoity by Meena Rhatore gangs. There are also some cases by Jats, Malis, Rajputs, Gujars, and brahmans, but none by the Mewatis.

The ethnographer Drake-Brockman describes the Mewatis as thieves who come from Bharatpur and Gurgaon. A police conference on criminal tribes to devise means of checking "depredations" in Bharatpur, Dholpur, and adjoining districts, however, shows the police's primary concern with the Kanjars, and the Bharatpur State prescribes a Kanjar settlement.[54] Besides, the Criminal Tribes Rules of 1914 of the Bharatpur state identifies the Sansias, Kanjars, (Chaukidar) Minas, Marwari Kherara, Malwi, and Munghias or Baorias, Badaks, Shikaris, Behelias, Aherias or Baherias, Berias also called Kabootries, Nats, Chakras or Chagras, and all others of the "gypsy class" as criminal tribes.[55] The Meos are noticeably absent from this list. In Alwar also the concern is with the Minas.[56] With reference to Drake-Brockman's accusation against the Gurgaon Mewatis, the Village Criminal Justice (Punjab) Bill, names the Gujars, Dogars, and Wattees Kharros but not the Meos.[57]

In addition, crime committed by higher castes such as brahmans and Rajputs is generally overlooked in official reports. Kolff mentions the considerable evidence of high-caste plundering and raiding such as among Bhati Rajputs. Lockett shows that criminal gangs comprised a combination of persons drawn from different castes and tribes and the simultaneous involvement of Shekhawati Rajputs, banias, brahmans, and Minas.[58] This suggests the shift between the early and late nineteenth-century colonial discourse on crime. The colonial accounts in the early phase take far greater cognizance of intercaste alliances, networks, and gangs.

The paucity of evidence against the Meos in the later nineteenth century appears not to have mattered. Powlett had only to establish the Mina connection of blood. Since the latter were an "essentially criminal" race the incrimination of the Meos in ethnographic terms was definitive and final. Once created, the construct of Meo-Mina identity became frozen. The history of the Meos was annexed to that of the Minas. Unlike in the case of most criminal tribes who became "essential types *without history*" the Meos were bestowed with a new history.[59]

Substantial historical reconstruction followed. The Meos, ethnographers claimed, became separate from the Minas following their conversion. When a Mina was asked, following Meo conversion the question, Who are you? he replied "*hum mev nā*" (or *mainā*, meaning I am not a Meo). Mevna is said to have been the source of the later Mina.[60] Crooke holds that Mina comes from "Amina" Meo or "pure Meo," a term applied to those who did not become Muslims. The formulation presumes a frozen ethnic understanding postulated on sectarian division. However, evidence is contrary to this fragile "reconstruction." First, the Meos are acknowledged as having been converted in phases in the medieval period. Second, the "Mewati" or "Miwan" is a usage that antedates their conversion.[61] And even following conversion Hindu Mewatis continued to persist and are mentioned in the Census of 1881. So for that matter are Muslim Minas. Both Meos and Minas, therefore, seem to have been decontextualized and recontextualized. Ethnography involved the dual moves of erasure and overwriting with respect to their past.

Anthropological works on both Meos and Minas fail to sustain the thesis that "several of the respective clans are identical." The enumeration of Mina gotras made in texts such as Hervey's report and the *Rajputana Gazetteer* shows nothing in common with the Meo gotras.[62] The identity of pal names between Minas and Meos that Powlett found in Alwar was also problematic because a pal is territorial category and covers *all* castes living in the area. Thus not only Minas but also Chamars, Jats, Gujars, and others who inhabit the pal have the same pal name.

Ethnographies describe Minas as a well-defined group with a long past that antedates the Rajputs, a distinct territory and social structure. Mina territory or Minavati that is distinct from Mewat stretches from Alwar to the area surrounding Jaipur up to Bundi, Kota, Sawai Madhopur, and Udaipur. In making the Meo-Mina connection, colonial ethnography thus violated regional conceptions of geography, the known history of the Minas, and their demographic distribution.

The stereotype of Mina criminality is equally problematic and needs investigation. Certain observations need to be emphasized. First, that only a small population of Minas (eight hundred in 1901) in Gurgaon defines Minas. Second, that criminal gangs were generally mixed and drew from different castes. Third, the "evidence" of crime was often assumed rather than established. In one case the mere presence of a few Minas in Ajmer was taken as proof of a conspiracy. Approvers sometimes did not know the persons being tried. As regards the habitual dacoits, "their being away from their homes in a body was held to be reasonable enough proof of felonious intent."[63] Thus fact and fiction were inextricably interwoven to create the construct of invincible Mina criminality, which short-circuited British claims to provide universal justice.

Attributing an intrinsic criminality to various groups masked the inroads made by colonialism into the livelihoods of various groups. So-called tribal peoples belonging to forest communities were inducted into systems of settled agriculture as landless laborers and in unequal trade relations that led to debt bondage.[64] Administrative and ethnographic reporting merge crime and resistance. In the case of the tribes it was a consequence of the erosion of tribal access to the forest and its produce as forested tribal areas were penetrated and brought under settlements.

The construction of Meo criminality, hence, was founded not on case histories and police reports but originated from the premises of colonial intellectual practice. Although in this case the ethnographic and the judicial-administrative discourse were not identical, one can, nevertheless, see a dense intertextuality. The vocabulary of police reports was appropriated to define the Meos in essentialist terms as a predatory, turbulent, and notorious people who infest certain territories.[65] In Crooke's work the reasoning that the Meos and the Minas were "originally the same" made the latter "famed robbers" and the worst of the criminal classes, terms Younghusband had used for the Minas.[66] Interestingly, Hervey's comments on the tribes were largely appropriated from Malcolm's work on central India, where they are described as "barbarians," "desperate plunderers," and "degenerate." Crime, argues Hervey, is the profession of whole communities who are "plunderers by birth, education and profession."[67]

The history of the Meos that could alternatively have been read as one of peasant protest and resistance or as a struggle for power and local autonomy by warrior lineages was now read as one of crime. Thus Powlett's reading of *Dariyā Khāñ* had crucial implications as it constituted the master narrative on the Meos.

The Mewati Narrative of *Dariyā Khāñ*

Alternative readings of *Dariyā Khāñ* are possible, as a romance, as evidence of prevalent exogamy/hypergamy. My reading emphasizes the central narrative idea of Meo community, brought out through a stress on Mina otherness. A reading of the text as metaphor suggests that the narrative signifies the juxtaposition rather than the interpenetration of two groups of culturally distinct peoples, Meos and Minas.

Cunningham provides the first written account of *Dariyā Khāñ*. Only fragments are quoted, and the story is summarized. He describes it as a "famous tribal legend" and "the most popular song at all Meo marriage feasts." The narrative consists in the version of Mavasi Rao that I recorded of sixty-three dohas.[68] There is an astonishing identity in the episodic structure outlined by Cunningham and that detailed by Mavasi Rao's performance suggesting the continuity of a folk form for more than a century, although the latter tends to emphasize the romantic theme of separation-reunion rather than the politics of alliance and feud.

Mavasi's version of *Dariyā Khāñ* begins by presenting Todar Mal and Rao Bada, the respective chiefs of the Pahat Meo clan and of a Mina clan, as courtiers at Akbar's court. They fight a battle together. Rao Bada takes the Meo to his house where they drink wine together and become friends. They also decide on the marriage of their yet unborn grandchild and child. A granddaughter called Sasbadni is born to Rao Bada and a son named Dariya Khan to Todar Mal. Their marriage takes place in childhood. But during the course of the wedding ceremony a "*bigāṛ*," or conflict, occurs between the two chiefs. As a consequence, when Sasbadni comes of age, the *gauṇa* rite preceding her departure to her husband's place does not take place.

Sasbadni sends three messengers, Shyamla, a Balai, or shoemaker; Chimla, the barber; and Dada Dhaurangiya, the Mirasi, with messages to Dariya. All three belong to the service castes of the Meos. The Balai is an "untouchable" caste used as traditional messengers in Meo marriage ritual, like the barber or Nai caste. During rites of marriage or death the Balai collects the wood used to cook food for the ritual feast.

When the messengers fail, Sasbadni visits the tomb-shrine of Khwaja Pir (Mu'in-ud-Din Chishti) at Ajmer. The saint promises her a reunion with her husband, and she returns to her village. Meanwhile, in Mewat, Dariya Khan decides to fetch his bride. Sasbandi is told of his impending arrival and busies herself with preparations for the feast and consummation of her marriage.

The early half of the narrative, on the surface, seems to unfold as a romance very much in the style of the popular *Ḍholā Marū* epic.[69] Forbidden desire intervenes, suggesting the struggle that communities must perpetually wage to maintain boundaries. Sasbadni expresses her blossoming sexuality in a letter to Dariya: "My body is not satisfied, like white ants attacking the *khairī* [acacia catechu] tree" *(merī dehī ghuṇ jūñ bīṇdhiye jūñ khairī kī lāṭh)*. The existents of romance sequentially stated are the separation of the couple, the yearning of the woman who sends a series of messengers to no avail, and the final reunion when Sasbadni anticipates

dūjo pahro rain ko tūtā juṛai sneh
dhan to dhartī ho rahī merā tū pī sāvan kā meh

In the second part of the night[70]
parted lovers will reunite.
Like the parched earth in summer
I will soak in the first shower of rain.

At a deeper level, however, the narrative simultaneously builds up the constituents of Meo-Mina opposition. The clans of Sasbadni and Dariya belong to the Meo and Mina groups, respectively. The two chiefs have distinct territorial jurisdictions. Panhora is the headquarters of the Mina clan.[71] Minavati and Mewat as the respective areas of the two groups are the modes of classification of a folk geography and signify a demographic separation as well as a spatial one.

Frequent references are made to Mewat as a distinct territorial area. Sasbadni's mother tells her daughter, "you are married in Mewat" *(betī tū byāhī mevāt maiṇ dābak vāko gāñv)*. The carpenter exclaims, "what can I say of Mewat" *(kyā kahūñ bāt mevāt kī)* when he relates to Sasbadni how badly he has been mistreated by the Meos. When Sasbadni goes to the Khwaja's tomb she finds "all the Meo men and women" at a camp on their way to the fair. The woman collecting cow dung sees Dariya and runs to tell Sasbadni, "Dariya comes to this country" *(āyo daryiā khāñ yā des)*. Identities are spatialized in terms of the conception of *des*, or land.

The marriage of Dariya and Sasbadni is more in the nature of an alliance rather than a sign of kinship.[72] It comes about when the two chiefs participate in a battle together. But they are soon embroiled in a feud. Thus even in the early part of the narrative (where the mood is romantic) one may note the symbolic rendering of the divide between the Meos and the Minas. The unity engendered by the alliance has proved to be temporary and fragile. Sasbadni's yearning, which is an attempt to transcend the distance, in fact, reinforces it. Her messengers are mistreated: Shyamla is beaten up after being force-fed a mixture of millet and mustard oil, and Chimla barely manages to escape.

The arrival of Dariya can be seen as a narrative break. What has so far been suggested as underlying the description of events and existents now comes to the fore. The articulation of the Meo-Mina opposition, which I argue is the dominant motif of the narrative, explicitly emerges in the second half as the central concern. Dariya alludes to the antagonism between the two chiefs telling Sasbadni, "How could I come to the Rao's / to take you, my path was obstructed so." Sasbadni refers to difference in cultural terms when she says: "In your country Salona is celebrated, In ours Holi accompanied by revelry" *(tihārai des saloṇā māniye hamārī hoḷī manai kharī)*.

Dariya is completely identified as part of a father-son dyad and constantly referred to as the Rao of the "Panch Pahar." He represents the Pahat pallakra as well as the larger Meo group. When Sasbadni suggests that with the help of her grandfather Dariya can help break the power of his father, Todar Mal, Dariya dismisses her with a disparaging remark about her clan's status vis-à-vis the Pahats:

potī bādā rāv kī mosuñ kahā khaṛī bādai
tero dādā bādā ko kyā mājno jo merī sīkrī sūñ saras sādai

O granddaughter of Bada Rao
why do you unnecessarily argue with me.
What standing does Dada Bada have
that he can even compete with Sikri?

Dariya thus represents his territory as one with inviolable borders.

Given the antagonism of Meo-Mina relations, a battle is inevitable. When the barber is sent to call Dariya to the Rao's court, Sasbadni is already anticipating a conflict. Nine hundred uniformed Minas guard Rao Bada. He invites Dariya to a feast of wine and meat. The rejection of the food offering of the meat of a goat slaughtered by the *jhaṭkā* (single stroke) method, in contrast to the *halāl*, becomes the symbol of social and cultural distance. This distance is far more meaningful than the marriage alliance. Despite Sasbadni's advice that he should smartly evade a quarrel, he misunderstands her signal when she holds up two fingers, and instead strikes the Rao twice.

The impending clash between the Meos and the Minas has already been symbolically indicated in the narrative. A woman suddenly drops her basket of cow dung and runs to tell Sasbadni of Dariya's arrival who "comes with gleaming sword held high in his hand." The battle is presaged in Sasbadni's dream, where she sees, as she tells her friends, that "the fields of Panhora were all cleared, as Mal's son wielded his sword." Panhora, or Mina territory, seems to be razed and destroyed in her dream. The image of Dariya is "like Rama, when he descended on Lanka, with sixteen hundred noble men" *(solah sai sāvaṇt lank pai rām risāyo)*. And so "Ravana was killed in the sky, in seconds, Lanka was destroyed" *(rāvaṇ maro aggās maiṇ pal maiṇ laṇk gaī hī ṭūṭ)*. Dariya comes then not only to claim his bride but also to destroy the Mina des.

Following Dariya's blow, the entire guard of nine hundred Minas rush to their chief's defense. Rao Bada is sure that Dariya Khan is isolated and cornered. Sasbadni pleads with her brother, Randhir, to help them escape from the palace, and before dawn they are able to get far away from the pursuing Minas. But when they halt to rest, the Minas catch up with them. Dariya sends Sasbadni to urgently summon his uncle, Malak Jalal Khanazada, to come to his rescue. The wrath of the Pahat Meos now descends upon the Minas.

Dariya lives up to the Pahat image of valor. He rushes with the Malak Khanazadas to the battlefield saying, "my mace I will now wield, behold the commotion in the field." They attack and surround the Minas. Meanwhile Dariya's brothers also join the fray. The intensity of battle is conveyed by the noise that is heard in nearby villages. The Minas are defeated in the battle by the Meos. Dariya Khan escapes with his bride.

The narrative maps human society within the region into two opposing groups. The antagonism between the Meos and Minas is expressed in terms such as bigar and bair (conflict, antagonism) and is reinforced by a series of events climaxing in the battle. Both groups of Minas and Meos are subdivided into clans constituted by the principle of patrilineal descent. In the narrative, however, intragroup differences, such as the division between pals, is obliterated. The Pahat are rendered synonymous with the Meos, and Rao Bada's clan becomes representative of the Minas.

As a Meo, Dariya has multiple identities, but the two levels of allegiance to his pallakra and the Meo group are meshed. He is a Pahat: witness his refusal to let Sasbadni and Rao Bada interfere with the Pahat clan's territory. The Islamic prohibition against eating the meat of an animal killed by the single-stroke method becomes the cause for the battle. But the conflict can hardly be called a religious one. The Meo community is conceived of in a kinship idiom as a "family." The "family," however, encompasses dependent castes such as the barber, leather worker, even the "untouchable" Mirasi, and others — some of whom might be non-Muslim. Addan Mirasi expresses this larger kinship sensibility, protesting when he is accidentally wounded, "Dariya of Todar Mal / you have killed one of your own family" *(daryiā ṭodar mall kā huyo tū ghar ko mārṇiyā)*. What Schneider calls the "possessive pronoun" is used here. The Mirasi is included in the Meo family, whereas the Minas are beyond this unit of shared understanding.[73] To wound a Mina is legitimate, which is not the case when a Meo kills or injures another Meo or a Mirasi. Dependent castes are subsumed in the "community."

Meo community is constructed through "sameness" in the narrative, a conception of the Meo self-being central to it. The idea of Mina otherness is constructed through the two metaphors, of battle and the personality of Sasbadni. Both these metaphors enable the narrator to make an explicit shift from symmetry to hierarchy in the representation of intergroup relations. The initial symmetry of Meo-Mina relations is indicated, for instance, by the copresence of the two chiefs at Akbar's court, their participation in a battle together, the sharing of food and wine after the defeat of their enemy, and the subsequent marriage alliance. Although the alliance has the potential of overcoming the sociocultural division of the two groups, it fails to do so, and the enmity of the two groups reasserts itself.[74] In the antagonism also there is a symmetry of relationship that is, however, negated by the Mina defeat in battle and the victory of the Meos. Mina otherness, which has thus far been based on exclusion, now becomes characterized as inferior.

The character of Sasbadni is also a crucial signifier. Dariya and Sasbadni's relationship is far more than an expression of mere gender relations of a peasant community. Whereas Dariya's position as leader of the bride-takers indicates Meo status, Sasbadni represents the subordination of the Mina bride-givers. When Dariya makes a scathing remark about her clan's status vis-à-vis the Pahat Meos, she replies passively in honeyed tones:

pāñch pahāṛ kai rāv jī terā khilaiṇ batīsuñ daṇ t
jāṇai gūñthī nag jaṛo merā dhan karīgar kaṇ th

O Rao of the Five Hills
may your teeth always gleam in a smile.
Like a gem set in a ring
I am beholden to Him who crafted you.

She goes on to say:

pahlo pahro rain ko bhojan huā taīyār
jīmo dhaṇ kā sāybā terī nār parosan hār

In the earliest part of the night
the food is prepared.
You will feast, my husband,
while your woman serves happily.

Sasbadni's subordination to her affinal home is complete. She becomes, as Dariya is told, "*terī nār*" (your woman). The gauna ritual she must undergo is a rite of separation that detaches her from her age and sex group, from her family and village, and from her clan and the Mina group. Following this, she is to acquiesce in the attitudes and actions of her affinal kin, even when the Meos kill her clansmen in battle. Sasbadni's subordination hier-

(a)

(b)

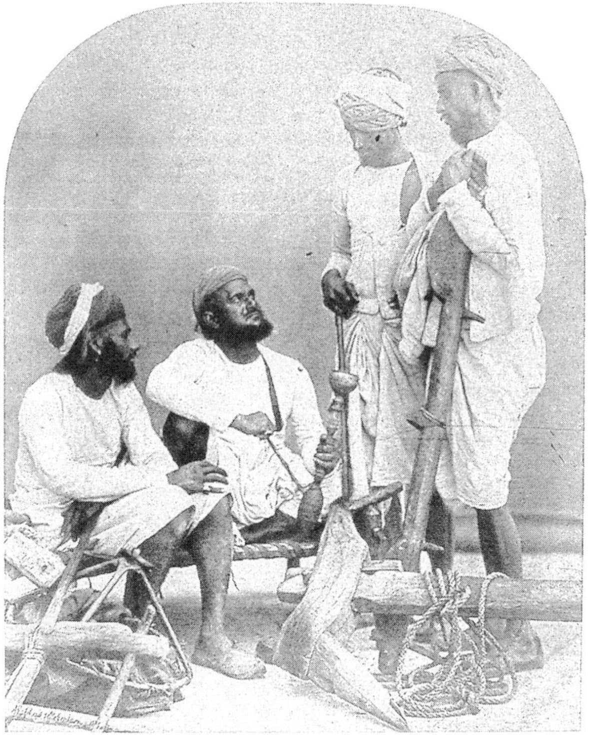

(c)

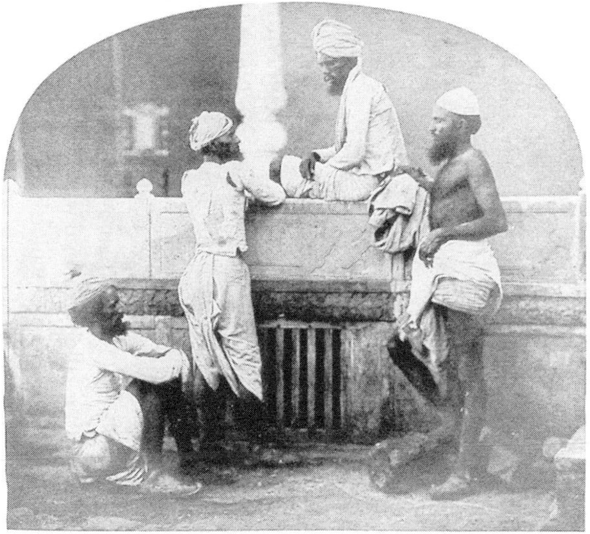

(d)

FIGURE 7

People of India: *(A)*, Meos; *(B)* Khanzadas; *(C)* Mewattees; *(D)* Meenas.

J. Forbes Watson and John W. Kaye, *The People of India: A Series of Photographic Illustrations of the Races and Tribes of Hindustan*, vol. 4 (London: India Museum and W. H. Allen and Co. 1874), 202.

archizes the Meos and negates the earlier symmetry of friendship/alliance/enmity.

Ethnographers in their reference to *Dariyā Khāñ* have uniformly *used* it for their own purposes rather than understood it as a text within a given cultural context. A given narrative structures the flow of events. The direction, the culmination has to be taken into account to understand its signification. In *Dariyā Khāñ* the brief period of amity described in the first few verses (hence the marriage) climaxes in a violent encounter. All ethnographers who refer to the story interestingly mention only the beginning. They ignore the negation of alliance by Meo-Mina enmity. Both Crooke and Rizvi completely undermine the violence that attends successive Meo-Mina encounters. The meaning of the text as a whole is not considered. Quite clearly what is being sought is a history of crime not a social history.

In this chapter I juxtapose the ethnographic text that feeds into both the historiographical and the anthropological accounts and the indigenous text. In the colonial period in India, the systematic construction of a mythology of criminality took place under the guise of "scientific" modes of enquiry and description. This was done by both census and gazetteer writers and the writer-administrator compilers of ethnographies.

Modes of classification orient both oral and written texts. To see ethnographic accounts as "objective" and empirical and to ignore the intellectual underpinnings (in this case of an evolutionist and essentialist approach to "crime") is inadequate. It is as unjustified as the attempt to class all folk narratives as mere lore and tales. Folk narratives reveal ideological boundaries. Mina otherness then becomes central in a reading of *Dariyā Khāñ* rather than the identity, common origin, and shared blood that British ethnographers tried to establish on its basis.

Intergroup relations and cultural identities, however, are not to be viewed as frozen or fixed but as highly localized, transient, and permeable. With respect to the Meo-Mina relation, intermarriages took place in southern Alwar around the Lachmangarh, Thanaghazi, and Rajgarh areas. In *Ghurcharī Mev Khāñ*, Sugariya and Umda Mina are keen admirers of the Meo bandit brothers and even team up with them. Currently, only the Meos of the Daimrot Pal interdine with the Minas and attend each other's weddings.

The unfinished part of the story is that Dariya Khan and Sasbadni live happily in the village Palka until Dariya is killed in a feud with Gujars. After killing Dariya Khan the Gujars return his corpse, which is placed on his mare, Bichan. His brother promises Sasbadni vengeance as the story closes.

Interestingly, however, the Singal clan of Meos are locally regarded as being close to the Gujars.[75]

The oral text thus brings into question Crooke's characterization of them as a "robber tribe" and the "boldest of the criminal classes" by locating it in a larger perspective that also viewed them as "thriftless, extravagant and lazy."[76] The category of "criminal tribe" is a cluster concept that subsumes a network of interrelated associations concerning evolution, tribal status, productive capabilities, and so on. The construct was in obvious contradiction to the empirical evidence that the Meos had emerged as the major landowning group of the region and were regarded as an *ūñchī jāt* (high caste) who possessed much of the fertile land in the Alwar and Bharatpur States. This association with land, their contribution to the fiscal base of the kingdoms, and their participation in the colonial army eventually prevented their being notified as a criminal tribe.

Nonetheless, it was the written word, the ethnographic image, that proved to be far more powerful. It created a mode of classification that has dominated colonial and postcolonial writing on the Meos. It has also made a deep impression on the group itself and how they conceive of their past. "We were looters and robbers," they often say today about themselves.

The Meo "other" of the English ethnographer helped create the "self" of the Meo group as the categories of the former continue to structure the popular imagination. Thus writing underlies utterance.

7 Crime, Feud, and Resistance in Early Nineteenth-Century Mewat

A notorious pirate is caught and brought to justice at the court of Alexander the Great who asks him, "How dare you molest the sea?" The pirate replies, "How dare you molest the world?" He continues before being executed, "Because I do it with a little ship only, I am called a thief; you, doing it with a great navy, are called an Emperor." The short story from Noam Chomsky's book *Pirates and Emperors* is a parable for kings and bandits throughout history.

State and history collapse crime and resistance. Crime is most often described by texts of history and governance as the act of disorderly sections. The discourse of colonial writing went as far as identifying entire groups as characterized by criminality. Needless to say, there is no account of state crime. Among the silences of the historical record is the suffering experienced by women as a result of this. Women are rendered the objects of feud, battles, and war but their voices have hardly ever figured in the historian's description of the event.

The communal memory of early nineteenth-century precolonial–princely state formation is encoded in its oral tradition. This describes the struggle of the local community as it was brought under the control of statist institutions and practices. Scholars such as Heesterman, Inden, Shulman, Stein, and Fox have pointed out the "paradoxes," the ambivalence and contradictions within Indian kingship that prevented the center from establishing a unitary, integrated polity such as the absolute or nation-state in Europe.[1] The existence of enclaves of autonomous self-governing communities in precolonial states has been emphasized. What does the existence of such an enclave in a Rajput State and its narrativized identity tell us? What were the nature of tensions with the state that arose out of the attempted absorption of such enclaves? How does the picture this helps build comment on the argument of the segmentary state or the galactic polity in the Asiatic context?

Regrettably much of the debate on the precolonial and princely state under paramountcy has been oriented to a statist or king-centric perspective. Fortunately in the Meo case considerable material from the oral tradition is available for the nineteenth century. Three texts are used in this and the following chapter to obtain an insight into the subjective perspective on state formation and the nature of resistance during this period. *Kaulānī* is a narrative that provides us with an account of successive Meo revolts in the early nineteenth century. The second text consists of fragmentary verses collectively called the *Gadar*, which is also the regional term for the anti-British revolt of 1857. The official versions of both the Alwar State and the colonial-British power are also available for these events. *Ghurcharī Mev Khāñ*, a bandit narrative, is a similar countertext of the late nineteenth century and assumes an entire prehistory of resistance.

This corpus of material from the Meo cultural performance tradition describes moments of protest or what can be called, paraphrasing Guha, the cultural symbols of negation.[2] One can see the close relation here between verbal symbols (speech acts) and nonverbal (actual acts). Austin refers to them as performative acts in which illocution means that to utter the word is to perform the speech act.[3] The three narratives take us through the reigns of three rulers of the Alwar State. The thematic of the oral tradition indicates a repeated disquiet in the Mewat countryside against both colonial and princely regimes. This continues in the early half of the twentieth century.

The kingdom of Alwar had been established in 1775 in northeastern Rajputana by the Naruka Rajputs. This cadet lineage of the ruling Kacchavaha Rajput lineage of the Jaipur State had established its presence in the area much earlier when a dispossessed head of a sublineage was given an estate in the area in 1388. Much later the Narukas were able to carve out the Alwar State with land seized from the Mughal Empire, the Jaipur State, and from Rajput and non-Rajput owners, including the Meos.

Kaulānī is a narrative from the corpus of the Meo oral tradition that indicates the character of the late eighteenth-to early nineteenth-century Rajput State and provides an account of successive Meo revolts. I first heard a performer singing a version of the narrative at a Meo wedding. Regrettably he only knew a few verses. Some time later I chanced upon a written version of the narrative in the possession of Dalpat Khan, Chaudhari of the Meo Baghora clan. He had got his genealogist (from the caste of Jagas) to write it down for him. Instead of an oral text that is sung to audiences drawn from the wider Meo community at rites of passage by groups of Mirasis (a "low" caste for the Meos), the "fixed" text is now in the possession of Dalpat, who maintains it as an account of the history of his family and clan.

Kaulānī then, belongs to an oral-written class of texts. It problematized for me both the components of the category "oral tradition," challenging its "oral" character as well as the nature of "tradition." Here was a written version of a performed text. One that was essentially "flat," lacking the performer's intonation of voice and the use of gesture to create mood, as well as an audience whose *hunkārā*, or interjection, is so central to performance. The aural-visual aspects of recited verse and the drama of musical accompaniment have been lost in the process of being reduced to writing. I was confronted also with the transformation of the oral tradition itself. Cultural performances usually take place at Meo rites of passage. Previously the bridal party stayed in the village for five to six days. Each of the many rites was accompanied by cultural performances. But the duration of marriage ceremonies has been shrinking and so are narrative performances. It is hardly possible now to find the performance of an entire narrative cycle. Nonetheless, *Kaulānī*, however problematic its orality, belongs to the Mewati oral tradition and the larger genre of heroic narratives called bat. The composition was oral to begin with. So was the initial context of the transmission of the narrative that depended on the patronage of Meo jajmans.

The discovery of the narrative was one of the crucial moments that helped me unpick the tangled knots of the nineteenth century. It became one of the crucial pieces in a jigsaw puzzle. Despite its frozen, written character, the text in its entirety made vivid a perspective on kingly state formation. A mere mapping of the Mewati terms for state and authority, as well as for resistance, produces a marvelous picture of the period. *Kaulānī* is one of the few narratives in the Meo oral tradition that is Meo rather than Mirasi authored. The poetic-prose account is of a witness as composer. Jai Singh, who used to herd cows, was present at the Battle of Kaulani; he was the Meo chief Rai Khan's wife's brother and a Meo of the Gorval clan. In this case the subaltern is certainly empowered by voice.

Another moment of transition from orality to writing is the version of the story printed in the *Chirāg i Baghorā: Alvar rājya kaulānī kile kī laṛāī*. This version superimposes onto the text a dating from the English calendar. The succession of battles that occurred between 1798 and 1825 are described. The printed version describes *Kaulānī* as a "history" *(tawārikh)*, specifically of the Tonvar clan of Meos. An early section of the text retains the form of bat and bansabali or genealogy from the Meo oral tradition. Thus the genealogy of the Tonvars consists of a narrated text in the oral-aural mode with no periods.

State Formation and Meo Resistance

The context of the narrative relates to the late eighteenth century, a period of intensive state formation. With the decline of Mughal power, Mewat had become a contested terrain fought over by several rival claimants, such as the Jats, the Marathas, the English, and the Rajputs. The Marathas were defeated in the battle of Hindan by the English army led by General Lake. At the battle of Laswari, fought twenty miles from Alwar on the border of Mewat, Lake fought Daulat Rao Scindia, who led the Maratha army in 1803.[4] G. B. Malleson rightly calls it one of "the decisive battles of India."[5] Three days later the British occupied Delhi as inheritors of the Mughal Empire. In 1803, following a British victory in the Battle of Delhi, a permanent British Resident was installed. The power center shifted from the Red Fort to the Residency.

At the imperial level the British replaced the Mughals. Alwar signed an "Offensive and Defensive Alliance" with the British. The support of the British restabilized the Rajput State system and underlay the Naruka Rajput State from its inception.[6] At a later stage, at the regional level Mewat was divided into two types of regimes, the princely under British Paramountcy and the directly administered territory of the British Empire that included the Gurgaon District of southeastern Punjab.

The action of *Kaulānī* is situated in northern Alwar around Ramgarh and Ghata near Firozpur. The Naruka Rajput rulers of Alwar were rewarded with territories in Mewat and Rath from the British for their assistance against the Marathas. Bakhtawar Singh, ruler of Alwar (r. 1791–1815) also acquired Tijara and Tapukra, semiurban settlements in northeastern Mewat, in exchange for the region of Haryana and a hundred thousand rupees. Firozpur was under the rule of Nawab Ahmad Baksh, a well-known former chief administrative official of the Alwar State. He had been rewarded with the principality of Firozpur for helping negotiate the 1803 treaty between Lord Lake and Maharaja Bakhtawar Singh.

Mewat, which had only recently become part of the Alwar territory, had yet to accept kingly control, and *Kaulānī* keenly expresses the sensibility of competing sovereignties and the community locked in a struggle with the regional state. It indicates the difficult incorporation of groups into the settlement regimes that had been initiated under the impact of nineteenth-century colonialism. This was a larger process of absorbing tribal, nomadic, and peasant groups who inhabited the forest and cultivated lands. The intrusion of cultivation/sedentarization into forest zones occurred in the several states that had developed after the decline of the Mughals.[7] In Mewat the conflict was more intense given the area's strategic location, close to Delhi, and the Meos' own traditions of resistance and social solidarity.

The Rajputs like the English inherited the sultanate-Mughal state's construction of the Meos as rebellious subjects. In Maharaja Bakhtawar Singh's old as well as new territory they are the "most numerous and troublesome of his subjects," who are characterized as "always notorious for their turbulence and predatory habits" and as plunderers, famous for their "raids and insurrections." "They gave much trouble to Lord Lake's forces in the Maratha War of 1803 while in the Mutiny they were conspicuous for their readiness to take advantage of disorder."[8] This construction fed into the colonial discourse of criminality. The question that needs to be asked is why resistance was read as crime.

There is ample evidence of peasant unrest in the two princely states. We know from conventional "textual" sources that several movements against the payment of revenue took place in Mewat: between 1806 and 1831 in northern Alwar and in 1818, 1829, and 1831 in eastern Alwar. In large measure the attempts at political control and revenue extraction of the princely regimes reinforced by colonial power and the consequent onslaught on hitherto relatively autonomous local power bases led to the several uprisings.

The fledgling Alwar State that was less than thirty years old required more revenue to face the challenges of state formation in difficult times, for its adventurist policies as well as for architectural investments such as gardens, cenotaphs, palaces, and forts. Bakhtawar Singh was attempting to gain control of politics in the neighboring Jaipur State by conspiring with dissidents. In 1811 he even sent the Alwar army to intervene.

While additional sources of revenue were required for state formation, the very nature of the Rajput polity made the jagirdari areas less accessible for the ruler. The kinship elite of the *bārah koṭrī* (literally, twelve chambers) or twelve Naruka lineages theoretically possessed a coparcenary right to land and power. As agnatic descendants of the founding conqueror, they could potentially provide an heir to the kingdom. As jagirdars they had to be pacified since not only had the monarchy been created at their expense but also the continued support of the bhai bandh, or brotherhood, was required for the monarch's state building policies. Hence the jagirs, or land grants, in the tehsils of Thana Ghazi, Bansur, and Kishangarh that displaced local landholders.[9] The areas in the south around Lachhmangarh and Rajgarh given to Naruka jagirdars virtually became frozen as a source of revenue. In addition, Bakhtawar Singh had to grant new jagirs to the Rajputs.

In the *khalsa,* or Crown lands, revenue was paid directly into the imperial treasury rather than the areas under jagirdari. The former were, hence, more favorable for the expansion of the fiscal base of the state. The Meos possessed the most fertile and intensely irrigated lands in the state. The sedentarization accomplished in the Mughal period had transformed a warrior pastoral economy to a peasant political economy. The cropping pattern shows a millet-producing area where pearl millet, sorghum, and barley were the chief crops of the Kishangarh and Ramgarh tehsils. Industrialization was negligible and commercialization of agriculture had not begun.

A series of attacks were launched against the Meo peasants by the Naruka Rajput State. We have a few fragmentary accounts from ethnographic sources. On the basis of a diary of a Muhammad Yusuf, Powlett mentions that the Meo population (of Tijara) was very rebellious. The diwan (administrative chief) took Indor "but there was much fighting with the Meos for years," especially in 1814 when the pargana (administrative unit for revenue collection) was measured. Multiple strategies were used to curb the "refractory" Meos including an alternation of the strategies of coercion and conciliation. Powlett describes the roles of a Rajput called Jahaz and of another called Bhagvan Dass:

> Tijara was placed by the Maharao Raja in the charge of one Jahaz, a *chela* or slave, who, by exchanging turbans with the principal Meos, established friendly relations with them, so that when ordered to send the leading Meos into Ulwur, he had no difficulty in getting them to come to a feast, where they were all seized, carried to Ulwur, and

> compelled to pay Rs. 10,000 for their release. One Bhagwan Dass was sent to realise the money, and oppressed the Meos much. He was joined by Jahaz, who plundered [the] villages Lapala, Palasli, Nimli, and Alapur. Khavani Meo of Lapala was an active insurgent, and being seized by Jahaz was put to death.[10]

The description encapsulates aspects of the Rajput State–Meo relationship: state oppression, duplicity and plunder, the dispossession of the rebels, and their reinforced insurgency. The same event is described by the Mewati narrative. Raja Bakhtawar Singh, Bhagvan Das, Jahaz, and Khavani Meo are the dramatis personae of the oral (later written) text. Powlett's written account consists merely of a single paragraph and there is only brief mention of the persons involved. The Meo narrative, on the other hand, captures in magnificent detail the textures of the early nineteenth century: the processes of state formation, power relations, land control, and modes of Meo protest and resistance. The oral tradition is often attributed with telescoping, but in this case it is clearly the purported history that telescopes the time span of half a century.

The Feud, State Crime, and Abducted Women

In *Kaulānī* as in the case of many south Indian epics, the battle is over land but the narrative has far greater resonances with the widespread north Indian genre of martial epics dominated by motifs of honor and revenge.[11] It takes us through two decades or more after 1806 (VS 1863) during which period the "subjugation" of the Meo villages of northeastern Alwar was substantially accomplished. The printed version of the narrative mentions that the conflict between state and community lasted for fifty-two years.

The oral text refers to a pastoral-agrarian society. The raids on cattle and the reference to cowherds *(gvāḷiyā)* and the girls who cut grass suggest the simultaneity of a bovine economy. The narrative is centered on the Bagh-orias, one of the most important of the thirteen Meo clans. State officials refer to them as belonging to a "wild" land *(bīhaṛ bhum)* and their chief or chaudhari as the Rao of the forest *(bīhaṛ pat rāv)*.

Kaulani is one of the major villages within the territory of the Baghora clan. The topography, landscaped by steep hills of the ancient Aravalli range, deep ravines, and uneven land crisscrossed by many streams and rivulets that flow from the mountains, gave the Meos "inaccessible fortresses." A later observer mentions the good soil and wonderful millet crops, excellent wells with sweet water, and the large herds of cattle.[12] Chaudhari Baksa Meo claims that his land is very fertile. The terrain includes arable land, pastures, and forests being brought under cultivation. Considerable internal autonomy is encoded in the narrative. Meo clans have horsemen, drums *(dhondhī)*, and headmen or chiefs *(chaudharis/raos)*.The chief's politico-juridical power is symbolized by his turban *(pāg)*, tied after the death of his father in a rite of patrilineal succession.

The story begins with an account of the feud between a Meo clan and two Khanazada headmen, Jabbar and Jhangir Khan.

> The two brothers, Jabbar and Jhangir Khan, live at Mubarakpur and are "informers" of the government. They have the power to give up to six months' imprisonment or the punishment of *kāṭh koyṛā*.[13] Maharaja Bakhtawar Singh gifts Jabbar Khan with a *siropāv* consisting of a horse, a woollen shawl, and turban for his work as an informer.
>
> Although Jabbar Khan's horse is stolen by a Meo from Sivana he thinks that the Meos from Kaulani who belong to the Baghora Pal have taken it. With this misunderstanding he catches Jalam, a Baghora Meo, in the bazaar. Rai Khan, the son of the chief of the Baghora Meos, protests to Jabbar Khan that he is trying to pick a fight. But Jabbar Khan's reply is that the stealing of the horse and the attack on the town is a question of his turban [i.e., of his honor].
>
> Rai Khan asks Jabbar once again to release Jalam. Rai Khan argues that he has been held captive on mere suspicion *[bodī bāt]* since the Kaulani Meos have not stolen the horse *[terā nāny haro ghoṛo]*. Rai Khan is angered when Jabbar collects all the Khanazadas of Mubarakpur and takes the matter to the court of the Alwar ruler. He threatens Jabbar that he will take revenge unless Jalam is released, "your cattle will be stolen, the town will be looted" *[terī dhāndī lūṅgo chīn lūt lū kasbo sāro]*. But Jabbar refuses to release Jalam.
>
> Fourteen Meo *thāmas* [patrilineages] advance and capture the Khanazadas' cattle in retaliation for Jabbar's act of injustice *[amāī]*. Jalam manages to run away and joins the attackers. Thereupon the Khanazadas collect, beat their drum in the city, and attack the Meo villages with their horses and men to release the cows. In the resulting battle at Kaulani the seven brothers of the Khanazada, Jabbar Khan,

> are killed. Jabbar buries their corpses in seven graves that are worshiped by the Khanazadas who consider them their *saiyyads* [ancestral heroes].

The worship of the spirits of martyrs in battle suggests a larger ideology of honorable death that the Khanazadas would share with the Rajputs.[14]

The conflict between the Meos and the Khanazadas follows the typical pattern of a feud. Anthropologists define "feud" as prolonged and intermittent hostilities among groups who exist in intimate relation.[15] The Khanazadas' action of arresting and keeping Jalam detained in the *kāth*, or torture contraption, is regarded as an injury to the whole group to which the victim belongs. In effect, it produces what Radcliffe Brown describes as group liability, that is, an expression of collective solidarity in which any member of the offender's group may be slain for the crime of his relative.[16] The feud approximates the classical model with the three stages of injury, revenge, and counterrevenge. Both groups see themselves in terms of difference, as a *qaum*, or separate group. There is, of course, a close relation between qaum and *kuṭumb*, or extended family, as groups define themselves through the metaphor of kinship. Ideas of village and clan honor are expressed in Rai Khan's insistence that he will extract tribute in revenge for the defamation of the Meos, as the matter has gone up to the court of Alwar.

Kaulānī describes how a feud between two local groups, the Meos and the Khanazadas, is transformed into a conflict between the Rajput State and the Meos. Earlier I referred to single group identity of the Meos and the Khanazadas who are referred to by the Persian chroniclers as "Mewatis." The Khanazadas emerged as an important regional power when a section of the Mewatis began taking a greater interest in court politics and were coopted by the late sultanate. Known as Khanazadas now, they entered into marriage alliances with the Mughals, and their ritual practice tended toward greater purity in an Islamist sense. The Meos continued to have a more distinctly liminal identity. Their marginality, liminality, and resistance fed into each other.[17] *Kaulānī* indicates also the political distancing of the Khanazadas and the Meos as the former collaborated with the Alwar State and later with the British in the mid-nineteenth century. The narrativized conflict between the Meos and the Khanazadas is in explicit contrast to *Dariyā Khāñ*, where they are described in kin terms and jointly fight the Minas. In the *Pālon kī Bansābalī* Julla Khanazada is referred to as an ancestor of a Meo clan. Julla was the Khanazada nawab of a fortified village called Ghosavdi around the 1760s. The Mewati oral tradition thus presents a constantly shifting kaleidoscope of intercommunity relations that might be mapped in terms of kinship, alliance, friendship, feud, and enmity.

Social conflict becomes a play of attack and counterattack. *Kaulānī* vividly describes mutual looting, the formation of attacking hordes *(dhāṛ)* consisting of both men and horses. Census records of the later half of the nineteenth century describe both Meos and Khanazadas as predominantly Muslim groups. But the shared religion hardly signifies as a critical variable in defining community. What matters far more are group interests and the structure of alliances. In the Meo view the Khanazadas obtained the support of the Mughals and the Rajputs. Indeed, Meos claim that they stopped intermarrying with the Khanazadas because of the latter's marital alliances with the Mughals.[18] In contrast, to the malleable Khanazadas, the Meos were considered deviant Muslims and difficult and troublesome by both the Mughals and the Rajputs. Clearly, power helps define fluctuating coalitions. As collaborators with the ruling elite of Alwar, the Khanazadas and Pathans were addressed as "Khan Sahib."[19]

There is an obvious shift from the Rajput-Khanazada conflictual relationship that characterized the initial rise of Naruka Rajput power in Alwar. Pratap Singh (r. 1775–91), the founder of the Alwar State, had sought the assistance of a Rajput, Sarup Singh, to suppress the local power of the Khanazadas that then extended over Bharatpur and Alwar. The Khanazada chief had built a strong fort in Ghasauli near Govindgarh. Sarup Singh, said to be "bound by ties of friendship and [marriage?] alliance" with the Khanazadas had, however, refused to help. In 1776 Sarup Singh, who had also refused to present a *nazar* (prestation conventionally given at a ruler's accession), was put to a gruesome death with a strip of wet hide bound over his head. His fort was also taken away. Pratap Singh then laid the foundation of the fort and temple of Lachmangarh. Of the two parganas with the Rajput, Mubarakpur was taken and Khilora was subsumed under the tehsil of Ramgarh. The Khanazadas managed to maintain their independence through Pratap Singh's reign and continued to be based at the fort of Ghasauli. In 1803 Bakhtawar Singh, with the help of the Marathas, expelled the Khanazada leader Zulfikar Khan. The fort was demolished, and the foundations of the fort and town of Govindgarh were laid by Bakhtawar Singh.[20]

The narrative obliterates this evidence of the displacement of the Khanazadas by early Rajput state formation. The quelling of Khanazada power was simultaneous with their induction into the state apparatus. *Kaulānī* demonstrates the kingly gifting of the siropav (literally, head to toe, usually a robe) to Jabbar Khan. This was an established practice in several Indian polities. This gift of the sovereign for the lesser chief/subordinate was often given along with the right to levy taxes. This is a widespread strategy of ritual incorporation into sovereignty intimating the sharing of ruling authority. The king's sacrificial role in this case is replaced by gift-giving whether of titles or lands, food or clothing. As Dirks points out, the publicly and dramatically displayed transaction carries reciprocal expectations of obedience, loyalty, and service. Ritual gifting takes place in a variety of situations, including offerings to the brahman or the bard, and parallels the transactions of puja, or worship of the gods. It suggests the political redefinition of caste hierarchies.[21]

In the narrative a consensual procedure for deciding to do battle is described, so that the Meos only advance after the entire clan confers at the customary feast usually held preceding the battle. This is in contrast to the more hierarchical pattern of state decision-making where war-making is projected as dependent on the will of the ruler. Hence, the narrative describes the maharaja as prevailing over the diwan who advises him against a later attack on the Meos. The narrative perspective on the kingly mode of power is of command for the subject-slaves *(dīno hukam rāv bakhtes dās ne bīṛo khāyo)*. In the Rajput polity, however, the raja was quite likely to consult his brotherhood. Although the narrative might have distorted procedure, it provides an interesting popular perspective on monarchy. *Kaulānī* also describes the means of politics that include the use of informers: when General Hathi Singh camps at Ramgarh he asks first for the *bhedī*, the person who collects intelligence about the tehsil. The *chobdār* (the military official responsible for communicating messages and keeping the musical instruments) approaches a merchant named Prabhu Singh to reveal "the secrets of the tehsil," coaxing him:

ham bāman tam bāniyāñ nā laṛbā kī ṭev
samar bhumm dhartī kisī hīṇ ko kisyo markhaṇo mev

I'm a brahman, you're a baniya,
unused to fighting.[22]
What is that land like
from where these brave Meos come?

Not-so-subtle mockery here of the upper-caste brahmans and baniyas lacking in masculinity from a warrior-ksatriya perspective.

The next frame of *Kaulānī* describes the intervention of the Alwar State in favor of the Khanazadas. Following the battle of Kaulani, Jabbar complains at the Alwar darbar that seven of his brothers have been killed: "All the Tanvar [Meos] attacked, broke the power of Pata [a village with a large concentration of Khanazadas]."[23]

In fact the real destroyers of Khanazada power had been the Naruka Rajputs in the 1760s. But it is indexical of their absorption into structures of power that in the narrative, Jabbar Khan plays upon the threat to Rajput rule from the Meos particularly of the Baghora clan:

tero amal uṭhāi det hāñ apṇo alvar gaṛh saj rākh
dagṛā chalañ hāñ thabaktā suṇkar baghoṛā kī dhāk

They challenge your power
guard your Alwar fort.[24]
Travelers fear to walk the roads
for the terror of the Baghora.

The Khanazadas exaggerate the threat from the Baghora Meos at the court. The challenge to the Khanazadas of Pata is made into a threat to all the Alwar State: "The Baghora Meos will end your *hukūmat* [rule]. If this continues then your rule will extend only up to Alwar city." The maharaja is worried. Jabbar Singh arouses his Rajput *josh* [sense of honor] instigating the prince, "the throne is eternal [but] the Tanvar [Meos] want to take over the land."[25] He urges, "the people of Rath Bighota [even] give them the tax." He refers to the Meo *bagāvat* [rebellion] and refusal to pay revenue to the state. Jabbar plays upon the Meos' having taken away "thousands of cows" and the symbols of sovereignty: the valuable turban and the horse gifted by the raja.

The Khanazada-Meo feud conjoins with the Meo refusal to pay revenue. The topographical term "*bīhaṛ bhum*" bears connotations of rebelliousness. The state's diwan, a brahman called Bhagvan, advises the maharaja to desist from interfering in the local dispute. He urges the ruler, "They [Khanazadas and Meos] live close together and their fighting is constant. They have not harmed the village, Raja, don't accept the [Khanazada] complaint." But the ruler insists on intervening on behalf of the Khanazadas. This makes a fundamental shift in what has up to now been a local conflict.

The state's advent is symbolized by the playing of military-musical instruments: the *dhaunsā* (bugle), the *tambūr* (kettle drums), and the *jaṇg kā bigūl* (battle bugle). The last hints at the penetration of the colonial war musicology. The army is led by the Rajput general Hathi Singh. With the intervention of the state the equivalence implicit in the notion of the feud is disturbed. The imbalance continues in the conflict spread over some decades. The narrative is a commentary on the state's violation of the rules of the feud. Traditionally the negative reciprocity of feud cognizes the rules for the stranger. For example, that fighting be suspended by mutual consent after sundown and messengers and mediators remain unharmed. The state's involvement in vendetta takes the form of death through execution, violating the rules for the stranger. The Meo chief, Chaudhari Baksa, is killed, despite his having been promised protection by the state. The commemoration in collective memory of Baksa's "betrayal" and execution by Rajputs as a form of sacrificial death and of remembered violence reproduces the heroic community. The pattern is repeated in Powlett's account of the death of Khwani quoted above. The state is also implicated in the abduction of Meo women.

General Hathi Singh reaches Firozpur and the army pitches its tents. The politics of another kingdom intervenes. The narrative expresses the Meo sense of otherness for the Firozpur ruler, Nawab Ahmad Bakas, referring to him as a "Mughal." Mansa, a Daimrot Meo chief of Ghata, captures Hathi Singh's horse. Nawab Ahmad Bakas tells Hathi Singh, "Ghata is rebellious which is why the Daimrot Meos have taken your horse." He adds that although he has "broken the villages of all the raiders of the country, Ghata remains rebellious and doesn't pay the revenue of the state" *(jitnā dauṛā des kā sabkā maiṇe liyā gāñvrā toṛ/jamā bharaiṇā rāj kī mosū ghāṭo raho āmoṛ)*. The verse brings out the underlying relationship between stigmatization and the nonpayment of revenue. It legitimizes state action against the so-called bandits *(dauṛā* or *dhaṛait)*. The intensity of Meo resistance to the measurement of agricultural land has been mentioned. The peasantization of the community is responded to by retaliatory raiding.

The state counters resistance and raiding are by an identical coercive strategy:

baṛ phajar dhāvo karo gaṛh ghāṭa pe jāy
sattar pakṛā ādmī inkī nosai chīnī gāy

ahmad bakas navāb ne bāt kahī bhārī
gaṛh ghāṭā kū toṛke pakaṛ lī do sai dubyārī

Early in the morning
fort Ghata is attacked.
Seventy men are caught
nine hundred cows are seized.
The Nawab Ahmed Bakas
speaks commandingly.
He breaks the fort Ghata
captures two hundred girls cutting grass.

Dubyārī refers to the girls' task of cutting fodder for the cattle they graze. The two hundred girls, nine hundred cows, and seventy men are shut up in the fortress of Firozpur.

The narrative of state formation leaves no space for state crime. Social contractualists from Hobbes to Rawls describe instead the state as the agency of order, and even justice. Ideologies of ruling groups such as the Rajputs emphasize the role of the ruler as protector of the kingdom.[26] *Kaulānī* suggests the involvement of Meos and Rajputs in cattle raids. Bruce Lincoln has pointed out that the cattle-raiding myth is paradigmatic as the warrior establishes his sovereignty. There is a quest of the hunter-pastoral-nomad for booty and treasure. He points out that the raid has cosmogonic implications, being a model for world creation or expansion. In the case of the Rajputs there is the added act of bride-stealing that expresses the masculinity of the states headed by the maharaja and the nawab.[27]

The narrative from the oral tradition describes both state crime and the division of the "loot" between the nawab and the maharaja. Musi and Maddi, the abducted daughters of the Daimrot Meo chief, are made captives of the Alwar ruler and the Firozpur nawab, respectively. Musi protests strongly after she is caught and put into a *dol* (palanquin) by the Rajputs. Maddi is made to undergo *nikāh* with the nawab despite her protests and is subsequently sent to Loharu. To her and Qutb-ud-Din Loharu was born the unfortunate Shams-ud-Din, later hanged by the British. A Charan (Rajput bardic) account, however, redescribes Musi as an orphaned Rajput girl who was bought up by a prostitute and given a home and protection by the king. The story indicates contestatory oral traditions and the Rajput attempt at reinscription of Musi's identity (as well as the messiness of Rajput liaisons with women of other castes and religions) implying an honorable ruler who married a "fallen" woman's daughter.[28]

"Folklore" is a seemingly innocent category. But more often than not it is deeply imbued with politics. The genre of the *marsiyā*, or the death elegy, is derived from Indian Shi'ism. It consists of poetic compositions on Imam Husain's death in the Battle of Karbala or expresses praise of a dead person. This genre is transformed into an elegiac Rajput account that erases the ruler's role in abduction.

The colonial account of the conflict provides another instance of the overwriting of history that might well be called communal in the subcontinental usage of the term. According to O'Dwyer, the Meos were "instigated" by the neighboring nawab of Firozpur, Ahmad Baksh, who had "quarreled with his old master on account of Bakhtawar Singh's cruel persecution of his Musalman subjects, and therefore worked up the Meos against him."[29]

The oral account clearly contradicts colonial and kingly "histories," the "communal" and statist readings that impute an exclusive "Muslim" identity to the Meos. In the Meo perspective both Nawab Ahmad Baksh and Maharaja Bakhtawar Singh along with his Rajput ruling elite are liable for state crimes and the abduction of the Daimrot sisters. Their alliance continues through subsequent battles with the Meos. According to the printed text of the narrative, Anvar Khan, the commander of the army of the Firozpur kingdom, repeatedly assists in the battles of Bhopal Singh and Kanvar Jahaj that follow.[30] The event hardly denotes any religious mobilization. Indeed, *Kaulānī* mentions by name representatives of Mughal and Pathan families who fought alongside the Rajputs against the Meos. On the other hand, other castes, including brahmans, are allied with the Meos. This raises a major set of questions with respect to the historiographical-ethnographic construction of identity politics.

The complexity of religious belief and practice is further foregrounded in the episode of the Battle of Hathi Singh or the Jhir ki larai (the Battle of Jhir). The two conflicts of the Meos with the Khanazadas and the Firozpur ruler develop into a larger Meo-Rajput confrontation in the second part of the narrative. The Rajputs demand that the cows be returned to the Khanazadas but are silent on the question of the Rajput army and nawab's joint raid on the Daimrot Meos and the booty thereof. Instead, the Rajput army is dispatched under Hathi Singh. It camps at the pilgrimage site of Jhir to take the sacred bath on *sūmotī amāvas (somvatī amāvasyā)*. Incidentally, this day of the new moon that falls on a Monday is regarded as particularly auspicious by both Rajputs and Meos. The narrative suggests the Meos participation in śakta traditions of the worship of the goddess. Meo and other devotees still visit the Jhir goddess' temple where the *snāna*, or purifying, sin-destroying bath, is taken.[31]

In the narrative it is the Rajputs who take the ritual bath although the goddess eventually intervenes on the Meos' behalf. The Meo counterattack is led by Rai Khan and his father, the Baghora chief called Baksa. The Rajputs are besieged and all access to the Jhir valley blocked. The Meos of several clans such as the Gorval, Dairhval, Baghora, and Ravat, present a combined front of the "brotherhood." Hathi Singh is killed, and the Meos are able to rescue the two hundred girls, seventy men, and nine hundred cows after breaking into the fortress of Firozpur. The self-image of the Meos is described in terms such as "*markhaṇo*" (brave). It is underlined by the image of Rajput duplicity, for Hathi Singh's family calls Baksa Meo under false pretenses and kills him.

The long drawn-out conflict is over power *(amal)* and land control. In the second part of the story, called "the Battle of Kaulani," Raja Bakhtawar Singh's mother's brother, called Bhopal Singh, takes up the challenge to "conquer the wild," the region of the Baghora Pal. Bhopal Singh's attempt to break Meo power is supported by his Rajput kin and by the Pathans (Afghans) Abdal Khan and Sabdal Khan and the "Mughal" Anvar Khan. Another Meo chief called Mukati has been refusing to pay the revenue due for the past twelve years *(jamā jo bārah baras kī tolū hargaj desū nāny).*

Bhopal Singh leads an army. He summons two informers, Syalti and Bhagmal, who are Nai Meos, to tell him the names of Meo leaders. Mark again the alliances that cut across religious affiliation that are obfuscated in the "history." The betrayal by the Nai Meos intimates the fissures within the Meos that provided a possible space for manipulation by the Alwar State.

Bhopal tries to lure Baksa by promising that he will make him the "chief of the wild." The offer is rejected. Syalti and Bhagmal come to Kaulani and suggest that the Meos pay the government 8 annas per plow, and the rest will be absolved of the remaining outstanding amount. Rai Khan agrees to give 8 annas per plow but in lieu of the outstanding twelve-year payment and 650 annas are collected. At first the entire village collects 8 annas per plow. But Sale Khan refuses, stating, "I accept no man's authority." The rest also take their coins back. Bhopal Singh now attacks Kaulani. The battle of Kaulani is waged for three days until Bhopal Singh is killed.

The third part of the story, called "Kanvar Jahaj ki larai," begins when

> Bakhtawar Singh writes to his nephew, Kanvar Jahaj, a Rao of Jaipur, to take up the challenge of avenging the death of Bhopal Singh. Jahaj declares he will break up the Meo pals, defeat Kaulani and establish a fortress there.

Powlett mistakenly refers to Jahaj as a "*chela* or slave," but the Meo narrative describes Kanvar Jahaj as belonging to the Chela Rajput clan of Jaipur.

> Jahaj is warned of the rebellious land of Kaulani and is told, "You cannot control Kaulani for the Meos rule there" *[tero kaulānī baskī nahīn thāro tapai mev ko rāj]*. But the Rajputs hope "control over the land will be ours" *[kabjā rahgā hāth maiṇ donū khaṛā jhujjār]*.

The force reaches Baghor, near Tijara, located thirty miles northeast of Alwar. Jahaj attacks Kaulani along with his five hundred men. But the Meos surround the Rajput force. Wave after wave of the Rajput onslaught is turned back.

The mythic tradition records the role of the leaders of the Meo community, Rai Khan, Sarup Singh, Khawani, Syalti, Madari, Dalmod, Dhan Singh, Abdulla, and others, who lead the fourteen Meo thamas (patrilineages). The Meos have the support of other local castes as well, such as the brahmans, Gujars, Nais, Kumhars, and Chamars. Repeated attacks are fought back. On the Rajput side, the Pathans are killed and so are several Rajput thakurs (heads of their households and lineages). Ram and Bhopal Singh's families are compensated with the land grants of Jhareda and Hathi Singh's with that of Hadreda located near Kaulani.

In Meo narratives, gods, goddesses, and saints frequently come to the aid of Meos in trouble. Jalam manages to escape from the Khanazadas when he prays to the Pir to help him against Jabbar Khanazada who is showing his strength *(jabbar jorī kar raho merī madat karā ne pīr)*. The saint mediates with the Lord *(khudā)* who responds to the pleas of Jalam, and he manages to break out of the cagelike contraption and join the Meos. When the Rao "of the fifty-two forts" (a metaphor for the Alwar ruler) attacks Kaulani, Gora (Parvati) wakens her sleeping husband, Shiva:

> *vā bihaṛ pat rāv pai chahṛo saglo des*
> *vāsū kaise jīte bihṛo ṣivjī molū baṛo sandes*

The Rao of the wild
is attacked by the entire country.
How can those of the wild be victorious
Shivji, what is your message?

Shiva, of course, foretells the victory of the Meos.

Kaulani is described as protected by the undulating landscape and the goddess of Jhir so that even the (Mughal) Badshah's generals, Hamdani and Harnath, attacked but could not conquer it:

bāgī bhūmm gidāvaṛo hūñ devī ko thān
bādsā bī hārgā jinkā rahgā dhol nisān

The rebel land is hilly
with the goddess shrine.
The (Mughal) Badshahs were also turned back
left their drum and flag behind.

The dhol and nishan are symbols of power. The community's victory is seen as an aspect of the power and protection of the goddess who is herself the embodiment of śakti, or cosmic energy.

The Meos begin the battle of Kaulani "after having remembered the 'thirty-three crore' [or 33 billion] gods" *(roḷo teg uṭhāy kiroṛ tetīs manākar)*, which is a conventional enumeration of the number of deities in Hindu mythologies. Along with their allies from other castes, they manage to burn the ammunition deposit and alcohol store of the Rajputs. The Rajputs and Pathans possess the superior technology of cannon fire, and fifty-one Meos die in the battle of the cannon. But the Rajputs are finally routed and Kanvar Jahaj flees.

The resistance of Kaulani continues for twelve years. Finally, the Alwar ruler sends Thakur Bhairu Singh of the Jaipur kingdom. He lives disguised as a Meo in the fort for another twelve years and is eventually able to become a *pagṛī palaṭ* brother of the Meos. The term suggests how a relation of alliance assumes a ritual character with the exchange of turbans. The possibilities of "fictive" kinship present a mode of bridging difference and of incorporating the Meos into the state. His descendant, the present thakur of Raghunathgarh, confirmed the details of Meo cultural memory when I interviewed him.

The violence of the state continues. History, written mostly from the vantage point of the state, records its struggle with the Meos through the nineteenth century and its eventual victory. The conflict extended also to the productive and prosperous terrain of the Nai and Duhlot Meo Pals spread over the villages of Naugaon, Charaonda, and Nikach that possessed very rich land.

The powerful Nai Meos along with the Khanazadas were owners of the twenty-two villages that are said to have given Bakhtawar Singh "much trouble."[32] Kingly control was established by building a fortress and breaking up the large villages. The rule of Maharaja Banni Singh (1815–57), Bakhtawar Singh's successor, was not substantially different. The ruler, who was a great builder, also came to be known for his oppression. With the help of two Muslim brothers from Delhi known as the "Delhi Diwans," he undertook stringent administrative reforms including a tightening of the fiscal regime. Powlett writes that the Meos of Nikach, in the valley nine miles northwest of Ramgarh, "were so troublesome that Banni Singh drove the people away from their village under the hill, near which a fort called Bajrangarh was built, and compelled them to live in a number of small hamlets scattered about the village lands."

Banni Singh "attacked and burnt" Kaulani in 1818.[33] The pattern is by now familiar: armed attack, dispersal of the population of the large villages, confiscation of their grazing lands, and establishment of "a fort to overawe the rebellious." The appropriation of grazing lands suggests the sedentarizing impetus of the state. Less than two decades later, in 1831, the same moves are repeated in the same area. Two versions of the revolt in the Ramgarh area are documented in Lockett's *Narrative*.[34] This text foregrounds the relationship between revenue default and "crime." Lockett noted the financial difficulties of the state because of "its treaty responsibility to divide revenues with Tijara [from where Bakhtawar and Musi's son ruled after the division of the kingdom], but more importantly because of the continued reluctance of the Meos in eastern Alwar to pay the state's land revenue demands."

The elements of princely state policy are clearly spelt out in Lockett's account. At the first stage the group is defined, classified, and categorized. State policy follows as a matter of consequence. The rao raja (Banni Singh's) version is represented as troubled mainly by his

> refractory Mewattee subjects, who were in constant rebellion and kept out his troops many months in the year. A large body of them had at

> this very time assembled in a menacing attitude at *Koolanee,* near Ram Gurh, and he was sending out a strong force against them, consisting of Cavalry, Infantry and Guns. His intention was he said, to exterminate a portion of them, by way of example — to demand hostages from some of the principal Zamindars for their future good behavior, and to erect a strong Gurhee in some convenient spot which would enable him to [keep] troops in readiness to overawe them at all times. He and his Ministers seemed to think that this course of proceeding against the Mewattees would have a most salutary tendency, and restore in a short time order and tranquillity throughout the Country.[35]

Later a police post was established at Ramgarh.

The Alwar army inflicted "signal chastisement" as it burned entire villages and carried off cattle.[36] Banni Singh attempted to break the backbone of Meo resistance by resorting to the military option and a policy of "hamletization. The large [turbulent!] villages were broken up, and the residents were resettled in smaller hamlets closer to the fields, which were cultivated under the supervision of occupying armies." As a result "the popular consciousness which could spawn united political action" was dispersed and "the Meo peasants were placed under the control of the troops of the central government."[37] The authority of the Alwar State was thereby established over Kaulani. The village lies in ruins to this day. The new Meo settlement is at Raghunathgarh.

In 1835 Maharao Banni Singh once again broke up and burned the large Meo village of Nikach and established a fort when its inhabitants refused to present a *nazar,* or ritual prestation.[38] Faulkner records this action as having accomplished the difficult task of bringing "the most troublesome of his subjects . . . into a condition of complete order and submission."[39] The brutality of state policy caused considerable alarm among the Muslims of Delhi, who threatened an invasion of Alwar. Bahadur Shah, the Mughal emperor, also complained to the British Agent. Powlett describes the outcome as a success of state policy commenting that "since their complete subjection by Bakhtawar Singh and Banni Singh . . . they have become generally well behaved." Although, he adds, they return to their former habits when opportunity occurs.[40]

Nonetheless, Lockett is able to get another version, divergent from the monarchical, on the events at Kaulani. In his report the correlation between Mewati action and peasant concerns is clearly established, as "many respect-

Figure 8
Meo villagers of the new settlement called Raghunathgarh, which was established in the early nineteenth century after the battles with Kaulani.

Figure 9
Meos of the Baghora clan at Raghunathgarh with Chaudhari Dalpat Khan *(far right)*, descendant of Rai Khan.

able persons" with whom he conversed during his stay at Alwar gave him "a very different account" of the matter: "They attributed the whole of the disorders to the Rajas *[sic]* personal character combined with the proceedings of the administration, which were calculated they said, to drive the people to open rebellion. They represented the whole system of administration as radically vicious."[41]

Lockett's concern was to represent the Rajputana states in a condition of Hobbesian anarchy in order to create grounds for colonial penetration and far-reaching systemic "reform." His description of the contract system of revenue collection is vivid: "the districts were rented to the highest bidder for the year, or the season, without any, or very little respect to the character of the contractor. During his short tenure, he exercises every species of severity and exaction on those placed under him and is himself in turn, fined, degraded, expelled and frequently imprisoned. . . . [T]he Country is consequently in the hands of a number of greedy, unprincipled adventurers."

Revenue collection was made in accordance with the contract system according to which "all land in Alwar (including temples) is farmed out . . . to the highest bidder" with the understanding that half the revenue would be remitted. This had become a fairly widespread practice among rulers in the days of the later Mughals.[42] Lockett gives two examples of revenue contractors from the baniya caste. In Lachhmangarh, land was farmed to Jiwa Ram for Rs. 175,000. Four districts of the Rao Raja's dominions including Alwar were farmed to Nand Khan, "a man of property" who "assumed the dress and appearance of a Rajpoot."[43]

Not surprisingly, complaints were made at Alwar against the Jaipur State for giving shelter and protection in their territory to "refractory and defaulting zamindars" who had fled from Alwar. Govindgarh is described as being in such a distressed state at the collection of 75 percent of its net assets, and "revenue in some of the villages was so high that it was marvellous how the people paid it at all."

Administrative response by the Meo peasantry was predictable. Protest and nonpayment of revenue was largely seen as a law and order problem and called for a repressive response. Hence, the emphasis on "reducing" the peasantry in correspondence and dispatches. British administrators also conceived of the problem in essentialist terms, drawing upon a larger theoretical paradigm. The Meos were an erstwhile "Dravidian tribe" given to predatory activity. Meo self-knowledge is cited in defense of the administrative policy of *pahle lāt, phir bāt*. This dictum of "first kick them then talk to them" is

FIGURE 10
Architectural signs of internal colonization: the Rajput Thakur's fortress at Kaulani-Raghunathgarh.

justified for the (Meos) "themselves admit, they are good only while kept under.'[44]

Without the Meo oral-written version of the events of the early nineteenth century the statist-colonial account of history would have prevailed. The narrative makes it possible for us to prise open both the character of state formation and statist discourse as it appears in document, report, history, and ethnography.

An account of early nineteenth-century state formation is intimated by Kaulani's political lexicon. The princely state (referred to as *hukumat, riyasat*) is characterized by the monarchy including his court and throne *(darbār, singhāsan)*, a network of informers *(mukbar, siyāmkhor)*, and messengers *(harīlo/ailchī)*. Peabody points out that in the eighteenth century Rajasthan kings were highly conscious of the polity's centrifugal tendencies and attempted to mitigate them by sending news-gatherers to spy on provincial administrators and jagirdars, and practicing divide and rule in local conflicts.[45] The Alwar State's coercive power comprises the military with platoons of soldiers *(fauj, palṭan)*, generals, policemen, and a network of police *chaukīs* (posts). One of the major functions of government is the collection of revenue *(jamā)*. The revenue administration includes officials such as the tehsildar and the lambardars of a tehsil who might be village leaders. That Mughal administrative units continue is evidenced by the use of terms such as "*mauza*" and "*pargana*'." State power penetrates with the expanded network of thanas and fortresses. The Alwar ruler was considerably preoccupied with the building of forts, palaces, and temples. *Garhīs*, or forts, not only were architectural symbols of rank and power but also served to control local politics, quell resistance to revenue collection, house arms, and station the militia, including infantry and cavalry. Frequently the fort also marked the expansion of the state into an inner frontier or served as a police post.

Court prestation is a mode of ritual subordination, like bowing or offering tribute. As with the Mughals, the presentation of the nazar symbolizes ritual acceptance of the sovereign's overarching authority. Clearly there are continuities with ideas of ritualized sovereignty derived from precolonial practice in which the ruler is responsible for the limited functions of warfare, the service of the gods, ritual prestation, and justice.

The narrative also indicates the occupational roles the major castes are associating themselves with. A brahman is the state diwan; Rajputs are ruling chiefs, generals in the princely army, and hold other high-level official positions. A certain level of economic development is indicated by references to the qasba or town and mandi (grain market). The town itself developed out of and around the grain market. The baniyas are merchants and moneylenders, or "mahajans," literally, the great and rich people of the town, but are also now revenue contractors and sometimes revenue officials. Kayasths have begun to figure in the nineteenth-century revenue administration, suggesting the growth of literate lineages that comprised the service gentry who moved into landholding by virtue of their official position and the mortgage and purchase of land.

Debating Kingship

How does this material comment on the extensive debates on Asiatic kingship and the precolonial Indian polity? Disturbed by a Eurocentric understanding of the state, there has been for the last three decades a quest for alternative formulations of the state that would better describe the non-European experience.[46] There was to begin with strong criticism of ideas of "feudalism" and "oriental despotism" derived from Marx.[47] The idea of the "segmentary state" drew upon research on the African "acephalous" kin-based polity. Geertz's model of the theater state has been particularly influential. It is closely related to the African anthropologist Southall's conception of a segmentary political universe. Geertz saw the court and capital of the Balinese State as representing a microcosm of the cosmic order. This exemplary center is replicated by subsidiary centers. Ceremony and ritual create sovereignty and authority. He writes, "mass ritual was not a device to shore up the state; the state was an enactment of mass ritual."[48]

The idea of the segmentary state has been applied to South Asia by Fox and Stein.[49] Stein applies the model to the early medieval Chola Empire, which existed from the ninth to the thirteenth century. He criticizes the view of ancient and medieval states as unitary, bureaucratized monarchies, and highlights their political decentralization. Stein identifies the local, political order as a "stateless" one since there is no formal state. Functions of government are embedded in multiple and autonomous "nuclear areas of corporate institutions" including caste, kinship, occupational groupings, and religious bodies. There is, he points out, much evidence of local taxation and of kingly warriors engaged in predatory warfare against chiefs nominally subordinate to them. The segmentary state, Stein argues, suggests at a pyramidal structure. Actual political control of the Cholas was only in the central domain, while ritual sovereignty held together intermediate and peripheral zones. The framework of legitimacy came from a religious ideology grounded in the Shiva cult. Chola ideas of a dharmic universe were realized through sacral kingship. In *Peasant State and Society in Medieval South India* Stein extends the idea of the segmentary state to the sixteenth-century Vijaynagar Empire pointing out that the empire subsumes many kinds of states.[50] Stein describes vertical segmentation in which the lowest levels of the village are linked to the highest level in their recognition of the ritual sovereignty of the highest central office. He demonstrates the existence of a ritually incorporative kingship in which sacrifice is the means by which the king is made sacred and is the means by which all other elements of the realm are incorporated and controlled.

The problem with the ritual sovereignty thesis arises when kingly ritual becomes a mode of violence, and kingship is not incorporative but exclusivist.[51] This understanding of premodern kingship has an implicit elite/state-centric orientation. It ignores the challenge to ritual hegemony posed by peasant groups, pastoralists, bandits, and other defiant groups that might reject state authority. Sacral kingship then has to be understood not only in terms of rāja dharma or ideological and performative aspects of the state but in terms also of its (il)legitimacy in popular perception, as an aspect of political process. In this case the focus is on the moral dimension of governance and of kingly authority, the perceived sense of justice or its absence.

Fox applies Southall's model to the traditional north Indian state. Fox describes the segmental organization of corporate kin groups or castes into the state and focuses on the relation between kinship and state. Stratified agnatic lineages "form local territorial cores onto which other kin groups are attached and settled affinally or cognatically." Stern, Rao, and Cohn are among the scholars critical of the segmentary state model. Cohn points out that the segmentary model was an outcome of the colonial understanding of the African polity.[52] Stern extends Dumont's argument emphasizing the importance of affinal rather than lineal kinship. Rao prefers to view the Ahir polity as federal.

Dirks and the Chicago School's transactional analysis have challenged the Dumontian structuralist view based on the disjunction between the realms of the king and brahman derived from the distinction between religion and power. Dirks examines the only princely state in Tamil Nadu, called Pudukkottai. He points out that the redistribution of tax-exempt land through the royal gift *(inām)* was a performative that constituted Hindu kingship and the Hindu polity. In Pudukkottai in the late nineteenth century more than two-thirds of territory was gifted, a conception quite difficult to explain in terms of the revenue rationality of neoclassical economics. Dirks questions Dumont's conception of "homo hierarchus," pointing out that caste was mutable. Dirks builds on Marriott's view of the importance of transaction or continuing exchanges in "coded substances" and also on Sahlins's statement that "chiefly pooling and redistribution of goods establishes a ranked centricity within groups." Dirks maintains that the king's gift to his political clients suggests the sharing of his divine persona, a politically established hierarchy, and the incorporation of the receiver into the kingdom with the king at its center. As he puts it, "The substance of the gift—the land rights, the titles, emblems, honors, and privilege of service, usufruct and command—was the partial sovereign substance of the king."[53] Note, however, that the gift represents simultaneously both incorporation and the *exclusion* of nonrecipients. This is demonstrated by the Khanazada/Meo case. But we will let this pass. Dirks's view restores the centrality of political process and the state marginalized by Dumont.

On the basis of his study of the Kota State, Peabody maintains that "Dirks has developed an overly formal 'top down' view of the traditional state that is largely unresponsive to 'ground up' centrifugal tendencies that simultaneously tend to undermine it." Symptomatic of this perspective, he points out, is Dirks's treatment of Pudukkottai in isolation rather than in a field of similarly constructed but overlapping polities, paramount powers, and political dependencies. As a result, Dirks failed to see how each of these centers advanced rival claims to kingship, sovereignty, and divinity, and how this affected the arrangement of territory. This is possibly because, Peabody states, Dirks's data are derived from late nineteenth-century land records and because colonial penetration had eliminated all other rival claims to sovereignty within the kingdom. Pudukkottai was the sole princely state in Tamil Nadu, in contrast to Rajputana where the contestation of sovereignty continued in the twenty-two contiguous "states and chiefships."[54]

Peabody's argument is akin to certain other writing on Indian kingship that has demonstrated how kingly power despite its claims to divinity was compromised by the counterpower of various groups such as rural caste panchayats and urban mercantile guilds. Inden maintains that divine kingship required perpetual reestablishment and reconstitution. This was done, for instance, by the king's annual performance of the Dashehra festival, which not only proclaimed the victory of good over evil but also affirmed the centrality of the king. The rites with their multiple *abhiṣeks*, or affusions, into sovereignty suggest that "kingship was less of a fixed state than an unending process that granted a vital place to its nemesis." As Inden puts it, the forces of darkness and evil could not be eliminated for once and all. They had to be constantly placated. The continuing battles between gods and antigods metaphored the constant struggle for sovereignty.[55]

Peabody rightly urges a dynamic and processual view of sovereignty in the precolonial state. He argues that Dirks mistakenly sees colonial (or Muslim) penetration as the source of change. His study of Kota highlights the jagirdar's constant resistance to royal authority. "For Dirks the Hindu state was decisively center-oriented and the pressures of unity far outweighed those of fragmentation. Contra Dirks, I argue that rebellion was not only common but it was a defining feature of the Hindu polity."[56] Peabody extends Tambiah's argument of the "galactic" polity beyond Southeast Asia. The term "galactic" is derived from the spatial symbol of the Indo-Tibetan notion of *mandala* that comprises a core surrounded by concentric circles of differentiated constituents. The mandala can be seen in terms of celestial and political arrangements such as the imperium of the cakravartin, the king of kings or universal king. Applied to the polity it encodes a "conception of territory as variable space, control over which diminished as royal power radiated from the center."[57] Tambiah points out that in the galactic polity the cultural/cosmological and the pragmatic/logistical cannot be disaggregated, unlike in Geertz's theater-state model. The divide between ritual and politicoeconomic action is spatialized into the king, court, and capital, on the one hand, and the "lower orders in the countryside" on the other. The "symbolic" dimension of the royal gift had far-reaching effects on the structure of royal power. In the regional contexts, the polity is "part of a large field of coexisting galaxies," indeed a highly competitive political universe. In Southeast Asia several core domains and satellite regions shifted affiliation and caused the fluctuating frontiers of various polities. At its weakest the galactic polity included a center coexisting with several "decentralized 'autonomous' petty principalities of chiefdoms." The highly ritualized sovereignty was based on the distribution of titles, honors, and regalia. A strong center could, however, control the juridical institutions of the periphery, levy taxes, and control trade. Centralizing trends were, however, countered by the ability of the satellites to shift loyalties to rival kings when they perceived their autonomy to be threatened.

Peabody points out that the advantage of the galactic polity over the segmentary state model is its derivation from indigenous rather than African categories. Further, it builds on the meanings that actors themselves self-consciously attach to their political relations. Second, the totalization rejects the radical disjunction between state power based on ritual sovereignty and local power based on agrarian management that characterize the Fox and Stein analyses.

Peabody sees the eighteenth-century Rajput kingdom of Kota as a circle of kings. Within the nucleus controlled by the king were the areas of khalsa (Crown) and jagir (noble) land. Here he was the nodal authority responsible for the redistribution of land, honors, and service tenures. He also distributed other "embodiments" of royal grace such as royal portrait paintings, turbans, robes of honor, and "pedigree" horses and weapons. "These sanctified objects indexed contact with the Maharao's divinity and they were, in turn, redistributed by jagirdars to their clients." Beyond the central domain were the realms of "tributary" or middle kings. The rulers of these conquered kingdoms retained their thrones and territory but had to pay Kota an annual or biennial tribute as well as special taxes (*peśkaśī* and *nazrānā*) on the occasion of marriages, the birth of an heir, or accession to the throne. They also constantly strove to assert their own authority. "In the prevailing context of decentralised administration and locally organised militias, peripheral actors continually tried to assert greater degrees of sovereignty and the central royal authority endlessly tried to undermine them."[58] The latter succeeded in the case of the Kotriat Thikanas. But there were occasions when nobles such as those of the Jhala clan established an independent kingdom. Political boundaries in eighteenth-century Rajasthan constantly shifted, and new centers in the galactic field came into prominence while others receded from view.

Peabody criticizes Dirks's center-oriented view of the Hindu State as he maintains that the pressures of unity far outweighed those of fragmentation. Peabody argues to the contrary that rebellion was not only common but it was a defining feature of the Hindu polity. Colonialism, argues Dirks, decapitated caste and allowed for the creation of an apolitical or civil society that was articulated by the brahman and was useful to the British. "The demise of kingship was accompanied by the steady ascendancy of the brahman, as the maintainer of the social order and the codes of caste. Brahmans reached a new high under British colonialism both in their participation in the development of the Hindu Law and in their preponderance in colonial administration."[59] Peabody takes Dirks to task for his "Raja-centric view of the pre-colonial state that underplays its active centrifugal tendencies."

Although Peabody's conception allows for far greater dissent and contradiction within the polity, he does not go far enough. Regrettably he only sees the rebellion within the ruling class. Paraphrasing his critique of Dirks, Peabody offers only a "top down" view of rebellion. Indeed historically speaking rebellion was not only of kingly lineages but also of groups who staked claims to kingly genealogies. The quasi-autonomous character of pastoral-peasant groups further foregrounds the "paradoxical" character of Indian kingship. These were also among the multiple and competing sovereignties laying claim to territory. The existence of "cross-cutting relations of dependency between clients and multiple overlords and patterns of fractured territorial sovereignty" that Peabody identifies in Kota cannot be seen in terms of Rajputs alone.

Dirks argues that the king was the source of legitimate power in the Hindu polity and expressed this through the distribution of the royal gift, of which land was paradigmatic. But there were competing chiefly distributors of the gift conceived as dana rather than inam that sociologists came to view as dominant castes. As Dumont points out, they wield the royal function at the local level. Hence the multiple and competing sources of legitimate power. Peabody does not unravel the implications of his own statement that "the meaning of caste always remained open to subversive non-royal interpretations, and, therefore, useful to anti-royal groups, even as they aspired to eventually reconstitute caste in a royal light (with themselves at the centre)."

Clearly Peabody improves upon Dirks's raja-centric view of the precolonial state with what one might call a "jagirdar-centric" view of rebellion. But the "paradoxes" of Indian kingship must include a greater diversity of axes of differentiation, such as gender and caste, including groups that were not ksatriya. Regrettably it ignores forms of political organization that were antithetical to state formation and that I have called "antistate." This is not to deny that antistates were not influenced by state practice or did not on occasion display an impetus to state formation themselves. The intertextuality of the literary is mirrored in the political realm. Indeed, the Indian polities can be seen as comprising a dialectic between state and "antistate." Cohn identified the levels of the polity as comprising the imperial, the secondary, the regional, and the local layers. But the situation is far more complex, and it is important to recover this history of political diversity.[60]

Tilly has argued that war and state making are the largest examples of

FIGURE 11
Portrait of Maharaja Banni Singh (r. 1815–57), variously addressed as maharao, rao raja, and maharaja of Alwar.

organized crime. War makes states, he writes.[61] History, which is in large measure the record of state formation, is silent on the question of the destruction of local communities and particularly on gender issues such as the abduction of women. Zuidema shows how the Inca Empire demanded women for the Andean community for secondary marriages.[62] Musi, the Daimrot Meo's daughter, becomes the concubine of the Alwar maharaja. When Musi is caught by the Rajputs she says:

FIGURE 12
The present Rajput thakur of Kaulani-Raghunathgarh, descendant of Thakur Bhairu Singh of Kotijhana in the Jaipur State, displaying his genealogy.

hūñ maiṇ beṭī mansā rāv kī bachan bharūñ hūñ tīn
tosū añg bhitāūñ nā jīvte kahā moy karā dīn bedīn

I am the daughter of Mansa Rao,
and vow three times.
I will not embrace you as long as I live
why have you violated my faith?

FIGURE 13
Cenotaph of Maharaja Bakhtawar Singh, popularly identified with the sati Musi "Maharani" *(below)*.

The woman who makes a strong statement of the violation of her *dīn* (body and being) in the narrative tradition, we know from other sources, committed sati following the death of the maharaja. The woman's voice mediated by the poet and bard that appears sporadically in the Meo oral tradition is erased in the patriarchal construction of the Rajput *riyāsat*, or kingdom. Here her only identity is that of sati or the self-immolated woman, the norms of domesticity regulating her "public" meaning. Musi's sati suggests at kingly control of female sexuality. Yet in death she was known as "Maharani." The legitimacy conferred by the title and the Charan's bardic account made it possible for her son by Bakhtawar Singh to claim to be heir. The six-year-old Balwant Singh's claim to the throne was forwarded by the Nawab Ahmad Baksh Khan, who also tried to dislodge Banni Singh. Not insignificantly the "private," communal account suggests the more demonic sources of the alliance, the partnership in raiding and abduction, and the absorption of the Daimrot sisters into ruling patrilineages. The Alwar State was divided after Bakhtawar Singh's death, with Balwant Singh ruling from Tijara until his death in 1845 and Banni Singh ruling from Alwar. As Balwant Singh died without an heir, the Alwar territories reverted to Banni Singh.

What the processes of transformation of Musi's self from Meoni to Rajput concubine and sati were we will never know. Yet on this was postulated the possibility of the beautiful architectural monument, the carved marble and red sandstone cenotaph near the City Palace of Alwar, popularly known as the "Musi Maharani kī chatrī," and her son's succession to a part of the Alwar kingdom in 1825.

8 The Prose and Verse of Rebellion: The Gadar of 1857

What does the narrative tradition offer in terms of an explanation of crime/resistance? How was resistance transformed into rebellion in 1857? And why the intensity of the Meo response in 1857? Although I have questioned the thesis of criminality, it would be romantic to deny the absence of crime. *Kaulānī* shows how *lūṭ/dhāṛā* might be an aspect of the politics of feud or raiding rather than merely of criminality. The mutual looting of cows and horses and fighting of battles, for instance, are modes of both conducting and settling disputes. The prevalence of feud is widespread and gives rise to alliances across caste. The ruling juridical structure however reads feud as crime. Regimes claim architectonic power on the grounds of the social contract that purports to establish order and law, the other of "crime." But, in fact, crime is also an integral aspect of state formation and not limited to socially deviant groups.

Unlike the statist attribution of crime to the social group, popular consciousness constructs crime as individual and gang based. Agency is attributed, for instance, by naming a Meo called Ravat from Sivana who is held responsible for stealing a horse from the Khanazadas. In the Mirasi's account the Singal Meos come from Sivana, referred to as a village of thieves near Khairthal in tehsil Kishangarh. The Meo Rao Madari is described as a *dhaṛait*, or bandit, and so is the Rajput Bhairu Singh. The latter makes the Meo promise to contribute his mercenary force of five hundred men to the Rajput attack on the Meos of Kaulani who will discipline the wild, rebellious land. Criminal elements, more often than not, lend their assistance to conquest and the expansion and reproduction of state power.

What is labeled as "crime," I argue, often has connotations of resistance to the revenue demand. Hence, the nawab of Firozpur proudly claims that he has destroyed the villages of the bandits of the country who are the persons who "don't pay the revenue of the state."[1] And the Alwar ruler has a similar tirade against the unyielding Meos of Kaulani. But one can well imagine the stresses created by doubling the amount of revenue collected during a twenty-year period in the early decades of the nineteenth century.[2] For the Meos, raiding represented not crime but redistributive justice.

Anticolonialism and Rebellion in British and Princely India

Under British influence both Alwar and Bharatpur remodeled their revenue administration, beginning in the 1840s, according to the norms of Victorian bureaucratic rationality and the standards set by the Punjab bureaucracy. Alwar was regarded as a "model" for all other states in Rajputana. Metcalf, however, points out the considerable distance with the ruled, that is, the enhanced hierarchization of kingship as a result of the concentration of coercive power, which explains the outstanding number of forts built by both Alwar and Bharatpur during the period.[3]

In the Jat-ruled state of Bharatpur the Meo population inhabited the tehsils of Nagar, Gopalgarh, Kaman, and Dig. Jat landholdings were concentrated primarily in Dig and Bharatpur. There were periodic rebellions by the Meos of the Nagar and Gopalgarh tehsils. In 1844 about ten thousand rebels surrounded the diwan and his group, who were rescued only after the intervention of the Darbar Regiment. In 1853, when the Naib came to collect the revenue at Saimla in Nagar, he was shot at, and two of his party including a Gujar Risaldar were killed. The diwan brought a strong force of cavalry and artillery to avenge the incident but the Meos had meanwhile fled to Alwar. The whole village was outlawed and occupied by state troops for two years.

Armed revolt occurred at Sikri, Bharatpur, in 1854 and again in 1855. Both the Lawrence and O'Dwyer reports blamed the diwan, the princely state, and the "native" land revenue administration.[4] But, in fact, the ruler, Jaswant Singh who inherited the throne in 1853, was very young, and the administration was conducted by the agent and a Regency Council until 1869. In view of popular resentment, the demand was reduced by 3.5 lakhs in the Summary Settlement of 1855–56 to 1857–58. But the political agent did not concur with the justification for reduction and thought the state had been put to an unnecessary loss. Despite the criticism by Lawrence, agent to the governor general, concerning the high previous revenue rates and the considerable expression of peasant dissatisfaction, the revenue was enhanced by 12.5 percent in the Three-Year Settlement (see table 5). This obviously violated colonial professions of intent and "had far-reaching adverse effects on the subsequent fiscal history of the land revenue payers."[5]

What was happening in the areas under direct rule? In 1838 Mewati and Rajput zamindars of Shahjahanpur were reported to have led men against

TABLE 5 Settlements of the Bharatpur State

Years	Settlement[a]	Demand (in Rupees)	% Revenue Increase/Decrease
1856–58	Summary	1,406,922	–19.8[b]
1859–62	Three-Year (Henry Lawrence)	1,551,261	+12.5
1862–68	Six-Year[c]	1,666,154	+6.0
1868–69	Six-Year Revised[c]	1,352,837	–19.5
1870–71	Six-Year Revised Again[c]	1,488,122	+10.0
1871–72	Maharaja Jaswant Singh	1,858,000	+24.8
1873–83	Ten-Year Settlement	2,015,724	+8.5
1883	Revision of Assessment[d]	1,694,799	–5.9
1885–1900	Fifteen-Year	1,790,803	–8.7
1900–1920	O'Dwyer's First Regular Twenty-Year Settlement	1,298,000	+20.5

[a]Settlements were revised because of famine and crop failures and the resulting difficulties of collecting unrealistically high revenue demands.

[b]This decrease occurred because of widespread protest by various groups, including Jats and Meos.

[c]The Six-Year Settlement was to have expired in1868 but because of famine it was extended, first to 1869, then to 1871.

[d]Revision of the Ten-Year Settlement followed the famine of 1877–78.

Source: "Final Settlement Report of the Bharatpur State," typescript, 1932.

the towns, and the Mewati military gentry to have resumed their depredation on the route between Delhi and Mathura. Significant events occurred between 1830 and 1857, including the Meo involvement in the strange murder case of the Delhi Resident, the repeated expressions of unrest, and the conflagration of "the Mutiny."

William Fraser, who was appointed to the powerful position of Resident in 1833 was murdered by the son born of the marriage of Nawab Ahmad Baksh Khan with the abducted Meo woman Maddi. According to William Dalrymple (related to Fraser through marriage and who hence had access to his correspondence) Fraser was a close friend and business partner of the nawab.[6] Fraser became involved in the violent inheritance dispute that broke out between the nawab's sons after his death in 1834. In the course of this controversy Fraser forcibly ejected from his house his own ward the nawab's eldest child, Shams-ud-Din. Dalrymple describes Shams-ud-Din as a raffish Mughal nobleman who started the dispute by seizing his younger brother's share of the family property. But he mentions that rumors were circulating in the bazaars of old Delhi that Fraser had made sexual advances toward Shams-ud-Din's sister. There were rumors also of Fraser's insanity. "Like Mr. Kurtz in Conrad's *Heart of Darkness*, [Fraser] saw himself as a European potentate ruling in a pagan wilderness; like Kurtz, he would brook no challenge to his authority." According to Dalrymple, Shams-ud-Din "began to plot revenge" and eventually had Fraser murdered on 22 March 1835. Fraser was returning from an evening's entertainment (he was particularly fond of performances by Delhi's famous bands and nautch girls) at the house of his friend the maharaja of Kishangarh. He was shot point-blank by a figure who had been riding ahead of him then slowed down. Charles Metcalf's nephew, Tom Metcalf, who succeeded as Resident of Delhi, quickly solved the murder from the incriminating correspondence between the assassin and Shams-ud-Din. Another accomplice gave evidence. Shams-ud-Din and the assassin were publicly executed.

Dalrymple sees a fundamental shift in the political culture of the empire with the departure of the early Delhi Residents, the Scotsmen Ochterlony and Fraser, and the new series of English Residents. The Scotsmen self-imaged themselves as Mughal gentlemen. Fraser, for instance, was a scholar of Persian, composed poetry in that language, befriended the great Urdu poet Ghalib, and loved to discuss ancient Sanskrit texts. He was a brilliant scholar, metaphysician, and philosopher. Fraser followed Indian customs, wore Indian clothing and a Rajput-style beard, refused to eat pork and beef, and was virtually "half a Hindoostanee." He so shocked Lady Nugent, the wife of the British commander in chief who "thought of him as Hindoo as much as Christian" that she reminded him sharply of the "religion [he] was brought up to." Fraser was regarded as having a great trust in and fondness for the natives and their customs. William Fraser's brother Aleck remarked on Fraser's isolation and distance from Europeans in Delhi and that it was only with his servants that he chatted or joked.

Fraser had a harem and many wives (the seniormost being a Jat woman). He was fond of hunting the Asian lion and of battle. Dalrymple suggests the vulnerability of Delhi in these early decades of the nineteenth century and how William Fraser helped build up its military and had his own personal army. Around 1808 Aleck wrote home, "In the district of Mewat (immediately west of Delhi), which he was stationed in, to civilize it, he built a fort and called it 'Fraser Ghur' in which he maintained 1000 sepoys of his own raising and disciplining. There he lived like a Nawab, being [as] absolute in his domain as Bonaparte in France." When Aleck moved from Calcutta, where he was studying to Delhi, he found his brother unrecognizable and described him as "iron in constitution and bodily force . . . his chest is wonderfully broad and round, his limbs full and well-turned." Later he wrote as he was dying that William had become wild, manic, and obsessive. This was the man who undertook to civilize "the wild inhabitants" of the region around Delhi. "When Willie civilized" them "he took hostages from the chief inhabitants of the most turbulent districts as security for the good conduct of the rest. The most ferocious have become the most faithful. These men — formerly robbers and perhaps murderers, certainly the relations of such — now sleep by our couches and would at any time risk their lives for us." William's massive staff of seventy household servants included Gujar and Mewati bodyguards.

Fraser's body was exhumed and reburied by his friend James Skinner. Skinner was founder of the cavalry called Skinner's Horse. He had received a title from the Mughal emperor Nasir ud-Daulah and became known as Col. James Skinner Bahadur Ghalib Jang, but was also referred to as Alexander the Great. Skinner's lineage bestowed on him the liminal identity that Fraser was so fond of sporting. His mother was a Rajput princess, and he is described as Moor-like in appearance. Skinner became one of the first to receive a commission in the Indian army. But he was seen as a person with mixed blood (a *chī-chī*), as Dalrymple points out, and his cavalry was absorbed only with great difficulty into the British army.

Delhi and its environs in the early decades of the nineteenth century with its "wild" inhabitants is almost a throwback to the Delhi of six centuries earlier following the establishment of the sultanate. In both cases the Meos are on its fringes. One can only speculate on the yawning gaps writing leaves in its wake, What were the deeper factors behind the Fraser murder? What were the deeper changes in property and inheritance taking place? What happened in the wake of the attempt to "civilize"? Particularly as, in this case, when it was the "wild" (William, according to his own brother) civilizing the "wild." And what were the repercussions among the families, clans, and friends of the hostages Fraser thought he had domesticated and rendered faithful? In any case, the net result of the Fraser murder was the absorption of Firozpur into the British domain, its nawabs left with the shrunken principality of Loharu.

The Meos in the Gurgaon area concentrated in the Nuh and Firozpur tehsils were almost immediately brought under a new revenue regime. These southern areas populated virtually exclusively by Meos suffered from low productivity of land and lack of available water. In Firozpur, land holdings were small and there was hardly any well irrigation.[7] In contrast, the Jats and Ahirs who comprised about one-tenth of the population owned villages in the fertile Bangar plain and in the west around Rewari, which had naturally irrigated land. British revenue settlements were launched in Gurgaon in 1836–37 in a context when agricultural production had declined and peasant discontent had considerably increased, reflected in the number of disputes.

The high assessment and the stringent collection of revenue in the Regular Settlement of 1837–38 was regarded as responsible for the famine of 1837–39, and several bad crop years followed in succession.[8] The new assessments were especially burdensome in the Meo areas of Palwal and Firozpur, where they broke down entirely and had to be revised. In 1841 Gubbins, author of the Settlements of Firozpur and Punhana, reduced the demand by 20 percent for the term of the settlement and remitted all balances. Although the Final Revised Assessment of 1842 reduced the demand, it was still considered steep, especially for Firozpur and Rewari. Thus the Settlements of 1838 and 1842 were regarded as particularly heavy, and much land came under mortgage (see table 6).[9]

Little wonder that there were widespread expressions of anticolonialism in the entire Mewat area during the revolt in 1857. Amitav Ghosh has rightly pointed out that the movement of 1857 is "universally acknowledged to be

TABLE 6 Settlements of Gurgaon District

Years	Settlement	Demand (in Rupees)
1837–77	Lawrence Regular	1,400,000
1842–77	Final Revised	1,114,000
1882–1902	Channing	1,100,000 for 7 years; 1,225,000 for remaining years

Source: F. C. Channing, *Land Revenue Settlement of the Gurgaon District*; Land Revenue Assessment in Alwar, Jaipur Agency, Rajputana CRP, R2/152-149, IOL.

the single most important anticolonial uprising in modern history" and "possibly the most important event in all modern Indian history." It is an event in which the absolute coerciveness of empire is foregrounded. Ghosh makes the point about the absolute, resounding silence in Dipesh Chakrabarty's *Provincializing Europe* and in other writings of the Subaltern Studies group on 1857. Chakrabarty's work, Ghosh maintains, deals with resistance but rarely refers to the coercive side of colonialism, the apparatus of empire.[10] How do we explain the events of 1857 through the Meo prism? Is political economy an adequate explanation? Was the expression of discontent an outcome of scarcity, of famines and agricultural deterioration? Or was religion a more decisive factor? I revert briefly to a semblance of what the English called "The Narrative of the Mutiny" in the region to piece together the events of 1857.

Gujars and Meos from villages in Alwar and the neighboring British provinces are said to have given trouble "by their rebellions and predatory habits." The Meos of Bharatpur joined their kin in Gurgaon in plundering Firozpur, Nuh, and other towns. A special British force had to be placed on the Khairagarh border to guard against their incursions and those of the Bharatpur Gujars.[11] In Alwar the Meos were the "first tribe to rise against British power." At Naugaon, a village 15.5 km (9.6 miles) northeast of Ramgarh, the Meos defeated a force sent by Maharaja Banni Singh of Alwar to relieve the Alwar garrison.[12] They were on their way to Firozpur with one hundred Raj bullocks for the use of the British troops. The escort was attacked just beyond Naugaon by the Meos and the Baniyas. They were surrounded and their commandant, Man Singh, was killed along with many of his men.[13] At

Ramgarh, which had been the scene of uprisings (including Kaulani), the Meos were said to have plundered large hordes of treasure that they continued to hold till nearly half a century later.[14]

Rebels are also described as having collected at Narnaul and Tapukra.[15] Lawrence and Newall commented, "throughout the late crisis this State was in a position of great difficulty. Her territory was overrun with our mutinous soldiery; the infection spread to her own troops and her Goojar and Mewatie population were not slow to follow the example of their brethren in our rebellious provinces."[16] The role of kinship was significant in spreading the revolt.

As was the case all over Rajputana, the ruler and his subjects were on opposite sides. The Alwar monarch "proved his loyalty to the British government by his attempt during the Mutiny to assist the beleaguered garrison at Agra."[17] Captain Nixon and others led a force of twenty-five thousand men sent to Mathura to obstruct the mutineers from Delhi and Meerut. It was to cooperate with the Alwar and Bharatpur princely states. The Bharatpur ruler lent his army, and they were joined by a force of twenty-five soldiers from Alwar. But at Hodal in Gurgaon, the force refused to attack the Mathura rebels. Instead they turned against the British officers and the Rajputs of the Alwar army and joined in the plunder of Kosi. Nixon had to flee for his life.

There was considerable Meo presence in the United Provinces, where they worked in the army, were given land, and established villages. While Allahabad had a major presence of about one hundred thousand Meos, Bijnore only had a small population. The Mewatis were adversely affected by the dual pressure of taxes and new regulations, which left them with no savings to send home. Large numbers deserted from the army. In Jhansi they destroyed bungalows and were insurgent in Bijnore. In Allahabad the Mewatis were said to be "the real contrivers of the rebellion of the sepoys and Risala."[18] Mewatis arrested for "talking in a seditious manner" were sent to Allahabad because of the perceived danger of their "infecting and tampering" with the VI Native Infantry.[19] Mewati rebels faced prosecution and punishment, and many were executed. In the Central Provinces on July 1 the revolt at Indore was led by the Meo leader Sadat Khan inspired by the slogan "move ahead, kill the sahabs." At Mandsor and Neemuch also the Meos led the revolt besieging the Neemuch station.

In the "gadar," as the Meos referred to the revolt of 1857, the role of the Meos of Gurgaon was particularly prominent. Indeed it was among them that the fiercest last-ditch resistance was mounted to the final reimposition of British rule once Delhi was retaken in late September. In June, Captain Eden had been surrounded by the Meos on the route between Taoru and Sohna. His cannon saved him from disaster and he retreated to Jaipur. In Gurgaon, the Meos fought the Khanazadas and the police; killed the assistant collector, Mr. Clifford and other officials in Raisina; and plundered Taoru, Sohna, Firozpur, Punhana, Pinangwan, and Nuh.[20] Stokes refers to this as an "orgy of plunder."[21] In Firozpur, Mewatis collected, planning an invasion of Naugaon and Ramgarh in Alwar. Later ninety Mewatis were arrested. Captain Eden rescued several Europeans and "engaged his force in punishing" the Mewatis in between Mathura and Palwal, writes Lawrence.[22] Brigadier Shower's column was occupied for weeks in the work of "pacification" and "reprisal," and some fifty villages were burned.

Since the foregoing account has been based largely on contemporary English sources, it is illuminating to counterpose the description with a Meo-authored text authorized by the All-India Meo Sabha of Delhi and Madhya Pradesh. The text is dedicated to the Meo martyr Sadat Khan, who was hanged at Indore on 1 October 1874, and is particularly interesting for its construction of the Meo past.[23] It describes the battles fought with the English at Taoru, Sohna, Firozpur Jhirka, and Pingavan. The text mentions Clifford being killed in Raisena on 31 October 1957. Clifford had attacked a number of villages after the killing of his sister in Delhi's busy market, Chandni Chowk. Sixty army personnel were killed near Raisena, and the Englishmen referred to as "firangi" were forced to walk on thorny bushes. The English took revenge by appropriating Meo land in Raisena, Haryahera, Jalalpur, Majra, Nanera, and Harchandpur. The force led by Showers continued the onslaught on the Meos. On 7 November 1857 the English army under the command of Lieutenant Grant attacked and looted the villages of Barka, Revasen, and Ghasera. A fierce battle was fought the next day in which 150 Mewatis were "martyred." Another large force led by Drummond, Temple, and Hudson attacked Rupraka confronting 3,000 Mewatis in a battle in which 400 were killed. Sometime later Meos led by Sadr-ud-Din were "martyred" in the battle at the village Mohna. All the land adjacent to Pingavan was destroyed by the English, who had seized the lands of peasants and headmen.

Heesterman describes the 1857 rebellion as "a chaotic resurgence of the inner frontier."[24] This massive confrontation with the English has left but a mere fragment in the oral tradition. The attack on British officials by the Meos of the Ghasera Pal of Raisina is celebrated in the following dohas:[25]

baṇglā maiṇ man nā lagai sūnī dīkhai sej
rāseṇa ke gaurve dekhā binā sīs añgrej
rāsena kā mev nai bhalo jagāyo dīn

kakkai mārā sassai kursī khālī kar dī tīn
gaṛh ghāseṛo gāñv pāl ko baṛo bharoso
rājā rām chandra autār rāj rāvaṇ ko khoso

The English wife is crying:
In the large bungalow the mind wanders
and the bed is desolate.
In the open space outside Raisena
the headless Englishman was seen.
The Meos of Raisena
performed a great religious act.
Hit so hard
they emptied three chairs.
The Meos of the (Dhaingal) pal
are proud of the fort Ghasera village.
(Like) the incarnate Raja Ram Chandra
seized the kingdom of Ravana.

Mark the reference to religion in the verses suggesting an Islamic identity. Simultaneously the Meos's onslaught on the British Raj reenacts Rama's epic destruction of Ravana's city, Lanka. I referred earlier to the dominance of the Dhaingal Pal in Gurgaon's Mewat area who attribute their origin to the village of Raisena. This clan is also referred to as the Ghasera or Bargujar Pal of the Meos and claims descent from Rama.

The local community is obviously conscious of the impact of its action on the Raj:

rāsenā hai gāñv raub bārū pālan maiṇ
kursī khālī hogī tīn huī charchā landan maiṇ

The village Raisena
carries weight among the twelve pals.
Three chairs were vacated
(the matter) was discussed in London.

The "chairs" refers to the heirs of the estates of English nobles who were killed.

Debating 1857

How have scholars explained this large-scale protest? Stokes advances an agrarian ecological explanation to explain the events of 1857. He argues that it was the Jat-led multicaste faction located in the "thirsty," unirrigated tracts to the west who bore the brunt of the high revenue assessment that revolted, not the Jat and non-Jat factions who had profited from the opening of the East Yamuna Canal. Certainly the participation of caste factions in the revolt of 1857 was contingent and arose from regionally specific causes. In the case of the Gurgaon Meos, it arose from a combination of overassessment of revenue, lack of adequate irrigation, and the mortgages, indebtedness, and land transfers that accompanied successive settlements. The Bharatpur revolts, however, came from a much better irrigated area with a different agrarian ecology. Though the Gurgaon tehsils are dry and relatively unproductive, the northern and central tehsils of Bharatpur (where revolts occurred in the mid- and later nineteenth century) and the Govindgarh tract of Alwar (epicenter of the rising of 1932) are rather well inundated and fertile. Kaman and Nagar could hardly be characterized as "thirsty" tracts. The agrarian ecology explanation, I argue, only possibly and partially explains the role of the Gurgaon Meos in 1857. It does not explain the occurrence of revolt in general, which is far more contingent.

The "religious factor" is indicated by rebel proclamations suggesting a perception of the colonial power as promoting conversion and encouraging the considerable activity of Christian missionaries. A circular from a preacher in the Bengal army, for instance, stated that it was time to convert Muslims to Christianity. Several petitions were sent to Bahadur Shah Zafar protesting this.[26] Ashraf attributes a prominent role to Islamic revivalists who had come to be called the Wahabis.[27] But at least in the area of Mewat in Rajputana the presence of the so-called Wahabis dates to the late nineteenth century.[28] It was the high levels of mortgage and indebtedness that contributed significantly to the buildup of anticolonial sentiment among the Gurgaon Meos. The rapid agricultural expansion of the early century, ecological changes, and high assessment rates resulting from the British advent had exhausted the productive forces of the countryside.[29] Another reason may have been loyalty to the rebel "king." Raisena's Kale Khan is said to have been a *topchī* (cannon driver/gunner) of the Mughal Badshah and was preparing his force to fight at the Delhi fort. A single motive then can hardly be attributed. One might agree with Bayly's formulation that the rebellion of 1857 was not one movement, but many.[30]

Amitav Ghosh points out that the silence on 1857 is an aspect of the larger silence on race in Indian historiography and in Indian narratives generally, almost a refusal to acknowledge it.[31] He quotes Uday Mehta who cites a powerful passage from James Fitzjames Stephen about "how the British Empire represents a belligerent civilisation, and no anomaly can be more striking or so dangerous as its administration by men, who being at the head of a Government founded on conquest, implying at every point the superiority of the conquering race . . . shrink from the open, uncompromising assertion of it." Ghosh argues that "race was the foundational social fact of the post-1857 Empire—an idea embedded more in practices than in discourse—and it grew ever stronger from the mid-19th century onward." "Race was much more than just a tool of Empire: it was (in the Kantian sense) one of the foundational categories of thought that made other perceptions possible." Ghosh refers to the unwritten stories of the British Indian army, of the sepoys who kept on mutinying, over and over again. In his response Chakrabarty makes the distinction between imperialist attitudes in settler-colonial countries and colonies where imperialists acknowledged the existence of a prior "civilization." Europeans never dominated India in the way they pulverized and wiped out aboriginal societies. Chakrabarty points out that there were deep dilemmas at the heart of European thought introduced by seventeenth- to eighteenth-century ideas about being human, hence the ambiguity that lies at the heart of liberalism (and within the Enlightenment) between the universal applicability that it claims for itself (such as of ideas of equality) and the unacknowledged racism that runs through it. Ghosh's counterpoint is that egalitarian and liberatory impulses of nineteenth-century Indian society did not just derive from Enlightenment, and that within Indian and most other philosophical traditions also there is an ambiguity. He argues that antihierarchical thought in India has had a long past and that the British not only reinforced hierarchical aspects of Indian society, they introduced hierarchies of their own. Racism, Ghosh emphasizes, is not just exclusivist or supremacist ideology: "It is an ideology that is founded on certain ideas that relate to science, nature, biology and evolution—a specifically post-Enlightenment ideology in other words."

While Chakrabarty's arguments are cogent, Ghosh's question is one we must leave hanging. Do Indians flinch from the question of race because of an instinct for self-preservation or because it contaminates liberal Western thought on which our own hopes of social betterment are grounded?

The gadar of 1857 then was a foundational event for ruler and ruled. Ghosh has rightly underlined that it was only in the aftermath of 1857 that most north and central Indians acknowledged their sense of despair: nothing could be done about the British regime and resistance could only be on the conqueror's terms. It was responsible for a transformation of the Indian psychosocial self that Nandy refers to as "the loss of self," hence the interiority of English attitudes that corroded from within. The question is also, as Dipesh Chakrabarty puts it, whether 1857 can give us a new narrative, a new understanding of colonialism? The siege and recapture of Delhi by the British on 14 September 1857 was seen as one of the great moments of empire, the massacres commemorated in monuments erected all over. The Mutiny Memorial, Dalrymple states, lists the dead on both sides as bowling averages and suggests a Delhi that was very different from what the Raj might have been under Ochterlony and Fraser. Fraser's rule was hardly benevolent, but it was only under his successors that the distancing from the natives became more fully practiced. What Ghosh underestimates is how fundamentally and dramatically the events of 1857 modified the nature of British presence instituting a new governmentality. The Raj introduced the rule of law and the apparatus of codes and courts. On the other hand, the hierarchy with the colonial subject produced a racism that underwrote institutional practice. Racism was not just present in the army, as Ghosh suggests. Grafted on to an understanding of caste and tribe, racism produced the ideology and administrative practice of the criminal tribe.

A contemporary explanation offered by a Meo for the revolt of 1857 is that it was against the English who had snatched Delhi *(dillī añgrezoṇ ne chīn lī)*. "We called it *mulak badsāh rāj kampanī hukam*" (the country with the Mughal Emperor and the authority of the Company). But the rule of the company authority was to give way to *añgrejī rāj* (British Raj), calling for a further Meo response in verse and action.

9 Kings, Peasants, and Bandits

How is the British Raj perceived in the Meo oral tradition? This chapter explores banditry as an oppositional cultural form through the lens of a bandit narrative called *Ghurcharī Mev Khāñ*. This might be read as an anticolonial text, which is not to negate the existence of other facets, other saliencies; for most certainly a narrative is a polysemy of voices. Here I identify what seems to be one of the dominant notes: that of an indictment of the colonial system. The term "colonial system" rather than the colonial *state* is used because the spatiotemporal context of the narrative is the princely state. The princely state is seen as underwritten by the British Empire and as a part of the colonial system. Although in this bandit narrative we get a strong sense of a critique, it lacks a conception of a utopia, that is, what is the desired alternative to the colonial-kingly regime. Nonetheless, *Ghurcharī Mev Khāñ* is a text on power and dissent, and a commentary on the ideology and the nature of the monarchical and colonial state.

Banditry is a widespread form, in fact, a universal mode of protest in South and Southeast Asia, Australia, Latin America, Europe, and Islamic societies. There has been a great deal of documentation and analysis of peasant resistance and social banditry the world over in the last couple of decades. Bandits, Hobsbawm writes, are not simple criminals. On the contrary, such protest is symptomatic of individual or minority protest in peasant societies. The bandits are looked upon as honorable, as heroes. They symbolize a struggle for justice and the redress of grievances and thereby represent an alternative code.[1] The paradigm instance of the noble robber is, of course, Robin Hood.

The bandit narrative is a popular form in preindustrial societies. In England it existed up to the early seventeenth century, in tsarist Russia until the mid-eighteenth century. The Balkans, Italy, Spain, Greece, Colombia, Peru, and Brazil all have similar stories. But about India, Hobsbawm remarks, "A possible or partial exception might have to be made for the peculiar caste-divided societies of Hindu southern Asia, where social banditry is inhibited by the tendency of caste robbers, like all other sections of society, to form self-contained castes and communities."[2] Yang also maintains that there is little firm evidence for banditry in South Asia.[3]

The bandit narrative is not an unfamiliar form in Indian caste society.[4] Richards and Rao analyze *Papadu*, a story about a Telugu folk hero and bandit who abducts women from elite sections, both Hindu and Muslim.[5] Pandian describes "heroic ballads" prevalent among the subaltern classes, such as the story of *Muthupattam* about a rebellious bandit.[6] In the Shekhawati area of Rajasthan there is a popular *dhaṛaaitī* tradition of *bagī* stories about raiders. There is a similarly large repertoire of bandit stories among the Bhil forest communities of western India. Habib Tanvir's contemporary theatrical rendering of a Chattisgarhi story called *Charandas Chor* is again the paradigmatical good thief who robs the rich but helps the poor. Quite clearly a folk text cannot be regarded merely as the expression of heroic rasa (mood) as in the tradition of Indian literary criticism or as an aspect of a panegyric tradition signifying its degradation for those associated with the Raj. Art has an aesthetic but also a subversive function.

Paramountcy and the Princely State of Alwar

In the considerable literature on banditry, scholars have highlighted its association with weak states so that it is in inverse correlation to state formation. In this section I refer to the intensification of state formation to indicate that this need not always be the case. The simultaneous assertion of colonial paramountcy and kingly authority, which characterize the late colonial period, is the context of the bandit story.

By the early nineteenth century British paramountcy was established through a series of treaties with more than six hundred kingdoms. Their establishment as British protectorates was symbolized by British control over succession and foreign affairs and the appointment of a Resident. The substitution of Mughal by British rule revalidated the Rajput-ruled kingdoms that now came to be known as princely (not kingly!) states.[7] This has been seen in the literature as the freezing of these states, but the substitution of the Mughals by the British also led to far-reaching transformations of the Rajput polity. The Rajput state system had hitherto been based on close kinship ties of the raja and his clansmen consisting of warrior-landholders and on the coparcenary right of the heads of the ruling lineages to participate in ruling. Often the clansmen did not owe the possession of their estates to the raja. These were a result of conquest by ancestors and predated the state. The raja was not their lord.[8] In return for protection the clansmen gave him military support and assisted in governance. The British now sought to reformat this polity based on shared power in accordance with a model of what they thought was Rajput feudalism.

Colonial policy on occasion supported monarchical authority, as in the case of the Jaipur kingdom's ruler Ram Singh. On the whole, however, throughout Rajputana, colonial rule deliberately undermined monarchical authority. The Rajput nobles were seen as "loyal allies," props to colonial power, and a check against monarchical absolutism. In strengthening the nobility, the British sought to restore what they imagined was feudalism. Tod's work provided the intellectual design of a grand theory of feudalism among the Rajput states.[9] As Stern puts it for the neighboring state of Jaipur,

> By positioning the British government above the inevitable disputes between a feudal prince and his nobility, as lord *impartial* arbiter of such disputes, the Company officers believed that they could establish a patron-client relationship with the Jaipur *durbar* that was not only stable and legitimate but entirely controllable by the patron. Again, the British were mistaking an agglomeration of noble landlords for a noble class. They were also mistakenly assuming that there was a pyramidal structure to Rajput feudalism.[10]

In several of the "native" states the councils, consisting of nobles and presided over by the agent, were identified as the agencies for renovating feudalism in Rajputana.

The independence of the Alwar State was severely compromised following the transfer of power from the East India Company to the Crown. This was despite the treaty of 1803 that provided a guarantee of noninterference (article 3). The Alwar ruler had supported the British against the Marathas in 1803 and again during the Revolt of 1857. The British, however, preferred strategically to bolster the nobility to counter the power of the raja. A rebellion of the jagirdars led by Lakhdir Singh, thakur of Bijwar, in 1858 was used as an excuse to dismiss and exile the two Muslim administrative chiefs, called the Delhi Diwans, appointed by the Alwar ruler. The reforms they had undertaken since 1838 were seen as strengthening the raja's position. A Council of Regency for the management of the state was established by Captain Nixon, political agent of Bharatpur.

The Council of Regency was eventually viewed by the British as an unsatisfactory arrangement and was replaced by a political agent for Alwar. During maharao raja Sheodan Singh's reign (1857–74) political agent Captain Impey undertook a major reorganization of every branch of administration. In 1869 the Political Agency was removed, and the agent to the governor general in Rajputana himself supervised matters relating to the Alwar darbar. Alwar was brought briefly under the Eastern Rajputana States Agency. But in 1870, following another rebellion of the nobility, a political agent was appointed, independent of the Eastern Rajputana States Agency, who continued till August 1911. Political agent Captain Cadell ruled through the council. The thakur nobles were made council colleagues, with the agent at the apex of the pyramid as president of the council, while the raja had a seat but no power to veto its decisions or interfere in the executive rulings.[11] A warning was issued to the ruler threatening his expulsion if the "disturbances" occasioned by the Rajput rebellion continued.[12]

Aitchinson's tenure as foreign secretary in the 1870s inaugurated a period of intensified intervention by the colonial power in most of the princely states. Alwar was included in a list of "Mediatised, Guaranteed, and Petty Chiefs."[13] The state became signatory to an Offensive and Defensive Alliance of "Permanent Friendship." According to a *sanad* agreement, Alwar could not enter into any negotiations or agreements without the consent of the British. In Alwar, as in many other princely states, control was now established over coinage, infrastructure including posts and telegraph, railways, and salt production.[14] Following an agreement, restrictions were placed on the minting of currency. In 1873 an English coin had been issued, and after 1877 British Indian currency became prevalent. A file on the "Coinage of new Alwar State" registers the ruler's protest against the closing of the Alwar mint since currency "is a sign of prestige and sovereignty."[15] Ironically the British granted the ruler the title of maharaja in 1889.[16] But in the same year the salt agreement prohibiting its manufacture in the state was concluded. In Alwar and in Bharatpur salt production was severely crippled. In addition, import, export, and transit dues on all articles except drugs were forbidden, and work on more rigorous revenue settlements was inaugurated.

The Rajput State that had developed thus far was a patrimonial system with a plural distribution of authority in which the ruler was primus inter pares. It now came under increasing strain. On numerous occasions Raja Sheodan Singh was obliged to accept British interference, as when he was prevailed upon by the political agent to give all land free of cost for the Rajputana-Malwa railway, although the majority of the adjoining states received compensation.

The Meo narrative identifies both the Rajput thakur of Bijwar, Lakhdir Singh, and the ruler with the state and does not refer to the internal schism between the raja and the Rajput nobility. The totalization of the Rajput State in the Meo perspective does not cognize internal dissensions. The thakur of Bijwar had been an important member of Captain Impey's three-member council that ruled the state. He had headed the Regency Council during Raja Sheodan Singh's minority up to 1863 and, in a sense, dominated the politics of the Alwar princely state for several decades. The correspondence on the induction of Lakhdir Singh into the council reveals colonial sensibility with respect to the Indian "princes" that bolstered the position of the Rajput nobles.

In Alwar, rule through the council was preferred by the British and proposed as an alternative to the maharao as "absolute ruler." The viceroy himself advocated a new government with the political agent and a council of five thakurs to "meet every requirement" and "entrust themselves with the task of reconstruction." The government of the council of thakurs and Lakhdir Singh was identified as particularly pro-British. Cadell had pointed out the need to induct him as a member of the council as the very condition of its success. Following his cue the British government emphasized that Lakhdir Singh, the leader of the thakurs, could be relied on as a counterbalance to the maharaja, which would strengthen the hands of the political agent.[17] Lakhdir Singh had also opposed the revenue and reforms and reorganization of state institutions sponsored by the Delhi Diwans. Cadell ended up nominating the entire council and rejected Sheodan Singh's nominees. The council was inaugurated following Lakhdir Singh's return.[18]

British control was to be operationalized in alliance with Naruka Rajput nobles through the council. The raja was accused of conspiring against Captain Impey's authority and of "interfering with the conduct of the affairs of the State";[19] of "Mahommedan proclivities" resulting in the domination of all official positions by Muslims;[20] and of oppressing the thakurs, confiscating their lands, and depriving them of all influence in the state. A declaration of emergency in the state was even considered by the British in view of the "treasonable intrigues" of the former Delhi Diwans.[21]

Cadell submitted a report giving the impression of a grave situation verging on civil war and suggested that the British determine upon active interference. He even advocated the ruler's deposition and the placing of the state under British management. The Hobbesian anarchy depicted in British documents shows all subjects in a state of revolt; the many complaints against criminal courts and police arrangements that cannot be worse; the protest from the Punjab government and the superintendent of the Thagi and Dacoity Department that have remonstrated against the present condition of the administration in which life and property have been rendered unsafe in Alwar and disorder has spread to neighboring districts, both native and British.[22] The officiating agent prohibited any expenditure from being made without the council's consent.

The Alwar ruler protested the formation of the council and the "suspension of his authority." He complained to the agent, "since Captain Cadell's arrival I have done my best to meet his wishes in everything."[23] His comments on Lakhdir Singh are enlightening, as the latter is alleged to "have made use of his power and influence to create a great disturbance by plundering the country and murdering the people two years after the Agency was removed."

Lakhdir Singh made a claim to the Alwar throne after the death of Sheodan Singh, but it was Mangal Singh (r. 1874–92) who inherited this captive position. The narrative of *Ghurcharī Mev Khāñ* is contextualized in the reign of Mangal Singh. This makes possible an approximate dating of the events, if not the actual composition of the work, which could have been later.[24]

It was not only the assertion of paramountcy that had a major impact on princely regimes but also, as Eric Stokes puts it, processes of industrial capitalism that "required the opening up of the country as a market and primary producer for British industry with all that this implied — a market society of legal equals under the rule of law, modern judicial and administrative institutions, private property rights in land, taxes reduced to fixed imposts in cash, and the general monetization of the economy."[25] The railways were to make possible the integration of the Indian economy with the global economy. The pervasive changes reverberate through the Mewati narrative.

FIGURE 14
Portrait of Maharaja Mangal Singh of Alwar (r. 1874–92).

Revenue and Resistance

Unlike other kingdoms in Rajputana, in both Alwar and Bharatpur, Crown (khalsa) lands predominated, where taxes were paid directly to the state. In Alwar 86 percent of the state constituted Crown lands, and the remainder was under jagirdari land tenure arrangements. O'Dwyer describes the Meos as a "proprietary body . . . distinct from and superior to ordinary cultivators." That is, they held proprietary rights, provided by hereditary and long-standing land titles. Although the state had sovereign rights over land, the titles entitled the cultivator protection in land ownership rights so long as revenue was paid. Meo concentration was in the northern tehsils of Tijara and Kishangarh, and the central tehsils of Govindgarh, Ramgarh, and Alwar (see table 7).[26]

While the Meos primarily inhabited the Crown lands, the Rajput landholdings fell in the jagirdari areas. In Alwar in the early nineteenth century the Rajputs held one-sixth (800 square miles) of the villages.[27] Their jagirs concentrated in the south of the state were untouched by the Settlement of 1896. Unlike the Mughal jagirs, the Rajput jagirs were hereditary landholdings and rarely resumed. The Rajputs provided military support, and up to the twentieth century the landholding rights of the jagirdars, which were the basis of their political, military, and economic power, were not interfered with. As the council was sympathetic to the interests of the nobility, the kinship elite was given a major role in decision-making.

Fiscal regimes that characterized the areas of direct colonial rule in the nineteenth century were extended to areas under "paramountcy." Impey undertook a three-year and later a ten-year settlement in 1858 and 1861, respectively. In Alwar following British-sponsored reorganization, revenue doubled within sixty years.[28] The summary settlement of 1872 refers to the privileged tenure of "favoured classes being assessed at lower rates." The estates owned by Shaikhawat and Chauhan Rajputs in the Bansur and Man-

TABLE 7 Tehsils of Alwar State

Northern	Central	Southern
Tijara	Govindgarh	Kathumar
Govindgarh	Behror	Lachmangarh
Mandawar	Ramgarh	Rajgarh
	Alwar	Thana Ghazi
	Bansur	

Source: P. W. Powlett, *Gazetteer of Ulwur* (London: Trubner, 1878).

dawar tehsils were assessed "below the standard." Major Powlett personally supervised the Settlement in the Meo tehsils of Alwar, Lachmangarh, Ramgarh, and Tijara, while others were left to his assistant. In these three areas the standard of two-thirds net was claimed as land revenue besides 2 percent for cesses.[29] The Twenty-Year Settlement (1898–1900) hiked the demand to 2.27 million (see table 8).[30]

In Mewat, land was most valuable because it was most intensely irrigated.[31] The *muwāzanas* of Kishangarh dated 1740 enable comparable figures of revenue collection of the Mughal period with the Settlement Survey of 1876 (see table 9). Cadell's statement on receipts and disbursements of the state from 1857–58 to 1869–70 shows more than a 20 percent increase in land revenue within a decade, from Rs 1,404,275 to Rs 1,734,641.[32] Revenue collection, thus, offset the benefits to the peasant from the rise in prices. Moreover, the year of 1877–78, just after the settlement was introduced was "marked by perhaps the most severe famine that ever devastated Rajputana and the southern Punjab. It was most severely felt in the Mewat tehsils, where the failure of rains was greatest."[33] Although the state remitted all arrears, Cadell's report of 1871 describes the decimation of the rural population, the general exodus, the grain robberies.

The Tragedy of Heroism: The Bandits Ghurchari and Mev Khan

This narrative is unusual in that it contests a twofold dominance, of the colonial and the princely regimes. Although the oral tradition uses the sole characterization of bat for the genre of narratives about the past, *Ghurcharī* can be seen as a folk epic since the narrative covers the cycle from birth to death of the hero, Ghurchari.

The narrator begins by describing the context. In the princely state of Alwar, around the tehsil of Kishangarh Bas, is the area of the Baghora Pal. In the village of Chaundavta lives Khuda Bakas, the son of Jaunhari, with his wife Jivni. Two sons are born to Khuda Bakas, Mev Khan and Ghurchari. Bandits are distinct from robbers and other criminals in terms of the moral connotations of their acts, their social concern, and their noble birth. The Meo brothers are described as belonging to a noble lineage. Their father has been appointed chaukidar (watchman) by the mukhiya (headman) because of the complaints of baniya merchants against the constant thieving

TABLE 8 Settlements of Alwar State

Year Initiated	Settlement	Officer	Demand (in Rupees)	% Increase
1858	Three-Year	Captain Impey	1,465,615	5.0
1861	Ten-Year	Captain Impey	1,753,425	20.0
1876	First Regular	Colonel Powlett	2,011,128	6.0
1898–1900	Second Regular	Colonel O'Dwyer	2,073,486	10.0

Source: Land Revenue Assessment in Alwar, Jaipur Agency, Rajputana CRP, R2/152-149; *Alwar District Gazeteer*, 447.

TABLE 9 Revenue Collected in Kishangarh (Alwar State)

	1740		1876	
Pargana	Area (Akbari) Bighas	Revenue (in Rupees)	Area (Akbari) Bighas	Revenue (in Rupees)
Pur	16,234	4,253	14,149	19,680
Behror	35,731	8,766	26,865	32,839
Govindgarh	—	1,994	—	2,950

Source: Compiled from P. W. Powlett, *Gazetteer of Ulwur* (London: Trubner, 1878), 136, 141, 143.

of their *mandīs* (grain markets) by the Minas. The appointment of Khuda Bakas as watchman refers to actual practice. Under a system introduced by L. T. Tomkins two thousand watchmen were appointed in the state under the supervision of headmen as agents to control crime.[34]

The greatness of Ghurchari, the younger son, is presaged at birth by the brahman astrologer who foretells: "You have given birth to such a son, Jivni, as has never been nor ever will be" *(tainai ī sut janmo jīvṇī aiso huyo nā ojū hoy)*:

laṛko gaṇḍhārī gaiṇvar ghaṇo āñkhan surkhī ḍoro lāl
nām nikāḷaigo pāl ko ghurchaṛī meṭaigo ī rājan ko naṭsāl

The boy's eyes are red veined
he will be authoritative and a helper of the poor.
Ghurchari will bring great name to the pal,
he will challenge the king.

Ghurchari's forthcoming role, antagonistic to the state, is presaged here, as he is *gaṇḍhārī*, or a source of authority.

Bandits and mountains are frequently associated. Both relate to remote and inaccessible areas.[35] Ghurchari and Mev Khan constantly seek refuge in the wild mountainous terrain of the Kala Pahar (Black Mountain). Growing up, the boys spend their time grazing goats, indicating a pastoral lifestyle. They are fond of hunting, learn to aim well, and get bows and arrows made. This does not, however, mean they are "predatory"; instead, they kill predatory animals such as the lion, tiger, and panther. The metaphor is extended later in the story to their annihilation of the predatory social elements/classes.

Early in life the brothers express a fascination with the new colonial technology, particularly the means of violence. When the brothers ask Khuda Bakas for a double-barreled gun, he tells them to select one of the weapons in the passage in their home. The brothers take a gun and go for a hunt. A policeman tells them of the availability of arms at Lahore. They decide to go to Lahore and rob the English *palṭan* (platoon). The two rob the arms depot there and leave with a rifle. They take the bus to Firozpur that takes them through Delhi.

Coercion figures centrally in the signification of the colonial regime that is staffed with military platoons and equipped with depots, well stocked with arms and ammunition. To "steal" from a colonial power is seen as legitimate because the colonial power has itself disturbed the code of right and wrong. So far the attack against the colonial state has been on its military stores, later its means of communication and control, the railway, will be targeted. The brothers' fondness for *shikār* and claims of access to the forests and its wildlife suggests how the kingdom's newfound control over natural resources will also be contested later in the story. Indeed, the state apparatus itself is directly challenged.

Interspersed with these events is the brothers' assault on social structure. The objects of banditry are persons with ample resources, the Kasai or butcher, the Sunar or goldsmith, the Randi or prostitute, and the baniya or merchant. They are identified as exploitative sections of rural society. The Kasais had emerged in the Gurgaon region during this period as a fairly prosperous caste who often lent money to indebted Meo peasants.[36] A butcher called Nanva is returning home after selling some calves. Two hundred fifty rupees are tied to his waist. The brothers accost him. Nanva pleads his religious affinity with them since he is also a Muslim and asks the brothers to let him go in the name of the Prophet *(duhaī nabī rasūl kī, moy tū musalmān kar choṛ)*. Mev Khan is sympathetic and asks Ghurchari to leave the butcher, but Ghurchari discounts the consideration of a shared religion. He takes half the money Nanva has tied around his waist. The remaining 125 rupees are to be delivered on the eighth day. They are collected from his house, outside which there is a huge pile of bones. The butcher is looted of his profit. In this case banditry acknowledges no religious distinctions: the profiteer is evil whether he is Hindu or Muslim.

At a shop where the brothers are eating sweets, the villagers are talking among themselves about the return of the baniya's marriage party and all the wealth it will bring back. Alerted, the brothers ask, "whose *bārāt* (bridal party) has gone and where?" "Naugavan," they are told. The brothers head in the direction of the bridal party, and at the base of the hill they loot the baniya who is both merchant and usurer. The exploitative triumvirate of sarkar, zamindar, and sahukar (or state, gentry, and merchant-usurer) is well known in rural society. Mewat did not fall under the zamindari tenure where the roles of zamindar (revenue collector turned landowner) and sahukar (usurer) were conflated as in Bengal as a consequence of British intervention. But the privileged status and power of the jagirdar in the Rajput polity emphasized the discrimination against the peasantry.

The narrative evokes a popular distrust of wealth. One of the more significant developments of the late seventeenth and early eighteenth century in north India was of the "intermediate classes." This included the sahukar or the big merchant of the city, the usurer, the mahajan or rural merchant and the baniya or village grocer.[37] The virulence against both sarkar-sahukar is conspicuous in the narrative and suggests the impetus to commodification associated with industrial capitalism. Several signs symbolize the qualitative change in the countryside. The presence of a money economy is signaled by the weights and coins used by the baniya and the money tucked around the butcher's waist. The growth of qasbas, or small towns, implies the expansion of privileged strata who can patronize novel forms of entertainment such as the *mujrā*, or dance performance, of the courtesan and can afford gold ornaments. The emergent stratification within the Meo community is indicated by the presence of persons of wealth and deep fissures despite kinship relations. The baniya's own wealth is epitomized by his household's wedding procession:

bahlī āvai chamakṇī jāpai paṛdo lāl
kahe ghurchaṛī suṇ mev khāñ yāmaiṇ koi lūṭaṇ lāyak māl

The palanquin comes glittering
a red curtain drawn across.
Says Ghurchari "Listen Mev Khan
looks like something we can loot."

The brothers come near the palanquin attracted by the ornaments that glitter from a distance. Ghurchari catches hold of the reins and asks the driver of the cart to halt. The baniya's image as a relentless, extractive Shylock is pervasive in Indian culture. He is the stereotypical moneylender, the symbol of wealth exploitatively acquired by the appropriation of the value of labor. To deprive him of wealth suggests the empowering of the marginalized.

Banditry is frequently supported by the lower orders of society. To begin with the baniya's driver takes offence, but when he recognizes Ghurchari and Mev Khan his tone is softer, "You are eternally blessed by the Lord, He loves you more than others" *(jin pai mihir sadā bhagvān kī jyādā rab ko pyār)*. The brothers are not only popular among the underprivileged but also described as being favored by God. The driver almost seems to assist the bandits in their actions against the societal "villains." Mev Khan holds the ropes of the bullock cart while Ghurchari climbs onto it and loots the jewelry crafted by the goldsmith.

Ghurchari and Mev Khan are bandits but to the local populace they are also heroes who help the poor and weak. This is foregrounded in an episode describing their encounter with a Gujar woman. Like the Meos, the Gujars are a peasant-pastoral group. As the brothers pass through the hills around the shrine of the Pir Chudh Sidh with a newfound ally, Umda Mina, they come across a Gujar woman who is crying, for a tiger has killed her cow. Ghurchari suggests to Mev Khan that they investigate the situation. Ghurchari asks the Gujari to tell them where the tiger is hiding or to send a man to help locate the animal so that he "will avenge this, mother, before the night is half over." Unaware of the brothers' identify, she replies that only Ghurchari-Mev Khan can kill the tiger, revealing touching faith in the bandits.

Vanquishing the tiger and conversely protecting the cows, the heroes are the defenders of the underprivileged, the weak, and the vulnerable. There is a constant emphasis on their masculinity. The Gujari tells them, "The tiger is your father; the tigress is your mother" *(siṅg tihāro bāp siṅgṇī terī māī)*. Similarly, at the end of the narrative in the *chāp kā dohā,* or signature verse, the author concludes, "Choto Thaniyo tells the story of two tigers." The bandit brothers are the "real" tigers who kill the predatory, carnivorous tiger. Ghurchari and Mev Khan cut the ears off the tiger and tell the Gujar woman, "Listen, mother Gujari, we have destroyed your enemy" *(suṇiyo mātā gūjarī hamnai tero meṭ diyo naṭsāl)*. Later in the story Ghurchari also rescues an Englishwoman and her child from a tent that has caught fire. Like bandits the world over the Meo brothers protect women (with the exception of those like the prostitute) in contrast to the nawab of Firozpur and the Rajput general who abduct women.

Ghurchari refuses the Gujari's offer of a buffalo and some cows as a reward, saying, "If we accept such rewards, they will amount to many haystacks." Assisting people in distress is a way of life for them. Instead of accumulating wealth and power, they represent an ascetic ethic that even their "enemy" uncle admits.

The counterfoil to the "goodness" of the bandits is the villainy of the princely state. The repeated reference to the Alwar maharaja's control over fifty-two forts symbolizes the state's concentration of the means of violence *(vā alvar mahārāj ko bāvan gaṛh maiṇ sor)*.[38] State power is evoked through the constant references to a network of thanas, chaukis or police posts, and officials such as the jamadar/thanedar, intelligence "reports," and the presence of jails, prisoners, and fugitives.

The baniya lodges his complaint at a police post. A furious search is launched to find Ghurchari and Mev Khan. Meanwhile an "untouchable" Bhangi joins Ghurchari and Mev Khan. He goes to the goldsmith's shop and hides there at closing time, planning to rob it. But then he ponders, "What will I do alone? Only if Khuda Bakas' sons come can the task be done." The Bhangi calls the brothers and they break into the shop. Ghurchari takes all the gold, the silver money, and a folding sword. They go inside where the goldsmith is sleeping. A large metal box is kept near him containing weights. In the dark it falls down with a clatter and wakes up everyone. The Bhangi and Ghurchari run away. The police surround the place. Mev Khan climbs the stairs and jumps out of the two-story house but the police catch him.

As Ghurchari waits for Mev Khan and draws on the *hukkā* (water pipe) he sees the horse cart of the courtesan *(randī)* of Kishangarh on the road. She is returning to her village after her dance performance at Bahadurpur. A Meo called Dandad who is returning to his village meets her horse cart. Attracted by her jewelry Dandad joins Ghurchari. They rob the sleeping dancer of all her jewelry, which Ghurchari wraps up in a bundle. He returns to his father and goes to sleep. In the morning the courtesan complains to the police. The police official replies, "But when you don't mention any name who should I register the complaint against?" She recalls, "I heard one voice saying 'Dada Dandad let's go.'" The jamadar takes a policeman and leaves to capture Dandad, who is beaten and interrogated.

The brothers' acts of banditry challenge through symbolic inversion both social structure and the state, colonial and princely. When Ghurchari wakes up he sees the marks from the policemen's horses hooves all around him. His father tells him that the jamadar came at night to inform him that Ghurchari was summoned to the raja's court. Ghurchari twirls his moustache and goes to the jamadar who accuses him of having caused a commotion in the state *(jamārāj kai bīch kahā tainai dund machāyo)* by defying "the rule of Mangal Singh (that) no one can defy" *(maṇgal sing kā rāj maiṇ nāny kisī kī tāp)*.

Ghurchari responds by identifying himself with the preceding history of Meo resistance and the events described in *Kaulānī*. In the "mythologization" of memory Meo defeat earlier in the century is transformed into victory and the state is vanquished. He proudly tells the jamadar referring to the past resistance of the Baghora Pal:

pahle bāghoṛā maiṇ huyā lūṭ kai duniyā khāī
duniyā gaī bīch maiṇ bhūl dūsrī rīt chalāī
rājā kaulāṇī pai chaṛho chahaṛ kai kāṇ ghaṭāī
vākī jitnī palṭaṇ gaī bagad nā ulṭī āī
jaṇg juṛai bhārat mañḍhai merā hūñ dekhiyo hāth
terā mangal siṇg mahārāj sūñ maiṇ karṇī chāhūñ do do bāt

They were born first in the Baghora (Pal)
who looted and destroyed the world.

In-between the world forgot
again we start the tradition.

The Raja attacked Kaulani
his image was destroyed.
The entire platoon that went
had to come back (defeated).
When the battle breaks forth
watch my hand.
To your Mangal Singh Maharaja
I'd like to say a thing or two.

The jamadar makes Ghurchari sit down. Under pretense of conversing with and pacifying him he gestures to the policeman who handcuffs him. Duplicity typifies the actions of state officials. With an angry flourish of his pen, the jamadar sentences Khuda Bakas and Ghurchari to four years imprisonment each. Sovereignty expresses itself in penal authority. It is defied by the bandits. At a later stage Ghurchari asserts, "The chains of the state have been broken with a stone" *(hamnai beṛī kāṭī rāj kī dī patthar sūñ kāṭ)*, and "we have become the thieves of the regime" *(chor huyā sarkār kā)*.

While Mev Khan is in the Gurgaon jail, Ghurchari and his father are held in custody at Alwar. After a heavy rain the mud walls of the jail collapse and Mev Khan escapes. Passing through the mountains he goes home to learn from his mother that his father and brother are in the Alwar jail. He asks her to call the ("untouchable") Sumra Bhangi, whose daughter is married to the sweeper of the Alwar jail. Mev Khan sends a note through Sumra to Ghurchari.

Meanwhile Umda Mina from the Jaipur region also hears about Ghurchari's exploits and comes to Alwar. The police have been watching his movements and he is arrested at Alwar and put in the lockup, next to Ghurchari. Umda, like the brothers, refuses to acknowledge the authority of the regime *(jāko rāj tapai ho des maiṇ maine ū bhī gāñṭho nāny)*. Ghurchari and he become *pagṛī palaṭ* (turban-exchanging) brothers. Friendship is anthropologized as fictive kinship but in fact suggests a bond as strong as that of brothers. Ghurchari and Umda decide to escape from the jail. Ghurchari tells Umda to go ahead as he wants to make a noise before leaving to proclaim their escape. When Ghurchari thinks that Umda must have covered some distance he shouts loudly for everyone to hear *(terī bhagar chalo hūñ jeḷ sūñ ghurcharī kahgo helo der)*. Ghurchari catches up with Umda and they head home.

Thus, at various points Ghurchari's career is linked to representatives of other subaltern groups. The bhangis from the caste occupationally consisting of sweepers and bearers of human excreta euphemistically called "night soil" and considered to be the most ritually polluting of the "untouchable" castes are allied to the bandits. Umda Mina is an important collaborator. The Minas (like the Bhils) had been displaced ever since the Rajputs ejected them from their citadels and established the dynastic rule of their clans such as the Rathors, Sisodia Chauhans, Kacchavaha, and Haras all over Rajputana and, were, in addition, marginalized by the colonial discourse of criminality.

In the narrative, Umrav, the brothers' uncle, symbolizes an upper strata of the Meo peasantry that had benefited in wealth and position from colonial and princely rule. He is a favorite of the maharaja and, as suggested by his large landholdings and the different sheds for his livestock and cattle, a man of considerable means. The association between wealth and regime is typical of bandit narratives. The three fugitives seek refuge with Umrav at his village. But in the Meo versus state conflict Umrav sides with the latter. Ghurchari uses a contemptuous word, "*muñhcharhā*," or pampered by the raja, for him. At Umrav's son's engagement the Mirasis are singing, but the brothers have not been invited. Umrav instead of offering them protection demands money from them. Ghurchari had given his uncle the sword and seventy rupees taken from the goldsmith, but now Umrav threatens to go to Alwar and report the matter to the maharaja and get them locked up in jail again.

The destruction of Umrav signifies the brothers' antistatism. Ghurchari sets fire to the goat shed, the cow shelter, and the haystack. At night they burn the camel shed, shoot a camel and prop it up as though alive, then return and pray to Mahadev. The battle between the two is described in epic proportions as akin to the killing of the cruel and wicked king of Mathura, Kansa, by Krishna; of Hiranyakashyapa by Vishnu (in his half-man and half-lion incarnation of Narasimha); and of Kichak (the evil brother of the queen of Bairath who had designs on the Pandava brothers' wife, Draupadi) by Bhim. The metaphors are pauranik, "Like the Hatnapur Pandavas fought I will battle your Mirzapur" *(jaise hatnāpar paṇdū laṛā kar dūñgo terī mirjāpar bhaunchāṛ)*.

In Meo narratives women are sometimes imaged as possessing powerful intuitive capacities, capable of seeing into the future. The destruction has been presaged in Umrav's wife's dream where she sees him teasing a "sleeping tiger." Umrav is perturbed and consults Tulla Joshi, a brahman astrologer, about the meaning of the dream. Tulla predicts division *(phūṭ)* among the brothers. In the morning Umrav's sons see that all has been burned. Umrav harnesses his horse and goes straight to the maharaja.

The issue of revenue that was strongly evoked in *Kaulānī* recurs here. Umrav complains in his petition to Mangal Singh that Ghurchari is appropriating the revenue of Mirzapur:

yākai nā paṭvārī sāth sipāhī nā hai pyādā
asal ghuṛchaṛī huyo jamā kuch mañgai jyādā

No patwari is with him
no policeman nor foot soldier.
Such a man is Ghurchari
he takes some extra revenue.

Ghurchari writes a note to Umrav explicating the idea that law creates the criminal. "You reported (us) to Alwar, made us fugitives from the law" *(taine alvar karī rapot baṇā ham dīnā bāgī)*. Ghurchari informs him "I have blown up all your capital, set fire to your village" *(terā diyā pūñjḷā phūñk gāñv maiṇ āg lagādī)*. The tone is virulent; the act is one of revenge. Ghurchari proudly declares, "We have been to Jhir for a pilgrimage but we haven't left our land." The order to arrest Ghurchari comes from the maharaja and the punitive apparatus is mobilized: "both the thanas attack; the police uses its full force" *(donū thāṇā chaṛhā pulas nai jor lagāyo)*.

The policeman articulates the brothers' attempt to constitute a new moral universe and establish an alternative source of authority:

ek rāj añgrej ko dūjo karai rihāṛ
tījo rājā ghurchaṛī mev ko jāko kiḷo kāḷo pahāṛ

One state is of the British
for the second you are fighting.
The third raja is Ghurchari Meo
whose fort is the black mountain.

There is a manifest sensibility of diverse systems of power here including the colonial, the kingly, and the community minus the exploiters that constitutes the moral universe. The verse suggests the bandit brothers' self-perception of wielding a separate source of power and thereby posing a major challenge to the state. The act of writing (read, command) is seen as one over which the ruler would like a monopoly, but the bandits encroach on this. Hence, the raja's complaint that Ghurchari "has written letter after letter (and) boldly shouts his orders" *(kāgaj pai kāgaj likhai hukam suṇālai tej)*. Umrav and the maharaja are represented as the structural opposite of the Khan brothers. The latter also stand in opposition at various points to the British Empire. With the strong attack on the collusiveness of the princely and imperial regimes, they are totalized as a single enemy. The established confronts the countercultural; the dominant is defied by the dissenting. This is analogous to the ecological opposition of the cultivated plains and the wild, rugged mountain terrain of the Kala Pahar, which is the refuge of the bandit brothers.

Ghurchari and Mev Khan head for the jail where their father is imprisoned. In the narrative, Thakur Lakhdir Singh of Bijwar, the leader of the nobles' revolt and the cornerstone of British design to use the nobility to reduce the power of the king, appears as "Lakhji Thakar," veritable symbol of state juridical power as he stands guarding the jail. When Ghurchari tells him to move out of his way, the thakur draws his dagger from its sheath. Ghurchari kills him, signifying an attack on the corporeal aspect of power. This does not, however, refer to an act that was *actually* committed. Lakhdir Singh died in Jaipur in 1875.

Unlike the state that uses modes of duplicity and treachery, the bandits' methods are honest and open. Ghurchari wants to acknowledge the killing and tells Mev Khan to break the lock of the baniya's shop and "bring a pen and some ink. Let us write before we leave that we have killed him so that no one else is caught." The bandits' actions are honorable and clearly distinct from crime, the latter being an act for which one would like to avoid responsibility. Ghurchari's effort on the contrary is bold, loudly proclaimed, and dramatic; he writes a verse with his blood and hangs it on the door. It has the desired effect for "in all Alwar there is an uproar when all the policemen gather" *(sarai alvar hogo sor pulas jab huī ikaṭṭhī)*.

The next target is the colonial empire. The brothers walk along the rail line. The "wire" of the rail makes a sound indicating an approaching train. Ghurchari proclaims, "Let it be known that Ghurchari passed by today." He climbs the pole with the help of his wooden staff, cuts the wire, and ties a paper to one end of the wire declaring, "I write you a letter Raja, how do you dare hold my father?'

jo tero base chakattā des ko kāgaj vāku dījyo bhej
dherai baṇd karūñgo rel kūñ dekhai mero kahā karaiñ añgrej

Inform the highest railway official
send him this note.
I will capture and stop your rail tomorrow
let's see what my Englishmen will do.

The mocking verse is read at both ends of the line by *babus*, or petty officials, of both the colonial and princely bureaucracy. Ghurchari's threat to the rail is direct and unambiguous. By cutting the "line of the English" the bandit brothers have terrified all Alwar *(tār kaṭo añgrej ko jā dinā sārī alvar tharrāī).*

The rail line for the Delhi-Alwar route on the Rajputana Railroad opened on 14 September 1875 and was expanded over the next few decades.[39] On 6 December 1876 trains ran from Delhi to Bandikui. The rail was the imperial symbol par excellence as E. M. Forster points out. Paul Theroux writes, "The Raj had no shortage of symbols, but the railway was the greatest of them. . . . It was the imperial vision on a grand scale." The innocuous goal of extension of communication and transport facilities required the backing of state power. As an imperial project, the rail sought to manipulate and transform the colonized. Its technology was purportedly concerned exclusively with conquest and control, and it ignored the disruptive impact on the life-world of the colonized.[40] In the areas under "indirect" rule it was the means by which the interventionist state directed itself toward penetration of colonized territory that was nominally under the suzerainty of the princely state.

The rail was the means whereby not only was the kingdom subordinated to the imperial power but also its economy was closely entwined with it. Railways linked up industrial produce with vast new markets in the rural hinterland. They helped produce the considerable famine and agrarian indebtedness that became alarming in the 1870s. Simultaneous with increasing commercialization of agriculture and a remarkable internal colonization (as the sown area of Punjab and Haryana doubled between 1850 and 1925 to 30 million acres), the small landholder was threatened with pauperization.[41]

Ghurchari and Mev Khan's act of "cutting the line" is an attempt to redress the unfavorable power structure, to decolonize their life-world. At a deeper level it questions the rhetoric of progress, industrialization, and modernity since the rail symbolizes the dominant ideology and is regarded as an amoral intrusion. Through this feat the brothers attempt to communicate "negative thinking," a precondition for any emancipatory project. Not surprisingly, the disruption of the rail became a symbol of an anticolonial posture in other places as well such as in Lucknow. In the narrative the rail becomes the site of conflict between colonial power and the fast-eroding local polity. The bandit brothers' fuzzy conception of "line," which is sometimes described as the rail and sometimes as the telegraph line, is an index of their marginality to the technocratic empire. Their attitude to technology suggests the ambivalence of the colonial subject, for earlier they have demonstrated a fascination with the new range of weaponry introduced by the British.

The brothers' next act is deliberately antiprincely. They go to the hill of the Meo saint called Pir Chudh Sidh. Umda Mina is waiting with food for them at the temple of Mahadeva. They eat and also feed the dogs. The distribution of food is a metaphor for an ideology of the sharing of the natural resources — land, water, and forests. It imagines a larger relationship between the human, animal, and natural world within a cosmos that incorporates Mahadeva, the goddess, and the Meo saint. It is in contrast to the privatization of the forest as a domain of royal play.

In the forest, tiger bait has been laid as Maharaja Mangal Singh is coming for a hunt. Ghurchari, however, kills the tiger and stands it up as though it were alive. The brothers hide with their guns and wait for the maharaja. He comes seated on an elephant surrounded by Rajput thakurs who converse among themselves of the "specially strong type of tiger." The maharaja fires his gun and the tiger immediately falls to the ground. The brothers stand up and Ghurchari says that an animal that had already been killed has been shot. The maharaja reacts angrily, for this is a gross violation of kingly legislation and the code for subjects based on deference to the regime and its incumbent. That the tiger, which was meant for the maharaja and would confirm his hunting prowess, in a sense his power, had already been shot is an act of supreme defiance, for "In the kingdom of Mangal Singh no other hunter can place a foot" *(maṇgal sinh kā rāj maiṇ nā koi dharai sikārī pāñv).*

Ghurchari introduces himself:

terī gayā jeḷ sūñ nikaḷ ghurchaṛī mosūñ bolaiṇ
ler dunāḷī hāth hīn parbat maiṇ dolaiṇ
jhapaṭ chalāī tār kūñ jaise panjo gāṛai hai bāj
ham to terā chor haiṇ hamkūñ kyā pūchai mahārāj

I escaped from your jail
Ghurchari is my name.
A muzzle loader in my hand
I roam across this mountain.
We have snapped your wire
like the vulture digs in its claws.
We are your thieves
what do you ask of us Maharaja?

To this the maharaja replies, "We are mere caretakers; the wires belong to the English." Ghurchari responds contemptuously, "We will not extend our hand toward you and won't come near you. On this stone is a token gift of Rs. 11. Take it. Whether you are a Maharaja or a *thekedār* (contractor) the answer to this we already have."

There is on the surface of Ghurchari's statement a pretense of deference that is deeply ironical, approximating what Booth calls "ironic satire." In calling themselves "thieves" Ghurchari parodies the ruler's speech. Parody is grounded in the mimetic as it imitates and mocks the other.[42] The so-called sovereignty of the Alwar State is ruptured by the evocative image of the "phirangi" (foreign) English and the maharaja as a "contractor" who is a mere caretaker. The powerlessness of the regime is further underlined by the maharaja's own acknowledgment of this and his relenting on the question of the release of Khuda Bakas from jail. The maharaja has submitted to the English, now he agrees to release Ghurchari's father. Ghurchari's token offering is what Bourdieu calls a challenge-gift that in the context of the Moroccan Berbers "is a provocation, a provocation to reply. . . . The receiver of a gift is caught in the toils of an exchange and has to choose a line of conduct which, whatever he does, will be a response (even if only by default) to the provocation of the initial act."[43] The limits of Ghurchari's parody remain, since it cannot really alter power relations.

The colonial intersects with the kingly as they mutually reinforce each other. The dominant British model of governance in the princely states led to the adoption of a Western model of "scientific forestry." This, in turn, led to the privatization of forest land. Village common lands had been used as pastures and a source of firewood and were controlled by the local community. There had been no question of access, rights, concessions, claims, and fences, except for the conventional taxes on grass and wood. But by virtue of "settlements" forests now became government land under the control of the revenue or forest department. In Alwar these became princely hunting preserves that fell into the categories of protected or reserved forests. The state proclaimed its control over forest land, and its produce and wildlife. The forests became a major arena of contestation in the decades that followed.

In the episode of the tiger hunt *Ghurcharī Mev Khāñ* explicitly articulates the conflict between the state and the peasantry over land and natural resources. This conflict has historically been a near-universal issue. It occurred in the German Peasant War of 1525 and in France between the sixteenth and the eighteenth centuries. In England it was reflected in the large instance of "forest crimes" such as timber theft and violation of game laws following the enclosure of land by the aristocracy.[44] The bandit narrative is replete with antihegemonic symbolism. Ghurchari shoots the tiger streaking through the forest. He preempts the maharaja's hunt for which the bait had been carefully laid. This is an act of supreme defiance since the object of attack is the apex of state power.

Ghurchari's mocking tone ridicules the power structure, which is really powerless: it is only capable of knocking down victims that are already dead. A hunter has not only entered prohibited premises but also destroyed the prey meant for the maharaja. It suggests the vacuity of the system and the yawning gap between promise and performance. The bandits are now locked in a direct face-to-face confrontation with Maharaja Mangal Singh. He addresses Ghurchari and Mev Khan as chatri (ksatriya), acknowledging their claim to the varna of rulers and thereby a symmetry of power.

There is a simultaneity of victory and tragedy in the mythic tradition. Umrav complains to the jamadar that he has seen both brothers at Jhirka. The jamadar promises to arrest the bandits and send them to Kishangarh, provided he is rewarded. Umrav virtually bribes him with the offer of "a hundred rupees, a turban, a headdress, and a cow." The jamadar attacks with a few hundred policemen *(jamādār chaṛh diyo sipāhī lārai līnā)*. They surround the Jhir police post, leaving not a single path unguarded so that, "Death encircles them; time takes such a turn."

As defeat of the bandits becomes inevitable the gods intercede. In the *Pāñch Pahāṛ* a faqir had intervened on the side of Meos battling with the Mughal-Rajput army. The bandit brothers remember Mahadeva (Shiva) and plead with him. His consort Gorja (from Gora or Parvati) urges her husband on the mountain Kailash to urgently reach "our sons" who have been surrounded today *(yā parbat kailās maiṇ daī gaurjā ṭer/pahoṇchai kyū ñai jognā āj liyā balakā gher)*.

Mahadeva disguises himself as an old Meo. From the goddess's shrine at Jhir he goes on to Jeroli where a crowd has collected at the house of a Meo elder called Badlu Chaudhari. Mahadeva comes to the rescue of the brothers who are surrounded by the menacing crowd of Umrav's men and "changes the plans of the attackers." He draws on the *hukka* (water pipe) and reprimands Badlu Chaudhari. A battle ensues. Ghurchari wounds one of the leaders of the opposing group called Haji Mall (the name refers to one who has been on the annual *hajj* pilgrimage to Mecca) but the battle is inconclusive. The shrines of the goddess and the Pir Chudh Sidh are part of Mewat's sacred geography and pilgrimage for both Hindus as well as Muslims. The pilgrimage sites figure again and again in myths of the nineteenth century.

Shulman remarks on the tension between the center constituted by the throne and the transcendent world. Shiva is the god of the remnant and outsiders.[45] Here he intervenes on behalf of his Meo "sons." The mythic past underwrites the present. Ghurchari and Mev Khan are likened to the Pandu (the Pandavas). They are connected with them genealogically as well, since the Baghora clan is said to have descended from Arjuna. The bond derives from an identity of "action" in the world that represents virtue and truth. Even though Jarjot (the Mewati name for Duryodhana) harassed the Pandu "their (intrinsic) goodness remained unchanged" *(burī karī jarjodh nai bigṛā nāṇy subhāv)*. The analogy establishes a moral universe. The methods adopted are rendered legitimate by the end, which is the destruction of evil.

Injustice and treachery within the community are major concerns. It is almost as though the Meo oral tradition is forestalling the constant fragmentation of the community by fostering group cohesion. Umda goes back to his land, and the two brothers go to Bhagmal, their uncle. They describe to him the problems and injustice Umrav caused them; how he metaphorically stabbed them in the back and made them leave their home *(mānā ko umrāv ḍob dagṛā maiṇ mārī, mānā kā umrāv nai dīnā julam gujār)*. Umrav goes to Meda, another Meo elder, and asks him to work out a reconciliation with Ghurchari. Umrav also pleads with Bhagmal to repair his quarrel with Ghurchari and Mev Khan. Bhagmal tells him that the brothers are in the hills but promises that when he takes their food he will speak to them. At sundown Umrav accompanies Bhagmal. Umrav and his men hide in the hills. Ghurchari has a premonition that his uncle has come to trap him from several ominous signs, like the howling of the wild animal and the bellowing of the cow. It is almost as though nature attempts to warn them.

The treacherous Umrav has sent the news of the brothers' hideout to Mangal Singh, and the soldiers of his army wait in hiding. Umrav says, "Let us eat together. Place your gun here." Ghurchari lays it aside and is caught. The brothers are tied with a rope, and a blanket is draped over them. But Ghurchari has a knife that he passes to Mev Khan, who cuts his own ropes. Ghurchari consoles his brother, "You cannot do anything; go leave this place." Ghurchari had escaped from the platoon that had gone "decorated with weapons and its officers" but is caught and brought to Alwar by the Meos. Meo complicity in the arrest suggests fissures within the group. Clearly a prosperous section of the Meo peasantry sides with the regime.

The rani of Maharaja Mangal Singh intercedes on Ghurchari's behalf, "to such a chatri (ksatriya) male, raja you must give a reward" *(aisā chatrī marad kūñ rājā toy deṇī chāhai ināṁ)*. But the raja himself acknowledges that he dare not, for if he "releases him he will have to bear the English anger" *(je maiṇ yakū choṛ dūñ mopai gusse hoy añgrej)*. The next day Ghurchari is imprisoned in an iron cage and sent to Lahore. Tormented by hunger his soul utters a curse so that the entire tent in which food is being cooked catches fire. The English *sahab* (official) panics, for his wife is being burned alive. He promises to acquit Ghurchari if he saves her. Ghurchari's cage is opened and he plunges into the fire wrapped in a blanket:

dīnī maim bhagāy bagal maiṇ bacchā līnā
sāhab khusī ho gayo bāñdhā yālū phaiṇṭa dīnā

The mem *[English woman] is rescued*
the child tucked under his arm
The Sahab is happy
ties a turban on his head.

The colonial official's order releases Ghurchari from the mud-walled jail. Till the order of clemency comes, Ghurchari stays with the official in Lahore. The English woman develops a passion for him, but Ghurchari spurns her. She poisons him and he dies.

Ghurchari's masculinity, which accepts no prison chains, no iron cage, culminates in his death. The romantic love of the Englishwoman is as unacceptable to him as the colonial regime. In response to her rejection she poisons him. Shulman comments that there is an *identity* between bandits and kings — attributes of royal birth, the reliance on brute force, and divinity.

The king-bandit opposition can be read in caste terms. In contrast to the king the bandit represents the ascetic denial of power. In Ghurchari's case the asceticism is sexually charged. But it is the bandit's link with tragedy and sacrificial death that marks him out from the king.[46] Ghurchari dies a free man, proud and defiant to the very end. The real tragedy is that the bandit is marginal by virtue of his relation to central values and symbols and that his death has no impact on the center, colonial or kingly.

Let us return to some of the major controversies that have surrounded the discussion on banditry. Hobsbawm's pioneering work interpreted it as primitive rebellion in transitional societies where tribal and kinship organization is disintegrating prior to the development of agrarian capitalism. Hobsbawm also characterized the social brigand as a "pre-political phenomenon" among "primitive rebels" who "appears before the poor have reached political consciousness."[47] He saw it as characterized by nostalgia for a pre-political just world and as preventing peasant mobilization and solidarity.

Banditry, however, may represent a deeply political act that questions the legitimacy of both the juridic-legal and social order. Rebellion in precapitalist and preindustrial monarchies has been seen as "customary rebellion."[48] It castigates officials for nonperformance of their duties but does not challenge the king whose authority is seen in the context of divine right and paternalism. The heroes of the Meo narrative, however, challenge the maharaja, attack the state apparatus, and rupture the very legitimacy of princely rule. That divinity is associated with the bandit heroes rather than an attribute of the king challenges the legitimation of monarchical rule.[49] Resistance need be no mere "subtext" of the dominant ideology.[50] In this case the oral tradition creates a countertext to the hegemonic ideology that outlines the nature of dominant political authority.

Hobsbawm viewed banditry as antithetical to class consciousness, a phenomenon that fades with the growth of peasant consciousness. Blok goes even further, arguing that banditry terrorizes peasants with depredations on large-scale landholdings, and this renders peasants docile.[51] Gallant points out that bandits are lone wolves and that this is not a family affair (let alone a clan or group one).[52] The Meo narrative hints at some of the tensions within the peasantry and the community that banditry produces. The large landholder is quite hostile to the bandits, despite a kinship connection, and they are eventually turned over to the princely state by a faction of their own group. The Meo bandit brothers, nonetheless, have a wider support—that of subaltern groups. The alliance encompasses symbolically the "untouchable," the "tribal-criminal," and the poor peasant-pastoralist Meo. This support from the lower rungs of the social hierarchy is a support that cuts across lines of caste, religious affiliation, and gender. The money-spinning prostitute is robbed, but caring protection is extended to the vulnerable Gujar woman referred to as "mother."

The mythology of banditry is subversive of property, but also of power. Indeed the very celebration of the bandit in the tradition of storytelling suggests how he is emblemized in terms of heroic resistance and even martyrdom. Cassia argues that myths of banditry resurface and get incorporated into nationalist/regionalist rhetoric. The bandit is romanticized and thus, bandit texts have a life of their own, giving them a permanence and potency that transcends their localized domain and transitory nature. A process of mythification incorporates Greek bandits into nationalist rhetoric.[53] The Meo critique of colonialism contributes to the making of Meo nationalism in the early twentieth century. The Meo bandits are celebrated again and again and invoked in the large-scale peasant movement of 1932–33 that mobilizes nearly one hundred thousand Meos. The critique of the state is evoked again in the oppositional moment. On this occasion it leads to the displacement of the monarchical regime.

10 Conclusions

I deliberately use the term"conclusions" rather than the conventional singular since this work has unfolded through multiple contentions about the nature of written and oral texts. The argument of the preceding chapters can be reduced to three major issues. The first concerns the constitution and character of marginality that arises from a close relation between state and history since history constituted a hegemonic imaginary that was transmitted across time and was associated with a series of state formations. The second is an analysis of the nature of resistance of a subaltern group. This group not only resisted state authority and struggled against the historical process that was, in a sense, "against them" as it consigned them to the margins but also contested historical representation. Third, while this resistance was read negatively by state formations, the group's oral tradition provides clues to its own counterperspectives on the past. It enables an exploration of constructions and contestations of state and sovereignty "from below" and of perceptions of power from a subject perspective relating to multiple state formations. Oral tradition as cultural memory not only yields a divergent perspective on the past but also suggests a sensibility indicating the unfolding of collective identity and the shifting character of intergroup relations.

The Meos provide a case study of a defiant community that has resisted successive state formations, the sultanate, the Mughal and British Empires, and the regional kingdoms. They are an example of how a group sustains its identity over time, which is especially important since the group does not succeed in history but is repeatedly defeated.

Social identity is created by articulating and keeping alive collective memory. The memorialized past permeates individual memory and shapes both self and society. The community is one of descent and rules of exchange that include marriage and gift giving, but it is also the community of remembrance. Solidarity is constituted through the memory of conquest and conflict, friendship and alliance, heroism and tragedy.

The community is also produced by the intellectual systems of ruling groups that are inextricably linked to institutional practices of governing. The sovereign must ontologically construct the other in order for it to be controlled and domesticated. This is the very condition of the social contract and the act of ruling. The exploration of domination, the exercise of power, then requires an investigation into the processes of knowledge that continuously structure the social world.

State formation implies a particular orientation to resistance. The activity involved in state formations between the thirteenth and nineteenth centuries ranges from "conquest" through co-optation to "control" so that the resistant group may be "reduced" or disciplined. Wildness is a metaphor for the legitimacy of rule carrying gendered implications of a chaotic sensuality that must be chastened. The metaphor is also ecological as it requires the forest to be cut down, the wasteland to be colonized, and the population to be sedentarized. In the writing in English, resistance is overwritten by ideas of race and criminality sponsored by colonial ethnographic texts.

The genre of colonial ethnography is derived from post-Enlightenment disciplines but its content borrows from the Indo-Persian histories where the Mewatis have already been imaged as turbulent and rebellious. The imperial center attempts the subordination of "subjects" by the extermination of particularly rebellious segments to destroy the wherewithal of rebellion, by besieging and ravaging their territory, extracting revenue, and "subduing" the population. The dialectic becomes all too familiar, repeated as it is in so many works. Representation is a prelude to state action and legitimates state formation, which is often an exercise that will curb subversion and insurgency. With colonialism the relationship with science is consolidated.

Oral traditions such as these open up the question, Is objective history possible? Is there any event independent of human interpretation? For without interpretation an event ceases to be a human event and remains a natural event. Most history has been written from the vantage point of the state. History like ethnography, then, is no merely descriptive or mirror account of "reality." In fact, it both constitutes and transforms this reality through language, its metaphors and other figures of speech. However, it often attempts a pseudoimpersonality. Voice assumes the appearance of a masquerade, projected as impartial and distant. It disguises the "I" that writes. In the case of oral texts the "I" is not screened off, but is identified with the speaker or author. There is also a built-in transparency, in contrast to the opacity of writing. The Meo oral texts are an imaginative construction of the world, one that is beautiful and painful, aesthetic and anguished in relation to the community.

Two dimensions are important with respect to examining how the written and printed word impinge on lived social worlds. The first is the question of representation, the epistemological processes whereby groups, their past and their actions, are portrayed. Second, how consciousness exists in a dialogical (albeit asymmetrical) relation with written texts. The inscription of history profoundly affects orality and memory. What results is a complex of both critique and protest, and the internalization of the form and content of written texts and the categories and practices of ruling.

Myth, memory, and the oral tradition, in this sense, are not the absolute other of history, of writing. Mewati folk texts exist at the juncture of writing and orality; at the intersection of several languages, Persian, English, Urdu, Brajbhasha, Khari Boli, Hindi, Marwari, and so on. They are decisively influenced by the written and spoken articulation in Persian (the language of the sultanate and the Mughal States and to some extent of the Jaipur kingdom as well), English (the language of the British Empire), and by Urdu (the official language of the kingdoms of Alwar and Bharatpur). This compromises the autonomy of subaltern consciousness.

The Mewati mythic tradition helps question much received wisdom on Indian civilization.[1] They are neither ultraspiritual nor renunciatory, and they demonstrate a preoccupation with ordering the past and with history and institutions.[2] They make possible the juxtaposition of two perspectives on a given event: one in which the ruling group classifies its universe, and alternatively the way in which a subject group perceives and represents its historical context and that of the other. Through the latter we have an alternative construction of historical encounter, a subject and subaltern perspective on different state formations. Mythic memory helps counter official memory or "history."

In the previous chapters I attempt to chart the course of Meo marginality. This is done through an understanding of the semantic fields of three kinds of "record": historical texts, administrative documents, and the cultural forms of the subject community. The historical texts written between the thirteenth and seventeenth centuries give a sense of the gradual destruction of Mewati centers of power. Along with the administrative documents of the eighteenth century, they demonstrate the inroads made into the Mewati polity and the undermining of the Meo peasantry. The oral narrative pertaining to the seventeenth century indicates the conflict and tension between state formation and a pastoral-peasant group concerned with its autonomy.

The past is open to multiple readings. The Mewati past can be read in at least two ways. First, as the Persian chroniclers did, as a record of insurrection. Alternatively, by looking at the interstices of the same works, it can be read as one of resistance against the repeated onslaught of the centralizing power. The Meo narrative contextualized in the Mughal period is a poignant description of an imperial system in ascendancy and the subordination of the local polity. It tentatively indicates how the Meo structured their world to incorporate the fact of Mughal-Rajput domination and their own loss of power. The culmination is necessarily tragic. The story is a universal one of the erosion of local and decentered modes of political organization.[3] It relives a tension that has existed globally between the universal state and the local polity.

Polities of conquest, however, tend to generate an underlife among displaced and marginal groups. Their antithesis is the counterculture of these groups available to us in their oral traditions. The paradox of the *Panch Pahar* is that although it is tragic it is also subversive. Its real achievement is the inversion of the categories of the Persian knowledge system. Fasad mewan and mufsidan mewati are the categories by which the Meos were defined from the thirteenth to the eighteenth centuries. The state's own self-projection was as the embodiment of order and justice ('adl). 'Adl is exposed in the narrative as its other, aniti or injustice. The otherness of the other is both redescribed and interrogated. The three Mewati categories jang, jama and julam are used to contest the imperial order. In the Meo view jang (war) rather than fasad (disorder, insurgency) characterizes their condition; resistance arises from the enforced collection of revenue, or jama; and julam, or injustice from an oppressive tyranny, is what characterizes the centralizing imperial regime in contrast to the legitimacy of the local polity. The oral-folk-popular cultural tradition challenges the Persian texts' careful construction of the imperial state as representing "order" and the Mewatis as representing disorder and chaos. Indeed, it exposes the Mughal-Rajput collaborative alliance as the perpetrator of violence in the region and as the primary factor responsible for the constant uprisings of Mewatis repeatedly referred to in the administrative documents of the period.

Women are particularly vulnerable to processes of state formation. This possibly explains the multiple stories of the abduction of Meo women in the oral tradition: Akbar's capture of a Meo woman; the daughters of a Meo chief kept captive by the Alwar raja and the Firozpur nawab; and of Rajni of Bisru who is said to have been taken away by the Mughals.[4] Sangari refers to several Charan bardic stories of the lustful Akbar.[5] Are these mere narrative tropes derived from a pan-Rajasthan cultural tradition? Why are Akbar, Shah Jahan, and the medieval Rajput noble memorialized by Mewati myth in a particular way? Surely the construct does not encompass the totality of the Mughal-Meo and Rajput-Meo relationship, which was far more complex. Then why the remembering, which is itself an act of cultural selection? And why the retelling suggesting that the memory be kept alive? This may suggest ways in which myth encodes the dominant form of the encounter. Inca myth in similar ways intimates the nature of the Indian-white contact and conquest; domination and the imposition of social hierarchy are central themes of Andean myth.[6] The mythic becomes a mode of understanding the nature of the encounter as well as the source of empowerment against domination.

In the Meo myth commenting on the Mughals, the central opposition is to the soldier who symbolizes an extractive state. The antagonism is not only to the imperial state but also to the emergent Rajput system. Kolff has argued that the sixteenth century meant for the Rajputs a shift away from the gregarious, pastoral, pre-Mughal world, and a new emphasis on brahmanical values, renunciation, endogamy, and exclusion. But another major shift took place during the seventeenth century regarding Rajput practices of power. This was the period of secondary Rajput state formation as distinct from the primary phase of the twelfth to thirteenth century. The phase witnessed an attempt to structure sovereignty and sociopolitical hierarchy through symbols such as the Rajput's exclusive right to ride horses and play the drum, and the demonstration of control through a network of forts and armed gangs.[7] The looting of Mughal treasure, the battle and the women's insistence on performing their ritual and playing the drum, which the *Panch Pahar* describes, become legitimate acts of resistance against the imperial state. The story culminates in the tragic fulfilment of Mughal-Rajput aggrandizement and the ultimate defeat of the local community following its prolonged struggle. Not surprisingly, administrative documents, likewise, indicate that from the mid-sixteenth century onward it was the Rajput "plunderers" and "oppressors" who were the main object of complaints made by Meo and other peasants.

That resistance was simultaneous with the internalization of the ideologies associated with Rajputs is also powerfully coded in the narrative tradition: in the Meo preoccupation with honor and heroism defined by bravery in battle; the shared attributes of kingship such as a fort, an army, treasure and genealogists; women's self immolation following a husband's death in battle, and so on. Pamela Price argues that the potential for subaltern autonomy in the Tamil country was "seriously compromised by the participation of subalterns in local institutions of worship and rule."[8] This was not the case with the Meos. The sharing of ideas of kingship, honor, and worship with the Rajputs did not preclude oppositional politics. Resistance does not require religious difference nor must it be defined in an absolute, linear sense, because it is simultaneous with interaction and exchange. Indeed the violation of kingly dharma can itself provide an ideology for revolt.[9] Dissent can use mythic and other aspects of the dominant culture to subvert the latter.

If the *Panch Pahar* is a critique of the imperial (Mughal) regime, *Ghurcharī Mev Khāñ* is a searing indictment of the colonial regime. It highlights how a significant shift takes place in the case of the Meo perception of the state, as technology is seen as central to the industrial-capitalist colonial system. The question becomes one of reacting to an essentially new kind of hegemony that is far more centralizing and extractive than that of the Mughal Empire. Contextualized in the late nineteenth century, the Mewati bandit narrative is a powerful folk commentary on colonial and princely regimes and the perceived nexus between them.

Dirks maintains that "the violence of the bandit is illegitimate, and it represents and causes the disorder that the legitimate violence of the king must control. Kings are not only legitimate, they define the realm of the legitimate."[10] But one needs to ask why the state should monopolize the definition of the legitimate. The use of bandits and pirates by several states itself sunders the boundary between legitimate and illegitimate violence. Surely the subject must also have a role in defining legitimacy. Indeed, in the community's perspective, it is the "legitimate" violence of the oppressed expressed as banditry that ruptures the proclaimed legitimacy of kingship.

The raja, the army, police, guns, the penal system (jails and courts), the patwari, and "babu" (mainstays of colonial-princely bureaucracy) are modes of power that subject the social body. The rail and the forest imply altered land use, new forms of land control, claims over resources, and a revolution in communications. Throughout the narrative the institutional structure of the colonial and princely states are questioned again and again. Through their looting, the brothers challenge the upper strata of the emergent social and juridical-legal order. The coercive and penal apparatus is confronted and the sovereign denigrated. The colonial state is assailed in the act of robbing the military platoon and by the attack on the arms depot and railway. The bandit brothers' emergence as a source of counterauthority is seen as a threat to state and sovereignty.

A moral boundary is suggested in the figures of the poor (Gujar) "mother," whom the bandits help, and the prostitute and "predatory" exploitative elite (including the merchant and butcher), whom they loot. But the deeper tragedy the narrative expresses is how the emergence of capitalist accumulation, exchange relations, and the commodity market have transformed the Meo community, creating fissures within itself. In some senses the text points to the community's partial reconciliation with the reality of state formation.

The telling and retelling of the fictionalized past at repeated gatherings on ritual occasions in different villages shows how local power corrodes centralist tendencies, how subversion is transmitted through cultural performance. The narrator's use of the personal pronoun "we" activates collective memory for the audience. The present tense is particularly important because it celebrates action. Through the use of direct speech, the past is (re)enacted in the performative text. Although the Meos were eventually forced to accept, and even acquiesced in, the imposition of centralized rule, nonetheless, they presented for at least seven centuries a serious challenge to different state formations. Heroes and other stereotypes are the creative cultural resources of a group under stress, particularly when they have access to a communicative media and an audience. By re-creating the past in a cultural performance attempts are made to mold the present, control the future. Precedents such as of a *laṛai*, or battle against the ruler, described in the oral tradition, offer a possible repertoire of collective action on future occasions. The oral tradition creates the ever-present potential of mobilization.

The debate on myth and history has moved center stage in the context of recent developments in Indian politics. A large number of contemporary theorists identify history with modernity, nationalism, and the state. They argue that it perpetuates the dominance of the West, and some have even heralded the "end of history."[11]

But for the same reason that myth is, as Clayton puts it, "a powerful oppositional technique" and its transmission reproduces the community of resistance, it can also be a potent source of the national political community. Both Gyanendra Pandey and Ashis Nandy argue that what contemporary Hindutva offers in India is the past packaged as history, as linear time.[12] But to deny the mythic aspects of the historical construction offered by organizations committed to the ideology of Hindu nationalism is to fail to see the tremendous power and energy of the myth model that involves the dramatic reenactment of the epic struggle between good and evil. Thus Rama comes again and again to fight the overpowering strength of adharma (in this case that of Islam). There is at work a larger appropriation of myth by history.[13]

Ashis Nandy in refutation of Obeysekere and my work critiquing the myth-history dichotomy argues that not all constructions of the past are history.[14] Surely, but to argue that "historical consciousness" is only the product of the West seems to establish an Occidentalism, a reverse orientalism. Myth tends to become the residual other of history sustained by nonmodern societies in this argument. To view myth exclusively as the language of threatened or victimized cultures, as Nandy does, is to deny the role of myth as a significant aspect in the exercise of hegemony. Myth and history cannot be seen along a moralization/totalization axis.[15] One only has to refer to the puruśasukta myth in the Indian context that describes the origin of four varnas (caste clusters) from the body of the primeval man. Or the ways in which Shankaracharya and numerous commentators on his work used the Satyakama Javal story to marginalize both women and lower castes from ritually "pure" status and access to learning.[16] A long tradition of anthropological investigation by theorists such as Durkheim show how myth relates to society's attempt to maintain order and cohesion. Guha brilliantly demonstrates how myth can be a congealed structure of power when it legitimizes brahmanical domination of dalit groups.[17]

Admittedly the term "myth" itself is a product of the Enlightenment.[18] Further, to see the mythic exclusively as an aspect of subalternity or the cultural product of non-Western cultures is to deny the continuous production of the mythic in the modern West. One has only to refer to the influence of the Rambo myth in the American public sphere or sections of the argument Barthes develops in *Mythologies* as he unravels the myths of everyday life.[19]

The historical imagination that fulfils the deep aspiration of the human self to discover its belongingness, identify its home, has assumed various shapes in different cultures. Islamic history located chronology in continuation with the history of Islam. In the Greek case the genres of history, epic, and lyric were intimately related. In Indian traditions the past was narrativized in several genres, particularly in the itihasa puranas of caste-communities that are best translated as cosmic genealogies. Europe projected its model of history in terms of its difference as an objective and empirical discipline. But it might be useful to view European and other histories also as itihasa purana since it helped locate the self in the world. Thus it is not, as sometimes has been argued, that Tod adopted a genre of Indian history writing (the "genealogical") but that he brought out what is implicit in Western genres themselves. Memory bridges myth and history, helps us explore different forms of the historical imagination in the past, and may be useful in furthering the vision of an alternative history. Let us not forget that when post-Enlightenment Europe consigned all other cultures to the category of backwardness, unreason, and nonlinear time it did so to premodern Europe as well. But it is important to recover from pre-Enlightenment Europe the notion of multiple histories that can potentially counter the totalizing impact of (universal) history.[20]

Certainly history has been associated with forms of power, and to simultaneously maintain, as Nandy does, the ahistoricity of myth is to deny the possibility of an alternative history. This is not unlike Levinas's contention that for the other to remain other or retain alterity it must not derive its meaning from history but must instead have a separate time distinct from historical time.[21] This and the "end of history" argument establishes a closure of what we have come to see as the professional discipline of history. It can only result in the apolitical move of production of accounts on the lines of ethnohistories or their nonhistorical equivalent rather than a vibrant conception of history as the battleground where mythic, remembered pasts and other representations are brought center stage. Multiple interpretations and diverse perspectives on pasts must feed into this. Both "myth" and the "documents" of nonstate actors need to be taken equally seriously as historians currently struggle with the challenge of conceiving of "alternative archive."[22] Dube and Skaria are outstanding examples of how myths can help build a completely different picture of the pasts of low-caste (untouchable) and forest communities.

What implications does this have for the constitution of subalternity? Dube makes the criticism that subaltern studies depends heavily on the binary opposition of state and community. My criticism of that criticism is that the opposition be treated not as an absolute division but as a measure of emphasis. Communities are not immune from practices of the state and are themselves permeated by hierarchies of caste, gender, and other power relations. Nonetheless, the absolute coerciveness of the state emerges from the intermeshing of the axes of sovereignty and history, and in the case of the colonial state the additional axes of industrial technology and ethnological science.[23] The subalternity of the Meos in history extends from the period of the Arab/Turkish conquest but deepens through the period of colonial rule and after.

Subaltern studies is one of the most interesting recent exercises attempting a history "from below." Some years after I had begun my work on the Meos I realized the close methodological affinities with the eclectic group that had published its research in the Subaltern Studies series and elsewhere. I have subsequently joined the collective. All through I have been strongly aware of the differences in approach and method within the group. One of the areas from which my own disagreement comes is from the relative neglect of the precolonial, by virtue of emphasis on the colonial and postcolonial. The very category "precolonial" homogenizes what is a range and diversity of human experience and institutions, rendering it a virtual prehistory. Chakrabarty acknowledges the close relation between state and history but only in the modern context. What happens before colonialism thus tends to get effaced. Guha points out the ways in which history writing is statist, in that it "authorizes the dominant values of the state to determine the criteria of the historic."[24] The Persian historiographical tradition also singularizes time, an exercise that is apparent in the category tawarikh or date. The question is of how the premodern is translated and transformed by the modern. For instance, perspectives on forest and other communities have already been forged in the Persian statist discourse in terms of the categories "mawas" and "bihar," the idea of a wild people inhabiting a wild terrain. The former comes from an Arabic root that means to oppose or to rebel. It is used as a legitimation for agricultural expansion and sedentarization.[25]

The colonial, then, is no absolute break with the past. Modes of knowledge and categories get translated across state systems. The marginality of castes, communities, and other groups even as they are the outcome of colonial construction, have extended histories.

States were not static, but highly dynamic political forms that responded in various ways to the interaction with their subjects. I do not propose an anarchic rejection of the state as a political entity. Indeed, the purpose of the discussion of the Meo polity is to show that there have been historically different modes of the organization of political power. Further, states are also capable of responding positively to critique and protest.

The question is how to address the problem of individual subjectivity within a mythic system. Although both Durkheim and Levi-Strauss suggested the powerful structuring quality of myth, they failed to see any tension between the two.[26] For Halbwachs (a member of the Annee Sociologique group formed by the followers of Durkheim) collective memory constitutes individual memory and thereby reproduces society. As Tonkin points out, the missing term in Halbwachs's account is socialization, defined as the ways and means by which the multiplicity of subjects internalize the external world.[27] Indeed, myth indicates conflicting individual subjectivities.

Several writers have recently protested the romanticization of resistance. Ortner points out that the account of everyday modes of peasant resistance must provide a parallel story of everyday modes of peasant collaboration.[28] In the Meo case resistance is simultaneous with acquiescence and collaboration. There were brief interludes when Meo chiefs were "king makers" at the imperial court. Some Meos became commanders and soldiers in Mughal armies and were employed as Akbar's *dāk*, or post runners, or as domestic servants by the Lodi kings. Mewati narratives demonstrate that one cannot totalize the world of Mewati subjecthood. The version of *Dariyā Khan* I obtained from Kaalu suggested some Meo collaboration with Mughals:

> When the Dholpur Rajput ruler revolted against Akbar the Meos contributed a force and destroyed the Dholpur kingdom:
>
> *kāñpai dillī bahādurā kāñpai rāj mahall*
> *ādha maiṇ akbar badshāh ādha maiṇ pāhaṭ ṭoḍar mall*
>
> *The brave of Delhi trembled*
> *palaces trembled too.*
> *Half (the land) was Akbar Badshah's*
> *half belonged to the Pahat, Todar Mal.*

In the colonial ethnographer's interpretation, half the loot went to Akbar and half to the Pahat chief![29] But the verses suggest the deployment of petty chiefs in furthering the imperial design. Among the Meos there were also factions that helped the British in their struggle against the Marathas.

The evidence of substantial intra-Meo conflict emerges from the narratives themselves. The bandit Ghurchari's uncle is a strong supporter of the Alwar king. Frequent allusions are made to the treacherous and colluding members of the community. In *Kaulānī* Rai Khan writes to the Meo, Rao Madari, who has been approached by the Rajputs for help:

rāv madāri khāñ kā the chuglī khāī
rājā to pyāro lāgai kahā toy burā lagā bhāī

Rao Madari,
you carried tales to the Khan(zadas).
Is the raja so dear to you
that you think badly of your brothers?

The bitter irony of the statement castigates the Meo who violates the norms of loyalty to his brotherhood. Eventually the Rao Madari is prevailed upon to withdraw his support of the Rajput attack. The Rajputs, however, continue to have the support of the Mughals.

In the process of writing this work, I have considerably revised original notions of "community" and "boundary" that characterized my initial thinking on the Meos, ideas that are genealogically derived from an older anthropological tradition. The Meo oral tradition hardly turned out to be the homogenous universe I expected it to be. Indeed the mythic suggests numerous controversies, disputes, and conflicts that are part of lived historical pasts. Identity, it needs to be emphasized is not a thing but a relation. It is crisscrossed by other kinds of relations, other lines of fissure. The oral tradition strives to create the community that constantly threatens to dissolve into myriad fragments, multiple subjectivities. Human desire repeatedly defies communal and racial boundaries. The stories of Dariya Khan and Ghurchari indicate the underside of communities disrupted by passions that are not sanctified by state and society. Sasbadni and Dariya seek a consummation prohibited by the Meo-Mina blood feud, and the English official's wife, the memsahab, is overwhelmed by a sexually charged attraction for the bandit hero.

The community can hardly be nostalgically rendered as a nonhierarchical, egalitarian site. It is imbued with much violence as is evident from the rich vocabulary of terms used for the army such as *dal, fauj, lashkar,* and so on, to the celebration of violence and the repertoire of weapons available to peasant groups including the *bhālā, bāḍhāḷī, teg, sāṅg, sel, talvār, pharsā,* and *khaṇjar* (all these being variants of the sword, dagger, lance, and spear). One narrative, after a gruesome account of killing, describes this violence metaphorically as Holi, or the festival of colors played with vermilion *(gulāl)* symbolizing the blood that flows in battle. Indeed, the battle is a sacrificial act, and violence helps constitute community. This is foregrounded by the story of Meo-Mina conflict where a formerly equal relationship between the Meos and Minas is repudiated and the Meos victoriously subsume the Mina bride givers, as the husband subsumes the identity of the wife in marriage. Warrior ideologies and gender relations mirror each other.

The Meo sense of identity is developed in relationship to other groups as much as in opposition to state forms. These relationships shift over time, as when the Khanazadas forged political ties with the Mughals leading to a distancing with the Meos. So also when the Jats developed a ruling lineage moving from their warrior-peasant past to statehood or when the Minas were relegated to a lower (and officially criminal) status than even the Meos under colonialism.

I have referred to the nineteenth-century world of incessant feud. Let me correct the impression of unrelenting intergroup strife by indicating the simultaneous presence of a vast universe of interaction and the shared mythic space among rural communities, "Hindu" and "Muslim." This is in contrast to the ethnic binaries presumed by current ethnic studies and historiographical research. As eminent a historian as Chris Bayly has called upon researchers to work on the "prehistory of communalism." In this privileging of ethnic conflict, what is ignored is the much larger evidence of collaboration and alliance across the boundaries of what are currently regarded as ethnic fault lines.

Meo villagers worshiped forms of the goddess and inhabited a world populated by deities and spirits. Verses from *Kaulānī* evocatively render this. When the Meos of the village call upon the goddess for protection, the Rajputs threaten her with their wrath, telling "Mother" Jvala that though they have offered her many sacrifices, she has not come to their rescue and that if they lose the battle they will destroy her shrine. On behalf of the Meos and other (Hindu and Muslim) castes, the brahman Moti goes to the goddess

Jvala's shrine with a flag and coconut and lights a flame before the goddess promising that if they win the battle they will make her an offering. It was customary to make promises of gifts to a goddess preceding battle if she would bless the army with victory. Moti's plea is heard, and the goddess appears in the temple:

bhīṛ bhagat pai paṛī hūñ jvālā bhorāī
āg kī aṇgāṛī uṛ rahī bhavan kai andar āyī
tū jā rai motī lauṭjā tam jitogā jaṇg
chappan kalvā chauñsaṭh joganī laṛaiṇgā bāvan bhairū sang

As the flame is revealed
crowds of followers come.
Sparks of fire flying
she enters the shrine.
"Go Moti, return
you will win the battle.
The 56 souls, 64 yoginis
the 52 (Bhairu) will fight with you."

The flame is the goddess herself. The major shrine of the goddess Jvala is located in District Kangra in Himachal Pradesh. Presided over by the "deity of seven flames" the temple draws Hindu and Buddhist pilgrims. Jvātā mukhī literally means flame mouth and is believed to have been created when the tongue of Sati fell at Nagarkot. This followed her sati and bodily dismemberment, since the grieving Shiva was creating cosmic havoc.[30] The image of the goddess as flame suffuses the verse. The yoginis are said to have been creatures of the body of Shiva's consort, Durga, who created them to help her fight the demon Mahishasura. They are the female forms that inhabit battlefields, take off with heads of corpses, and drink blood from their skulls. The fifty-two Bhairu are the terrible, gruesome forms of Shiva who are worshiped at the center of a circle of mothers or yoginis in Kaula tantra. The fifty-six *kalvā* refers to local tantrik practice whereby the souls of dead children are brought under control and made to do as desired. Moti brahman, the Meos and Hindu castes, on one side, and the Rajputs with the help of the Pathans (Afghans), on the other, appeal to the goddess alternating between threat and inducement. She intervenes in favor of the

Meos and their allies. As scholars of popular religion remind us, its cosmos tends to be horizontal, and divinity is immanent in the world.

Lest an absolute "Hindu" identity be deduced from the foregoing, it must be emphasized that the Meos also simultaneously have an Islamic identity. Dariya apprehends ritual pollution from eating defiling, prohibited food such as pork. There is a simultaneous violation of Islamic injunctions against drinking, with Meo warriors indulging in much orgiastic drinking in this narrative describing events of the sixteenth century. The *namāz*, or the canonical prayer required of Muslims, might be irregularly performed and there are few persons who have been to the Mecca for the *hajj* pilgrimage, but pirs, faqirs, Sufis, and their insignia mark the landscape of memory. The focus on speech communities that have different ways of thinking and speaking highlight also the departure of real-life processes from a textbook model of Islam.

Meo identity then is a complex of multiple identities that are seen as normal and usual, even though they draw upon sources that are considered the total opposite of each other and, therefore, mutually exclusive.

The Meo oral tradition reveals a universe of shared beliefs, interaction, and exchange between several groups. The Mina chief's daughter Sasbadni, unable to bear the pain of separation from her beloved Dariya, appeals to the great thirteenth-century Muslim saint Pir Khwaja Gharib Nawaz, to whose shrine people go to have their wishes *(murād)* fulfilled. She travels to the saint's tomb in Ajmer, where she "sweeps" the shrine, a ritual act that is widely performed by worshipers in South Asian Sufi shrines irrespective of denomination. Her desire is acknowledged, and a proclamation is made by the Pir's darbar that she will be united with her beloved. Mewati narratives intimate local and household cults ranging from the veneration of saints and *sayyads* (martyred ancestral heroes) to *shrādh*, or ancestor worship.

The *Pālon kī Bansābalī* is an instance of the celebration of what Ricoeur calls a "founding event" that often exists at the core of group identity. Simultaneously it indicates shared myths and genealogical and other literary genres among pastoral and peasant castes such as the Jats, Gujars, Ahirs, Meos, and others. The oral tradition demonstrates the existence of larger wholes and other cultural contexts with which symbols, images, and tropes are constantly exchanged. In terms of form there are obvious continuities with Western and pan-Indian folk traditions, pauraṇik, and Persian pre-Islamic and Islamic mythic traditions.

When Ghurchari is cornered he prays to Mahadev:

terai bohot chaḍhāyā khomchā bohot bhajī māḷā
mahādev kitlū gayo āj merā tū jhir tīrath vāḷā

We have made you many offerings
stroked the beads many times.
Mahadev of my Jhir pilgrimage
where are you today?

The mode of address to the gods is one of familiarity. Half a century later the Meos will be accused of having desecrated the site of their own pilgrimage, the Shiva temple at Firozpur Jhirka. The joint front of different (Hindu and Muslim) castes in the Kaulani battle will be replaced by anal and other forms of bodily torture, rape, arson, the mass abduction of women, and genocidal violence against the "Muslim" Meos by alliances of members of Hindu castes in the context of the partition of the subcontinent.

Appendix: Meo Narratives in Summary

Dariyā Khāñ

A summary of the version of Mirasi Mavasi recorded at Alwar on 30 September 1987.

Rao Bada Mina and Todar Mal are two chiefs. Todar Mal belongs to the Pahat clan of the Meos. The poet visits Todar Mal at Dabak and tells him that half the area of Mewat is his and half is under Rao Bada. Both chiefs were at Akbar's court. Rao Bada and Todar Mal vanquish Dholpur. After their victory Rao Bada takes the Meo chief to his house, where they drink wine together. They become friends and decide to arrange the marriage of their unborn grandchild and child, respectively. A granddaughter called Sasbadni is born to Rao Bada and a son named Dariya Khan to Todar Mal. They are married but a *bigāṛ*, or conflict, between the two chiefs occurs at the ceremony. Sasbadni's *gauṇā* [rite preceding her departure to her husband's place] does not take place.

In the month of *sāvan* [the Indian monsoon] Sasbadni and her friends are swinging in the garden. They ask each other the names of their husbands. All of them come to Sasbadni and ask her. She says she will find out from her mother. Her mother tells her she is married to Dariya Khan, the son of Todar Mal.

Sasbadni sends three successive persons with messages for Dariya. Syamla, a Balai, or shoemaker, and Chimla, the barber, are both beaten by Todar Mal. The Mirasi Dada Dhaurangiya is then summoned by Sasbadni. He tells Sasbadni to dress up and adorn herself and pass by the court *[kacherī]* of Rao Bada, where women are not allowed. When Sasbadni passes by, Rao Bada asks who the woman is. "She is your granddaughter, Sasbadni

Bai," who has "grown up," Dhaurangiya informs him. "Go to Mewat and call Dariya Khan," Dhaurangiya is told.

Dhaurangiya visits Todar Mall. He greets and placates him saying he has not been on speaking terms with Rao Bada ever since the fight at the wedding. Todar Mal is feasted with rice and gifted with gold coins. He comes to learn that Dariya lives in Palka. Some men carrying liquor are going there and Dhaurangiya follows them.

Dariya Khan recognizes Dhaurangiya as having come from his bride's home. He distributes wine among his brothers and companions. When they are all intoxicated and fall asleep, Dariya is able to talk to Dhaurangiya and ask for news of his wife. Dhaurangiya gives him Sasbadni's letters.

Meanwhile all the men and women in Mewat leave for the Khwaja Garib Nawaz [Urs] fair held at Ajmer. They halt at night in the forests of Panhora. Sasbadni is told by her maid-companions that the Pir fulfills desires *[murād]*. Sasbadni goes to the dargah and sweeps the floor with her long scarf. A proclamation from the tomb tells her that her husband will be with her soon. Sasbadni returns to her village.

Dariya leaves home to fetch his bride. His brothers have refused to accompany him. A woman collecting cow dung encounters him and his companion in the forest. She runs to Sasbadni to inform her. Sasbadni is very happy and adorns herself in "sixteen ways." Sasbadni's companions call Dariya Khan into her room where Sasbadni has arranged bottles of wine all around. He gets intoxicated. Sasbadni reproaches him for not having come to her for so long. Dariya informs her that he was unable to because of the enmity with Sikri. He spends the night with Sasbadni.

In the morning Bada Rao sends a barber to summon Dariya Khan. Bada Rao has nine hundred uniformed Minas who guard him twenty-four hours a day. Sasbadni is anxious that a battle might ensue as a result of their meeting. Dariya enters Bada Rao's court. Everyone is offered wine, and Rao Bada himself gives Dariya Khan wine and meat in which five gold coins have been hidden. Dariya Khan tells the Rao that he has sworn on Khwaja sahab not to eat meat or drink wine.

Sasbadni who is watching from a balcony holds up two fingers, indicating that he should obey Bada Rao but then throw up the meat he consumes using his two fingers. Dariya thinks she has gestured to him to strike the Rao twice. He pushes the Rao with one hand and says, "stay away, *dheṛ*" [low-caste cow eater]. The nine hundred Mina soldiers pull out their swords and are determined not to let the Meo get away alive. Dariya Khan pulls out his sword. Sasbadni sees this and goes to plead with her brother, Randhir, asking him to defend her husband. Randhir arranges horses for the couple. Sasbadni disguises herself like a man and the two escape.

As they rest in the forest the force of nine hundred Minas mounted on horses catches up with them. Sasbadni fights some of the Minas and then wakes up Dariya. He asks her to fetch his father's elder brother, Malak Jalal Khanzada. Malak Jalal and Dariya surround the Minas. Dariya Khan escapes with his bride.

Dariya Khan's brothers also arrive. They attack the Khanzada group, being under the impression that they are holding Sasbadni forcibly. After half of them have been killed Dariya's brothers learn that they are their own kin. Addan Mirasi is sent to fetch Dariya. Dariya mistakes him for an approaching Mina. He shoots an arrow that pierces Addan's arm. Dariya tells Addan to inform his brothers that they are well and happy. The brothers ask forgiveness of Malak Jalal Khanzada and return.

Dariya and Sasbadni live happily in the village Palka. A fight with the Gujars of Parmandla takes place. The Gujars kill Dariya Khan and send his corpse home on his mare, Bichan. Dariya Khan's brother tells Sasbadni to have patience as no one lives forever and that his spirit will create havoc on the following day.

Ghurchaṛī Mev Khāñ

A summary of the version of Mirasi Abdul recorded at Alwar on 25 May 1990.

The singer mentions that he is beholden to [the goddess] Isri and his *ustad* [guru].

Khuda Bakas, the son of Jauhari, lives with his wife, Jivni, in the village of Chaundavta. This is in the Baghora Pal of the tehsil Kishangarh Bas of the Alwar kingdom. The Minas of Rath Bighota trouble the people of Kishangarh Bas by the constant thieving of the grain market. The baniyas, the important people of Kishangarh Bas, hold a meeting of the villagers and appeal to the mukhiya [headman] of Baghora. He appoints Khuda Bakas a chaukidar [watchman] for the area.

A son is born to Khuda Bakas. His name is Mev Khan. When Mev Khan is nine years old another son is born to Khuda Bakas. Jivni sends Sumra Bhangi [from an "untouchable" caste] to fetch her husband from Kishangarh. Khuda Bakas returns with a brahman. After studying the newborn's horoscope the brahman predicts greatness for him and suggests that he be named Ghurchari. The boys grow up. They learn to hunt with the bow and arrow.

Ghurchari and Mev Khan ask their father for a double-barreled gun. A Kasai, or butcher, from Chandoli called Nanva is returning to Jindoli after selling some calves at the cattle market. Five hundred rupees are tied to his waist. The brothers rob him of half the money. They learn from a policeman of the Alwar State that his gun has been made in Lahore. They buy a ticket for the train and leave for Lahore. They rob the [English] platoon and return with a rifle. The brothers catch the bus to Delhi and come to Firozpur, where they buy some sweets. At the shop villagers are talking about the return of the baniya's marriage party and all the wealth it will bring back. The brothers are alerted. They go to Naugaon. The ornaments can be seen glittering from a distance in the palanquin. Ghurchari climbs onto the bullock cart and loots all the jewelry.

In Alwar an uproar results as a search is launched for the brothers. Ghurchari and Mev Khan are joined by a Bhangi from Mirzapur. The three break into a Sunar's, or goldsmith's, shop. Ghurchari takes all the gold, the silver rupees, and a folding sword. A large box containing weights falls and awakens everyone. The Bhangi and Ghurchari run away. Mev Khan jumps out of the house but is caught by the police who have surrounded it. Ghurchari leaves the money and sword with his uncle Umrav.

As Ghurchari waits for Mev Khan, he sees the dancer of Kishangarh returning to her village after a *mujrā* [dance] performance. A Meo thief called Dandad joins him. They rob the prostitute of all her jewelry. The prostitute complains to the jamadar and mentions that she heard them speaking the name Dada Dandad. The jamadar goes to Dandad, who is beaten up and interrogated. He says that he was with Ghurchari. The jamadar visits Khuda Bakas and insists that Ghurchari surrender to the police. Ghurchari goes to meet the jamadar. Under the pretense of carrying on a conversation with him the jamadar handcuffs him. Ghurchari and his father are sentenced to five years.

Ghurchari and Khuda Bakas are jailed in Alwar while Mev Khan is in the Gurgaon jail. The mud walls of the jail collapse after a heavy shower of rain and Mev Khan escapes. He goes home and sends a note for his brother with Sumra Bhangi. Meanwhile, Umda Mina of Jaipur is also jailed along with Ghurchari. The two become *pagṛī palaṭ bhāī* [turban-exchanging brothers] and manage to escape from the jail. They seek shelter with Ghurchari's uncle Umrav. Umrav refuses to return to them their loot and instead asks for seventy rupees. Umrav threatens to complain to the Alwar maharaja Mangal Singh. Ghurchari sets fire to Umrav's goat shed, the cow shelter, the stack of fodder, and the camel shed. He shoots a camel and sets it up as though it were alive. Umrav's wife has a dream in which the seated camel cannot get up. Umrav is perturbed and consults Tulla Joshi, a brahman astrologer who lives in Mirzapur, about the meaning of the dream. Tulla predicts division among the [Meo] brothers. In the morning Umrav's sons see that all has become ash. Umrav goes to the maharaja and complains that Ghurchari is appropriating the revenue. Ghurchari makes two attempts to kill Umrav. The brothers go and pray to Mahadev.

A warrant to arrest Ghurchari is issued by the maharaja, but he eludes the police. Ghurchari, Mev Khan, and Umda Mina come to Balji, the [Rajput] thakur. Balji reprimands Ghurchari for wandering while his father is still in jail. The brothers arrive at the jail as Lakhji thakur is making the rounds. When he obstructs their entry he is killed. Ghurchari hangs a note on the door confessing to the killing.

The brothers walk along the rail line, where a train is approaching. Ghurchari uses his wooden staff to climb [the pole]. He cuts the wire of the rail and ties a paper to the two ends. His message is received by clerks at Alwar and the rail official at Padisal. It tells them to inform the highest railway official that he will capture and stop the rail on the following day.

The brothers go to the hill of [the Meo saint] Chudh Sidh. They learn that the Maharaja Mangal Singh is to come for a hunt and tiger bait has been laid. They kill the tiger. The maharaja asks who has dared to kill the tiger meant for his hunt. Ghurchari introduces himself as a bandit of the state. The maharaja informs Ghurchari that news about him has spread to Lahore and that the English to whom the "wires" belong are searching for him. Ghurchari tells him, "Whether you are a Maharaja or a *thekedar* [caretaker], the answer to this we already have." He offers him a token gift and asks the nawab to release Khuda Bakas, to which the nawab agrees.

After fetching Umda Mina, the brothers go to the hills. They meet a Gujar woman who is in tears, for a tiger has killed her cow. When Ghurchari tells her that he will avenge this by killing the tiger, she informs them that only the brave Ghurchari and Mev Khan can accomplish this task. The brothers reveal their identity. They shoot the tiger. The Gujar woman wants to reward them but they refuse. She blesses them. Roaming the hills the three pass the shrine of the Pir Chudh Sidh and come to the temple of Mahadev.

Umrav complains to the jamadar and promises to reward him if the fugitives are arrested. The jamadar along with several hundred policemen surrounds the brothers. The brothers call upon Mahadev for aid. Gorja [Parvati] urges her husband to go and help their sons who have been surrounded. Mahadev disguises himself as an old Meo and goes from Jhir [his shrine] to Jeroli. A crowd has gathered to attack Mev Khan and Ghurchari at the house of Badlu Chaudhari. Mahadev also arrives there. He changes the plans of the attackers. A battle results, in which Haji Mall is killed.

The brothers go to Bhagmal, their father's sister's husband. Umrav also arrives. He pretends to Bhagmal that he wants to repair the enmity with the brothers. Bhagmal takes Umrav with him to the hills where the brothers are hiding. Umrav reveals their hiding place to Maharaja Mangal Singh. The soldiers of his platoon lie in wait for the brothers. Umrav asks Ghurchari to lay aside his gun while they eat. Ghurchari puts it aside and the brothers are caught. They are tied with a rope and a blanket is draped over them. Ghurchari gives the knife in his pocket to Mev Khan who is able to cut his ropes. Ghurchari urges Mev Khan to run away. Mev Khan escapes and Ghurchari is left behind.

Ghurchari is locked in an iron cage and taken to Alwar. Mangal Singh's queen comes to see him and appeals to her husband to release him and reward him instead of punishing him. He refuses, and the next day Ghurchari is put back in the iron cage and sent to Lahore. At Lahore he is kept hungry. Ghurchari's soul utters a curse and the entire tent where the food is being cooked catches fire. The English official's wife is inside the burning tent. The official sees Ghurchari and promises that he will dismiss the case against Ghurchari if he rescues his wife. Ghurchari wraps a wet blanket around himself and brings out the wife and child from the burning tent. Until the order of clemency comes Ghurchari stays with the official. The Englishwoman falls in love with him. Ghurchari refuses her. She poisons him and he dies. His tomb is in Lahore.

Kaulānī kī laṛāī

A summary of the script obtained from Chaudhari Dalpat Khan, Alwar, having been written down by his genealogist. A printed version is available in *Chirāg i Baghorā: Alvar rājya kaulānī kile kī laṛāī* (Alwar: Ram Shyam Printer, 1997). It has been published by Chaudhari Nasruddin Tanvar, president of the Meo Mahasabha, Rajasthan.

The first story is called the Battle of Hathi Singh, or the Jhir kī laṛāī [the battle at Jhir]. Two brothers, Jabbar and Jhangir Khan, are Khanzada chaudharis. They live at Mubarakpur and are "informers" for the government. They have the power to give up to six months' imprisonment or the punishment of *kāṭh koyṛa*. The maharaja of the Alwar State, Bakhtawar Singh, gifts Jabbar Khan with a *siropāv*, or horse, woollen shawl and turban for his work as an informer. Jabbar Khan's horse is stolen by Ravat Mev of Sivana. He thinks the Kaulani Meos of the Baghora Pal have taken it. Jabbar captures Jalam, a Baghora Meo, in the bazaar. Rai Khan, a chaudhari of the Baghora Meos and the son of Baksa, protests to Jabbar Khan that he is trying to pick a fight. Jabbar Khan's counteraccusation is that the stealing of the horse and the attack on the town are a question of his turban [honor].

Rai Khan asks him again to release Jalam, who he claims has been held captive on mere suspicion since the Kaulani Meos have not stolen the horse. Rai Khan is angered when Jabbar collects all the Khanzadas of Mubarakpur and takes the matter to the Alwar court. Rai Khan threatens to take revenge unless Jalam is released: "your cattle will be stolen, the town will be looted." Jabbar refuses to release Jalam.

Fourteen Meo *thāmās* [agnatic lineages] advance and capture the Khanzadas' cattle in retaliation for Jabbar's act of injustice. Jalam manages to escape and joins the attackers. The Khanzadas gather together, beat their drum in the city, and move to attack the Meo villages with their horses and men in order to release the cows. They are obstructed by the Meos on the hillside of the Balad Nala. In the resulting battle at Kaulani, the seven brothers of the Khanzada Chaudhari of Mubarakpur, Jabbar Khan, are killed. He acknowledges defeat and pretends to friendship *[yārī]*.

The Khanzadas exaggerate their complaints to the Alwar ruler. The challenge to the Khanzadas of Pata is made into a threat to all the Alwar State. "The Baghora Meos will end our *hukūmat* [rule]. If this continues then your rule will extend only up to Alwar city."

The diwan and Hathi Singh are sent to avenge the Khanzadas' defeat. Hathi Singh's army reaches Firozpur and pitches its tents. Ahmad Bakas, the nawab of Firozpur, belongs to the Mughal *qaum*, or group. Mansa Meo, a Daimrot Meo of Ghata Basi called the Rao sahab of Ghata, takes the horse of Hathi Singh thinking it belongs to a gypsy. Ghata has been refusing to pay the revenue of the state. Two hundred cowgirls, nine hundred cows, and seventy men are captured by Nawab Ahmad Bakas and the army and shut up in the fortress of Firozpur. Among them are Musi and Maddi, the daughters of the Daimrot Meo, Mansa of Ghata. Hathi Singh shuts Musi into a *dol* [palanquin] and sends her to Tijara. Maddi, who is made to undergo *nikāh* with the nawab despite her protests, is sent to Loharu. To her and Qutb-ud-Din Loharu is born Shams-ud-Din.

The diwan of Alwar commands that Kaulani's Baksa, the chief of Ratangarh and Kehargarh, return the Khanzadas' cows, otherwise his village will be attacked after the Rajputs take their ritual bath. While the army bathes at the temple of the goddess at Jhir, the Meos close all the routes and attack them from all four sides. The Gorval, Baghora, and Ravat Meo clans combine. Hathi Singh is killed by Khavani Meo. The Meos are able to obtain the release of the two hundred cowgirls, nine hundred cows, and seventy men after breaking into the fortress of Firozpur. The Daimrot Meos have ever since been grateful to the Baghora Meos for this. This is the battle of Hathi Singh, or of Jhir. The headless corpse of Hathi Singh is buried at Jhir, where a cenotaph was erected.

Baksa refuses to pay the revenue for Mohammadpur. The diwan summons Baksa, swearing on his religion not to harm him, but gets him killed. His corpse is sent back to Kaulani. Sarup Singh threatens the diwan, saying he will avenge the betrayal by killing him. The diwan asks for greater military reinforcements from the camp at Naugavan.

The second part of the story is called the Battle of Bhopal Singh, or Kaulani kī laṛāī. Bhopal Singh is Raja Bakhtawar Singh's mother's brother and belongs to the Gaur Rajput clan. Bhopal Singh takes up the challenge to "conquer the wild." His army camps at Pata and he calls his informers, Syalti and Bhagmal, who are Nai Meos to tell him the names of Meo leaders and to spy on the Meos. Bhopal tries to lure Baksa by promising that he will make him the "chief of the wild." The offer is rejected. Syalti and Bhagmal arrive at Kaulani and suggest that the Meos pay the government the rate of eight annas per plow and the rest will be absolved. At first the entire village collects eight annas per plow. But Sale Khan Meo refuses to give the eight annas or accept another's authority. The other Meos also take their money back.

Syalti and Bhagmal inform Bhopal Singh about the preparations for battle at Kaulani. He attacks Kaulani. The battle of Kaulani continues for three days. Mahadev predicts in a conversation with his wife, Gora, that the Meos will win. Afraid of the continuous firing of the cannon, the Meos retreat into the hills. Bhopal Singh stops the firing under the impression that they have run away. He moves to investigate the Meo fortress of Kaulani. Just then the Meo drum plays *[nagāṛā]*, the sound of which has always symbolized a victory for the Meos. This is a signal for the Meos to attack again. After three days of fighting Bhopal Singh is killed by the spear of Moti brahman. Bhopal Singh's brothers are given the jagir of Jhareda as compensation.

The third part of the story is the Battle of Kanvar Jahaj. Kanvar Jahaj, of the Chela Rajput clan, takes up the challenge to avenge the death of Bhopal Singh and defeat Kaulani. The Meos, along with the Hindus of the village, worship the goddess Jvala Mukhi who appears before them. She predicts their victory. Kanvar Jahaj retreats and runs back to Bakhtawar Singh.

Bakhtawar Singh calls for the astrologer, asking him how he might repair the enmity with Mewat. The pandit predicts a battle for twelve years and peace after twenty-four. The Rajput thakur Bhairu Singh lives at Kotijhana in the Jaipur kingdom. Bakhtawar Singh sends Bhairu Singh to Kaulani. He arrives and exchanges turbans with the Meo "brothers." The fortress of Raghunath is decorated. Twelve years have passed fighting with the kings.

The last part of the story summarized from the *Chirāg i Baghorā: Alvar rājya kaulānī kile kī laṛāī* adds the following to the above description of events:

Kanvar Jahaj attacks Kaulani along with five hundred men. Anvar Khan, the chief commander of the nawab of Loharu, comes to help Kanvar Jahaj. . . .

The shock of Kanvar Jahaj's retreat and defeat leads to the death of Bakhtawar Singh. In 1815 Banni Singh succeeds to the throne. In 1821 he summons his astrologer. The astrologer predicts that battle will wage for fifty-two years and there will be peace after sixty-four. The Alwar king asks the Jaipur king for help against the Meos. He suggests the name of Bhairu Singh, a Naruka Rajput from Kotijhana, in the Jaipur kingdom. Bhairu Singh disguises himself as a dacoit. He comes to Kaulani with a lot of wealth. Bhairu Singh collects all the Meo chaudharis and tells them that he is a rebel *[bāgī]* of the Jaipur State and that his life is in danger. Goats are sacrificed and the wealth he has brought is distributed among the Meos. Bhairu Singh "exchanges turbans" with them. He repairs the fortress. In 1826 Banni Singh sends an army of twelve thousand to Kaulani. Fifteen cannon are fired. A statue of Raghunath [Rama] is placed in the temple in the fort. Ever since then, in the government records the village has been known as Raghunathgarh.

Pāñch Pahāṛ kī laṛāī

A summary of the version of Mirasi Dina Rai of Gvalda, Tijara, Alwar, recorded at Alwar on 24 April 1988.

The Pahat Meos loot the treasure and camels of the Mughal Badshah Shah Jahan that are on their way to Akbarabad [Agra]. The only soldier of the Mughal army who manages to escape complains at the court of the Badshah about the Meos' looting and the destruction of the entire army.

In the Badshah Shah Jahan's court Shaikh, Saiyyad, Mughal, and Pathan are seated and there are also the thirty-six chairs for the Rajputs. The Adlipat ["just"] Badshah asks, "Who will avenge the defeat and bring the treasure back?" Raja Ahlad Singh, the Chauhan Rajput, picks up the betel leaf roll [symbolizing a challenge]. He puts the naked sword back in its sheath, vowing to defeat the Meo clan and bring it under control. But he is worried when he returns to his palace. His queen warns him that the Meos are a group to be feared. Ahlad Singh, suffused with Rajput vigor, insists that he will defeat the Meos and recover the treasure. Ahlad Singh moves towards Ajangarh [the headquarters of the Pahat Pal] with a force of twelve thousand men. They halt at Gurgaon where the boundary of Mewat begins and worship the goddess. Ahlad Singh is advised to write a letter to Rai Bhan, the Pahat chief.

At Ajangarh the Pahat Meos are celebrating their victory. Wine is flowing; Mirasis are singing; and the Meos are gifting them. Rai Bhan reads Ahlad Singh's letter asking him to concentrate on his peasant tasks and return the treasure. He promises to reward them with as much land as they desire. Rai Bhan tears the letter into pieces and says that even if the force of the twenty-two subas provinces were to come or the Badshah himself in person, he would not return the treasure. Ahlad Singh writes another letter in a more conciliatory tone, cajoling him with references to the brotherly feelings between the Meos and the Mughals. Rai Bhan replies that the camels have all been taken away by the Mirasis. Ahlad Singh now writes to another Pahat elder, Masand Godaliya, offering him a jagir land grant. The offer is rejected again and once again when he is offered Braj. Masand reprimands him for attempting to divide the Pahat Meo "brothers."

In spite of the famine in the Alwar kingdom, the revenue is sent to Delhi. A force of twelve thousand under Dharam Singh, Ahlad Singh's wife's brother, has been sent to enforce collection. Revenue is brutally collected by the Mughals and Rajputs. Dharam Singh kills many people and beheads the eighty-four-year-old Meo elder Kutba Chaudhari, who had come with the revenue of the eighty-four villages of the Pundlot Pal. His son, Hari Singh, refuses to eat or drink till the death of his father is avenged. Hari Singh's wife calls his nephew, Badal Kalaliya, to avenge his death. She also complains that the Mughals have surrounded the water sources and her clan is dying of thirst. Badal Kalaliya kills Dharam Singh.

Ahlad Singh's wife reproaches him again for having taken up the emperor's challenge. She asks the Badshah Shah Jahan to send the entire force of the twenty-two subas [Mughal provinces] against the Meos. She insists, and finally he agrees to let her son, Hamir Singh, go with his force of twelve thousand. The Meos and Mughals now confront each other in battle. Both sides lose many men. The Meo Badal Kalaliya kills the Rajput Hamir Singh, and his wife commits sati. The Mughal force of twelve thousand is cut down, and Badal Kalaliya's wife also immolates herself. Ahlad Singh's wife rebukes him again for having taken up the challenge. Ahlad Singh besieges Ajangarh.

After forty years a grandson is born to Jodh Singh, the son of Rai Bhan. Jodh Singh's wife, Lali, insists that she must perform the rite of the sixth day after childbirth *[chatī]* at the well of the Pir Alakh. Lali refuses to eat or drink or feed the baby till her demand is met. Rai Bhan explains to her that all the Pahat men will be killed since the Rajput army lies there, but she is adamant. Rai Bhan is forced to ask Ahlad Singh for safe passage for the women. Ahlad Singh agrees to let them have access to the well on condition that there will be no celebratory singing or playing of the *ḍhol*, or drum.

The Pahat women proceed to the site. But they refuse to accept Ahlad Singh's condition. The rite cannot be performed without the playing of the drum. As soon as the drum is heard, the Rajputs attack and battle ensues. The younger son of Rai Bhan, Baj Khan, severely depletes Ahlad Singh's force. But he is killed by Ahlad Singh. Another force of twelve thousand armed with maces comes to their rescue. The Pahat Meos are defeated. Only five men survive.

Notes

Chapter 1

1. Nathan Wachtel, *The Vision of the Vanquished: The Spanish Conquest of Peru through Indian Eyes, 1530–1570,* trans. Ben Reynolds and Siân Reynolds (Sussex: Harvester Press, 1977).
2. Chief Joseph, Letter, *North American Review* (April 1879).
3. Ruth Finnegan, *Oral Literature in Africa* (Oxford: Clarendon Press, 1970). One needs to also make the proviso that oral traditions have increasingly been reclaimed by social science following the "narrative turn."
4. Derrida considers only spontaneous speech and writing. He does not examine oral traditions that are committed to memory and transmitted across generations and years, sometimes centuries. Hence his discussion of textuality is also circumscribed. This is not to gainsay his brilliant reworking of the notion of writing that "overflows" from the printed page and pervades the realm of the spoken. Jacques Derrida, "Plato's Pharmacy," in *Dissemination,* trans. Barbara Johnson (Chicago: University of Chicago Press, 1981), 61–84, and *Of Grammatology,* trans. Gayatri Chakravorty Spivak (Baltimore: Johns Hopkins University Press, 1976), 142–44.
5. According to Ong, the oral imagination is evanescent to the degree that oral cultures have to depend on formulas to ensure its transmission. Milman Parry's analysis that Homeric epics used metrically tailored formulas has been demonstrated in oral traditions throughout the world. Goody follows Parry and Lord's work to demonstrate that shifts from magic to science, from prelogical to a more rational state of consciousness, or from Levi-Strauss's "savage" mind

to domesticated thought can be explained as shifts from orality to literacy. Walter J. Ong, *Orality and Literacy: The Technologizing of the Word* (London and New York: Methuen, 1982), 29; Milman Parry, *The Making of Homeric Verse: The Collected Papers of Milman Parry*, ed. Adam Parry (Oxford: Clarendon Press, 1971).

6. Alfred Bates Lord, *The Singer of Tales* (Cambridge, Mass.: Harvard University Press, 1981 [1960]); Gregory Nagy, *Poetry as Performance: Homer and Beyond* (Cambridge: Cambridge University Press, 1996) follows Lord's contention that performance and composition are like parole and langue. Plato and Aristotle distinguished between diegesis and mimesis. Narrative and (dramatic) reenactment represent the latter. Both epic and lyric in ancient Greece were a medium of mimesis.
7. This is not to deny the emancipatory role that writing has played, such as in the struggle for individual rights.
8. Jack Goody, *The Interface between the Written and the Oral* (Cambridge: Cambridge University Press, 1987), 132, 160.
9. See Jack Goody's *Domestication of the Savage Mind* (Cambridge: Cambridge University Press, 1977), and his introduction to *Literacy in Traditional Societies*, ed. Goody (Cambridge: Cambridge University Press, 1987), 1–26. Skaria's sensitively written account shows how peasant rebels both appropriated and destroyed writing. He provides a thoroughgoing critique of Goody's and Henige's orientalist myth-models that privilege writing and highlight the magicality of writing for the nonliterate person. Ajay Skaria, "Writing, Orality, and Power in the Dangs, Western India, 1800s–1920s," *Subaltern Studies: Writings on South Asian History and Society*, vol. 9 (Delhi: Oxford University Press, 1996), 13–58.
10. Mukund Lath suggestively argues that the Sanskrit terms *margī* and *deśī* are an improvement, since they are unlike the spatial categories, classical and folk, that demarcate the urban center and the country. The desi can even be produced by the king, and the category is indicative of the extent of local autonomy and freedom. Personal conversation, 14 June 1997. An early and highly problematic application of dichotomous categories to Indian civilization can be seen in McKim Marriott, "Little Communities in an Indigenous Civilization," in *Village India*, ed. McKim Marriott (Chicago: University of Chicago Press, 1955), 171–222.
11. Natalie Zemon Davis's work shows how readers read aloud to those who could not read. *Society and Culture in Early Modern France* (Stanford: Stanford University Press, 1975), 97–122. Carlo Ginzburg's *The Cheese and the Worms* (New York: Penguin, 1980) describes a sixteenth-century miller who could read but used the interpretive devices of an oral tradition and its myths so that the church saw him as heretical.
12. Finnegan and Street rightly challenge the notion of any pure oral cultures. Ruth Finnegan, *Oral Traditions and the Verbal Arts* (Cambridge: Cambridge

University Press, 1992); Brian Street, *Literacy in Theory and Practice* (Cambridge: Cambridge University Press, 1984).

13. Richard Terdiman, *Discourse and Counter-Discourse* (Ithaca: Cornell University Press, 1985); Michel Foucault, *Language, Counter-Memory, Practice*, ed. Donald F. Bouchard (New York: Ithaca, 1977), 139–64.
14. For a discussion of Paul Ricoeur's notion of a text see his *Hermeneutics and the Human Sciences: Essays on Language Action and Interpretation* (Cambridge: Cambridge University Press, 1981), chap. 8. Ricoeur states, "we must enlarge the space of reading to include everything written, historiography as well as literature." Why can the practice of reading not be extended to oral texts/performances? One wonders whether the act of listening cannot be analogous to that of reading, enabling a participation in the referential dimension of the text. Only in his later work does Ricoeur qualify his Eurocentric approach to texts by stating that the refiguring of praxis on the plane of human acting and suffering also occurs through orally communicated texts. He continues with the caveat that "without thereby neglecting the oral tradition, the effectivity of the historical past can be said to coincide in large part with that of texts from the past." *Time and Narrative* vol. 3 (Chicago: University of Chicago Press, 1988), 101.
15. Ganesh Devy, "Inaugural Presentation," Oral Epics of the Bhils, for Loka: The Other Voice series, Sahitya Akademi, Delhi, 28 Sept. 1996.
16. Daniel Bell, *The End of Ideology: On the Exhaustion of Political Ideas in the Fifties* (rev. ed., New York: Free Press, 1962); Ninian Smart, *Beyond Ideology: Religion and the Future of Western Civilization* (London: Collins, 1981).
17. Joseph Campbell, *The Masks of God: Occidental Mythology* (London: Souvenir Press, 1964), 522.
18. Claude Levi-Strauss, *Tristes Tropiques*, trans. John Weightman and Doreen Weightman (Harmondsworth: Penguin, 1976); Levi-Strauss, *The Savage Mind* (Chicago: University of Chicago Press, 1966).
19. There need not be as Brückner argues, a suspension of linear, chronological time in myth. Heidrun Brückner, "Kannalāye: The Place of a Tuḷu Pāḍdana among Interrelated Oral Traditions," in *Flags of Fame: Studies in South Asian Folk Culture*, ed. Heidrun Brückner, Lothar Lutze, and Aditya Malik (Delhi: Manohar, 1993), 283–334.
20. Jan Vansina, *Oral Tradition as History*, trans. H. M. Wright (Harmondsworth: Penguin, 1985). Contrast this approach with that of Henige, who seeks chronology in Charan bardic chronicles but finds instead the telescoping and lengthening of time. David P. Henige, *The Chronology of Oral Tradition: Quest for a Chimera* (Oxford: Clarendon Press, 1974), appendix B "The Jodhpur Chronicles." Skaria points out that this approach involving a "denial of difference (between oral traditions and history) emerged from the decolonizing im-

petus in Africa, a radical move that claimed that the colonized were not without history. But this is itself a form of participation in the discourse of lack. The constant appeal to the tribunal of literate historical standards is after all primarily an evaluation of these traditions by their suitability for conversion into sources for the professional discipline of history," "Writing, Orality, and Power," 3.

21. Jonathan Hill, introduction to *Rethinking History and Myth: Indigenous South American Perspectives on the Past* (Urbana and Chicago: University of Illinois Press, 1988), 5, 6. I do not, however, agree with Hill's contention that mythic consciousness gives priority to structure whereas historical consciousness gives greater weight to agency and social action in the present. In fact, it is the former that details the agency of Meo rebels such as the bandit hero Ghurchari and that by celebrating the heroic, makes possible a recurrence of rebellions.
22. Michael Taussig, *The Devil and Commodity Fetishism in South America* (Chapel Hill: University of North Carolina Press, 1980). See also Gananath Obeysekere's *The Apotheosis of Captain Cook: European Mythmaking in the Pacific* (Princeton, N.J.: Princeton University Press, 1992). Contrast this with Bronislaw Malinowski, *Magic, Science, and Religion, and Other Essays* (New York: Doubleday, 1954 [1926]). Leach critiques Malinowski for his argument that myth and ritual are complementary and that myth is a charter for ritual action and sanctions social behavior developed in his famous text *Myth in Primitive Psychology* (New York: W. W. Norton, 1926). Leach points out that there are several competing versions of a story. Myth and ritual are a "language of signs in which rights and status are expressed but it is the language of argument, not a chorus of harmony. If ritual is sometimes a mechanism of integration, one could as well argue that it is often a mechanism of disintegration." Edmund Leach, *Political Systems of Highland Burma* (London: London School of Economics and Political Science, 1954), 278.
23. Ronald Wright, *Stolen Continents: The "New World" through Indian Eyes* (Boston: Houghton Mifflin, 1992); also the publications in the Cambridge University Press series Oral and Literate Cultures, ed. Peter Burke and Ruth Finnegan.
24. Barthes views myth as the naturalization of meaning or the moment when meanings take on givenness and fixity, and when the processes that have created meanings become invisible. Roland Barthes, *Mythologies* (London: Paladin, 1973); Friedrich Nietzsche, *The Birth of Tragedy* (New York: Doubleday, 1956), 51–2, 137.
25. Maurice Halbwachs, *The Collective Memory* (New York: Harper and Row, 1980).
26. Lucette Valensi, "From Sacred History to Historical Memory and Back: The Jewish Past," *History and Anthropology* 2 (1985): 207–24. The special issue of

this journal dealing with "between memory and history" surveys research in the previous two decades.

27. Claude Levi-Strauss, "The Structural Study of Myth," *Structural Anthropology*, trans. Claire Jacobson and Brooke Grundfest Schoepf (New York: Basic Books, 1963), chap. 11. Most Western writing on myth sees it in terms of the primordial time of the beginning made available through a dissolution of the categories and experiences of concrete time and space. Memory, however, relates "primordial" and "concrete" time. It does not therefore annihilate (as Cassirer and Eliade hold *mythos* does) the profane but might even align it with the sacred. Ernst Cassirer, *Language and Myth*, trans. Susanne Langer (New York: Harper and Brothers, 1946), 32–33; Mircea Eliade, *The Sacred and the Profane*, trans. Willard Trask (New York: Harcourt, Brace and World, 1959).
28. Anika Lemaire, *Jacques Lacan*, trans. David Macey (London: Routledge and Kegan Paul, 1979), 170.
29. Burton Stein, *Peasant, State, and Society in Medieval South India* (Delhi: Oxford University Press, 1980). Also Stein's "All the King's *Mana:* Perspectives on Kingship in Medieval South India," in *Kingship and Authority in South Asia*, ed. John F. Richards (Delhi: Oxford University Press, 1998), 133–88; and "State Formation and Economy Reconsidered," *Modern Asian Studies* 19 (1985): 387–413; Stanley Tambiah, "The Galactic Polity in Southeast Asia," in *Culture, Thought, and Social Action: An Anthropological Perspective* (Cambridge, Mass.: Harvard University Press, 1985), 252–86.
30. See, for example, Stanley Tambiah, "The Galactic Polity," and his *World Conqueror and World Renouncer: A Study of Buddhism and Polity in Thailand against a Historical Background* (Cambridge: Cambridge University Press, 1976); Clifford Geertz, *Negara: The Theatre State in Nineteenth-Century Bali* (Princeton: Princeton University Press, 1980). For a critique of the ritual sovereignty thesis see my *Resisting Regimes: Myth, Memory, and the Shaping of a Muslim Identity* (Delhi: Oxford University Press, 1997).
31. Tambiah,"The Galactic Polity," 241.
32. Johannes Fabian, *Time and the Other: How Anthropology Makes Its Object* (New York: Columbia University Press, 1983). Historiography has undeniably been closely related to what Guha calls statism. Ranajit Guha, "The Small Voice of History," *Subaltern Studies*, vol. 9, ed. Shahid Amin and Dipesh Chakrabarty (New Delhi: Oxford University Press), 13–58.
33. Michel de Certeau, "Walking in the City," in *The Practice of Everyday Life*, 91–100. In more recent work Foucault develops the notion of heterotopias through which he examines unusual ("other") places that are different from the normalized understandings of place and social relations. Through a disturbing effect of unsettling regular categorization of social relations, they can serve as conceptual and material spaces for resistance in other lived spaces.

Michel Foucault, "Of Other Spaces," *Diacritics--A Review of Contemporary Criticism* 16 (1986): 22–27.

34. Hashim Amir Ali, *The Meos of Mewat* (Delhi: Oxford and IBH, 1970), 28.
35. Stuart Hall, "Cultural Identity and Diaspora," in *Identity, Community, Culture, Difference,* ed J. Rutherford (London: Lawrence and Wishart, 1990), 222–37; Michael Taussig, *Shamanism, Colonialism, and the Wild Man: A Study in Terror and Healing* (Chicago: University of Chicago Press, 1987); bell hooks, *Yearning: Race, Gender, and Cultural Politics* (Boston: South End Press, 1990); Anna Lowenhaupt Tsing, *In the Realm of the Diamond Queen: Marginality in an Out-of-the- Way Place* (Princeton, N.J.: Princeton University Press, 1993).
36. Ong maintains that writing makes possible the great introspective religions such as Buddhism, Judaism, Christianity, and Islam. He seems ignorant of the fact that the Vedas were the product of a "primary oral culture." According to him, narrative is more important in primary oral cultures. Orality is associated with illiteracy, which in turn, is held to imply ignorance. In Ong's work one just might substitute the term "oral" for"savage" or "primitive." Ong, *Orality and Literacy,* 105, 179.
37. Renato Rosaldo, *Culture and Truth: The Remaking of Social Analysis* (Boston: Beacon Press, 1989), 208.
38. Mary Douglas, *Purity and Danger* (London: Routledge and Kegan Paul, 1966), 120–21.
39. Ganesh Devy, *After Amnesia* (Delhi: Orient Longman, 1993).
40. Presentation, Mukund Lath, Jaipur History Center, Jaipur, 16 Feb. 1997.

Chapter 2

1. Elliot traces a further genealogy of migration. He follows Cunningham in tracing the Meos to an Indo-Scythian group settled beyond the Danube that is mentioned by Herodotus. He also cites Cunningham's *Report of 1863–64,* which maintains that the Meds, or Mands, were the representatives of the Mandrueni who lived beside the Mandrus River to the south of the Oxus in Central Asia. They accompanied the forced Jat migration from the Oxus to the Indus. Both Meds and Jats are said to be descendants of Ham, the son of Noah. According to Virgil and Ptolemy, the Meds were present in the Punjab around A.D.30–40. Cunningham even traces place-names in the Punjab to the Meds (such as Lahore from Medhukur) to suggest that they "were once the dominant race in the Punjab" and "the first Indo-Scythian conquerors of the Punjab." From upper Punjab they are said to have moved southward to Sind around Minnagara (possibly Thath) and Saurashtra. This possibly led to the beginning of their rivalry with the Jats. H. M. Elliot, appendix, ED, vol. 1, 525–30.

2. See Abd al-Hayy ibn Zahhak Gardizi, *Kitāb Zayn al-akhbār*, ed. Tashih Muhammad Nazim (Berlin: Iranschahr, 1928); *Arab Classical Accounts of India and China*, trans. S. Maqbul Ahmad (Shimla: Indian Institute of Advanced Study, 1989), 4, 17, 21; and *India and the Neighbouring Territories in the Kitāb nuzhat al-mushtaq fi'khtiraq al-'afaq of al- Sharīf al-Idrīsī*, trans. and commentary by S. Maqbul Ahmad (Leiden: E. J. Brill, 1960), 118–19.
3. According to Al-Baladhuri the Mids had robbed a ship and taken orphan girls captive (slaves according to another account) who were being sent by the king of Ceylon as gift to Hajjaj, governor of Iraq. Hajjaj demanded their return, but Dahir replied that he had no authority over the pirates. This caused Muhammad Qasim's attack on Sind. *Futūh al-Buldān*, trans. Philip Khri Hitti (Beirut: Khayats, 1966). André Wink, *Al-Hind: The Making of the Indo-Islamic World*, vol. 1, *Early Medieval India and the Expansion of Islam, 7th–11th Centuries* (Delhi: Oxford University Press, 1990), 164.
4. 'Ali ibn Hamid Kufi, *Fathnāmah-i Sind: Being the Original Record of the Arab Conquest of Sind* also known later as *Chachnāmā* (Islamabad: Institute of Islamic History, Culture, and Civilization, Islamic University, 1983).
5. Wink, *Al-Hind*, vol. 1, 196–201. Wink's notion of fitna suggests how state formation did not take place by mere expansion of military power as in Europe but how alliances were forged and a variety of tactics deployed to win supporters against a given enemy that included gift-giving, conciliation, and winning over an enemy's local supporters so that force was used only secondarily. André Wink, *Land and Sovereignty in India: Agrarian Society and Politics Under the Eighteenth-Century Maratha Swarajya* (Cambridge: Cambridge University Press, 1986). David Shulman points out that what fitna seeks to do is revise an earlier "imperial" conception of state formation by demonstrating how ritual or symbolic hegemony rather than coercion created weak and decentralized medieval polities; *The King and the Clown in South Indian Myth and Poetry* (Princeton: Princeton University Press, 1985). I suggest that it conveys instead the primacy of politics and the deployment of diplomacy and tactics rather than merely jihad and military maneuvers.
6. Irfan Habib, "Jatts of Punjab and Sind," in *Punjab Past and Present: Essays in Honour of Dr. Ganda Singh*, ed. Harbans Singh and N. Gerald Barrier (Patiala: Punjabi University, 1976), 95–96. Wink seems to follow this argument, *Al-Hind*, vol. 1, 163. More recently Habib has given up the thesis of migration and the identity of the Jatts of Sind and the Jats of the Punjab. He now argues that "jat" was a generic term for most peasant castes and even Krishna's (Yadava's) parents are referred to as jat. Personal conversation, Aligarh, 30 Sept. 1997.
7. See *India and the Neighbouring Territories*, trans. and commentary by Ahmad, 44, 118– 19; Wink, *Al-Hind*, vol. 1, 142, 165–66.

8. Abdul Shakur, *Tarīkh Mev Chatrī* (Urdu) (Nuh, Gurgaon: Chaudhari Yasin Mev High School, 1974 [1919]), 93; personal interviews, Ajmer, Jan. 1998. Shakur argues that Mewat is a distortion of mevas or meras that etymologically derives from people who inhabit the mountains.
9. Elliot states, "During the whole period of their known history, they have been conspicuous for their lawless and predatory habits, from the time when four thousand Mer archers defended their passes against Pirthi-Raj, down to A.D. 1821 when their excesses compelled the British government to attack them in their fastnesses, and reduce them to complete obedience. Since which period, it is gratifying to observe that they have emerged from their barbarism." Appendix, vol. 1, 525–30. This account has also influenced histories authored by Meos. See Muhammad Habibur Rahman Khan Mewati, *Tazkirāh-i Sūfīyā-i Mewāt: Islāmī Hind kī tārīkh kā bhulā huā ek aham bāb* (Gurgaon: Mewat Academy, 1979), 39–40, 44–45, 53–54.
10. ED, vol. 2, 519, 532–33.
11. The Meos claim to have established many villages in Bulandshahr, Kol, and Etah and to have battled Ghaznavi along with the ruler of Bayana. Habibur Rahman Khan Mewati, *Tazkirāh-i Sūfīyā-i Mewāt*, 37, 46–50.
12. The *Imperial Gazetteer* cites Rajput clans of Bulandshahr and Etawah as claiming that the Meos were dispossessed at the order of Prithviraj Chauhan. *Imperial Gazetteer*, vol. 17, 313. The Bargujar raja, Pratap Singh, a relative of Prithviraj is "said to have cleared the region of the turbulent Mewatis which pleased the Dor raja, Chait Singh so much that he gave his daughter in marriage to him." E. B. Joshi, *Moradabad: Uttar Pradesh District Gazetteers* (Allahabad: Government Press, 1966), 38. Nevill maintains that it was the Meos who overran the Doab and expelled the Dors. But if this is so, it is surprising that a Dor raja called Chandra Sen was ruling when Aibak conquered the area in 1193. H. R. Nevill, *Aligarh: A Gazetteer* (Allahabad, 1909), 163. This account is reproduced in later gazetteers again without indicating the sources.
13. The *Imperial Gazetteer* mentions "local tradition" regarding the Meos' crossing of the Yamuna after Ghaznavi's invasion. *Imperial Gazetteer*, vol. 17, 313. H. R. Nevill, *Meerut: A Gazetteer* (Lucknow: Government Press, 1922), 150; H. R. Nevill, *Aligarh: A Gazetteer*, 163–65; E. B. Joshi, *Meerut: Uttar Pradesh District Gazetteers* (Allahabad: Government Press, 1965), 41.
14. Habibur Rahman Khan Mewati, *Tazkirāh-i ūfīyā-i Mewāt*, 37. Sections of Meos continued to inhabit the southern parganas of Meerut in the late thirteenth century. Joshi, *Meerut*, 34.
15. The capture of Baran by Aibak was followed by that of Mahaban, and Mathura. Kol (Aligarh) was conquered the following year. Hasan Nizami, *Tāj-ul Ma'āṣir*, ED, vol. 2, 204–43. Meerut was given to Malik Kishli Ulugh Khan when he came to visit Balban, according to a Persian inscription, ED, vol. 2, 4; *TNR*,

vol. 1. Gwalior, Kanauj, Awadh, Malwa, and Ajmer were also conquered. *Futūḥu's Salāṭīn* or *Shāh Nāmah-i Hind of Isami*, trans. and commentary by Agha Mahdi Husain (Bombay: Asia Publishing, 1967 [1938]), 68n, 196. In 1196 Mu'izz al-Din fought with the Bhatti Rajputs and their leader, Kumara Pala, the rai of Thangir (later known as Bayana).

16. In the fourteenth century "numerous Rajput adventurers are said to have poured into the defenseless country" of Bulandshahr and "expelled the Meos from their land and villages." *Imperial Gazetteer*, vol. 9, 49.
17. A significant population of Meos still lives in the villages that have now been incorporated into Delhi.
18. Brajadulal Chattopadhyaya, *The Making of Early Medieval India* (Delhi: Oxford University Press, 1994), 99.
19. Kishori Saran Lal, *History of the Khaljis*, A.D. 1290–1320 (Delhi: Asia Publishing House, 1967), 134–39.
20. *MT*, vol. 1, 359.
21. *TMS*, 204, 211, 213.
22. Bahadur Nahar, the son of Lakhanpal, was originally called Samarpal and renamed Naharpal by Sultan Firoz Shah because he killed a tiger. Lakhanpal's other son, Shoparpal, was called Chajju Khan. The conversion, it is speculated, might also have been a "change of heart" come about from Bahadur Nahar's association with the Sufi saint Nasir-ud-Din Mohammad, Chiragh-i Delhi (d. 1356), a disciple of the Chishti Shaikh, Nizam-ud-Din Auliya. Bahadur Nahar is said to have become rich and to have fallen in love with a Rajput Thakur's daughter. The Thakur, however, duped him and got him killed. Shaikh Muhammad Makhdum, *Arzang-i Tijārah* (Urdu) (Agra: Agra Akhbar, 1290 H.), 2–3.
23. Muhammad Makhdum, *Arzang-i Tijārah*; Habibur Rahman Khan Mewati also mentions that twenty-five Meo gots and pals have come from the Jadon. *Tazkirāh-i Sūfīyā-i Mewāt*, 87.
24. For a description of the period, see Satish Chandra, *Historiography, Religion, and State in Medieval India* (New Delhi: Har-Anand Publications, 1996), 228.
25. Satya Prakash Gupta, *The Agrarian System of Eastern Rajasthan, c. 1650–c. 1750* (Delhi: Manohar, 1986), 10.
26. V. S. Bhatnagar, *Life and Times of Sawai Jai Singh, 1688–1743* (Delhi: Impex India, 1974).
27. For details see Suraj Bhan Bhardwaj, "Socio-economic Conditions in the Mewat Region, 1650–1750 A.D.," Ph. D diss., Center for Historical Studies, Jawaharlal Nehru University, 1990, 16–17.
28. *Punjab DG*, vol. 4A, *Gurgaon District, 1910* (Lahore: Civil and Military Gazette, 1911), 21.
29. Muhammad Makhdum, *Arzang-i Tijārah*, 51.

30. Pratap Aggarwal's writings argue this forcefully. See his *Caste, Religion, and Power: An Indian Case Study* (New Delhi: Sri Ram Centre for Industrial Relations, 1971). See M. N. Srinivas's articulation of the concept of dominant caste in *The Dominant Caste and Other Essays* (Delhi: Oxford University Press, 1987).
31. Irfan Habib, *An Atlas of Mughal India* (Delhi: Oxford University Press), 18.
32. Sharfalla-ud-Din Ahmad, *Muraqqā'-i- Mewāt* (Mewāt kā itihāsa), trans. from Urdu to Hindi by Anil Joshi (Alwar: Kusum Prakashan, 1989), 53.
33. Burton Stein refers to this new phase as "states without communities," in contrast to earlier phases of Indian history when there were communities without states or communities were states or where communities and states coexisted and were incorporated into states. *A History of India* (New Delhi: Oxford University Press, 2001 [1998]), 20–31.
34. "Bharatpur State," in *Imperial Gazetteer of India*, vol. 8 (Oxford: Clarendon Press, 1908), 80–81.
35. Alexander Faulkner, *An Historical Sketch of the Naruka State of Ulwar* (Calcutta: Thacker and Spink, 1895), 2.
36. William Crooke, *Natives of Northern India* (London: Archibald Constable, 1980), 144.
37. "Bharatpur State," in *Imperial Gazetteer of India*, vol. 8, 79–80.
38. P. W. Powlett, *Gazetteer of Ulwur* (London: Trubner, 1878), 37–51.
39. Ismailism is said to have had a major presence in the Sind along with brahmanical and Buddhist culture. See *India and the Neighbouring Territories*, trans. and commentary by Ahmad, 118–19. The Jats are said to have been "converted" to Islam by the Ismailis. It was with Jat help that Ismailis gained power in Sind until they were destroyed forever by Mu'izz al-Din Ghuri.
40. Maulvi Mir Mahbub Ali Mewati attributes Meo conversion to Sayyid Salar Masud Ghazi, popularly known as Ghazi miyan, and to Hazrat Muhlab bin Abi Safra who came to India (from 44 to 225 H.) and "did *jihād* against the *kuffār* [infidels] so that the Hindis gradually accepted one God." Habibur Rahman Khan Mewati, *Tazkirāh-i Sūfiyā-i Mewāt*, 51–53, 57. Elsewhere Habibur Rahman Khan Mewati also suggests that it took several centuries to convert the Meos.
41. The *Farhang-e āsafiyāh* refers to the Meos as *nau-Muslim* (neo-Muslim) who were converted by Timur, when for twelve years he took revenge on the region between the towns of Rewari and Jhirka. *Farhang-e āsafiyāh*, vol. 4, compiled by Syed Ahmed Dehlawi (Delhi: National Academy 1944, Hyderabad reprint 1964, 1987), 512–13.
42. M. S. Ahluwalia, "Muslim Inscriptions as a Source of Early Medieval Rajasthan History," in *Sources of the History of India*, vol. 2, ed. S. P. Sen (Calcutta: Institute of Historical Studies, 1979), 52- –61. The Qadiriyya Silsila was

founded by Shaikh Abd al-Qadir Jilani (d. 1166). This oldest Sufi order came to India from their center in Baghdad in the fifteenth century when Delhi was sacked. The Naqshbandiyya Silsila was founded by Abu Ya'qub Yusuf al-Mamadani (d. 1140) but was more popularly associated with Muhammad Baha-ud-Din Naqshbandi (d. 1389).

43. Saiyid Athar Abbas Rizvi, *Muslim Revivalist Movements in Northern India in the Sixteenth and Seventeenth Centuries* (Agra: Agra University, 1965), 18. This is a point that André Wink also emphasizes, *Al-Hind*, vol. 2, *The Slave Kings and the Islamic Conquest, 11th–13th Centuries* (Delhi: Oxford University Press, 1999). See, in contrast, Habibur Rahman Khan Mewati's account in *Tazkirāh-i Sūfīyā-i Mewāt*, such as the section on Shah Chokha, 313–20.
44. See Punjab Census, 1901, 2835–36.
45. Shakur, *Tarīkh Mev Chatrī*, 641–45, 650–53.
46. For a case against the Rasulshahis, see Abdul Qadir Khan, *Waqā-i Abdul Qādir Khānī* (Aligarh MS), 179–84.
47. Saiyid Athar Abbas Rizvi, *A History of Sufism in India*, vol. 2 (Delhi: Munshiram Manoharlal Munshiram, 1983), 18, 30–31, 46, 109.
48. The followers of Shah Madar (Shaikh Badi-ud-Din, d. 1435) were a heterodox Sufi order known as the Madaris. Saiyid Athar Abbas Rizvi, *A History of Sufism in India*, vol. 1 (1978), 306; R. S. Bhatnagar, *Dimensions of Classical Sufi Thought* (Delhi: Motilal Banarsidass, 1992), chap. 9.
49. *Census of India, 1881*, Punjab, records 177,707 Mirasis and 40,009 Jogis in British Punjab (Bombay: Examiner Press, 1882).
50. Col. James Skinner, *Tashrīh-ul-Aqwām* (Persian, British Museum, 1824).
51. Powlett, *Gazetteer of Ulwur*, 38, 71; S. L. Sharma, "Religion and Ethnic Tradition among the Meos," in *Aspects of Social Anthropology in India*, ed. L. P. Vidyarthi, B. N. Sahay, P. K. Dutta (New Delhi: Classical Publications, 1980), 178, 169.
52. J. Forbes Watson and John W. Kaye, "Mewatees," in *The People of India: A Series of Photographic Illustrations of the Races and Tribes of Hindustan*, vol. 4 (London: India Museum and W. H. Allen, 1874), 202.
53. Watson and Kaye, "Mewatees," in *The People of India*; Pratap Aggarwal, "Islamic Revival in Modern India — The Case of the Meos," *EPW* 4 (1969): 1677, 1679–1681.
54. *BSARCT*, 26.
55. Powlett, *Gazetteer of Ulwur*, 70–71.
56. G. A. Grierson, "Note on the Principal Rajasthani Dialects," *Linguistic Survey*, vol. 9, pt. 2 (Delhi: Motilal Banarsidas, 1968), 1–15.
57. K. K. Sehgal, *Rajasthan District Gazetteers: Bharatpur* (Jaipur: Bharat Printers, 1971), 87.

58. Moti Lal Gupta remarks that Rajasthani dialects form a distinctive group that are more different from Hindi than, for example, Punjabi. Under no circumstances should they be classified as dialects of western Hindi. "Rajasthan and Rajasthani: Switching over from Hindi," in *Perspectives on Ethnicity*, ed. Regina Holloman and Serghei A. Arutinov (The Hague: Mouton, 1978), 341.
59. For a discussion see Mukund Lath, "Folk and Classical Music: A Dichotomy That Does Not Quite Work in India," *Sangeet Natak* 88 (1988): 44–46.
60. R. K. Barz and Monika Thiel-Horstmann suggest that texts move across genres within a single performative context and myth can have folktale, genealogies, and songs woven in. Introduction to *Living Texts from India*, ed. R. K. Barz and M. Thiel-Horstmann (Wiesbaden: Otto Harrassowitz, 1989), 1.
61. Charlotte Vaudeville, *Myths, Saints, and Legends in Medieval India*, comp. and intro. Vasudha Dalmia (Delhi: Oxford University Press, 1996), 274–75.
62. Dusan Zbavitel, *Dictionary of Oriental Literature* (New Delhi: Vikas, 1975).
63. See Amaresh Datta for a review of the literature. "Ballad," in *Encyclopedia of Indian Literature*, ed. Amaresh Datta (New Delhi: Sahitya Akademi, 1987), 340–56.
64. For example, a variant from *Ghurcharī Mev Khāñ* that I once recorded was

    khudā bakas kā ghuṛcharī baiṭho hī pāyo
    baiṭho ho jā sūrmā āj maiṇ ek takan dekh āyo

    Ghurchari is substituted by *chatri* in the version of Asin Khan who told me, "*baiṭho ho*" should be "*khaṛo ho jā.*" Abdul's response to this was "*tuk nā baiṭho*" ("it does not make sense").
65. Richard Burghart, "Itinerant Vaiṣṇavite Genealogists of the Ganges Basin," in *Flags of Fame*, 423–43.
66. Mikhail Bakhtin, "Epic and Novel," in *The Dialogic Imagination: Four Essays*, trans. Caryl Emerson and Michael Holquist, ed. M. Holquist (Austin: University of Texas, 1981), 35. Tambiah suggests that ritual performances of oral traditions move the present to the ideal or mythical past. Stanley J. Tambiah, *Buddhism and the Spirit Cults in North-east Thailand*. Cambridge Studies in Social Anthropology, no. 2 (Cambridge: Cambridge University Press, 1970). There is also a reverse move, however, to bring the past into the present.
67. Marcel Proust, *Remembrance of Things Past*, English trans. of *A la recherche du temps perdu* by C. K. Scott Moncrieff and Terence Kilmartin (New York: Vintage Books, 1982).
68. Kenneth Koch, *One Train* (Great Britain: Corcanet Press, 1994), 4.
69. See, for example, Brenda Beck's study of a Tamil folk epic, *The Three Twins: The Telling of a South Indian Folk Epic* (Bloomington: Indiana University Press, 1982).

Chapter 3

1. Brajadulal Chattopadhyaya is a representative example in his assertion that between the third and fourth and the sixth to tenth centuries monarchy became the "norm" of polity. *The Making of Early Medieval India,* 19. But as Stein points out both monarchies and communities continued to form the basis of state regimes in the Gupta period. Indeed, Chattopadhyaya's own work shows that the rise of royal lineages among Rajputs continued until the ninth century. States emerged from previous clan/communal formations, as in the case of Rajputs and Orissan rajas, or when imperial states emerged from local chiefdoms that were not eliminated but were incorporated into the state, as in the case of the Cholas. The simultaneity of community and state (as also their mutual hostility) dominated Indian politics until the eighteenth century. Stein, *A History of India,* 22–23.
2. Richard Fox, introduction to *Realm and Region in Traditional India,* ed. Richard Fox (Delhi: Vikas, 1977), ix–xxv; and Susanne Rudolph, "Presidential Address: State Formation in Asia—Prolegomenon to a Comparative Study," *Journal of Asian Studies* 46 (1987): 731–46.
3. Stein, *A History of India,* 19–20.
4. In view of the Jats' rejection of monarchy, they were actually called *arāshṭra,* or kingless. A. H. Bingley, *Sikhs: The Origin, History, Religion, Customs, Fairs, and Festivals* (New Delhi: Sumit Publications, 1984 [1910]), 4. For accounts of regional political systems such as those of the Jats, Ahirs, and Rashtrakutas, see Girish Chandra Dwivedi, *The Jats: Their Role in the Mughal Empire* (New Delhi: Arnold Publishers, 1989); Mahesh Chandra Pradhan, *The Political System of the Jats of Northern India* (London: Oxford University Press, 1966); Nonica Dutta, *Forming an Identity: A Social History of the Jats* (Delhi: Oxford University Press, 1999); A. H. Bingley, *History, Caste, and Culture of Jats and Gujars* (New Delhi: Ess Ess Publications, 1978 [1899]); M. S. A. Rao, "Rewari Kingdom and the Mughal Empire," in *Realm and Region in Traditional India,* 79–89; Ronald Inden, *Imagining India* (Oxford: Basil Blackwell, 1990).
5. E. E. Evans-Pritchard, *Nuer: A Description of the Modes of Livelihood and Political Institutions of Nilotic People* (London: Oxford University Press, 1940).
6. Pierre Clastres attacks the ethnocentrism of Western philosophy and anthropology, which sees the state as the destiny of all society and as the presupposition of civilization itself. It makes possible the good life, so we learned from Greek theorists. Clastres asserts that the state institutionalizes domination and introduces the hierarchy of classes. *Society against the State: Essays in Political Anthropology,* trans Robert Hurley (Oxford: Basil Blackwell, 1977).

7. Romila Thapar, *From Lineage to State* (Delhi: Oxford University Press, 1990).
8. Claude Levi-Strauss, *The Raw and the Cooked: Introduction to a Science of Mythology*, trans. from the French by John and Doreen Weightman (London: Jonathan Cape, 1970).
9. This version of the *Pālon kī Bansābalī* was recorded from Abdul Mirasi of village Maujpur, tehsil Laxmangarh, Alwar, on 29 Sept. 1989.
10. See, for instance, Romila Thapar's work on puranic genealogies of ancient India in "Genealogies as a Source of History," *Indian Historical Review* 2 (1976): 259–28; Maureen Patterson's description of family histories in her "Chittpavan Brahmin Family Histories: Sources for a Study of Social Structure and Social Change," in *Structure and Change in Indian Society*, ed. Milton Singer and Bernard S. Cohn (Chicago: Aldine, 1968), 396–411; Veena Das's analysis of caste puranas in Gujarat, *Structure and Cognition: Aspects of Hindu Caste and Ritual* (New Delhi: Oxford University Press, 1977); Ravindra K. Jain's account of the relationship between genealogies and the traditional history of the Bundela ruling groups in, "Bundela Genealogy and Legends: The Past of an Indigenous Ruling Group in Central India," in *Studies in Social Anthropology*, ed. John Beattie and R. G. Lienhardt (Oxford: Clarendon Press), chap. 3; A. M. Shah and R. G. Shroff's examination of the role of the Vahavancha Barots in castes, clans, and lineages in Gujarat in their "Vahavanca Barots of Gujarat: A case of genealogists and mythographers," in *Traditional India: Structure and Change*, ed. Milton Singer (Jaipur: Rawat, 1975 [1958]), 40–70.
11. J. A. Barnes, "Genealogies," in *The Craft of Social Anthropology*, ed. A. L. Epstein (Delhi: Hindustan, 1978), 101.
12. The vansh or kul (clan) is the largest kinship unit within the Rajput *jāti* said to derive from the sun, moon, and fire. Norman P. Ziegler "Some Notes on Rajput Loyalties during the Mughal Period," in *Kingship and Authority in South Asia*, 215–51. The Jadav and Tumar are lunar kuls; the Chauhans, a fire kul; while the solar kul includes the Rathors of Marwar and the Kacchavahas of Jaipur.
13. Interview, Abdul, Maujpur, 26 May 1987.
14. *dair̥hwāl yā banṣ main̥ jabrā rattāvat bālot*
    hain̥ lāḍhāvat chattrī jinko bāghor̥ā bar̥got
15. *saras kalesā bans kī chatar pāl rāṭhor̥*
    kursī nāmo bār pāl ko kañvar khāñ likh biṭhāyo jor̥
    bāvan bārah pāl ko liyo māyno chān
    terahvon pālan pai pallākr̥o hai mero pāhaṭ pe nirbān
16. Romila Thapar, *Cultural Transaction and Early India: Tradition and Patronage* (Delhi: Oxford University Press, 1987), 9; Surajit Sinha, "State Formation and

Rajput Myth in Tribal Central India," reprint no. 3, *Proceedings on Comparative Studies on South Asia of Duke University*, n.d.

17. Pamela Price, *Kingship and Political Practice in Colonial India* (Cambridge: Cambridge University Press, 1996), 19–25.
18. Aditya Malik, "Avatāra, Avenger, and King: Narrative Themes in the Rajasthanī Oral Epic of Devnārāyaṇ," in *Flags of Fame*, 239–67.
19. Susan Wadley points out that *Ḍholā* challenges Rajput status, even mocking the Rajput king, who is described as reluctant to fight. Personal conversation, Jaipur, 16 Oct. 1998.
20. Ajay Skaria, *Hybrid Histories: Forests, Frontiers, and Wildness in Western India* (Delhi, Oxford University Press, 1999), chap. 5.
21. Among Rajputs the layers comprise the jati, vansh, kul, shakh (branch), *khanp* (twig), and *nak* (twig tip). The last two have a relatively lower role in the formation of contemporary Rajput identity. A shakh is founded when the group breaks away from the kul, relocates and gains military and political power. Each is derived from a heroic ancestor. Intra-kul marriages are allowed if kul members belonged to different gotras (hazily defined as a group of people who claim spiritual descent from a preceptor or common Vedic sage). See Lindsey Harlan, *Religion and Rajput Women: The Ethic of Protection in Contemporary Narratives* (Berkeley: University of California Press, 1992), 25–30.
22. I. S. Marwah, "Tabligh Movement among the Meos of Mewat," in *Social Movements of India*, vol. 2, ed. M. S. A. Rao (Delhi: Manohar, 1979), 83.
23. Marwah, "Tabligh Movement among the Meos of Mewat," 83.
24. Paul Hershman, *Punjabi Kinship and Marriage*, ed. Hilary Standing (Delhi: Hindustan Publishing Corporation, 1981), 174–75.
25. The mahajanapadas, or "great community," characterized by collegiate forms of governance flourished in the pre-Mauryan period. Models of nonmonarchical governance go back to institutions from the later vedic period called sabha and samiti. The epics, on the whole, represent the precedence of monarchy over the rule by lineages.
26. Dwivedi, *The Jats*, 14.
27. Aggarwal, *Caste, Religion, and Power*, 25.
28. Skaria, *Hybrid Histories*, 81.
29. Louis Dumont, "The Conception of Kingship in Ancient India," *CIS* 6 (1962): 48–77.
30. Gloria Goodwin Raheja, *The Poison in the Gift: Ritual, Prestation, and the Dominance Caste in a North Indian Village* (Chicago: University of Chicago Press, 1988), 268n, 19, 212.
31. Skaria, *Hybrid Histories*, 145.
32. S. L. Sharma, "Religion and Ethnic Tradition among the Meos," 150.

33. Skaria, *Hybrid Histories*, 145. Shulman points out that the celebration of raids and other activities of bandits have close affinities to kingship. Shulman, "Bandits and Other Heroes," in *The King and the Clown in South Indian Myth and Poetry*, 365–66.
34. *Chirāg i Baghorā: Alvar rājya kaulānī kile kī laṛāī* (Alwar: Ram Shyam Printer, 1997).
35. *Punjab DG, Gurgaon District, 1910*, vol. 4A, 24–26.
36. On this theme see Thomas R. Trautmann, *Dravidian Kinship* (Cambridge: Cambridge University Press, 1981), 357–58; Velcheru Narayana Rao, David Shulman, and Sanjay Subrahmanyam, *Symbols of Substance: Court and State in Nāyaka Period Tamilnadu* (Delhi: Oxford University Press, 1992), 262.
37. Aggarwal, *Caste, Religion, and Power*. Erin Moore describes the effectiveness of the traditional panchayat compared to that of the modern *nyāya* panchayat. She contrasts the consensual system of justice of the former with the adversarial system of the American legal system, which through the process of hearing tends to escalate and accentuate conflict. *Conflict and Compromise: Justice in an Indian Village* (Berkeley, Calif.: Center for South and Southeast Asia Studies, 1985), 26. The availability of local juridical procedures and punitive measures often forestalled the entry of the police.
38. Mumtaz Khan, "Tracing Meo Settlement Through Oral History," draft paper and oral communication, 27 Sept. 1994.
39. In Bharatpur, for instance, at the turn of the nineteenth century, the Gopalgarh tehsil had 66.5 Duhlot villages and 26.5 Pahat villages; in Pahari tehsil the Daimrot had 32, the Chiraklot 14, and the Bargujar 6 villages respectively. In Kaman the Pahat had 15, the Baliana 11, the Nai 7, and the Kamaliya 7 villages. Eleven Pahat villages were located in the Dig tehsil. *ARCB*, 26. In Gurgaon, Doha in Firozpur is a Duhlot and Ladhavat area, and Doha along with Ghata Shamsabad a Daimrot tract. The Dhaingal pal is concentrated in northern Nuh, whereas the Dairhval are toward the south and the Chiraklot toward the southeast of Nuh, in Punhana. *Punjab DG*, vol. 4A, 26.
40. Eric Stokes, *The Peasant Armed: The Indian Rebellion of 1857*, ed. C. A. Bayly (Oxford: Clarendon Press, 1986), 131–32.
41. Aggarwal, *Caste, Religion, and Power*, 25. According to a Pakistani Meo called Rao Imrit Khan Khusab Sargodha (his *Tarikh-i Mev* was published in Pakistan in 1974), it was Balban who got Kakurana to divide them into pals when, even after repeated attacks on Mewat in 1248, 1252, and1258, he could not suppress them. Svaleh Khan (Bivan) maintains that the division into pals took place between 1388 and 1400 during the period of the rise of Bahadur Nahar. For a discussion, see Siddiq Ahmad Meo's article in, *Chirāgh-i-Mewāt*, 5 Sept. 2000.
42. Skaria makes the point that unlike the Marathas the British understood sover-

eignty as exclusive. They limited Gaekwadi Maratha rights in the coshared villages, created a fixed boundary between Dangs and Baroda, excluding Baroda officials from the Dangs. The overlapping rights of the Gaekwad and Dangi chiefs were reconstituted as part of two territories, bounded and exclusive of each other. Thus frontiers became substituted by mapped boundaries. The forest polity stood clearly marginalized under colonialism. Skaria, *Hybrid Histories*, chap 11. See also Wink, *Land and Sovereignty in India;* Stewart Gordon, *Marathas, Marauders, and State Formation in Eighteenth-Century India* (Delhi: Oxford University Press, 1994); and Gordon, *The Marathas, 1600–1818, The New Cambridge History of India* 2.3 (Cambridge: Cambridge University Press, 1998).

43. Eric Stokes, *The Peasant and the Raj: Studies in Agrarian Society and Peasant Rebellion in Colonial India* (Delhi: Vikas, 1978), 44.
44. *Punjab DG*, 140, 155, 173–74.
45. *Punjab DG*, vol. 4A, 25.
46. David D. Shulman, "On South Indian Bandits and Kings," *IESHR* 17 (1980): 283–306.
47. Pamela Price, "Revolution and Rank in Tamil Nationalism," *Journal of Asian Studies* 55 (1996): 359–83.
48. Geertz, *Negara: The Theatre State in Nineteenth-Century Bali.*
49. Gyan Prakash, *Bonded Histories: Genealogies of Labor Servitude in Colonial India* (Cambridge and New York: Cambridge University Press, 1990).
50. Paul Hershman writes that before 1947 even the Jats had Mirasis who went to Pakistan. *Punjabi Kinship and Marriage*, 26.
51. According to Kautilya the kingdom consisted of seven natural elements including the *svāmī* (master/ruler), *amātya* (royal household from which is appointed the ruling class), *janapada* (country/*janah* or people), *durga* (fortified town), *kośa* (treasury), *daṇḍa* (legitimate force), and *mitrānī prakṛtayah* (ally/friend). *Arthaśastra*, trans. R. Shama Shastry (Mysore: Mysore Printing and Publishing House, 1967). Versions of Marxist structuralism do recognize the importance of the ideological state apparatus.
52. Romila Thapar describes the *dāna-stuti* hymns composed in favor of patrons (often clan chiefs) following cattle raids. In return the bard was lavishly gifted with cattle, gold, slave-girls, and so on. The stuti itself reiterated his right to be raja. The *praśastis*, or eulogies, that subsumed genealogies were important as claims to kingly status. *Cultural Transaction and Early India*, 26. Chattopadhyaya shows how early Rajput state formation emphasized genealogies and it was only a later stage that saw the emergence of several subclans. Jonas Kristjansson points out the relation of kingship to sagas of kings in *Icelandic Sagas and Manuscripts* (Reykjavik: Saga Publishing House, 1970).

Chapter 4

1. Ziya' al-Din Barani,"Tarikh-i Firoz Shahi," ED, vol. 3, 93–268.
2. Henry Louis Gates, "Critical Fanonism," *Critical Inquiry* 17 (1991): 457–71. Spivak herself disclaims this criticism. Personal conversation, Jaipur, Jan. 2001. But her writing validates Gates's critique.
3. Max Weber, *The Protestant Ethic and the Spirit of Capitalism* (London: Allen and Unwin, 1930); Karl Wittfogel, *Oriental Despotism: A Comparative Study of Total Power* (New Haven and London: Yale University Press, 1963); Karl Marx and Frederick Engels, *On Colonialism* (Moscow: Foreign Language Publishing House, 1959).
4. See Edward Said's various writings such as *Orientalism* (London: Routledge Kegan and Paul, 1985 [1978]), and "Orientalism Reconsidered," *Race and Class* 27 (1985): 1–15.
5. Ortner points out that Spivak's own agency is that of trying to articulate the perspective of Bhuvaneswari who had committed suicide without sharing with anyone the moral dilemma she was caught in. Sherry B. Ortner, "Resistance and the Problem of Ethnographic Refusal," *Comparative Studies in Society and History* 37 (1995): 173–93.
6. Reinhart Koselleck, *Futures Past: On the Semantics of Historical Time*, trans. Keith Tribe (Cambridge, Mass.: MIT Press, 1985).
7. Wolseley Haig, *The Cambridge History of India*, vol. 3, *Turks and Afghans* (Delhi: S. Chand, 1965), 233, emphasis added.
8. Robin George Collingwood's classical formulation viewed history as a science "to study events inferentially, arguing to them from something else which is accessible to our observation, and which the historian calls 'evidence' for the events in which he is interested." *The Idea of History* (Oxford: Oxford University Press, 1993 [1946]), 251–52.
9. See Roland Barthes, "The Discourse of History," in *Rhetoric and History: Comparative Criticism Yearbook*, ed. Elinor Shaffer (Cambridge: Cambridge University Press), 7, 18. Barthes criticizes the "realism" of narrative. "Introduction to the Structural Analysis of Narrative," in *A Barthes Reader*, ed. Susan Sontag (London: Jonathan Cape, 1982), 251–95. Structuralists such as Levi-Strauss suggest that "historical knowledge" is hardly distinguishable from the mythic lore of "savage" communities; see his *Savage Mind*, chap. 9.
10. Hayden White, *Metahistory: The Historical Imagination in Nineteenth-Century Europe* (Baltimore: Johns Hopkins University Press, 1973). A similar argument is made by Robert Young, *White Mythologies: Writing History and the West* (London: Routledge, 1990), and Ronald H. Carpenter, *History as Rhetoric: Style, Narrative, and Persuasion* (Columbia, S.C.: University of South Carolina Press, 1995).

11. Michel de Certeau, *The Writing of History*, trans Tom Conley (New York: Columbia University Press, 1988), 44–45.
12. Ricoeur, *Time and Narrative*, vol. 3, chap. 4. Ricoueur points out history's refiguration of time through its invention and use of reflective instruments such as the calendar, the succession of generations, and the recourse to archives, documents, and traces. These play a role as connectors between lived time and universal time. The calendar bridges lived and universal time and also invents a third form of time, which is mythic time. Myth suggests the idea of a great time that envelops all reality. Ricoeur maintains that the calendar consists of three features including a founding event that launches the era (birth of Christ, Buddha, etc.) as the axial moment that is responsible for dating other events—a point zero that brings together the physical and the cosmological; a bidirectionality or the possibility of traversing time in two directions; and the measurement of physical time on the basis of astronomical phenomenon. The calendar "cosmologizes lived time and humanizes cosmic time" and so contributes to reinscribing the time of narrative into the time of the world (109). Ricoeur argues that history has a fiction-effect that is augmented by various rhetorical strategies. An implicit pact of reading is established between the narrative voice and the implied reader. As a result the reader lowers his guard, suspends mistrust, and emanates confidence. According to Ricoeur, "what 'might have been' . . . includes both the potentialities of the 'real' past and the 'unreal' possibilities of pure fiction" (14), such that the past (what might have been) is a combination of both fact and possibility.
13. Ricoeur, *Time and Narrative*, vol. 3, chap. 10.
14. On Collingsworth, see n. 8 above; Bernard Cohn, "Notes on the Study of Indian Society and Cultures," in *Structure and Change in Indian Society*, 6–11.
15. Ronald Inden reviews European writing on India in his "Orientalist Constructions of India," *Modern Asian Studies* 20 (1986): 401–46, and in *Imagining India* (Oxford: Basil Blackwell, 1990).
16. Ranajit Guha, "Dominance without Hegemony and its Historiography," in *Subaltern Studies*, vol. 6, 283–84.
17. See André Wink for a critique of the periodization of Indian history and the notion of "Indian feudalism." *Al-Hind*, vol. 1, 220–25.
18. H. H. Dodwell, ed. *The Cambridge History of India*, vol. 6, *The Indian Empire* (Delhi: S. Chand, 1970); James Mill, *The History of British India*, vol. 2 (London: Piper Stemphenson and Spence, 1820); see also ED, vol. 1, xix.
19. Examples of such works are Upendra Nath Day, *Some Aspects of Medieval Indian History* (New Delhi: Kumar Brothers, 1971); Peter Hardy, *Historians of Medieval India: Studies in Indo- Muslim Historical Writing* (Cambridge: Cam-

bridge University Press, 1960); A. K. Warder, *An Introduction to Indian Historiography* (Bombay: Popular Prakashan, 1972); and Ishwari Prasad and S. K. Subedar, *Hindu Muslim Problems* (Allahabad: Chugh Publications, 1974).

20. Peter Hardy, "Some Studies in Pre-Mughal Muslim Historiography," in *Historians of India, Pakistan, and Ceylon*, ed. C. H. Philips (London: Oxford University Press, 1961), 115, 119; Francis Robinson, "Islam and Muslim Separatism: A Historiographical Debate," in *Communal and Pan-Islamic Trends in Colonial India*, ed. Mushirul Hasan (Delhi: Manohar, 1985), 356.
21. The purpose of history was didactic as it indicated a moral lesson, comments Jagadish Narayan Sarkar. "Personal History of Some Medieval Historians and Their Writings," in *Historians of Medieval India*, ed. Mohibbul Hasan (Meerut: Meenakshi Prakashan, 1968), 198–208.
22. Harbans Mukhia, *Historians and Historiography during the Reign of Akbar* (New Delhi: Vikas, 1976); and "Court Chronicles par Excellence," *Book Review* 14 (July–Aug. 1990): 10–11. This was with the exception of Abul Faz'l who, Mukhia points out, represents a radical break as he does not use mythico-religious chronicles or follow the tradition of praising Allah, the Prophet, caliphs, then sultans up to the current one. Instead he traces the descent of Akbar from Adam through a secular lineage, that of the rulers of Central Asia. This is possibly because his intellectual genealogy is that of the Mongol tradition of historiography. Harbans Mukhia, *Perspectives on Medieval History* (New Delhi: Vikas, 1993). Irfan Habib maintains that Abul Faz'l's vision is no longer of the court chronicles, as he uses diverse sources. Foreword to *Tarikh-i-Akbari* by Muhammad Arif Qandhari, annot., trans., and introd. Tasneen Ahmad (Delhi: Pragati Publications, 1993). Nonetheless, Abul Faz'l's history is even more closely identified with the state as he views Akbar as the climax of history.
23. Raymond Aron, "Thucydide et le récit historique," *Theory and History* 1, no. 2 (1960), reprinted in *Dimensions de la conscience historique* (Paris: Plon, 1961), 147–97. Muhammad Hasan and Afsar Umar Salim Khan, *The Political Theory of the Delhi Sultanate* (Allahabad: Kitab Mahal, 1961), 125; see the discussion in Iqtidar H. Siddiqui, *Perso-Arabic Sources of Information on Life and Conditions in the Sultanate of Delhi* (Delhi: Munshiram Manoharlal, 1992), 162.
24. *TNR*, 829. Saiyid Athar Abbas Rizvi, *Muslim Revivalist Movements*, 8.
25. Minhaj-us Siraj Juzjani, *TN*, 63–67; "Tabakat-i Nasiri," ED, vol. 2, 259–383; *TNR*.
26. Hardy, "Some Studies in Pre-Mughal Muslim Historiography," 118.
27. *TN*, 79–80.
28. Prostrating before the sultan is considered to be anti-Islamic and condemned

by sections of the ulama. But the practice, derived from Persian imperial traditions, was continued by the first four Khalifas and the Turkish sultans in India.

29. The Shamsi slaves later became khans. The possibilities of mobility for slaves among the Ghaznavides, Ghurids, and Delhi sultans suggests the far greater openness of early Islamic societies. Hermann Kulke and Dietmar Rothermund, *A History of India* (London: Routledge, 1990), 166.
30. This indicates an inversion of the Hindu classification of *dev* (deity) and *asura*. In the early Vedic period, Persian and Indian deities were common until later conflicts arose and the Indian *dev* became the Persian term for devilish.
31. See C. A. Storey, *Persian Literature: A Bio-bibliographical Survey*, vol. 1 (London: Royal Asiatic Society, 1970), 507. Ziya'-al-Din Barani, *Tarīkh-i Fīrūz Shāhī*, ed. Saiyid Ahmad Khan (Calcutta: Bibliotheca Indica, 1860–62); Tarikh-i Firoz Shahi, ED, vol. 3, 93–268.
32. Preface to Nizam al-Din Ahmad, *Tabaqat-i-Akbari*, 3 vols., trans. Brajendranath De, ed. Baini Prasad (Delhi: Low Price Publications, 1990 [1927–39]), xxvi.
33. Hardy, "Some Studies in Pre-Mughal Muslim Historiography," 116.
34. ED, vol. 3, 95. Mukhia contests Barani's eulogistic attitude vis-à-vis Balban, pointing out that the only ruler Barani genuinely admires is Ghiyas al-Din Tughlaq and also to an extent Ala al-Din Khilji, though he is severely critical of him too. Personal communication, Sept. 2001.
35. Mukhia, *Historians and Historiography during the Reign of Akbar*, chaps. 1, 3.
36. This discussion is based on *TFS*, vol. 1, 65–68.
37. The Persian term *rāhzan* is the equivalent of the Arabic *kate-tarīk*, that is, cutting across the path.
38. Stripping women, as the English translation goes, is pushing the word *barhana* to an extreme. It could also mean taking jewelry or an item of clothing. The Hauz Shams, a major water reservoir named after Iltutmish, was built in 1229–30 and covered a thousand acres of land.
39. Bada'uni refers to Firishta's description of the Kaitharis as "notorious robbers and brigands," *MT*, 29, 185n.
40. This account is largely based on *TF*. See also "Tarikh-i Farishta," ED, vol. 6, 207–36, and Mohammad Kasim Ferishta, *Tarikh-i Ferishta: History of the Rise of the Mahommedan Power in India till the Year* A.D. 1612, 3 vols., trans. John Briggs (Calcutta: R. Cambray, Indian ed., 1908).
41. Francis Joseph Steingass, *A Comprehensive English-Persian Dictionary* (London: Routledge and K. Paul, 1982), 1168.
42. This section is based on *TF*, vol. 1, 127–28, 134–35. Compare with Ferishta, *Tarikh i Ferishta*, trans. Briggs, vol. 1, 249, 238, 244–45, 255–56.
43. André Wink argues that the sultanate of Delhi accomplished the merger of two types of society, sedentary and nomadic. *Al-Hind*, vol. 2.
44. Preface to Nizam al-Din Ahmad's *Tabaqat-i-Akbari*.

45. 'Abd al-Qadir ibn Muluk Shah Bada'uni, *Muntākhab al-Tawārīkh,* vol. 1, trans. and ed. G. S. A. Ranking (Delhi: Renaissance Publishing House, 1986), 129, 185, 134.
46. Hardy, "Some Studies in Pre-Mughal Muslim Historiography," 120.
47. Saiyid Athar Abbas Rizvi, *Uttar Taimūr kālīn Bhārat* (Hindi), vol. 1, *History of the Post-Timur Sultans of Delhi,* pt. 1, *1399–1526* (Aligarh Muslim University: Department of History, 1958); See *TMS,* 160, 179, 192. Yahya bin Ahmad, "Tarikh-i Mubarak Shahi," ED, vol. 4, 6.
48. See preface to Nizam al-Din Ahmad, *Tabaqat-i Akbari;* also ED, vol. 2, 6.
49. *TA,* vol. 1, 256; *TMS,* 137–39.
50. *TA,* 260. A *nazar* gift of a pair of white parrots had also been sent to Timur. *Arzang Tijara,* 3.
51. Yahya bin Ahmad, "Tarikh-i Mubarak Shahi," ED, vol. 4, 27, 53–58.
52. This discussion is based on *TMS,* 179, 191–92.
53. *MT,* vol. 1, 365, 375, 381. Khizr Khan also had to suppress "rebellions" all through the Doab, in Kol, Etawa, and Gwalior. See *TMS,* 192.
54. Ferishta, Briggs trans., vol. 1, 512.
55. See also *MT,* vol. 1, 385; and ED, vol. 4, 61–65. The *TA* modifies the version somewhat: "laid waste and depopulated their country."
56. Tortured, according to Farishta, *TF,* 300; *TMS,* 211–12; *TA,* 279.
57. *TA,* vol. 1, 279–80; *TMS,* 212.
58. *TMS,* 227.
59. Mohammad Habib and Kaliq Ahmad Nizami, *Comprehensive History of India,* vol. 5, *The Delhi Sultanat* (New Delhi: People's Publishing House, 1987), 259, 628, 636.
60. For details see preface to Nizam al-Din Ahmad, *Tabaqat-i-Akbari.*
61. Powlett, *Gazetteer of Ulwur,* 7.
62. *TA,* vol. 1, 296, 303; Firishta, vol. 1, Briggs trans., 553. According to Ahmad Yadgar eleven parganas were wrested. *Tārīkh-i Shāhī* or *Tārīkh-i Salātīn-i Afāghinā* (Persian), or A *History of the Sultans of Delhi from the Time of Bahlul Ludi* (A.H. 855–94) to the Entry of Emperor Akbar into Delhi in A.H. 964, ed. M. Hidayat Hosain (Calcutta: Bibliotheca Indica, 1939), 11.
63. During Lodi rule several anecdotes were prevalent regarding thieving by the Mewatis. Personal conversation, Iqtidar H. Siddiqui, Aligarh, 5 Oct. 1997. Interestingly, despite this, Mewatis were widely employed as foot soldiers, servants, and lifeguards under Sikandar Lodi. According to Mushtaqi's work of the Afghan period (compiled in 1572), there was no noble in Agra, the site of Sikandar's capital, who did not employ Mewatis. Shaikh Rizqullah Mushtaqui, *Waqi'at-e-Mushtāqui,* trans. and ed. Iqtidar H. Siddiqui (New Delhi: ICHR, Northern Book Center, 1993).

64. Babar, *Tuzak-i Bābarī,* ED, vol. 4, 241.
65. Babar, *Tuzak-i Bābarī,* ED, vol. 4, 263.
66. This account is based on Zahiru'd-din Muhammad Babur, *Babur-Nama,* vol. 1, trans. from Turki by A. S. Beveridge (reprint ed., Delhi: Oriental Books, 1970), 577–78. Jagdish Singh Gehlot, *Rajputānā kā itihās: Jaypur vā Alwar rājyon kā itihāsa* (Hindi) (Jodhpur: Jodhpur Sahitya Mandir, 1966), 239. Babar, ED, vol. 4, 273.
67. *Tarikh-i Salatin-i-Afaghina,* ED, vol. 5, 35–37.
68. According to the *Babur-Nama* he fled after being wounded by an arrow, leaving behind his army.
69. *Akbar Nama,* trans. H. Beveridge (Bibliotheca India; reprint ed., Delhi: Rare Books, 1972).
70. Hakim Ajmal Khan's preface to Abdul Shakur's *Tarīkh Mev Chatrī.*
71. Mushtaqui, *Waqi'at-e-Mushtāqui,* 164n.

Chapter 5

1. *The Shah Jahannama of 'Inayat Khan, An Abridged History of the Mughal Emperor Shah Jahan,* compiled by his royal librarian, trans. A. R. Fuller, ed. W. E. Begley and Z. A. Desai (Delhi: Oxford University Press, 1990), 151. Yamin ud daula and Quli Khan were major nobles who held control over governance during the reign of Nur Jahan. Shaikh Farid Bhakkari, *Dhakhirat al-Khavanin,* or *Biographical Dictionary of Mughal Nobles* (Persian), vol. 2, ed. Syed Moinul Haq (Karachi: Pakistan Historical Society, 1961), 32–46, 397.
2. *The Shah Jahannama,* 148.
3. Farman no. 76, 16 July 1650. A nishan of Begum Sahiba Jahanara to Jai Singh later appreciates his service in expelling the mischievous elements from Kaman-Pahari and populating them with Rajputs, 24 Rajab 1060 AH/23 July 1650. S. A. I. Tirmizi, *Mughal Documents,* A.D. 1628–1659 (Delhi: Manohar, 1995), 97.
4. Farman no. 77, 28 Sept. 1650. See Nurul Hasan, "Further Light on Zamindars Under the Mughals--A Case Study of (Mirza) Raja Jai Singh Under Shah Jehan," *Indian History Congress Proceedings* 39 (1978): 498.
5. Irfan Habib, "Jatts of Punjab and Sind," 92–103; Chetan Singh, *Region and Empire: Panjab in the Seventeenth Century* (Delhi: Oxford University Press, 1991).
6. The Agra Suba included Alwar with an area of 2,777 square miles that paid a revenue of 39,832,204 dams; Tijara with 633 square miles that paid 17,700,460.5 dams; Sahar with 997 square miles that paid 5,917,569 dams; and Narnaul with 16 mahals that paid 50,046,703 dams. The Rewari Sarkar of the Delhi Suba consisted of 12 mahals and paid 739,268 dams. Abu'l-fazl 'Allami,

ā'īn-i- Akbarī, vol. 2, trans. Col. H. S. Jarrett and H. Blochmann, ed. Jadunath Sarar and D. C. Phillott (New Delhi: Munshiram Manoharlal, 1978).

7. Tariq Ahmad, "A Note on the Interpretation of Medieval Historiography," in *Bias in Indian Historiography*, ed. Deva Huti (Delhi: D. K. Publications, 1980), 247–50.
8. Irfan Habib, *The Agrarian System of Mughal India, 1556–1707* (New York: Asia Pub. House, 1963), 257.
9. John F. Richards mentions that the assessed revenue demand in the five provinces of the Gangetic plain doubled over 100 years from 1,784 million to 3,584 million dams. The total state demand grew from 5,864.6 million dams in the last years of Akbar's rule to 13,339.9 million dams in 1709. Richards, *The Mughal Empire, The New Cambridge History of India*, 1.5 (1993), 186, 188.
10. Habib, *Agrarian System of Mughal India*, 212, 319. The revenue rates also took into account variables such as the caste status of the peasantry, the specific crop, nature of the soil, market prices, and so on.
11. Richards, *The Mughal Empire*, chap. 9.
12. H. K. Naqvi, *Urbanization and Urban Centres Under the Great Mughals* (Simla: Indian Institute of Advanced Study, 1971), 160–86.
13. Douglas E. Streusand, *The Formation of the Mughal Empire*, (Delhi: Oxford University Press, 1989), 71.
14. Muzaffar Alam, "Aspects of Agrarian Uprisings in North India in the Early Eighteenth Century," in *Situating Indian History*, ed. S. Bhattacharya and R. Thapar (Delhi: Oxford University Press, 1986), 146–70; also his *Crisis of Empire in Mughal North India: Awadh and the Punjab, 1707–1748* (Delhi: Oxford University Press, 1986).
15. R. P. Rana, "Agrarian Revolts in Northern India during the Late 17th and Early 18th Century," *IESHR* 18 (1981), 158; John F. Richards and V. N. Rao, "Banditry in Mughal India: Historical and Folk Perceptions," *IESHR* 17 (1980): 95–120; Gautam Bhadra, "Two Frontier Uprisings in Mughal India," in *Subaltern Studies*, vol. 2, 43–59.
16. See Rana, "Agrarian Revolts," 307.
17. See Farman R.Y. 4 of Shah Jahan/1631, according to which Jai Singh was given a *sawār* rank of 4600 and 5 crore 2 lakh dams in *inām* (gift of revenue-free land); Satish Chandra, *Mughal Religious Policies: The Rajputs and the Deccan* (Delhi: Vikas, 1993), 105n.
18. Kaman (a jagir of 2 million dams) and three other parganas had been given to Jai Singh in recognition of his services against the Jats and Mewatis. Bhangarh was obtained with a revenue grant of Rs. 58,350; Naraina and Alwar with a revenue of Rs. 80,413. The Amber ruler was further promised Khori and Mathura if he suppressed the Jats. Vakil report 140/130, 24 Ramazan 1099 H./13 July 1688. Later he also obtained a jagir worth 15,000,000 dams in pargana

Toda Bhim according to vakil report 251/369, 28 Shaban 1102 H./17 May 1691. See also H. C. Tikkiwal, *Jaipur and the Later Mughals* (Jaipur: Hema Printers, 1975), 52.

19. These were held till 1678 when the mansab was reduced.
20. The faujdar was the imperial representative in the district. He was to maintain law and order; control the army; supervise police stations; guard frontiers; suppress rebellions, crime, and robber gangs; demolish illegal forts; and protect merchants. The amil was the second most important official after the faujdar. He was in charge of revenue assessment and collection and had considerable executive and punitive powers for punishing robbers and refractory and dishonest peasants. The faujdar was also to assist the amil in collecting revenue from rebellious and defaulting peasants. As in the later colonial system, the key officials were the amil, the qanungo, and the chaudhari. A large number of other officials, clerks, and gumashtas (agents) helped the amil. The discharge of the revenue function also required a thanedar (official in charge of a police post), patel (headman), and patwari (accountant).
21. In 1702 the ruler obtained the *zamīndārī* of parganas such as Jalalpur, Bharkol, Khilohra, Maujpur, and Vadhera.
22. The state emphasized *saguṇa bhakti,* or worship of an embodied deity. The subsequent correspondence of the Jaipur State invariably begins with the invocation to Rama ("Shri Ramji") or Krishna ("Shri Gopalji"). This shift parallels the creation of Braj and the growing importance of merchants.
23. The arhsattas of Ghazi ka thana indicate the extent of land grants to Rajput clans such as the Chauhans.
24. The son of a Meo chief states, "*ham dinnūñ turaṇg kudāvte khāte sakkar ghīv*" (All day we galloped on horses, eating sugar and ghee).
25. James Tod, *Annals and Antiquities of Rajasthan,* 2 vols. (Delhi: M. N. Publishers, 1983).
26. Gupta, *Agrarian System of Eastern Rajasthan,* 180–81.
27. I use the term "zamindar" with respect to the Meos following Nurul Hasan's third category of primary zamindars as distinct from autonomous chiefs (such as the Kacchavaha) and intermediate zamindars (such as the Jats). See "Further Light on Zamindars Under the Mughals," 497–502.
28. *Chihī* to the amil, pargana Khohri, Asadh Vadi 4, Vikrami Samvat (henceforth VS) 1797/1740, Mahakma Khas.
29. Bhardwaj, "Socio-economic Conditions in the Mewat Region," 220–30.
30. Bhardwaj cites a large number of cases, ibid., 139–40, 220–30.
31. Studies of the agrarian economy of Mewat demonstrate that most of the area was under food grain cultivation. Cash crops such as cotton and mustard were grown only over approximately 10 percent of the area. Thirty-two *kharīf,* or spring, and twenty-four *rabī,* or winter, crops were cultivated, according to the

arhsattas. *Māl*, or tax, on the crops was the major source of revenue, according to *jamā'bandī* records. Revenue was paid in both cash and kind.

32. See Rana, "Agrarian Revolts," 290. Satish Chandra and Dilbagh Singh's study of the *yāddāshtī* documents highlights the differential rates that were applied to the lower and higher castes. Rajputs generally paid about 33 percent and brahmans 12 percent of the revenue rate. Minas, Gujars, Jats, Muslims, Chamars, Kolis, and others, on the other hand, paid up to 76 percent. "Structure and Stratification in the Village Society of Eastern Rajasthan," *Indian History Congress Proceedings* 33 (1972): 196–203.
33. Dilbagh Singh, "Caste and Structure of Village Society in Eastern Rajasthan during the Eighteenth Century," *Indian Historical Review* 2 (1976): 299–311.
34. Gupta's work on the arhsattas highlights the strain on the peasantry that had to pay 44 percent of the produce and an additional tenth directly or indirectly. Gupta, *Agrarian System of Eastern Rajasthan*, 148.
35. Famines occurred in 1630–32, 1660–63, 1694–98, 1717–18, leading to a tremendous disruption of agricultural produce. Habib, *The Agrarian System of Mughal India*, 319, 332–34, 342– 46; also his *Atlas of Mughal India*. Bhardwaj, "Socio-economic Conditions in the Mewat Region," 40–41, 103.
36. Madhavi Bajekal's study of the amil's correspondence shows that cultivators were assaulted and dispossessed of land, and constantly complained that jagirdars arbitrarily increased the rate of revenue in violation of conventional dastur rules. "Rural Disputes in Eastern Rajasthan in the Eighteenth Century," M. Phil thesis, Centre for Historical Studies, Jawaharlal Nehru University, 1980.
37. Bhardwaj, "Socio-economic Conditions in the Mewat Region," 190, 231.
38. Chitthi to the amil, Asadh Vadi 8, VS 1722/1665.
39. Gupta writes, "[A] large number of *chiṭṭhīs* testify to forcible occupation of the villages, oppression and terror by the *bhomīas*, which enhanced the misery of the peasantry." *Agrarian System of Eastern Rajasthan*, 138.
40. Bhardwaj, "Socio-economic Conditions in the Mewat Region," 103–8.
41. The petitions written by amils and faujdars (chitthis and *'arzīs*) articulate either the complaints of officials or of the people regarding the violation of their land rights. Besides the *'arzdāsht* and *akhbārat*, the vakil reports from persons who were virtual ambassadors at the Mughal court and send accounts addressed to the rulers of Jaipur are also examined. The documents are from the Mahakma Khas, the historical section of the Jaipur Records at the Rajasthan State Archives, Bikaner.
42. Rao Banai Singh to Maharaja, arzdasht, 1133 H./1720.
43. Lal Mohammad to the Maharaja, arzdasht, 1131 H./1718.
44. Vakil report, Mangsir Vadi 9, VS 1769/1712.
45. The word "mufsid" means one who is mischievous, pernicious, corrupt, depraved, a destroyer, an author of evil and seditiousness. Steingass, *A Compre-*

hensive English-Persian Dictionary, 1286. It occurs in the Koran frequently, for example, as in Sunah ii 219, "God knoweth the foul dealer *(mufsid)* from the fair dealer *(muṣlih)*." See *Encyclopedia of Islam* (Leiden: E. J. Brill, 1960).

46. The raiyati and mawas contrast, J. C. Heesterman points out, is a classical Indian opposition between settled agriculture and the wastes/forests inhabited by the warrior and his war band. "*Mawāsi*" refers to "cattle" or "the life and practices of a *mawās* or leader of a horde of banditti." Heesterman's contrast is not altogether correct since raiding was as characteristic of peasant society as of transhumance or pastoral-nomadic social formation. Frequently agricultural cultivation and raiding were alternating activities dependent upon the agrarian cycle. *The Inner Conflict of Tradition: Essays in Indian Ritual, Kingship, and Society* (Chicago: University of Chicago Press, 1970), 169–70.
47. Megh Raj to Raja Ram Singh, vakil report, Ramazan 1103 H./13 May 1692.
48. Megh Raj to Raja Ram Singh, vakil report, 15 Ramazan 1105 H./30 April 1694.
49. Kesho Rai to Maharaja Ram Singh, vakil report, 16 Shawwal 1111 H./7 April 1699.
50. Mohammad Chain Sirchani to Maharaja Jai Singh refers to his own and Saiyyad Mubarak's appointment. Arzdasht, Jammadalawwal 1141 H./1709.
51. Baqir Khan to Maharaja, arzdasht, 1124 H./1712. Vakil Megh Raj refers, in particular, to the Mewatis complaints against the interference of Hathi Singh. Vakil report 1105 H./ 1693.
52. Arzdasht, Gobind Chand to Maharaja, 1123 H./1711.
53. Arzdasht, 1131 H./1718, and Jammadalawwal 1141 H./1709.
54. See Bhatnagar's *Life and Times of Sawai Jai Singh*, 175.
55. Gobind Chand and Mahar Chand to the Maharaja, arzdasht, n.d.
56. Govind Chand to Maharaja, arzdasht, 1133 H./1720. Nusrat Khan was faujdar of Sambhar and Didwana around the same period. Gupta, *Agrarian System of Eastern Rajasthan*, 13–14.
57. Rao Banai Singh to Maharaja, arzdasht, 1133 H./1720.
58. Arzdasht, VS 1750/1693. See also arhsattas of parganas Pindayan, Mojpur, Bharkol, Mandawar, and Naharkhoh, VS 1806/1749.
59. The vakil informs the maharaja that despite several requests from the writer, Kesho Rai, constant complaints have been received of the oppression suffered by the zamindars. A farman is issued for the maharaja to stop the oppression in Mewat. Vakil reports, 7 Rabiulawwal 1103 H./ 18 Nov. 1691 from Kesho Rai to Raja Ram Singh and 24 Muharram 1105 H./18 June 1693.
60. Arzdasht, Fagun Sudi 14, VS 1749/1692.
61. Vakil report, 24 Muharram 1105 H./18 June 1693.
62. Bhikari Das to Maharaja, arzdasht, 1120 H./1708.
63. Arzdasht no. 587/144, n.d.
64. Shyam Singh to Maharaja Jai Singh, arzdasht, 3 Kati Vadi, VS 1757/1700.

65. Gopal Das Rajawat to Maharaja, arzdasht, 7 Pausha Budi VS 1774/16 Dec. 1687.
66. Wazid (Byazid in other sources) Khan to Maharaja, arzdasht, 1133 H./1720.
67. Akbarabad is the old name for Agra. This was the Mughal capital until Shah Jahan shifted it to Shahjahanabad (Delhi) in 1638. The reference to both capitals indicates a compression of time and space.
68. *Adlī* refers to the Mughal emperor, the Badshah (in this case Shah Jahan) who ought to be both true and just.
69. Rajab Ali (a Saiyyad) is said to have been the sipahsalar, or commander, of the army in charge of the Badshah's treasure *(māl khazanā)*, which was being taken to Delhi. Possibly this is the name of the survivor who makes the complaint.
70. The "south" refers to the south of Delhi.
71. There is evidence that many Meos were co-opted into the imperial system. The *A'īn- i-Akbarī* informs that a thousand Meos (Mewras) worked as fine couriers in the imperial infantry and were also excellent spies. Some also worked as post carriers and messengers for the Amber rulers. See Bhardwaj, "Socio-economic Conditions in the Mewat Region," 16.
72. Khakla is a spring fodder crop derived from wheat or millet.
73. The description of the *kaband* comes from old myths where the corpse keeps moving even after it has been decapitated.
74. Ahlad Singh states, "fighting and killing we do daily, it is the work of Rajput clans" *(laṛṇo ghuḷṇo kaṭnon kāṭṇo ḍheḍhī hain ye rajpūtan kā kām)*.
75. Masand says:

āj mere takhat pos darbār galīchā gilal kachairī
asab kos asvār kuṇj bājat hā bhairī
daftar khān aur mudaftar khān jaise chār pahar hāiṇ rājā chahkai
algār umaṇg āhūñ pahar āj merī itnī gatī masaṇd kai

Today my court has stages
mattresses and carpets,
a treasury, horses with riders,
elephants and a horn that blows.
Rajas like Daftar Khan and Mudaftar Khan
are around me half the day.
Through the day my drums play
such is the status of Masand today.

76. Chitthi to the faujdar, Khori Pargana, VS 1784/1727.
77. In Rajputana a large number of battles and disputes have centered on the dhol, such as Bundi's conflict with Deogarh and Rao Jodha's with Bhikaji of Bikaner. In one account from the Patta Parwana Bahi (ledger) the Oswal right to the

dhol was challenged by the upwardly mobile Maheshwaris. The latter's newly acquired land control gave them a status that led them to question the Oswal right to the dhol that had symbolized their dominant social status and control of the pateli. I am grateful to Dr. Rajendra Joshi for this account.

78. Interview, Dalpat Khan, Alwar, 22 Sept. 1994.
79. Akbar also married Hasan Khan's daughter. Muhammad Makhdum, *Arzang-i Tijārah*, 8.
80. Samuel N. Eisenstadt, *The Political System of Empires* (New York: Free Press, 1969), 10– 12.
81. M. Athar Ali maintains that the Mughal polity reconciled opposing principles. This included the absolute and semidivine sovereignty of the emperor, an immense centralization, and the mansabdari system that was a unique and "unrivalled device for organizing the ruling class" with a normative framework. The latter involved the creation of a composite nobility. "Towards an Interpretation of the Mughal Empire," in *The State in India, 1000–1700,* ed. H. Kulke (Delhi: Oxford University Press, 1989), 263–77. Kulke refers to this position as representing "the Indian historiographical model of the pre-modern state." "Introduction: The Study of the State in Pre-Modern India," in ibid., 1–47.
82. Stephen P. Blake, "The Patrimonial-Bureaucratic Empire of the Mughals," *Journal of Asian Studies* 39 (1979): 79; Susanne Hoeber Rudolph and Lloyd I. Rudolph, "The Subcontinental Empire and the Regional Kingdom in Indian State Formation," in *Region and Nation in India,* ed. Paul Wallace (New Delhi: Oxford and IBH, 1985), 40–59; Heesterman, *The Inner Conflict of Tradition,* 166–67; Streusand, *Formation of the Mughal Empire,* 34–35, 72, 74. For a critique of "Western" scholars, see M. Athar Ali's "Mughal Polity–A Critique of "Revisionist" Approaches," *Indian History Congress Proceedings,* 52nd session, 1991–92, 303–12. For an excellent review of the literature, see Hermann Kulke, "Introduction: The Study of the State in Pre-modern India," in *The State in India, 1000–1700,* 1–47. Peter Hardy and John F. Richards seem to affirm Blake's model.
83. In particular, Muzaffar Alam and Sanjay Subrahmanyam's criticism is directed against Tapan Raychaudhuri's and Irfan Habib's contributions to *The Cambridge Economic History of India,* vol. 1, ed. T. Raychaudhuri and I. Habib (Cambridge: Cambridge University Press, 1982). Alam and Subrahmanyam argue that the Marxist (and nationalist) perspective of these historians makes them describe the Mughal Empire "as a vast, relatively uniform and centralized fiscal system, based on the collection of agrarian revenue" (13). They point out that these writers, along with John F. Richards, reflect the influence of the work of the British administrator-historian W. H. Moreland, *The Agrarian System of Moslem India.* Thus the colonial state is projected backward onto the late

sixteenth century. Introduction to *The Mughal State, 1526–1750,* ed. M. Alam and S. Subrahmanyam (Delhi: Oxford University Press, 1998), 1–71.
84. Richards, *The Mughal Empire.*
85. David Ludden, *An Agrarian History of South Asia* (Cambridge: Cambridge University Press, 1999).
86. Heesterman, *The Inner Conflict of Tradition,* 162.
87. Streusand, *Formation of the Mughal Empire,* 14, 152; Iqtidar Alam Khan, *The Political Biography of a Mughal Noble, Mu'nim Khan Khan-i Khanan, 1497–1575* (New Delhi: Orient Longman, 1973), xvi.
88. M. Athar Ali, "Towards an Interpretation of the Mughal Empire," 263–77.

Chapter 6

1. The criminality of entire groups was not merely a product of colonial rule. Behind the conceptualization were specifically English ideas that emerged from the Industrial Revolution, which created a large working class in England. The poverty and destitution of this class was widely regarded as the source of crime and revolution. The English experience intersected with theoretical developments. Evolutionary theory fostered by Darwinism and the Enlightenment notion of rationality foregrounded the idea of progress. All societies were placed on and evaluated in terms of a single evolutionary scale. Simultaneously, ethnology dominated by evolutionism became concerned with the classification of the human race in terms of racial types and segments with physical and behavioral characteristics. Wilhelm Koppers, "The Historical Basis of Ethnology," in *Essays in Ethnology,* ed. and trans. John V. Ferreira, J. V. Ferreira, S. Fuchs, and K. Kloster-Maier (New Delhi: Reliance, 1987), 18. For an example, see Herbert H. Risley, *The People of India* (London: W. Thacker, 1915).
2. See Sanjay Nigam, "A Social History of a Colonial Stereotype: The Criminal Tribes and Castes of Uttar Pradesh, 1871–1930," Ph. D diss., University of London, 1987. I am grateful to Sanjay Nigam for access to his dissertation.
3. For details see my "Criminality or Community: Alternative Constructions of the Mev Narrative of *Dariya Khan,*" *CIS* n.s. 25 (1991): 57–84. Also K. D. Erskine, *Rajputana Gazetteers: The Western Rajputana States Residency, and the Bikaner Agency,* vol. 3A (Allahabad: Pioneer Press, 1909); Stewart N. Gordon, "Bhils and the Idea of a Criminal Tribe in Nineteenth-Century India," in *Crime and Criminality in British India,* ed. Anand A. Yang (Tucson: University of Arizona Press, 1985), 128–39; Meena Radhakrishnan, "The Criminal Tribes Act in Madras Presidency," "Surveillance and Settlements Under the Criminal Tribes Act in Madras," *IESHR* 26 (1989): 269–96 and 29 (1992): 171–98; Marie Fourcade, "Les denommees 'Tribus Criminelles,'" *Puruṣartha* 16 (1993): 245–59.

4. The princely states were given blanket powers vis-à-vis the criminal tribes in their areas. See *Rules for the Guidance of the Indian States in Rajputana and Central India for the Control and Reclamation of Criminal Tribes,* RA Misc no. 14, 1911. The Criminal Tribes Act (CTA) of 1924 was repealed only by the CTA (Repeal Act) of 1952. In 1952 the Rajasthan Habitual Offenders Ordinance was passed, which decriminalized groups. It defined as a habitual offender any person who committed an offence three times.
5. Anand A. Yang, "Introduction: Issues and Themes in the Study of Historical Crime and Criminality: Passages to the Social History of British India," and "Bengali Bandits, Police, and Landlords after the Permanent Settlement," both in *Crime and Criminality in British India,* 1–47.
6. See Cohn, "Notes on the Study of Indian Society and Cultures," in *Structure and Change in Indian Society,* 3–28.
7. See, for instance, the works of P. W. Powlett, *Gazetteer of Ulwur;* M. A. Sherring, *Tribes and Castes of Rajasthan* (Delhi: Cosmo, 1975); Alexander Cunningham, *Report of a Tour in Eastern Rajputana in 1882–83,* Archaeological Survey of India (Series), vol. 20 (Varanasi: Indological Book House, 1969 [1885]); William Crooke, *Tribes and Castes of the North Western India,* vol. 3 (Delhi: Cosmo Publications, 1975); and Crooke, *Natives of Northern India;* Risley, *The People of India;* R. V. Russell, *The Tribes and Castes of the Central Provinces of India* (London: Macmillan, 1916); W. W. Hunter, ed., *Imperial Gazetteer of India,* 27 vols. (Oxford: Clarendon Press, 1908); Denzil Ibbetson, *Panjab Castes: Castes and Tribes of the People of Punjab* (Delhi: Cosmo, 1981).
8. Malinowski's claim that ethnography is a science has come under attack; Malinowski, *Magic, Science, and Religion,* 11. See James Clifford, introduction, and Talal Asad, "The Concept of Cultural Translation in British Social Anthropology," both in *Writing Culture: The Poetics and Politics of Ethnography,* ed. James Clifford and George E. Marcus (Berkeley: University of California Press, 1986), 1–26, 140–64.
9. Talal Asad, "Two European Images of Non-European Rule," in *Anthropology and the Colonial Encounter,* ed. Talal Asad (London: Ithaca Press, 1975), 103–18; Said, *Orientalism;* Inden, *Imagining India.*
10. See Evans-Pritchard, *Nuer.*
11. Clifford Geertz, *Works and Lives: The Anthropologist as Author* (Stanford Calif.: Stanford University Press, 1988).
12. A method formulated by Roman Jakobson, "Two Aspects of Language and Two Types of Linguistic Disturbances," in *Fundamentals of Language,* ed. R. Jakobson and M. Halle (The Hague: Mouton, 1956), 55–82.
13. On Powlett, see 90–92 FC, FD, GOI, Natl. Archives of India, New Delhi (NAI), 11 Sept. 1857. A year later intimation was sent that he had not yet passed college, 3319–24 FC, FD, NAI, 31 Dec. 1858. Powlett was appointed assistant

agent to the AGGR, and OPA and PA (from 3 Dec. 1870) to the ERSA, which was later amalgamated into the Jaipur Residency. See Rajputana no. 147 (no 2039P Fort William, 28 Nov. 1870), Political Branch, RA no. 12-Alwar (New). Following his work in Alwar he was promoted to the rank of colonel. Powlett was PA in Rajputana in 1881–84, 1886–89, and 1889– 92. See Erskine, *Rajputana Gazetteers: The Western Rajputana States Residency, and the Bikaner Agency*.

14. Powlett, *Gazetteer of Ulwur*, 38, emphasis added.
15. Powlett, *Gazetteer of Ulwur*, 42–43.
16. *Rajputana Gazetteer*, vol. 1 (Calcutta: Office of Superintendent, Government Printing India, 1879), 165, emphasis added.
17. Powlett, *Gazetteer of Ulwur*, 38.
18. *Rajputana Gazetteer*, 165; also Powlett, *Gazetteer of Ulwur*, 22.
19. RA File no. 79.
20. Skinner, *Tashrīh-ul-Aquām*, 71–77. Irfan Habib maintains that this is a text derived from brahmanical sources. Personal conversation, Aligarh, 1 Oct. 1997.
21. Powlett, *Gazetteer of Ulwur*, 40.
22. *ASSR*, 19; Powlett, *Gazetteer of Ulwur*, 5; and *Imperial Gazetteer of India*, vol. 9, 165– 66.
23. Watson and Kaye, "Mewatees," in *The People of India*, vol. 4, entry 202.
24. Quoted in Crooke, *Tribes and Castes*, vol. 3, 490, emphasis added.
25. *Rajputana Gazetteer*, vol. 1, 165; Jogendra Nath Bhattacharya, *Hindu Castes and Sects* (Calcutta: Temple Press, 1896), 252; and Crooke, *Natives of Northern India*.
26. Faulkner, *An Historical Sketch*, 32.
27. Ibbetson, *Panjab Castes*, 179.
28. Sherring, *Tribes and Castes of Rajasthan*, 90.
29. Alexander Cunningham, *Report of a Tour in Eastern Rajputana in 1882–83*, 27. Varying accounts are available on the question of Meo "origin." Although they are considered in the file on the *Imperial Gazetteer* article on the Meos and Mewat, the alternative answers are sidelined. Clearly, some of them would have refuted the idea that the Meos were an indigenous, aboriginal, and "Dravidian" tribe. In other words, ethnographic construction involved the selection of *one* from a multiplicity of histories, this selection being contingent on the image being constructed in the present.
30. The fluidity of the caste system has been emphasized by Chris A. Bayly. The practice of hypergamous marriages was common, and Rajputs married low-caste women and also kept concubines. *Indian Society and the Making of the British Empire, The New Cambridge History of India*, 2.1 (1987), 11–12. Dirk H. A. Kolff describes the Rajputs as an open status group until the sixteenth century. *Naukar, Rajput, and Sepoy: The Ethnohistory of the Military Labour*

Market in Hindustan, 1450–1850 (Cambridge: Cambridge University Press, 1990), 71–74, 82–84, 153–56. The Punjab Census of 1901 reports that intermarriage between castes was quite common.

31. S. H. M. Rizvi, *Mina: The Ruling Tribe of Rajasthan* (Delhi: B. R. Publishing, 1987), 27. Shakur's *Tarīkh Mev Chatrī* rejects the Meo origin from the Minas thesis, pointing out that one jati cannot be considered the source of another.
32. The *Pālon kā jas* refers to the marriages of Prithi Mal of Patan, Chakmal of Chahal, Atmal of Silkho, and Todar Mal of Dabak with Mina women.
33. Risley, *The People of India*, 49; William Crooke, *Natives of Northern India*, 143.
34. Quoted in Sherring, *Tribes and Castes of Rajasthan*, 78.
35. Marianna Torgovnic, *Gone Primitive: Savage Intellects, Modern Lives* (Chicago: University of Chicago Press, 1989).
36. *Imperial Gazetteer*, vol. 12, 405.
37. *BSAR*, 26; Drake-Brockman, *Muttra: A Gazetteer* (Allahabad: Government Press, 1905), 20, emphasis added.
38. *Report mardumshumārī Rāj Mārwār* (Hindi), vol. 1 (Jodhpur: Vidyapeeth, 1895), 110.
39. S. L. Sharma, "Structural Continuity in the Face of the Cultural Change," *Eastern Anthropologist* 22 (1969): 148; S. L. Sharma and R. N. Srivastava, "Institutional Resistance to Induced Islamization in a Convert Community—An Empiric Study in Sociology of Religion," *Sociological Bulletin* 16 (1967): 75.
40. Hashim Amir Ali, *The Meos of Mewat*, 78.
41. Haig, *Cambridge History of India*, vol. 3, 72, 88–89; Wink, *Al-Hind*, vol. 1, 164.
42. Pratap Aggarwal, "A Muslim Sub-caste of North India: Problems of Cultural Integration," *EPW* 1 (1966): 159–61, and his "Changing Religious Practices: Their Relationship to Secular Power in a Rajasthan Village," *EPW* 4 (1969): 547–51, emphasis added.
43. Aggarwal, *Caste, Religion, and Power*, 41.
44. Interview, Alwar, 31 March 1990.
45. Muhammad Ashraf Khan, *Miyo quam aur Mewāt* (n.p.: 1909).
46. The sixteen cases of "depredations," "aggression," and "robbery" reported to Lockett were committed partly by Rajawat Rajpoots and partly by the Minas. In Alwar certain Mina gangs set fire to villages, plundered, destroyed wells, burned children, and carried off animals, women, jewelry, clothes, and weapons. Lockett, *Narrative of a Journey from Bhusawar in Bharatpur Territory to a Part of North Western States (Ajmer)*, Foreign Department Miscellaneous Record no. 272, Files of the Rajputana Agency, National Archives of India, 35–36.
47. Lockett, *Narrative*, 76, 345–46.
48. OAGGR, FC, FPF, no. 425, 26 Dec. 1851, furnishes information regarding criminal cases; the secy. of state comments on the "outlawed Bheels and

Meenas in Nahir Hills." Dispatch from Court of Directors, no. 8, 13 Feb. 1850.

49. Captain Denny, Supt. Neemuch, to Major Eden, Officer Commanding Neemuch, no. 268 of 1859, Mt. Aboo, 8 June 1859, FPF. Sir H. M. Lawrence recommended that a body of one thousand troops be dispatched. OAGGR to SGOI, no. 37, 14 July 1855.
50. Major Brooke's report on the state of Mina districts refers to the Kherar as the parent country of the Minas where "every Meena . . . is or has been a robber." OPA, Harowatee, to Major Eden, OAGGR, Camp Deolee, no. 45, 19 Nov. 1859; Punjab Police Report, Legis. Dept. Progs., no. 54, Nov. 1871; and Lawrence's report, which shows British agitation over the Minas afer 1857 as they are said to stop all traffic on highways, rob camel loads of opium, and are active all over Rajputana. OAGGR to SGOI, Camp Ajmere, no. 6 of 1859, FPF, 16 Dec. 1859, 247–58.
51. Colonel Hervey, General Supt., to C. U. Aitchinson, SGOI, FD no. 1160A, Report on the Operation of the Thugee and Dacoitie [Thagi and Dakaiti] Dept. in the Native States, 1868, 12, 35. Statement C mentions 21 classes of Minas who are responsible for dacoities between 1864 and 1868. See also C. U. Aitchinson, *A Collection of Treaties, Engagements, and Sanads Relating to India and Neighbouring Countries*, vol. 3 (Calcutta: Office of Superintendent, Government Printing India, 1892), 77, 130.
52. The Mewatis are absolved by the Annual Police Reports of 1868 and 1869. Legis. Dept. Progs., no. 79-88, Nov. 1871. See also F. O. Mayne, Insp. Genl. of Police, to Secy., North Western Provinces, 28 May 1867. Legis. Dept. Progs. no. 57, Nov. 1871. Also note on "criminal tribes," 2 Feb. 1870, Legis. Dept. Progs., no. 48, Nov. 1871.
53. Hervey's report 35, 51. Enclosure no. 5, report of Lieutenant Blair, Asst. Gen. Supt. for the States of Rajpootana, 1866.
54. See ERSA no. 66, 1912.
55. ERSA file no. 215, 1934.
56. J. C. Brooke indicates his fear that tension between the Maharao Raja and Cadell, PA, might induce Minas to plunder highways. Camp Dhola, 27 March 1871, RA file no. 12, 204.
57. Legis. Dept. Progs. of May 1911. See the report of GGB Isaacs, SP, Ferozpur, 24 June 1908, Home (Police) Dept., no. 104. Several United Provinces gazetteers also describe the Mewatis as "thieves." See, for instance, Drake-Brockman, *Gazetteer of the Eastern Rajputana States: Bharatpur, Dholpur, Karauli* (Ajmer: 1905); and E. B. Joshi, *Moradabad*. Jats and Gujars are referred to in like terms. Further, it is not unlikely that in the eighteenth century disintegration that followed the invasions of Nadir Shah and Ahmed Shah Abdali, Mewati gangs may have indulged in "predatory activity," just as Jat, Gujar, Maratha, Pindari, Rohilla, Sikh, and Afghan gangs did.

58. See Lockett, *Narrative*, 75–76, 80–81, 208, 233, 238–39.
59. Sanjay Nigam, "Disciplining and Policing the Criminals by Birth," pt. 1, "The Making of a Colonial Stereotype: The Criminal Tribes and Castes of North India," *IESHR* 27 (1990): 131, emphasis in original.
60. *Report mardumshumārī Rāj Mārwār*, vol. 1, 115.
61. ED, vol. 3, 104n.
62. Contrast the enumeration in Saraswat Ravat, *Minā itihās* (Hindi) (Jaipur: Ajanta, 1976).
63. See Hervey's report, 44–45.
64. A. L. Raj, "Ideology and Hegemony in Jharkhand Movement," *EPW* 27 (1992), 200; also the writings of Verrier Elwin such as *The Baiga* (London: John Murray, 1939), esp. 76–130, and *The Agaria* (Calcutta: Oxford University Press, 1942), 121–22, 267–68.
65. Annual Police Reports no. 73, 105, Legis. Dept. Progs., 1871.
66. Compare Crooke, *Tribes and Castes*, vol. 3, 485, and Legis. Dept. Progs., nos. 101, 102, and 106.
67. Hervey's report, 5–6n, 34, 43.
68. Recorded at Alwar on 30 Sept. 1987.
69. *Dariyā Khāñ* is close to Kallol's *Ḍholā Mārū rā duhā*, a narrative of the thirteenth to fourteenth century. Kesri Singh, "Translation of Dingal Poetry," typescript.
70. The reference is to eight *pahar* into which the day is divided.
71. Panhora is situated in the present Rajgrah subdivision of Alwar district, where there is a high concentration of Minas.
72. Shamsuddin Shamsh agrees with this position. *The Meos of India: Their Customs and Laws* (New Delhi: Deep and Deep, 1983). Norman P. Ziegler argues that marriage was an important instrument in fifteenth- and sixteenth-century Rajasthan politics for the building of alliances and the settlement of *vair* (hostilities). "Marvari Historical Chronicles: Sources for the Social and Cultural History of Rajasthan," *IESHR* 13 (1976): 219–50, and "Some Notes on Rajput Loyalties during the Mughal Period," 242–84.
73. David M. Schneider, *American Kinship: A Cultural Account* (Englewood Cliffs, N.J.: Prentice Hall, 1968), 6.
74. The antagonism between the Meos and the Minas is also referred to in *Ghurchaṛī Mev Khāñ*, where the Baghora Meos are described as being constantly upset by the plundering Minas. The people of Kishangarh Bas go to the mukhiya (headman) of Baghora and request that a chaukidar (watchman) be appointed. Subsequently, a Meo called Khuda Baksh is appointed.
75. Personal interview, M. Subban, Delhi, 12 Aug. 1990.
76. Crooke, *Natives of Northern India*, 143, and Crooke, *Tribes and Castes*, 490; *Imperial Gazetteer*, vol. 12, 405.

Chapter 7

1. Heesterman, *The Inner Conflict of Tradition*; Shulman, *The King and the Clown in South Indian Myth and Poetry*; Stein, *Peasant, State, and Society in Medieval South India*; Stein, "All the King's *Mana*, 133–88; Stein, "State Formation and Economy Reconsidered," *Modern Asian Studies* 19 (1985): 387–413; Richard G. Fox, *Kin, Clan, Raja, and Rule* (Berkeley: University of California Press, 1971); Inden, *Imagining India*.
2. Ranajit Guha, *Elementary Aspects of Peasant Insurgency in Colonial India* (Delhi: Oxford University Press, 1983), chap. 2.
3. See John L. Austin's *How to Do Things with Words* (Boston: Harvard University Press, 1975), 3.
4. The battle was fought in Ramgarh tehsil, twenty miles from Alwar. Gehlot, *Rajputānā kā itihāsa*, vol. 3, 239.
5. G. B. Malleson, *The Decisive Battles of India* (Jaipur: Aavishkar Publishers, 1986).
6. See Edward Haynes, "Imperial Impact on Rajputana: The Case of Alwar, 1775–1850," *Modern Asian Studies* 12 (1978): 419–53.
7. C. A. Bayly, introduction to *Rulers, Townsmen, and Bazaars: North Indian Society in the Age of British Expansion, 1770–1870* (Delhi: Oxford University Press, 1992), 17.
8. P. W. Powlett, *Gazetteer of Ulwur*, 20, 14, 37, 2; *Imperial Gazetteer*, vol. 13, 314.
9. Haynes points out that the Alwar ruler was also seeking to extend his support base to the less-traditional kinship sectors and gave fifteen out of twenty-four new jagirs to non-*barah-kotri* families, that is, to Rajputs not part of the kinship elite. "Imperial Impact on Rajputana," 23.
10. Powlett, *Gazetteer of Ulwur*, 131–32.
11. Velcheru Narayana Rao points out that martial epics dealing with themes of heroism and masculinity were popular among the landed castes, while the left-handed castes had women-centered epics in which the female hero died not in battle but through self-immolation. "Tricking the Goddess: Cowherd Kaṭāmarāju and Goddess Gaṇga in the Telugu Folk Epic," in *Criminal Gods and Demon Devotees: Essays on the Guardians of Popular Hinduism*, ed. Alf Hiltebeitel (Albany: State University of New York Press, 1989), 105–21.
12. M. F. O'Dwyer cited in Wylie Settlement, Ramgarh Nizamat, vol. 1, Alwar Archives. Indeed the *dahrī*, or flooded alluvial catchment valleys, of Ramgarh were regarded as the most fertile areas in the state, particularly the tract watered by the Chudh Sidh stream.
13. *Kāṭh koyṛā* was a common instrument of torture used by the revenue administration of the princely states. The feet of the defaulting offender were pinned down by iron fastenings and he was beaten with a whip.

14. The worship of ancestors suggests a heroic cult popular among Rajputs, as Harlan points out. Paper presented on hero stones to Workshop on Framing, Narrative, Metaphysics, and Perception, Israel Academy of Sciences, Jerusalem, 23–27 May 1999. Memorial stones among Rajputs go back a thousand years as Chattopadhyaya shows. Goetz suggests their derivation from the *govardhanas*, or tribal memorial pillars of central India, Rajasthan and Gujarat, that are associated with a cult of dead. *The Making of Early Medieval India*, chap. 5.
15. See, for instance, Max Gluckman, "The Kingdom of the Zulu of South Africa," and E. E. Evans-Pritchard, "The Nuer of the Southern Sudan," both in *African Political Systems*, ed. Meyer Fortes and E. E. Evans-Pritchard (London: Oxford University Press, 1940), 25–55, 272–96.
16. A. R. Radcliffe-Brown, *Structure and Function in Primitive Society: Essays and Addresses* (London: Cohen and West, 1940).
17. A colonial text describes the Khanazadas as "originally Goojars, but [they] were converted to the Mussulman faith in the time of the Emperor Aurangzeb, and are said to have taken their rise from the issues of the Pathans' intercourse with Goojur women. Khan is the title that every Pathan (or Afghan) assumes; hence Khan Zada, the khan's offspring, or literally, sons." Watson and Kaye, "Khan Zada," in *The People of India*, vol. 7, entry 347.
18. Abdul Shakur, *Tarīkh Mev Chatrī*, 5.
19. *Punjab DG* vol. 4A, *Gurgaon District, 1910*, 83.
20. *ASSR*, 21.
21. Nicholas Dirks, *The Hollow Crown: Ethnohistory of an Indian Kingdom* (Cambridge: Cambridge University Press, 1987), 99.
22. The Baniya is mocked in another verse, "A standing Baniya is like one lying down / one lying down is like one dead" *(khaṛo baniyā paṛo barobar paṛā marā kī jāt)*.
23. Tanvar refers to the Meo clans claiming to have emerged from the Tanvar Rajput vansh and descended from Arjuna.
24. That is, watch your position in the Alwar State.
25. The word "*dvīp*" is used to mean subcontinent.
26. Harlan mentions that in older Rajput genealogies some lineages attached *pal* (literally protector) to their name instead of or in addition to *sinh* (lion). The ruler was responsible for internal security and also for guarding the safety and virtue of women. Hence the emphasis on Rajput chivalry in narratives. Several stories describe the rescue of women from lustful marauders. *Religion and Rajput Women*.
27. Bruce Lincoln, *Priests, Warriors, and Cattle* (Berkeley: University of California Press, 1991). Ruth Katz Arabagian holds that the cattle-raiding myth is related to that of bride-stealing. The booty in both cases is feminine and suggests the

masculine orientation of Indo-European pastoral nomadic groups and their warrior ideologies. "Cattle Raiding and Bride Stealing," *Religion* 14 (1984): 107–42.

28. The author of the elegy is a Charan contemporary of Bakhtawar Singh called Baraith Ummaid Ram. Personal conversation, Badridan Godan of Harmara, 17 Feb. 1997.
29. *ASSR*, 25.
30. Iman-ud-Din, the former nawab of Loharu, informed me that Ahmad Baksh urged Musi to commit sati so that her son would inherit a portion of the kingdom of Alwar. Loharu was a small principality that remained after the British appropriated the nawabdom of Firozpur Jhirka. The takeover was accomplished on grounds of the murder of Colonel Fraser by Nawab Shams-ud-Din, the son of Qutb- ud-Din Loharu. Personal interview, 28 Dec. 2001.
31. The conjoining of the sun and moon, which occurs two or three times a year on this occasion, is characterized by a fluidity of power and is regarded as suitable for making dana (gifting) and enhancing *puṇya* (merit). In popular worship *yajña*, or sacrifice, might be displaced by *yātrā*, or pilgrimage. On this theme see Ann Grodzins Gold, *Fruitful Journeys: The Ways of Rajasthani Pilgrims* (Delhi: Oxford University Press, 1989 [1988]). The Khandoba cult of Maharashtra is a similar Shaivite festival. For a description see Günther D. Sontheimer "King Khaṇḍoba's Hunt and His Encounter with Banai, the Shepherdess," in *Flags of Fame*, 19–80.
32. Powlett, *Gazetteer of Ulwur*, 153. There was a degree of conciliation also. A state report mentions the transfer of the estates of Nangal Chiraonda with the goddess temple adjoining Kaulani to the Nai Meos, which led to a hereditary feud with the Baghora clan. O'Dwyer cited in Wylie Settlement, Ramgarh Nizamat, vol. 1, Alwar Archives.
33. *ASSR*, 25.
34. See Lockett, *Narrative*. In a later period the Ramgarh area included 124 villages with an acreage of 109,282 according to M. M. L. Currie, *Alwar State Settlement Report*, Finance 26, 284f/B, no. 5878, Alwar State Records, Rajasthan State Archives, Bikaner.
35. Lockett, *Narrative*, 29–30.
36. Powlett, *Gazetteer of Ulwur*, 22.
37. Haynes, "Imperial Impact on Rajputana," 447.
38. *ASSR*, 25.
39. Faulkner, *An Historical Sketch*, 32.
40. Powlett, *Gazetteer of Ulwur*, 37.
41. This and the following passage are from Lockett, *Narrative*, 30.
42. Bayly, *Rulers, Townsmen, and Bazaars*, 14.

43. Lockett mentions that revenue collection had fallen from 2.5 million rupees in Bakhtawar Singh's time ("when the Mewattees were kept in very good order") to 1.8 million rupees in Banni Singh's time. *Narrative,* 26–31. Lockett records that Thakur Nahur Singh and his brother Simboo Singh farmed twelve villages around Hursorah for twelve hundred rupees, half of which was to be remitted. He mentions the corresponding figures of Abul Fazl's *Ain-i Akbari,* where it is described as one of the mahals of Alwar Sarkar with a revenue of 227,046 dams, or 5,677 rupees. Not only has the rent collection doubled since the Mughal period but Nahur Singh is said to have had a very "bad" character, so that he was even imprisoned briefly but was later given back his farm. Lockett describes how his return alarms the inhabitants of Hursorah particularly the numerous cloth printers who deserted the town so that not a single individual out of three or four hundred was to be found when he sent for some specimens of the quilts and counterpanes manufactured there. Lockett, *Narrative,* 42–43, 35, 186.
44. *Imperial Gazetteer* (Oxford: Clarendon Press, 1908), vol. 20.
45. Norbert Peabody, "*Kotā mahājagat,* or the Great Universe of Kota: Sovereignty and Territory in 18th-Century Rajasthan," *CIS* 25 (Jan. 1991): 29–56.
46. Richard Fox's introduction to a volume of a Duke University seminar describes the "application of European notions of the state to India, Africa, and other traditional polities" as an example of intellectual imperialism. The image of the state derived from European historiographical models of the absolutist and nation state saw polity "in terms of fixed boundaries and territorial administration, with recognized sovereignty and centralized authority, and with a monopoly of coercive force." Non-Western polities were seen "as state-less, acephalous, or tribal. This led to binary classifications of status and contract, societas and civitas, and so on." The "Eurocentric notion of the state" focuses attention on classifications of polity rather than the processural development of state organization. Fox adds that "it has ruled out kinship, caste or ethnicity as an important adjunct of certain forms of state." Introduction to *Realm and Region in Traditional India,* ix–xxv.
47. For a review and critique of oriental despotism, the Asiatic mode of production, and the debate around feudalism, see Romila Thapar, *From Lineage to State,* chap. 1; Kulke, introduction in *The State in India, 1000–1700,* 1–47; Rudolph and Rudolph, "The Subcontinental Empire and the Regional Kingdom in Indian State Formation," in *Region and Nation in India,* 40–59.
48. Aidan W. Southall, *Alur Society: A Study in Processes and Types of Domination* (Cambridge: W. Heffer, 1956); Clifford Geertz, "Politics Past, Politics Present — Some Notes on the Uses of Anthropology in Understanding the New States," *Archives Europeene de Sociologie* 8 (1967): 1–14, and *Negara: The Theatre State in Nineteenth-Century Bali.*

49. Fox, *Kin, Clan, Raja,, and Rule*, and introduction to *Realm and Region in Traditional India*, ix–xxv; Burton Stein, "The Segmentary State in South Indian History," in *Realm and Region in Traditional India*, 3–51; Stein, *Peasant, State, and Society in Medieval South India*, chap. 7.
50. Stein, "State Formation and Economy Reconsidered," *Modern Asian Studies* 19 (Feb. 1985): 387–413. See also his earlier piece, "The Segmentary State in South Indian History," and the subsequent *Peasant, State, and Society in Medieval South India*, chap. 7, and "The Segmentary State: Interim Reflections," in *From Kingship to State: The Political in the Anthropology and History of the Indian World*, ed. J. Pouchepadass and H. Stern, *Puruṣārtha* (1991): 217–38.
51. Mayaram, *Resisting Regimes*, chap. 1.
52. Henri Stern, "Power in Traditional India: Territory, Caste, and Kinship in Rajasthan"; M. S. A. Rao, "Rewari Kingdom and the Mughal Empire"; Bernard S. Cohn, "African Models and Indian Histories," all in *Realm and Region in Traditional India*, 52–78, 79–89, 90–113.
53. Dirks, *The Hollow Crown*, 129.
54. Peabody, "*Kotā mahājagat*," 32–34.
55. Ronald B. Inden, "Ritual, Authority, and Cyclic Time in Hindu Kingship," in *Kingship and Authority in South Asia*, 41–91.
56. Peabody, "*Kotā mahājagat*," 39.
57. See Tambiah, "The Galactic Polity in Southeast Asia," 252–86.
58. This and subsequent quotations are from Peabody, "*Kotā mahājagat*," 47, 50, 43, 54.
59. Dirks, *The Hollow Crown*, 10.
60. Fox's remarks on the Scottish Highlands as part of the "realm" lead one to conclude that the European absolutist state might also be more complex than has hitherto been allowed.
61. Charles Tilly, "War Making and State Making as Organized Crime," in *Bringing the State Back In*, ed. Peter B. Evans, Dietrich Rueschemeyer, and Theda Skocpol (Cambridge University Press, 1985), 169–70.
62. Reiner Tom Zuidema, *The Ceque System of Cuzco: The Social Organization of Capital of the Inca*, International Archives of Ethnography, trans. Eva M. Hooykaas (Leiden: E. J. Brill, 1964).

Chapter 8

1. *jitnā dauṛā des kā sabkā maiṇe liyā gāñvrā toṛ/jamā bharenā rāj kī mosū ghāto raho āmoṛ*
2. Powlett, *Gazetteer of Ulwur*, 129.
3. *Selections from the Papers of Lord Metcalfe*, ed. John William Kaye (London: Smith, Elder, 1855), 77.

4. Lawrence's report to Secy., GOI, 4 March 1857, cited in *BSAR*.
5. *Final Settlement Report of the Bharatpur State*, typescript, 1932, 8.
6. The following account draws from William Dalrymple, *City of Djinns* (London: Harper Collins, 1993), 108–42.
7. In the Meo and Jat areas two-thirds of the land was cultivated by proprietors themselves. Of the remainder 30 percent was held by tenants with rights of occupancy, who seldom paid any rent except to the government. Tenants-at-will usually paid their rents in cash. Channing, *LRSGD*. The following account draws considerably from this work.
8. Cited in Channing, *LRSGD*, 6; J. Wilson, *Report on the Revision of Mr. Channing's Settlement*, 1881, 5. Nuh was settled as early as 1808–9.
9. Later it was recognized that Mewat "had suffered from over-assessment in earlier times and much of it was heavily mortgaged." Channing conceded that the Meos had "suffered most from the misfortunes which have befallen the district" and that the realization of a heavier revenue than that which people had been accustomed to paying had added to the difficulties in 1877–81. But the old rate of Rs 2 per acre was retained by Channing and a further enhancement made from Rs 126,657 to Rs 149,085 or 18 percent, rates much higher than were prevalent in most parts of Punjab. Channing, *LRSGD*, 10–11, 13–14.
10. Amitav Ghosh and Dipesh Chakrabarty, *Correspondence on Provincializing Europe*, Amitav Ghosh Web site (Delhi: Permanent Black, forthcoming).
11. *BSAR*, 25.
12. FPF 492-P (S)/33, Crown Representative Papers, India Office Library, 75.
13. Powlett, *Gazetteer of Ulwur*, 153.
14. *ASSR*, 25.
15. Maulvi Mohumed Fuzuloolla Khan, Diwan of Alwar to Captain Eden, PA, Jaipur, 27 Nov. 1857, RA file no. 42, Dec. 1859.
16. General Lawrence and Lieutenant Newall, *Narrative of Mutiny in Rajputana, 1858–59*, RA, 34 Mutiny, 1858–59, 19.
17. *ASAR* 1910–11, 10.
18. See S. A. A. Rizvi and M. L. Bhargava, eds., *Freedom Struggle in Uttar Pradesh (FSUP)*, Source Material (Uttar Pradesh: Information Department, Publications Bureau, 1959); Ranajit Guha, *Elementary Aspects of Peasant Insurgency in Colonial India*, 118, 141, 321.
19. Secret Consultations, FD, 18 Dec. 1857. Also C. Chester, Commander IV Division to O'Brien, Offg. Commander, Allahabad Garrison, 7 Sept. 1858, Secret Consultations, FD no. 156.
20. *Punjab DG* vol. 4A, *Gurgaon District, 1910*, 24.
21. Stokes, *The Peasant Armed*, 123–24, 218.
22. Lawrence and Newall, "Narrative of Mutiny in Rajputana," RA, 1858–59, 2.

23. Rahim Khan, *The Meo Martyrs of 1857* (Hindi) (Delhi: All India Meo Sabha, n.d.).
24. Heesterman, like Bayly and Wink, uses the concept of an inner frontier to suggest areas that remained beyond the control of centralized polities. Heesterman, *The Inner Conflict of Tradition*, 170– 75.
25. Recorded from Chajju, Nagar, Bharatpur, 10 March 1991.
26. I am grateful to Iqbal Hussain, Aligarh Muslim University, for sharing with me his research on 1857.
27. Kunwar Mohammad Ashraf, "Muslim Revivalists and the Revolt of 1857," in *Rebellion 1857: A Symposium*, ed. P. C. Joshi (Delhi: People's Publishing House, 1957).
28. O'Dwyer mentions the spread of the influence of Wahabi tenets among the Meos from the sect's center in the Pahari tehsil in the late nineteenth century. *BSARCT*, 27. Stephen Fuchs's statement that the Wahabis kept aloof from the Movement of 1857 is incorrect. *Godmen on the Warpath: A Study of Messianic Movements in India* (Delhi: Munshiram, 1992), 269.
29. Bayly, *Rulers, Townsmen, and Bazaars*, 296–97.
30. Editor's concluding note in Stokes, *The Peasant Armed*, 226. Elsewhere a faction of Mewatis attacked a group supporting Bahadur Shah that had captured the treasure the British had abandoned at Gurgaon.
31. Information in this and the following paragraph is from Ghosh and Chakrabarty, *Correspondence on Provincializing Europe*, Amitav Ghosh Web site.

Chapter 9

1. Eric Hobsbawm, *Bandits* (London: Weidenfeld and Nicholson, 1969), 13.
2. Hobsbawm, *Bandits*, 15–16n. Hobsbawm's comments are not unlike Barrington Moore's thesis on the absence of agrarian protest, "submissiveness," and the "apparent political docility of the Indian peasantry." In his view "caste spells indifference to national politics." Barrington Moore Jr, *Social Origins of Dictatorship and Democracy: Lord and Peasant in the Making of the Modern World* (London: Allen Lane, Penguin, 1967 [1966]), 330, 335, 339. Dipesh Chakrabarty points out that Ranajit Guha challenged the usage of the political as it had been deployed in "received traditions of English- language Marxist historiography." Chakrabarty argues that a historicism underlay Hobsbawm's analysis, which was grounded in evolutionist paradigms of the nineteenth century. Guha in explicitly critiquing the idea of peasant consciousness as "prepolitical" suggested that the nature of collective action by peasants in modern India stretched the category of the "political" far beyond the boundaries assigned to it in European political thought. Chakrabarty, "Introduction," *Provincializing Europe:*

Postcolonial Thought and Historical Difference (Princeton: Princeton University Press, 2000).

3. Anand A. Yang, introduction to *Crime and Criminality in British India,* 1–47.
4. Sarat Chandra Mitra, "On the North Indian Folklore about Thieves and Robbers," *Journal of the Asiatic Society of Bengal* 1 (1895); David Shulman, "On South Indian Bandits and Kings," *IESHR* 17 (1980): 283–306.
5. Richards and Rao, "Banditry in Mughal India," 95–120.
6. M. S. S. Pandian, *The Image Trap: M. G. Ramachandran in Tamil Politics* (New Delhi: Sage, 1992).
7. For a discussion of the princely states see Barbara N. Ramusack, *The Princes of India in the Twilight of Empire: Dissolution of a Patron-Client System, 1914–1939* (Columbus: Ohio State University Press, 1978), and *Princes, People, and Paramount Power: Society and Politics in the Indian Princely States,* ed. Robin Jeffrey (Delhi: Oxford University Press, 1978).
8. Robert W. Stern, *The Cat and the Lion: Jaipur State in the British Raj* (Leiden: E. J. Brill, 1988), 15–16. There has been a considerable debate on the question of the applicability of the idea of feudalism to India. In the classical conception of feudalism, the state is the source of land endowments that lead to the emergence of a class of landed intermediaries. Marc Bloch's classic work saw European feudalism in terms of "a subject peasantry; widespread use of service tenement (i.e., the fief) instead of salary, which was out of the question; the supremacy of a class of specialized warriors; ties of obedience and protection which bind man to man; fragmentation of authority–leading inevitably to disorder; and, in the midst of all this, the survival of other forms of association, family and state, of which the latter during the second feudal age, was to acquire renewed strength." *Feudal Society,* trans. L. A. Manyon (Chicago: University of Chicago Press, 1964). For views for and against the Indian feudalism thesis see Ram Sharan Sharma, "How Feudal Was Indian Feudalism?" (revised and updated), and Harbans Mukhia, "Was There Feudalism in Indian History?" both in *The State in India, 1000–1700,* 48–85, 86–133. Mukhia points out that whereas European feudalism is seen as emerging from changes at the base of society, in India the establishment of feudalism is attributed by its protagonists primarily to state action in granting land in lieu of salary or in charity.
9. James Tod, *Annals and Antiquities of Rajasthan,* vol. 1, 155–56, 182–83, 190.
10. Stern, *The Cat and the Lion,* 16, 87.
11. Powlett, *Gazetteer of Ulwur,* 24, 25.
12. *ASSR,* 27.
13. See Statement on Aitchinson's Treaties, Army Branch, File no. 133 ch/1927, ASR, RSAB; and C. U. Aitchinson, A *Collection of Treaties, Engagements, and Sanads Relating to the States etc, in Rajputana in Political Relations with the*

GOI through the AGGR (Calcutta: Office of Superintendent, Government Printing India, 1892).

14. Ian Copland, *The Princes of India in the Endgame of Empire, 1917–1947* (Cambridge: Cambridge University Press, 1997).
15. See Council 308/1878, ASR, RSAB.
16. *ASAR* 1910–11.
17. Col. J. C. Brooke, Offg. AGGR to SGOI, FD, no. 168, Mt. Aboo, 2 Sept. 1870, Rajputana Agency no. 12.
18. Cadell to Brooke, no. 133, cited in RA no. 12.
19. Cadell to AGGR, Ulwur, 1 Sept. 1870, RA no. 12, 26.
20. Duke of Argylly, Secy. of State for India, to GOI, 16 Aug. 1870, no. 203 of RA no. 12.
21. See Capt. T. Cadell, V. C., Offg. PA in ERS to Offg. AGGR, no. 166, Camp Ulwur, 1 Sept. 1870, RA no. 12.
22. See C. U. Aitchinson, Secy., FD with Governor Genl. to Col. J. C. Brooke, Offg. AGGR, no. 46 AP, 22 Oct. 1870.
23. In matters such as restoring confiscated jagirs and reinstating cavalry men, see no. 142, Purport of *khureeta* from Rao Raja of Ulwur to AGGR, 7 Sept. 1870.
24. Copland points out that later there was a sea change in the attitude of the British, who began to see the native states as the epitome of resplendent ancient traditions, martial virtues, and loyal partners of the British raj. *The Princes of India in the Endgame of Empire*, 22–27.
25. Stokes, *The Peasant and the Raj*, 27.
26. *ASAR* 1912–13, 3.
27. *ASSR*, 27.
28. Powlett, *Gazetteer of Ulwur*, 21.
29. *ASSR*, 41.
30. See File on Imperial Gazetteer Article, 106/1906 Alwar State (Agency), RA.
31. Edward Haynes, "Changing Patterns of Dispute Settlement in Eastern Rajputana during the Late 19th Century," *Journal of Asian History* 8 (1979): 152–81.
32. No. 131, RA no. 12.
33. The autumn crop gave only 200,000 *maunds* (2,799 tons) or one-fifteenth of the normal yield. The winter crop also gave only a fourth of the normal of 1,200,000 *maunds* (44,789 tons). Cattle died by the hundreds. O'Dwyer writes, "By the end of July as general panic set in among the agricultural communities, especially the Meo, who began to desert their homesteads in thousands." *ASSR*, 41–42.
34. *ASAR* 1928–29, 55. There were more than 3,000 chaukidars in Alwar in 1934–38.
35. Hobsbawm, *Bandits*, 16.

36. Prem Chowdhry, "Contours of Communalism: Religion, Caste, and Identity in South East Punjab," *Social Scientist* 24 (1996): 130–63.
37. David Hardiman, *Feeding the Baniya: Peasants and Usurers in Western India* (Delhi: Oxford University Press, 1996).
38. The Alwar state court of arms declares "*gaṛh jīte sab ḍhāy*," that is, all the fifty-two forts have been won in war. This is set against a background of a shield, swords, and a tiger. Gehlot, *Rajputānā kā itihāsa*, vol. 3, 232.
39. File no. 131 (serial no. 167) Alwar II, 1910, proposes the construction of a railway line to Tijara and Tapukra and the meter gauge from Rewari to Mathura. See index, Alwar II, Foreign Secy., no. 5976, 1919, ASR. "The Rajputana Malwa line traverses the State North-South dividing it into two equal parts while the branch line from Bandikui to Agra runs along the South-East border of the State." See *ASAR* 1913–14, 1.
40. Paul Theroux, *The Great Railway Bazaar* (Boston: Houghton Mifflin, 1975). Ramchandra Guha, for example, shows the impact on the forest policy of the Himalayan region in *The Unquiet Woods: Ecological Change and Peasant Resistance in the Himalaya* (Delhi: Oxford University Press, 1989).
41. Stokes, *The Peasant and the Raj*, 9–11. The Alwar's *Annual Administration Report, 1909–1910*, mentions that there are "no statistics of rail borne traffic in this State, but from local enquiries it appears that about 75,000 maunds [2,799 tons] of wheat, barley, grain, oil seed, etc., were imported from Bhartpore and British territories, and that 200,000 maunds [7,465 tons] of grain were exported to Saugar, Jhansi, Ajmere, Cawnpore, Fyzabad, Jubbulpore, Ahmedabad, Burdwan, Calcutta and Bombay."
42. Wayne C. Booth, *A Rhetoric of Irony* (Chicago and London: University of Chicago Press, 1974).
43. Pierre Bourdieu, *Outline of a Theory of Practice*, trans. Richard Nice (Cambridge: Cambridge University Press, 1977).
44. See on this issue the discussion by E. P. Thompson, "The Crime of Anonymity," in *Albion's Fatal Tree: Crime and Society in Eighteenth-Century England*, ed. Douglas Hay et al. (London: Allen Lane, 1975), 255–344. Madhav Gadgil and Ramchandra Guha, *This Fissured Land: An Ecological History of India* (Delhi: Oxford University Press, 1992); also Ramchandra Guha, *The Unquiet Woods*, 28–61.
45. Shulman, "Bandits and Other Heroes," in *The King and the Clown in South Indian Myth and Poetry*, 365–66.
46. Shulman, "Bandits and Other Heroes," in *The King and the Clown in South Indian Myth and Poetry*, 344, 364.
47. On this question see Eric Hobsbawm and George Rude, *Captain Swing* (London: Lawrence and Wishart, 1969), 65; see also Ranajit Guha, *Elementary Aspects of Peasant Insurgency in Colonial India*.

48. The terminology is Max Gluckman's, who writes that custom "directs and controls the quarrels through conflicts and allegiances so that despite rebellions, the same social system is re- established through widest areas of communal life and through longer periods of time." See his *Custom and Conflict in Africa* (Oxford: Blackwell, 1956), 47, and *Order and Rebellion in Tribal Africa* (New York: Free Press of Glencoe, 1963).
49. Brenda Beck describes a similar popular bardic epic, *The Brother's Story*, which captures a peasant perspective on the dynamics of rulership. Also from a living tradition, it describes a small kingdom in an interior area of Tamil Nadu around the fifteenth century. The twin brother heroes are given a land grant but refuse to pay taxes. The epic describes the king, different caste groups, and the role of the goddess who guards territory and is concerned with prosperity and fertility. The king's political powers are symbolized through a merger of divine powers, his ritual prerogatives, and his rights over a local territory and population. The story culminates in the brothers' death, which is seen to be a cause of well-being and new life. "Indian Minstrels as Sociologists: Political Strategies Depicted in a Local Epic," *CIS* n.s. 16 (1982): 35–57.
50. For an example of this argument see Ramchandra Guha, who writes, "in every ideology that legitimizes domination there is a sub-text, a legitimizing ideology of resistance." *The Unquiet Woods*, 89. It is true that forms of domination enable and structure resistance and protest. But protest comes from an alternative ideology and mode of legitimation that questions the dominant ideology.
51. Anton Blok, "The Peasant and the Brigand: Social Banditry Reconsidered," *Comparative Studies in Society and History* 14 (1972): 493–503.
52. Thomas W. Gallant, "Greek Bandits: Lone Wolves or a Family Affair?" *Journal of Modern Greek Studies* 6 (1988): 269–90.
53. Paul Sant Cassia, "Banditry, Myth, and Terror in Cypress and Other Mediterranean Societies," *Comparative Studies in Society and History* 35 (1993): 773–95.

Chapter 10

1. Ronald Inden comments on the orientalist construction: "The Indian mind, they tell us, is inherently imaginational rather than rational: it thinks in mythic, symbolic (that is, iconic), and ritualist, rather than in historical, semiotic and practical terms." *Imagining India*, 263–64.
2. Mill's famous statement went, "It is allowed on all hands that no historical composition existed in the literature of Hindus; they had not reached that point of intellectual maturity, at which the value of a record of the past, for the guidance of the future begins to be understood." Mill adds that they have no sense of geography, chronology, or history. See his *History of British India*,

vol. 2, 47, 51. On this question see also P. Saran, "A Survey and General Estimate of the Importance of Historical Sources in Regional Languages, with Reference to Rajasthan and Gujarat," *Historians of Medieval India,* ed. Hasan, 198–208.

3. It is repeated, for instance, in southern India's Vijaynagar Empire where the *nāḍus* underwent a decline. Burton Stein, *Rural India: Land ,Power, and Society Under British Rule,* SOAS Collected Papers on South Asia (London: Curzon Press, 1983).
4. Interview, Dalpat Khan, Kaulani, 14 April 1998.
5. Kumkum Sangari, Presentation on Conversion, University of Chicago, 19 April 1994.
6. Jonathan D. Hill and Robin M. Wright, "Time, Narrative, and Ritual: Historical Interpretations from an Amazonian Society," and Peter G. Roe, "The Josho Nahuanbo Are All Wet and Undercooked: Shipibo Views of the White Man and the Incas in Myth, Legend, and History," in *Rethinking History and Myth: Indigenous South American Perspectives on the Past,* ed. Jonathan Hill, 78–105, 106–35; Wachtel, *The Vision of the Vanquished.*
7. Kolff, *Naukar, Rajput, and Sepoy,* 7, 16, 29.
8. Price, *Kingship and Political Practice in Colonial India,* 5.
9. See Mayaram, *Resisting Regimes,* chap. 1.
10. Nicholas Dirks, *The Hollow Crown,* 70.
11. Dipesh Chakrabarty, "Radical Histories and Question of Enlightenment Rationalism," *EPW* 30 (8 April 1995): 751–59; Ashis Nandy, "History's Forgotten Doubles," Opening Address to World History Conference, Wesleyan University, 25 March 1994, *History and Theory* 34 (1995): 44–67. On the death of history, see Jean Baudrillard, *Simulations* (New York: Semiotext[e], 1983); and Francis Fukuyama, "The End of History?" *National Interest* (summer 1989): 3–18.
12. Gyanendra Pandey, "Modes of History Writing: New Hindu History of Ayodhya," *EPW* 29 (18 June 1994): 1523–28.
13. See Shail Mayaram, "Communal Violence in Jaipur," *EPW* 28 (1993): 13–20.
14. Gananath Obeyesekere, *The Apotheosis of Captain Cook: European Mythmaking in the Pacific* (Princeton: Princeton University Press, 1992).
15. Nandy, "History's Forgotten Doubles," 45–47.
16. The Satyakama Jabala episode from the *Chandogya Upanishad* describes how the young boy, Satyakama, wants to enlist with a guru and is asked about his lineage. He asks his mother who his father was. She tells him that in the course of her work she visited many homes and knew many men and he must tell the guru he is Jabala's son. Shankaracharya and later commentators change the mother's response, moralizing its tenor and denuding the response of its boldness. Shankaracharya's interpretation of the story was that Jabala told her son she had forgotten to ask Jabala's dead father his lineage. Bibek Debroy

and Dipavali Debroy, *The Upanishads* (Delhi: Books for All, 1994). Daya Krishna, personal conversation, May 2003; Ranajit Guha, "The Small Voice of History," 1.

17. Ranajit Guha, "The Career of an Anti-God in Heaven and on Earth," in *The Truth Unites: Essays in Tribute to Samar Sen,* ed. Ashok Mitra (Calcutta: Subarnarekha, 1985), 301–28.
18. Gananath Obeyesekere has argued that the term "myth," which carries the implicit ideological baggage of unreason, should be replaced by alternative, indigenous terms. *Medusa's Hair: An Essay on Personal Symbols and Religious Experience* (Chicago: University of Chicago Press, 1981).
19. Barthes, *Mythologies.*
20. Koselleck, points out that prior to the eighteenth century in Europe the idea of the possibility of plural histories held sway, until it was replaced by the notion of a single history. *Futures Past: On the Semantics of Historical Time.*
21. Emmanuel Levinas, "The Trace of the Other," in *Deconstruction in Context,* ed. Mark C. Taylor (Chicago: University of Chicago Press, 1986); also Levinas, *Totality and Infinity: An Essay in Exteriority,* trans. Alphonso Lingis (Pittsburgh: Duquesne University Press, 1969), 52, 55.
22. For an elucidation see Dipesh Chakrabarty, "History as Critique and Critique(s) of History," *EPW* (14 Sept. 1991): 2262–68, and Gyan Prakash, "Writing Post-Orientalist Histories of the Third World: Indian Historiography Is Good to Think," in *Colonialism and Culture,* ed. Nicholas B. Dirks (Ann Arbor: University of Michigan Press, 1992), 353–88.
23. Dipesh Chakrabarty, in a marvelous exercise of dismantling the "hyperreal" Europe, shows how in the European context history became conflated with the idea of progress and civilization or rather the lack of these in the non-West. The construction of Europe as the source of reason and enlightenment, capitalism and modernity assisted the project of European global domination. Historical time became the measure of cultural distance that contrasted the West and the non-West. "Historicism–and even the modern, European idea of history — one might say, came to non-European peoples in the nineteenth century as somebody's way of saying 'not yet' to somebody else." Chakrabarty, introduction, *Provincializing Europe.*
24. Dipesh Chakrabarty, "History as Critique," 2162–66; Ranajit Guha, "The Small Voice of History," 1.
25. Wink, *Al-Hind,* vol. 1.
26. Emile Durkheim, *Primitive Classification,* trans. and ed. Rodney Needham (London: Cohen and West, 1963); Levi-Strauss, *The Raw and the Cooked.* Critics such as Tonkin have pointed out that Levi-Strauss sees myth as objectified thought and anonymous, a perspective that disregards the thinking subject. Elizabeth Tonkin, *Narrating Our Pasts: The Social Construction of Oral*

History, Cambridge Studies in Oral and Literate Culture 22 (Cambridge: Cambridge University Press, 1992).

27. Tonkin, *Narrating Our Pasts*, 104–5.
28. Ortner, "Resistance and the Problem of Ethnographic Refusal," 173–93.
29. *ASSR*, 24.
30. See Kathleen M. Erndl, *Victory to the Mother: The Hindu Goddess of Northwest India in Myth, Ritual, and Symbol* (New York: Oxford University Press, 1993), 44–47. Jvala is associated with the celebrated Jalandhar pitha of the tantric texts. Jalandharipa is one of the eighty-four siddhas of Tibetan Buddhist literature. According to Agehananda Bharati this is one of the four great pithas in Buddhist and Hindu tantrism. The shrine is also connected with Gorakhnath hagiographical literature.

Glossary

amil. The second most important Mughal official after the *faujdar*, with the power to punish refractory peasants and robbers.

anīti. Unrighteous action.

ānnās. 16 annas equal 1 rupee.

apabhraṇṣa (apabhransa). Literary language of northwest India, derived from Sanskrit and the Prakrits.

arhsaṭṭās. Revenue records.

'arzīs /'arzdāsht. Petitions written by *amils* and *faujdars* that articulate either the complaints of the people or of officials.

Baniya. Merchant; also moneylender and member of one of the commercial castes.

baṇs (vaṇśa). Clan.

baṇsābalī (vaṇśavalī). Genealogy.

bāt. Mewati narratives generically similar to Rajasthani *vāt*, meaning tale or epic or prose narrative (from the Sanskrit *vārtā*, meaning account). The term has a range of meanings from history to story. (Adapted from Sitaram Lalas, *Rājasthānī sabad kos* [Jodhpur: Rajasthani Shodh Sansthan, 1962–78], vol. 3, 2999.)

bhom. Land rights.

bhomiā. Lower gentry, usually Rajput, more or less equivalent to Mughal *zamindar*, as they held superior rights in land. The *bhomias* also constituted a local militia who held and maintained fortresses of the district.

bīghā. A measure of land equal to approximately 3,025 square yards or 5/8 of an acre.

chatrī. See *kṣatriya (chatrī)*.

chaudhari. Headman, usually of a village; generally a leading land-controller of the area who was responsible for collecting revenue from villages and *zamindars* and handing it on to agents of the emperor or the holders of land grants.

chaukī. Police post.

chaukidar. Village or town watchman.

chiṭṭhī. Letters to *amils* written by *diwans* and *faujdars* expressing complaints of officials or the people.

ḍahar. Alluvial catchment valleys.

dām. Copper money.

dāna. Ritual prestation.

dargāh. Saint's mausoleum.

Dariyā Khāñ. Mewati narrative.

dastur. Tax regulations.

deṣ. Land.

dhauṇsā. Battle drum.

ḍhol. Drum.

diwan. Chief of administration.

Doab. The alluvial plain between the Ganga and Yamuna Rivers.

dohā. Rhymed couplet.

faqīr. Muslim mendicant.

farmān. Imperial mandate or order.

fasād. Disorder.

faujdar. Governor or chief civil and military official of an area.

fitna. Arabic term for sedition, discord, riot, crime.

gadar. Revolt of 1857.

gaṛhī. Small fort, sometimes strengthened with mud walls that could withstand artillery.

Ghuṛchaṛī Mev Khāñ. Mewati narrative about bandit brothers.

got (gotra). Unit of exogamy in Hindu kinship.

Gujar. Hindu or Muslim caste of mostly pastoralists and cattle keepers.

ijāra. A contract to farm a particular tract that was usually part of a *jagir* and was leased for a short while. The amount due from the *ijaradar* was stipulated in the *paṭṭā*, or document of lease.

inām (in'ām). See *māfī*.

itihāsa-purāṇa. Indian genre of genealogical-mythic history.

Jagas. Genealogists of the Meos.

jāgīr. Assignment of revenue of a tract of land by the state to an officer or *jagirdar* in lieu of a salary in return for services rendered.

jamā. Total amount of revenue payable by a cultivator or a *zamindar*.

jamadar. See *thanedar*.

jajmān. Patrons of brahmans and other service castes.

jajmānī. A system according to which services are rendered by specialist castes. The Meos had such a hereditary patron-client relation with castes such as the brahmans, Mirasis, and Nais, or barbers.

jang. Battle.

jas (yaś). Praise.

jāti. Caste characterized by hereditary membership and endogamy.

jihād. Holy war.

joginī. Female forms that inhabit battlefields, take off with severed heads, and drink blood from skulls.

julam. From the Persian *zulm,* meaning tyranny or oppression.

***kafir* (plural, *kuffār*).** Nonbelievers, including Jews, Christians, and all those who believe in more than one god.

Kaulānī ki laṛāī. Mewati narrative of peasant protest in the late eighteenth to early nineteenth century.

khalīfā. Preceptors, preachers of Sufi lineages.

khālsā (khāliṣa). Crown land with revenue paid directly into the imperial treasury, not given in *jagir.*

khānqāh. Religious hostel or center associated with Sufi lineages.

khil'lat. Robe of honor.

kos. Measurement of distance that varies regionally but is just under 2 kilometers (1.2 miles).

Krishna. Cowherd deity and Hindu god.

kṣatriya (chatrī). Traditional *varna* of warriors and rulers.

Lal Das. Meo saint (1540–1648).

lambardar/nambardar. Village headman.

laṛāī. Battle.

lok gāthā. Literally, folk narrative; a highly developed tradition in India, especially after the twelfth century, simultaneous with the growth of apabhransa languages.

māfī. Gift of revenue-free land.

Mahabharata. Great Indian epic with many regional variations.

Mahadev. See *Śíva* (Shiva).

mahal. See *pargana.*

malik. King, or title given to high Indian officials.

manṣab. Rank or office.

Marathas. Group of warrior lineages that emerged from the Muslim kingdoms of the Deccan, established a kingdom in the mid-seventeenth century, and came to be regarded as a caste.

mawās. Wild and desolate terrain, the refuge of rebels and robbers.

Mirasis. Caste of Muslim musicians and poet-bards.

Naruka Rajputs. A sublineage of the Kacchavaha ruling lineage of the Jaipur State.

nazar. Prestation conventionally given at a ruler's accession.

nep āliyā. Meos who do not belong to the pals or clans.

pagṛī. Turban.

pagṛī palaṭ bhāī. Turban-exchanging brothers.

Pālon kī Bansābalī. The genealogy of the *pāls*.

pāls. The thirteen territorial clans of the Meos associated with an actual or mythical ancestor; they are both units of kinship and governance.

palṭan. Platoon.

pāltis. See *rai'yatī (pāltis or asāmīs)*.

paṇchayat. Traditional governing, arbitrating, and consultative body of elders of Meo pals and of other castes.

Pāñch Pahāṛ kī laṛāī. Mewati anti- Mughal and Rajput narrative.

Pandūn kā kaṛā. Mewati folk epic and version of Mahabharata.

pargana. Smallest administrative unit and the revenue district, which consisted of one hundred villages, with approximately one thousand villages per revenue circle.

Parvati. Shiva's consort and one of the forms of the goddess; also called Gora (Gaura).

patel. Village leader.

patwari. Village accountant and land record keeper.

peshkash. Fixed-revenue demand or offering generally given at the time of the ruler's accession or at the time of the grant of the *jagir*.

pīr. Saint, spiritual guide, or a person imbued with certain religious powers.

qanungo. Land and revenue record keepers.

qasbā. Small town.

qazi (qādī). Muslim legal expert.

rai. King.

rai'yatī (pāltis* or *asāmīs). Middle peasant castes.

ri'āyatīs. Castes and officials with privileged land tenure rights.

sahukar. Hindu or Jain usurer or merchant.

śakta. Pertaining to the worship of the goddess.

sawārs. Horsemen.

***sharī'ā* (Persian *sharī'at*).** Islamic religious/divine law.

silsilā. Sufi lineage.

sipāhsālār. Chief commander of armies.

siropāv. Gift of the sovereign for a lesser chief or subordinate.

Śíva (Shiva). One of the gods of the Hindu trinity and of nonvedic cultures.

subās. Mughal provinces.

talvār. Sword.

tankā (takā). Silver coin used in the sultanate period; valued at 172 grains of silver. It was roughly equivalent to a rupee but with far higher buying power, being able to buy some 75 kilograms of wheat.

tankhwāh jāgīr. Transferable assignment of land in lieu of salary.

tārīkh. Literally "date," referring to Indo-Persian tradition of writing called chronicles.

tehsīl. Revenue subdivision of a district.

thāmā. Agnatic lineage tracing descent from an actual ancestor known as *dādā (ek hī dādā kī aulād).*

thanedar. Officer in charge of police station.

thekedar. Lease-holder for collection of revenue on a contract basis.

***'ulamā* (singular, *'alim*).** Muslim theologians.

vakil. Virtual ambassador at the imperial court who wrote reports addressed to the rulers of Jaipur.

***vansh* or *kul* (clan)** Largest kinship unit within the Rajput *jati;* said to derive from the sun, moon, and fire.

varna. Traditional fourfold division of brahmanical social order consisting of brahmans, ksatriyas, vaisyas, and sudras.

vasūlī. Revenue collection.

vīr rasa. Heroic mood or emotion.

yajña. Vedic sacrificial rite.

zamindār. Landholder; also used to mean rent-receiving intermediary, holder of hereditary superior right in land, or even independent chief.

zorṭalab. Recalcitrant *zamindars.*

Index